JONATHAN F. VANCE

A HISTORY
OF CANADIAN
CULTURE

Jonathan F. Vance

A History of Canadian Culture

OXFORD
UNIVERSITY PRESS

OXFORD
UNIVERSITY PRESS

70 Wynford Drive, Don Mills, Ontario M3C 1J9
www.oupcanada.com

Oxford University Press is a department of the University of Oxford.
It furthers the University's objective of excellence in research, scholarship,
and education by publishing worldwide in

Oxford   New York

Auckland   Cape Town   Dar es Salaam   Hong Kong   Karachi
Kuala Lumpur   Madrid   Melbourne   Mexico City   Nairobi
New Delhi   Shanghai   Taipei   Toronto

With offices in

Argentina   Austria   Brazil   Chile   Czech Republic   France   Greece
Guatemala   Hungary   Italy   Japan   Poland   Portugal   Singapore
South Korea   Switzerland   Thailand   Turkey   Ukraine   Vietnam

Oxford is a trade mark of Oxford University Press
in the UK and in certain other countries

Published in Canada
by Oxford University Press

Library and Archives Canada Cataloguing in Publication

Vance, Jonathan F. (Jonathan Franklin William), 1963–
A history of Canadian culture / Jonathan Vance.

Includes bibliographical references and index.
ISBN 978-0-19-541909-2

1. Canada—Civilization.   2. Canada—Social life and customs.
3. Canada—History.   I. Title.

FC95.V35 2009   971   C2008-907008-9

Cover image: Gulls and Ravens, by Kenojuak Ashevak,
reproduced with permission of Dorset Fine Arts.

2 3 4 5 - 12 11 10 09

Oxford University Press is committed to our environment. This book is printed on
Forest Stewardship Council certified paper which contains 100% post-consumer waste.
Printed and bound in Canada.

The production of the title *History of Canadian Culture* on Rolland Enviro 100 Print paper
instead of virgin fibres paper reduces your ecological footprint by:

Trees: 44   Suspended particles in the water: 8 kg
Solid waste: 1,263 kg   Air emissions: 2,774 kg
Water: 119,519 L   Natural gas: 180 m³

FSC

Recycled
Supporting responsible
use of forest resources

Cert no. SW-COC-000952
www.fsc.org
© 1996 Forest Stewardship Council

Printed by Transcontinental. Text pages on Rolland Enviro 100, containing 100% post-consumer recycled fibres.
Eco-Logo certified, processed without chlorinate, FSC Recycled and manufactured using biogaz energy.

Table of Contents

Acknowledgements

This book was first suggested to me by my good friend Laura Macleod nearly a decade ago, when she was an editor at Oxford University Press. At the time, I was teaching a course on the history of Canadian culture and blithely assumed that I knew a fair bit about the subject. I am grateful to Laura, not only for coming up with a terrific idea in the first place, but for helping me to understand that I knew far less about Canadian culture than I imagined.

Jennie Rubio, who took over the project when Laura left OUP, has been a joy to work with, as have the other people at Oxford who have been involved, especially Christopher Hanney and Katie Scott. As always, I would like to thank Linda McKnight of Westwood Creative Artists for everything she did to see this project through to completion.

While working on this book, I was lucky enough to receive financial assistance from the Canada Research Chairs program and from the Government of Ontario, through its Premier's Research Excellence Awards program. This allowed me to hire a number of research assistants, including Dorotea Gucciardo, Anne Millar, Forrest Pass, and Helmi Trotter, to help sift through the mountain of sources on Canadian culture. I would particularly like to thank Julia Rady Shaw and Jeff Vacante for their excellent work in navigating the vagaries of government support for culture.

It would take far too much space to thank the various archivists, librarians, and public servants who have helped me over the course of this work. However, I would be remiss if I did not recognize a few people who offered all manner of assistance: David Bentley, Claire Campbell, Regna Darnell, J.L. Granatstein, Peter Neary, Mary Henley Rubio, Dean Ruffilli, Amy Shaw, Neville Thompson, and Mary Vipond.

Introduction

Some years ago, a joke circulated about the state of the arts in Canada:

> Question – What's the difference between Canada and yogurt?
> Answer – Yogurt has an active culture.

Two centuries earlier, one of Canada's first novelists had made a very similar point: 'I no longer wonder the elegant arts are unknown here; the rigour of the climate suspends the very powers of the understanding; what then must become of those of the imagination?...Genius will never mount high, where the faculties of the mind are benumbed half the year.'[1]

For centuries, Canadians have been hearing about the deficiencies of their culture. We have always been fond of the back-handed compliment, 'It's Canadian, but it's good'—as if the combination of the two adjectives was a contradiction in terms. In 1888, the novelist Sara Jeannette Duncan lamented that 'We hear too often "it is very well, considering ..."'—considering, of course, that it's Canadian. This belief—that where Canadian culture is concerned, high expectations are unwise—was a constant irritant to a woman who continually urged her compatriots to strive for higher cultural standards.[2] But in spite of the exhortations of Duncan and many others, we have long laboured under this inferiority complex. We have been told that our culture is derivative or imitative, provincial or parochial—as critic, essayist, and poet J.D. Logan put it in 1884, 'the fiction and *belles-lettres*, generally, have the limits of the municipality and the flavour of the log-hut.'[3] It has even been declared non-existent, and by more people than just the anonymous jokester. If this book attempts anything, it is to demonstrate the fallacy of that notion: Canada and yogurt, in my view, have at least one thing in common.

'Culture' is a tricky concept. It can encompass almost everything that characterizes a society—the customs, modes of behaviour, beliefs, values, and social practices and structures—but it can also be used in a much narrower sense (as it is in this book), as a synonym for the arts. Still, even that narrower definition leaves an enormous amount of ground to be traversed, from ballet and opera to circuses and cartoons, and everything in between. In trying to cover that ground, I have had to avoid straying from the narrower definition of culture to the broader. A discussion of music can feed into the study of religious practices; literature naturally raises questions about education; and folk art relates to aspects of ethnicity. But none of those larger themes could be accommodated in this book, except tangentially.

Instead, to make sense of the sheer quantity of material, and to maintain a focus on the arts in a specific sense, I have emphasized a number of themes that transcend time and place. Some, such as the slow growth of government intervention in the arts, require little introduction at this point; but others are more complex. One is the struggle between ballet and burlesque, between high (or elite) culture and low (or popular) culture. The former included forms of expression that were deemed to provide not only enjoyment but moral and spiritual improvement; for that reason, elites (in this context, the social, political, and economic elites were usually the cultural elites as well) believed that it was essential to disseminate forms of high culture as widely as possible. 'I reject the idea that the arts are for the rich,' businessman and philanthropist G. Hamilton Southam told an Ottawa audience in 1965. 'Truth and beauty, which are the business of the arts, their concern and glory, are the birthright of all mankind.'[4] But despite their good intentions, Southam and his like did not seem to realize that the very people who were in need of improvement did not necessarily share the notion that 'truth and beauty' were their birthright. For them, culture was a hand-carved toy, a dime novel, a vaudeville show, or a dialect song learned from a grandparent: these cultural artifacts arguably contained more truth than a comedy of manners or a rhyming quatrain. For them, the arts were less about intellectual engagement and moral improvement than they were about diversion, entertainment—and perhaps even poking fun at the very people who sought their betterment.

Connected to the struggle between elite and popular culture is the struggle between the traditional and the modern. 'We all of us grow older every day,' said Peter Dwyer, the director of the Canada Council, in 1968. 'There is some tendency towards the hardening of our artistic arteries, a danger of looking backward rather than forward...The only antidote is a constant respect for the reasonable excesses of the young even though the shocks they often contain may bring us into conflict with the more conservative elements of society who look to us to assist what is comforting in the arts because it has become familiar with time.'[5] But all too often, these reasonable excesses were too much of a shock to a conservative public. That is certainly how one theatre-goer felt after taking a grandmother to see the UBC Players' modernist interpretation of *Caesar and Cleopatra* in 1934: 'we both came away disgusted at the attempts of these amateur thespians. Instead of an evening of entertainment and amusement we came away from the theatre with a distinct bad taste in our mouths and my grandmother claims that her heart was affected...[the] shameful nakedness was *really* too much. Such a display of masculine limbs may have been all right in degenerate Egypt, but we really feel that some of the most obvious proprieties might have been observed on a *university* stage of all places.'[6] The fact was that theatre groups and art gallery owners, in their desire to advance cultural expression, came up against public resistance to anything new and different. A Vancouver theatre director recalled in 1948 that 'there was a time when we had to cut practically all our plays to prudish society's idea of decency.' But her group was no longer willing to pander to the public's conservatism: 'they have to take experimental and educational plays as we see fit to include them in the program,' for only that way would Vancouverites become 'theatre conscious, and appreciate the plays for their true worth, living pictures of assorted phases of life.'[7] Calgary's Irene Prothroe agreed, observing that a production of *The Enchanted* was a new kind of play as far as Calgarians were concerned: 'many of them will no doubt consider it to be too far out,' but such plays 'must be produced occasionally in Calgary, if this city is to continue its cultural development.'[8] Implicit in such comments is the belief that the popular taste was pedestrian and traditional, and needed to be updated by cultural elites, with their superior understanding of the arts.

It would be convenient if the dichotomy between traditionalism and modernism was simply a generational divide, as Dwyer suggested, but this was not the case. We might assume that novelist Hugh MacLennan was a young turk bubbling over with modernist ideology when he went to Oxford University as a Rhodes Scholar in 1930, but nothing could be further from the truth. By his own admission, he had eagerly read every book by Sir Charles G.D. Roberts and was very fond of Archibald Lampman and Bliss Carman; had never read anything by Morley Callaghan; and had not even heard of Joyce, Eliot, Pound, or Proust—the high priests of modernist literature. MacLennan was not even familiar with the Group of Seven.[9] Toronto financier Sir Edmund Walker, on the other hand, who looked for all the world like a stodgy old conservative where art was concerned, was one of the most consistent promoters of modernist art in early twentieth-century Canada. Not that he had anything against the Old Masters—like Dwyer, he simply appreciated the 'reasonable excesses' of artists who were pushing boundaries.

I have no doubt that many readers will be unsatisfied with this book, if only because I have left out a favourite painter, poet, or sculptor. Even before I started writing, it became clear that for this book to be a readable size, there would be many difficult choices about who and what to include. Those decisions were made as an historian, rather than as a literary scholar, an architect, or a dramatist; in choosing to include some lesser-known figures because they illustrated the central themes of the book, I had to leave out many well-known names. As a defence, all I can say is that much has been written about these people and the few lines I might have added would hardly do them justice.

The dissatisfied reader might draw comfort from the fact that at few times in our history have we been satisfied with the state of our culture—why should this book be any different? However, we have rarely doubted the importance of the arts, and this is implicit in the final theme: that our culture embodies elements of the cultures that shaped it—aboriginal, French, British, American—but at the same time it is also uniquely and identifiably Canadian. On one level, this book is about cultural nationalism (or the belief that indigenous culture had to be promoted as a keystone of nation-building), but more accurately it is about the role that culture has played in the creation of a national identity.

For if Canadians have long lamented the state of our culture, we have been even more concerned about the nature of our identity. Does it exist? Do we have a national identity, or a series of regional or ethnic identities, or do they all coexist uneasily at once? 'We hear it said that there is no Canadian identity,' Hamilton Southam told his Ottawa audi-ence. 'What nonsense! What may be true is that our identity is hidden yet in the Pre-Cambrian Shield, as the Pietà remained hidden in a block of Cararra marble until Michelangelo took his chisel to it. Give our playwrights a generation or two, chipping away at our stony reserve with their sharp minds, and I can promise you that our grandchildren will know who we are.'[10]

It is significant that Southam assigned the task of revealing and expressing the national identity not to the statesman, the soldier, the explorer, or the captain of industry, but to the artist. The former may have built the country in a political or economic sense, but it was the poet, the painter, the sculptor, and the composer who gave it life. This book is the story of their efforts to chip away at the raw material until a Canadian identity emerged.

Chapter 1

The First Artists

The earth, water, muskeg, and rock of this country have yielded some breathtaking pieces of art created by Canada's original inhabitants. A tiny ivory mask, some 3,500 years old, its eyes and mouth tightly shut and its face incised with lines that may represent tattooing. On a single limestone outcrop near Peterborough, Ontario, hundreds of painted images of people, animals, birds, reptiles, and boats. Shards of pottery, elegantly decorated with squares, diamonds, and fine rows of notches stamped into the still-damp clay, found in the grasslands of southern Saskatchewan. A delicately carved effigy pipe, in the shape of what may be a lizard, recovered from the site of a Huron village north of Toronto. From the work of archaeologists, ethnographers, anthropologists, and historians, we know that aboriginal culture was extraordinarily rich with confidently and strongly worked forms, vibrant and powerful colours, and vigorous and expressive dances and music.

But it was a culture that did not fit easily into European preconceptions. It made no distinction between objects that were utilitarian and those with only an aesthetic purpose; the European notion of art for art's sake was foreign to aboriginal society. Nor was there any division of cultural activity into a hierarchy, with the high arts like painting and sculpture at the top, and the crafts, like pottery and weaving, at the bottom. Native societies did not separate arts from crafts and, indeed, no native language has a word that corresponds to 'art' in the western sense. The Anishnabec use 'mijiwe-izhijiganan,' which literally means 'made with the hands.' The Haida language has words for objects that are carved, painted, or woven, but the word that corresponds most closely with 'artist' is 'stlanlaas,' meaning 'good with their hands.'[11] For the First Nations, culture was not a single, demarcated aspect of existence, as it often is in the western tradition; it was existence itself, and was inextricably bound up with everything else, from the religious to the social to the political to the practical. To conceive of a culture that was purely and solely aesthetic in the western sense is to imagine something that did not exist.

———•◦•———

In an account of his travels in the Arctic in the late eighteenth century, explorer Samuel Hearne tells of meeting an Inuit woman, the last survivor of an attack in which her entire family was killed. She had escaped from captivity and wandered the Arctic wastes for seven months; when Hearne and his party encountered her she was living the most precarious existence. However, Hearne was surprised to see that she was wearing beautifully decorated clothing: 'It is scarcely possible to conceive that a person in her forlorn situation could be so composed as to be capable of contriving or executing any thing not absolutely necessary to her existence; but there were sufficient proofs that she had extended her care much farther, as all her clothing, beside being calculated for real service, shewed great taste, and exhibited no little variety of ornament. The materials, though rude, were very curiously wrought, and so judiciously placed, as to make the whole of her garb have a very pleasing, though rather romantic appearance.'[12]

This anecdote reveals the difficulty of considering aboriginal art from a Eurocentric perspective. To put it simply, what should be considered art? To the western mind, a plain coat, spearhead, or clay pot is not art, but at what point does it become art? With the addition of one incised decorative line? Two lines? A pattern? There are no easy answers to such questions, and indeed the questions themselves would make little sense to the aboriginal mind. For the European explorer, the woman had used some of her precious energy and resources merely to decorate her clothing, a task that he regarded as 'not absolutely essential to her existence.' But for the nameless Inuit woman, it was not simply a matter of decoration; art was part of her essence, and to create what Hearne and his comrades saw as art was as much a part of life as eating or sleeping. After all, the Inuit word meaning 'to make poetry' is the same as the word for 'to breathe,' and both derive from the word for 'the soul.'[13] So, it pays to cast the net as broadly as possible in considering aboriginal culture; for in those early societies, everything was suffused with, and energized by, artistic activity.

Even so, there is a point in the prehistory of human societies at which art cannot exist. In his pioneering work *Primitive Art* (written in 1927 but not published until 1955), anthropologist Franz Boas argued that cultural works can only emerge when societies have the opportunity, the ability, and the inclination to produce them.[14] The creation of a work of art takes time, and a society in which everyone is constantly engaged in the struggle for survival is unlikely to have time to produce works of art. On the other hand, a tribe that secures the bulk of its food supply in a season or two, and therefore has one or more seasons of leisure, will have the opportunity for creative expression. By the same token, a society that is sedentary has a greater opportunity to create works of art. An artist is unlikely to complete an ornate basket or a woven cape in one sitting; she will put it aside occasionally, to be completed over a period of time. Nomadic peoples rarely had the luxury of being able to carry around half-finished works of art. A society must also possess the technical ability to produce works of art. The level of expertise, particularly in working with tools, must be such that the artists have the manual skills to render the object they want to render. Until a carver has the dexterity to carve something that resembles, even vaguely, a bird, sculpture cannot be said to exist. And finally, the inclination to produce decorative items must exist. Culture demands a degree of awareness; the artist must recognize a form to the degree that he wants to represent it in art, while the rest of that community must have a sufficient level of consciousness to recognize the form once it has been reproduced. There had to be some moment when the man took up a piece of bone and realized that he could use a flint tool to transform it into the image of a bird or a seal; there had to be a point at which the woman realized that hues could be daubed on an animal skin to produce designs. Until that realization took hold, there could be no art.

But even when all of these characteristics were in place, it was not necessarily enough; the last piece of the puzzle was an understanding that the artistic rendering of those forms had some value. In this regard, the spiritual dimension of art is crucial. There had to be the conscious-ness that art could improve an object, although not only in the western sense of making it more attractive. Carved weapons are a case in point. The finest examples are rendered with breathtaking skill, but it would be wrong to assume that the carving and incision was merely decorative. Rather, the decoration was part of the function. The skilled carver could transform a harpoon head into a more effective weapon by adding intricate incisions or designs. The images that were incised imparted their power to the object, making it more effective. Art, in this way, became a mystical act. But as we will see, this was a double-edged sword. It motivated a remarkable flowering of aboriginal art, but it also made native culture more vulnerable when the Europeans arrived.

It is difficult to say where and when the first art emerged in Canada; we can only deduce from what has survived, and acknowledge that this represents just a tiny fraction of what was produced over the millennia. Music and story-telling probably came first, for they were the most flexible of art forms. As Boas noted, the hunters roaming the prairie or the seal hunters waiting at the blowhole could not carve or paint while they hunted, but they could chant, sing, or tell stories to each other, either to pass the time or to bring the power of magic to their hunt. Story-telling, of course, was more than just a form of entertainment. Aboriginal nations were oral societies, and the stories told by native elders constituted the historical and spiritual traditions of the people. Stories and legends were the repositories of their religion, their history, their identity—everything from their creation myths to tales of great military victories in the distant past. In short, the oral tradition was every bit as important in native society as the written tradition was in European.

Music and dance were the features of aboriginal culture that appear to have made the strongest impression on the first Europeans who encountered them, so they often described them in great detail (according to their own cultural assumptions, of course). George Heriot, a British traveller and artist who visited Lower Canada in the early nineteenth century, watched native dancers; his account says as much about what he saw as it does about conflicting native-versus-newcomer views of culture:

> they are strangers to melody in their songs, being totally unacquainted with music. The syllables which they enounce, are *yo*, *he*, *waw*. These are invariably repeated, the beholders beating time with

their hands and feet. The dancers move their limbs but a little way from the ground, which they beat with violence. Their dancing, and their music, are uniformly rude and disgusting, and the only circumstance which can recompense a civilized spectator, for the penance sustained by his ear, is, that to each dance is annexed the representation of some action, peculiar to the habits of savage life.[15]

A rather more open-minded observer was George Back, a British naval officer and artist who accompanied Sir John Franklin's Arctic Land Expedition of 1819–22. At Fort Providence on Great Slave Lake, in what is now the Northwest Territories, Back witnessed a dance by a band of Slavey Indians, who had come to the fort to trade furs and bear grease:

Every one had four feathers in each hand—when one commenced moving in a circular form—lifting both feet at the same time— similar to jumping sideways—after a short time a second and third joined—and afterwards the whole band were up—some in a state of nudity—others half-dressed—singing an unmusical wild air—with (I suppose) an appropriate story—the distinctive marks of which were ha! ha! ha! uttered vociferously and with great distortion of body, the feathers being kept constantly trembling.[16]

Our knowledge of aboriginal music, dance, and story-telling derives largely from accounts by contemporary European travellers like Heriot and Back, or from scholars or Indian Agents of the late nineteenth and early twentieth centuries. But we can also deduce what those forms may have been like in the pre-contact period by working back from the way they are practised now, as long as we acknowledge that forms of expression have changed over the centuries. Musicologists have concluded, for example, that there was a great range of musical styles across the continent: the deep and throaty songs, sung in a narrow range, of the coastal peoples; the more lyrical and higher, almost vibrato songs of the mountain communities; the steady drumbeat and apparent monotony that characterized the songs of the Plains Indians; and the songs of the Inuit, which were almost invariably accompanied by dancing and drumming (for the people of the north, the drum was a spiritual

The timelessness of native culture: compare the etching done in 1823 with the photograph on page 7, taken in 1949.

instrument, and was referred to as the 'shaman's steed' or the 'door to the world of spirits'). Early European visitors found native singing to be a tedious repetition of a very few syllables: one missionary reported that 'for the most part, their songs are heavy, so to speak, sombre and unpleasant; they do not know what it is to combine chords to compose a sweet harmony.'[17] Later scholars, however, have concluded that the words themselves were less important than the images that certain sounds were intended to evoke. Indeed, many songs may have consisted of sounds rather than words (rather like the form of jazz singing known as 'scat'), and the sounds carried the meaning. Such interpretations of native music would not have occurred to contemporary observers like George Heriot, however; their first instinct was to apply European cultural standards to a non-European culture.

Music, dance, and story-telling were ever-present in aboriginal societies, but they came together most significantly in the ritual performances, like the Sun Dance of the Plains Indians, that were so important to aboriginal spiritual and social life. In imagining these ceremonies, though, we must exercise caution. They have been described by countless travellers and anthropologists, but we have no way of knowing the degree to which the ceremony they witnessed resembled those that occurred in the pre-contact era. With that caution in mind, we might

Inuit child dancing, 1949.

use as representative a description of the Sun Dance held by the Sarcee of Alberta, as recorded by anthropologist Diamond Jenness.[18]

There were five 'societies' in the Sarcee nation (Jenness translated the native names as Mosquitoes, Dogs, Those Painted Red, Those Who Make Others Their Associates, and Birds), and every Sarcee male belonged to one or more society through his lifetime. Each of the societies held a ritual dance during the summer, but everything culminated in the August Sun Dance, when the various Sarcee communities came together as the berries they relied upon were ripening. The ceremony lasted for nine days, the first four of which were taken up by the people assembling at the chosen site. On the fifth day, they built the Sun Dance lodge and, once a centre pole (the most important symbolic element in the structure) had been selected, the couple hosting the Sun Dance began the process of ritually painting their daughter and son with red and black paint. As they did so, they chanted two songs: one was associated with the red hue, and one with the black. Finally, the mother placed on her daughter's head the richly decorated Sun Dance headdress, now the property of that family. They then took part in the ceremonial raising of the centre pole, which involved a number of elements, including an old warrior recounting stories of the nation's military history and a ritual dance using whistles carved from the wing bones of eagles.

With the preparations complete, the ceremony proper began on the sixth day. The primary element was the ritual torture of a number of young men, as a way to mark their passage to adulthood, but the Sun Dance abounded with different kinds of cultural performances. One man fasted for the duration of the festival in order to achieve a spirit vision, during which he would learn a new Sun Dance song; he then taught the song to a group of elders, who performed it while the faster danced. A warrior told stories of his past military glories while another, dressed in full battle gear, performed a re-enactment of the deeds. A group of men danced in a circle around three or four drummers, while other members of the community chanted and sang.

The Sun Dance, like similar ritual ceremonies held by other native nations, combined religious observance, expression of social status, community celebration, and cultural display. The art was inseparable from the religion, which was in turn inextricably linked to the status and celebratory functions. It was, then, an affirmation of the degree to which cultural expression was inherent in all aspects of aboriginal life.

Any discussion of pre-contact dance, music, or story-telling is necessarily based on a large measure of conjecture; for obvious reasons, we have no unadulterated songs, stories, or dances from the time before

This petroglyph, from Writing-on-Stone Provincial Park in Alberta, shows the impact of contact in the native hunter pursuing his prey on horseback. Undated.

the Europeans came. Of the cultural artifacts that survive and do allow direct analysis, the earliest may well be the rock paintings and etchings that can be found across Canada. This earliest form of graphic art comes in two forms: pictographs, or images painted on a rock face; and petroglyphs, images engraved or incised into the rock. It is not entirely clear which came first, or whether they emerged at the same time. It may be that incising—which requires more time and effort—was reserved for images with greater significance; or perhaps the pictograph was a later art form that replaced the petroglyph as aboriginal artists discovered that it offered greater versatility.

Regrettably, more questions than answers surround these images. They were incised using simple stone scrapers and chisels, or painted on with sticks or fingers using a pigment made from powdered minerals, usually ochre (the vast majority of pictographs are red). But the precise nature of the compound is unknown; it has proven to be considerably more durable than modern commercial paints, for reasons that scholars do not entirely understand. It has not even been possible to date these images satisfactorily, for they are not amenable to the carbon-dating techniques that have been so useful to archaeologists in other contexts.

Petroglyphs in northwestern Ontario are believed to be as much as five thousand years old, but the oldest in British Columbia are perhaps three thousand years old.

We can readily describe the composition of these images: some are geometric, involving patterns of lines and dots, while others used stylized, abstract forms that tend towards the representational. Occasionally, they are accompanied by hieroglyphics, or symbols representing certain concepts or objects. As with many other forms of aboriginal art, there are no frames or groundlines, and no apparent effort to group images deliberately; the composition is dictated less by the will of the artist than by the shape and form of the rock. Crevices, hollows, and cracks become as integral to the image as the paint and the etching.

We can only guess, however, at the purpose behind this form of art. The fact that the content was clearly more important than the form suggests that they were intended to be functional rather than aesthetic. Some of the images are simply directional; they point the way for a traveller, or mark the boundary of a hunting ground or an ancestral homeland. Others seem to be narrative in nature, describing important events in the life of a community or individual. It is likely, however, that much of the art had a strong spiritual element. Petroglyphs on the intertidal coast of British Columbia may have been invocations to the fish, to draw them into the rivers where they could be caught. By the same token, an elaborately incised boulder near Herschel, Saskatchewan, is probably a kind of offering to the bison upon which the people of the region depended. Other images may have been executed by shamans to record the elements of mystic rituals, or to record the dreams and visions of youths who were engaged in a spirit quest.

Rock was the most durable of canvases, but aboriginal peoples found many other surfaces that were suitable for painting. The Saulteaux, of the Ojibwa language group, painted geometric and realistic forms on rock, but also on birchbark and leather; and other peoples of the western plains, who apparently did little carving of either stone or wood, were just as versatile. Tent covers, *parflèches* (carrying pouches made of folded leather), animal hides, articles of clothing—all were richly decorated in whatever colour scheme the community preferred. The Cree used mainly red, with embellishments in yellow, purple, black, blue, or green, while the Ojibwa liked either very dark or very light hues—reds, yellows, greens, blue-violets, browns, tans. All of the colours came from the world around them: mineral-rich clays yielded brown, red, and yellow tints; blacks came from charcoal or dark earth; purples, blues, and greens from berries. Here again, the spiritual element dominated. Blackfoot tipis, for example, were often painted in a scheme that reflected their view of the cosmos. A band of decoration along the bottom edge represented the earth, with animals, spirits, or significant events depicted above. The horizon line was often scalloped to denote the mountains, while the upper band represented the night sky, complete with the sun, the moon, and the constellations. As archaeologist Eldon Yellowhorn put it, the 'tipi literally is a canvas for sketching Peigan [Blackfoot] identity.'[19] The Cree would paint skins as a way to propitiate the animals they hoped to kill; geometric shapes might be combined with a silhouette of the animal that was being hunted as a way to ensure success. If the hunt was a good one, they would then paint lines, bars, dots, or crosses on the inside of the hide of one of the hunted animals, as an act of gratitude. The Anishnabe carried this spirituality one step further: painting and drawing was the prerogative of the shaman, who used art to record his beliefs and philosophy, and to teach sacred beliefs to new initiates.

It appears that virtually every aboriginal community also practised carving and sculpting to a certain extent; even the people of the western plains, who had little access to raw materials, still produced elegantly carved weapons. The Iroquoians of the Upper St. Lawrence excelled at carving stone pipes, used in the ceremonial smoking of tobacco, with images of humans or animals, particularly the lizards, turtles, and birds which were so central to their cosmology.

But of all the carving that has survived from the pre-contact era, it is the work of the Dorset people—the ancestors of today's Inuit—that has excited the most interest amongst historians, ethnographers, and archaeologists. Dorset carvers were not interested in landscapes, plants, or geometrics but only in humans and animals, and even then the spiritual element dominated; as anthropologist Robert McGhee puts it, they portrayed humans 'as actors in a magical world of animals and spirits' rather than as people engaged in the everyday acts of living.'[20] It is not the quantity of Dorset art that is remarkable. Only a few hundred pieces survive, because carvers generally preferred vulnerable organic

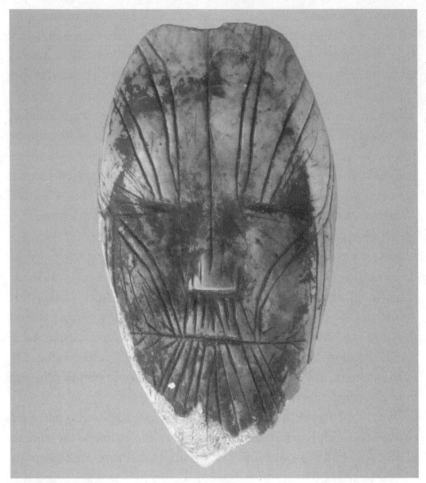

The skill of the Dorset Carver is evident in this finely worked mask, just 54 mm in length. c. 1700 BCE.

material—bone, horn, tooth, or wood (although wood was so scarce that it was reserved for bows and harpoons, or for special fetish objects or masks with religious significance)—to the more durable stone. But the items that do remain are of exceptional quality. Most of the pieces are small; walrus ivory, for example, yields only a small piece of carvable material; larger wooden objects had to be made from a number of small sections joined together. Even the tiniest pieces, however, are energetic, confident, vibrant, and extraordinarily well crafted. Typically they are not spatially oriented; there is no top or bottom, no background, and no groundlines or waterlines to situate the object in an environment. They float in space, and can be viewed equally well from any perspective.

Yet it was not until the 1960s that scholars began to devote serious attention to Dorset sculpture. George Swinton was one of the first to do so, and he posited that much of the sculpture was created by shamans who were skilled carvers and used art primarily for spiritual purposes. He imagined them to be akin to professional sculptors; they were probably mostly men, and they likely passed down their skills to their sons and grandsons. More recent scholars have not been so convinced by Swinton's analysis. Robert McGhee accepts that much of the art seems to have had a magical or religious purpose, in that it reveals the ways that the Dorset people tried to come to terms with a dangerous universe. However, he argues that the conclusion cannot be pushed too far. In the first place, there are enough extant pieces that do not seem to have been religious or magical in intent to demand a different interpretation. This comes out clearly in the treatment of various animals. The most common animal in Dorset sculpture is the polar bear, the animal with which they probably felt the closest kinship. Some are rendered in a highly naturalistic style, and their realism suggests that they had no purpose other than aesthetic; others, however, are stylized (like the flying or floating bear) and seem to refer not to a physical bear but to the bear spirit. Carved falcons were probably also executed for magical or religious purposes, either to signify a shaman's helper or to mobilize the spirit of the falcon to improve the skills of a hunter. Seals, on the other hand, were almost always carved naturalistically and in great detail, again suggesting that they were aesthetic objects pure and simple. By the same token, the wide range of ability reflected in the surviving works suggests that while there were undoubtedly some craftsmen of unusual skill, there was probably a relatively high level of general competence; it seems likely that many people in Dorset society had a sufficient level of skill to execute these carvings. For McGhee, this in itself suggests that art had a variety of purposes, including medical, magical, ornamental, and recreational. The most finely crafted works were medical or magical, while ornamental pieces or carved toys reflect a slightly lower level of ability, but still a capable hand.

Yet skilled carving could not save their way of life. Beginning in the eleventh century, and probably accelerated by the climate change that threatened their way of life, the Dorset were gradually swept aside by the Thule, a more technologically sophisticated society that was based on the whale hunt. McGhee suggests that this period witnessed a flowering of Dorset art because its spiritual content was magnified. The Dorset produced increasing numbers of carved religious objects as amulets or talismans to protect them in a rapidly changing world. It was not stability and prosperity that stimulated this renaissance, as Boas might have argued; it was the realization that their very way of life was under assault.

Most scholars agree, however, that the Thule were less sophisticated artistically, and their sculpture has suffered by comparison with that of the Dorset. It seems less original and inventive, and reflects a lack of variety—suggesting that the skill had been devalued in its practical and social significance. Where the Dorset figures floated freely in space, Thule figures were orientated using framelines, groundlines, or waterlines. Dorset geometric patterns were deeply incised, but Thule patterns use shallow dots or lines that may betray a kind of half-heartedness on the part of the carver. Perhaps for this reason, Thule art was especially vulnerable when ecological change began to affect the society. Through the sixteenth and seventeenth centuries, as the climate of the region changed, the communities that had been established to hunt whales began to disperse, and the Thule became nomadic. Just as Boas had theorized, nomadism meant the end of Thule art; it began to stagnate and no further development was witnessed.

The north was a birthplace of another art form that would eventually spread through the aboriginal communities of North America: ceramics. The art of making pottery was imported to Canada first by the Paleo-Eskimos who came across the Arctic from Siberia; the earliest examples, found at the Engigstciak site in the northern Yukon, are perhaps 3,500 years old. But those practices did not spread to the south; instead, a quite separate pottery tradition came north, originally from Mexico, but more directly from the North American heartland around the Mississippi River system, reaching what is now Ontario (where it became very significant in many communities) around 500 BCE. It reached the Maritimes (where it had less impact on the culture) some five hundred years later. As in many other art forms, pottery saw the merging of the utilitarian and the aesthetic. The earliest ceramics were probably unadorned, but in time their makers came to add patterns, initially simple geometric designs or decorative bands created by pressing a stick, a rope, or a piece of woven textile into the damp clay.

The ceramic arts reached the highest level of competency in settled agrarian communities, particularly the Iroquoian peoples of the St. Lawrence valley. Pottery, after all, is relatively fragile, and hardly suited to the lifestyle of nomadic people. Agrarians, on the other hand, because they tended to occupy the same villages for extended periods, found greater use for pottery and at the same time were able to develop an expertise, especially in the kiln technology that allowed them to create more durable pieces. As a result, the most striking achievements in the ceramic arts are to be found among the Huron, Petun, and Neutral peoples who inhabited southern Ontario and Quebec.

Two other crafts are worth mentioning because of the high artistic standard they attained: basketry and decorative clothing. A nineteenth-century anthropologist—writing with eighteenth-century sensibilities—labelled basketry as 'an art which may be called *par excellence* a savage art...[and] one of the most striking examples of savage patience and skill,' but his analysis was much more complimentary than these comments might suggest.[21] He found, as later scholars have, very high levels of creativity and technical skill in native woven baskets, as well as an astonishing range of techniques. The Kutchins, at the headwaters of the Yukon River, used tamarack roots for the basket itself and hair and porcupine quills for the ornamentation; all of the materials could be dyed using berries or grasses. For the Chilkoot of the west coast, the material of choice was the spruce root, split into long strips and sometimes dyed brown or black, with decorative red bands and highlights created by interweaving wild wheat straws. So tight and fine was the weaving that the basket could be made watertight. Their Salish neighbours preferred cherry bark, which they wove into coiled baskets using a technique known as imbrication. The Algonkians and Iroquois used fibres from birch and linden trees for basket-weaving, the white fibre being set off by bands of other materials dyed red, yellow, blue, or green. Their materials were modest; but from the accounts of the first Europeans who saw their work, their skill and design sense were remarkable.

In the case of decorated clothing, what appeared ornamental often had much deeper meaning. The nameless Inuit encountered by Samuel Hearne had not decorated her clothing simply to pass the time; for many aboriginal communities, ornament had specific practical or

'The dance of the Kutcha-Kutchi,' according to the title of this 1851 lithograph.

Nova Scotia artist Mary McKie's watercolour of a Mi'kmaq woman weaving baskets, 1845.

spiritual purposes that demanded the greatest skill from craftspeople. The clothing of the Mi'kmaq people in the Maritimes, for example, was rich in decorative elements—porcupine quills that were dyed red with bedstraw plant, black with boiled wood root, or yellow with boiled gold root, and woven, plaited, or stitched onto the hide; delicate moose

A native woman in the village of St. Regis, Quebec, drawn by Katherine Ellice in 1838.

hair embroidery; beads crafted from copper, stone, bone, teeth, claws, seeds, shells, or feathers; and paintings rendered with small tools made from bone. All of the ornament was carefully arranged into traditional designs and symbols that had magical significance, and crafted by women who were regarded as experts by their people; so highly valued was this skill that the craftswoman's tools were often buried with her.

And basketry was almost always done by women, for in most aboriginal communities there were clear gender distinctions in the production of crafts. Decorating articles of clothing was also largely the preserve of women, as was weaving, whether it be the false embroidery of the Tlingit, the twined spruce roots of the Haida, or the formline weaving of the Chilkat, and bark-biting. Designs bitten into tree bark (often birch) might be used as patterns for beadwork or porcupine-quill weaving, or they may have been used as decorative elements on their own. Carving, however, was largely the preserve of men, especially when it involved objects to be used in spiritual rituals or for medical purposes. Even in painting, there was a gendered division based on the implied importance of the item. Women often painted the geometric forms that served as decorative elements, while men rendered the supposedly more significant scenes of battles or visionary experiences. There may not have been a clear differentiation between high arts on the one hand and crafts on the other in native societies, but there clearly was a differentiation based on gender.

———•◦•———

The societies of the Arctic, the western plains, and the eastern woodlands took the arts to a high level of accomplishment, but the consensus seems to be that the finest flowering of aboriginal culture, and the one that brought together the greatest number of different art forms, occurred among the people of the northwest coast. It was also those communities whose view of art and culture most closely resembled the European; only there would the notion of art for art's sake have been comprehensible. What made these communities nearly unique was that the plentiful off-shore resources (primarily salmon) enabled a settled existence with considerable leisure time. It also meant that art was not primarily devoted to objects and ceremonies intended to improve the chances of a successful hunt. It still had a spiritual dimension, but in the rigid social hierarchy of these communities, art also came to have a secular, social element that was absent in other native nations. Art was a demonstration of social position, as song, dance, and carving enacted an individual's lineage and family linkages. It was a means to show status and prestige, and communities were used to seeing what amounted to cultural competition, as members expressed their claims to supremacy through the lavishness of their art. As a result, art belonged to the entire community, rather than being the sole preserve of the shaman. Everyone from slave to master participated in its creation, its performance, and its enjoyment. The result was a cultural life of extraordinary richness and vibrancy.

That richness has brought scholars to the field in unusual numbers, and consequently more is known about the art of the northwest than any other region. There is evidence of personal decoration dating as far back as 3000 BCE, and the first artistic renderings of life forms were probably done around 2500 BCE. Simply decorated tools probably came next, with the decorative motifs becoming progressively more elaborate through the generations, particularly as expanded trade networks brought in new materials such as amber, dentalium, jet, obsidian, and copper. A thousand years ago, animal or human forms began to appear in the art, putting in place the last piece of the puzzle that is now identified as the fully formed classic northwest style. This entire process took something like four millennia, in what anthropologist Roy Carlson sees as a perfect example of the Boas dictum: coastal communities slowly generated the system of shared beliefs and modes of thinking, as well as the general recognition of certain graphic symbols, that was necessary for art to exist. As Carlson put it, 'the accumulation of historical and mythological traditions by the corporate lineages of northern coast villages was approaching the threshold where graphic symbols of corporate identity became meaningful.'[22]

Notwithstanding the important differences in cultural practices between the peoples of the west coast, there were sufficient commonalities to allow us to speak of a 'west coast art' that is broadly consistent through the Tlingit, Haida, Tsimshian, Bella Coola, Kwakiutl, Nisga'a, Gitskan, and Nuu-chah-nulth (Nootka) nations. Without doing too much violence to the uniqueness of these communities, we can easily create a scenario that captures the richness and vibrancy of west coast culture.

Our story might begin with a headman who felt motivated to erect a new *gayang*, or frontal pole, at his dwelling. For some months he had become increasingly aware that his neighbours were erecting more ornately carved objects: mortuary poles to store the remains of the dead; memorial poles to commemorate clan members who had died elsewhere; and elaborately painted frontal screens for their houses. They were demonstrating their wealth—partly in material terms but more importantly in what anthropologists Bill McLennan and Karen Duffek called 'the intangible riches inherited from ancestors: the rights to dances, songs, names, masks, and regalia, as well as to crests and other prerogatives.'[23] Employing craftsmen to create these masterpieces and holding the ceremonial feasts to dedicate them were very public displays of their social position. But our headman's own fortunes had recently improved, and he felt that it was time to commission a new pole to reaffirm the privileges that went along with his status and lineage.

Like most of the men in his village, he was a skilled craftsman himself—he had spent many hours carving and decorating household implements—but the importance of the occasion demanded that he engage a professional. Had his family been larger, there would probably have been a master carver in it, but instead he had to call in an outsider, a local man who had been apprenticed in the art of carving by his father or uncle, and who was essentially a professional artist making a living from commissioned carvings (it is worth noting that this master carver was invariably male). His skill gave him status; he was regarded as a community leader, the equivalent of a high-ranking member of the noble class. Meetings were held and terms agreed, but a public announcement of the contract was necessary in this pre-literate society. The headman organized a feast, at which the contract was announced and a downpayment offered to the carver, who (along with an assistant or two) moved into the headman's dwelling while they worked on the pole.

Once a cedar of the proper height and girth had been selected and felled, the carver began to work, using crest images of animals with which the family was identified. As the pole took shape, some of the peculiarities of west coast art became evident. The carver disliked blank spaces, so the animal figures—whales, beaver, eagles, hawks, ravens—were elongated or compressed to fill the entire pole. Colours came next, although the carver did not have a large palette to work with: black, taken from soot, graphite, or manganese; red, orange, brown, and yellow from ochre; greenish blue from corroded copper; white from diatomaceous earth or burned shells. The images were strong and confident, and the contrasting colours made them even more striking.

At last the pole was ready and it was time for another feast to dedicate it. But this feast would be much more extravagant than the last, for it would mark a new chapter in the headman's social existence, a demonstration of his new level of status. Not only would the pole

Richly carved poles in a Haida village, Louise Island, British Columbia, 1878.

be raised and the carver paid, but elaborate performances would tell the tale of the headman's lineage for all the community to hear. Songs would be sung, some of which had been handed down from generation to generation while others were commissioned from the community's composer, a professional (again usually a man) who held the same exalted social rank as the master carver. He would devise the lyrics (he was particularly fond of plays on words that poked fun at certain guests) and the musical arrangements, although the accompaniment would be confined to percussion instruments like drums and tambourines. He would then teach the songs to the headman's kin, always in secret so the other guests would not know what to expect. There would also be dramatic recitations in which the headman's relatives would re-enact legends and great events from the clan's history, all accompanied by props, painted backdrops, and ritual dances. The distinctive appearance of the performers' ornate clothing was as important as its sound and its feel. Brightly coloured carved masks and headdresses trimmed with feathers, animal hooves that dangled from the hems and banged together rhythmically, expertly woven or embroidered tunics done by the women who preserved those arts—all came together in a riot of

The Haida village at Masset, British Columbia, 1890. Note how the traditional native architecture has been replaced by European-style buildings.

sound, music, colour, and sensation. And when it was finally over, the headman was well satisfied, fully aware that his neighbours would now regard his own display of status with growing envy.

This scenario probably never happened in exactly this way, for it brings together elements of a variety of traditions. But it is representative of the kind of cultural ceremony that punctuated the lives of the first peoples of the west coast. It combined artistic elements—dance, music, the plastic arts—with immense communal symbolism. In short, it made manifest the intimate connection between the arts and all other elements of social interaction.

This scenario also reveals the glory of west coast culture that was such a revelation to the first Europeans who encountered it, men who had been conditioned to regard aboriginals as savages devoid of cultural sensibilities. In contrast to what they had been led to expect, they found communities with cultures as rich, if vastly different, than their own in Europe. Fur traders were struck by the fact that virtually every public act in Haida life was accompanied by a song; every business transaction was prefaced and concluded with music. James Cook, the explorer who has been credited with staking British claims to the northwest coast, marvelled that 'nothing is without a kind of freeze-work, or the figure of some animal upon it…even upon their stone and bone weapons…The strong propensity of this people to works of this sort is remarkable, in a vast variety of particulars.' Explorer Étienne Marchand, who visited Haida villages on the west coast in 1791, was amazed to see 'paintings every where, every where sculpture, among a nation of hunters.' The Norwegian traveller Johan Adrian Jacobsen, who toured the same communities a century later, called them 'a nation of artists, for there is nothing they use that is not skilfully decorated with meaningful designs.' Such comments were echoed by Europeans elsewhere in North America. Samuel de Champlain, the explorer and cartographer often called the father of New France, was 'struck with wonder' at the carving skills of the native peoples living along the St. Lawrence River. For Marc Lescarbot, a French lawyer and author who came to Acadia in 1606, the porcupine quillwork practised by the Mi'kmaq 'coloured with red, black, white and blue, which are the colours they use, [was] so vivid that ours seem not to approach them.'[24] The shock of contact, in this small context, was felt by both sides.

But the arrival of those Europeans would have dire consequences for the very culture that so impressed people like Cook and Marchand. Even as native culture reached what was arguably its highest point of development, it was about to be placed under threat. The communities of the west coast were the last in Canada to be touched by the Europeans; as the First Nations to the east had already learned, native culture was being changed forever.

Chapter 2

The Meeting and Mingling of Cultures

There are few places where the impact of contact is as clearly expressed in art as in Writing-on-Stone Provincial Park, in the Milk River valley of southern Alberta. An important meeting place for the nomadic peoples of the plains, it is the largest concentration of petroglyphs and pictographs on the North American prairies, with rock art covering centuries of human history. Some of the earliest paintings show warriors on foot preparing to do battle, clearly depictions of warfare in the pre-contact era. A later drawing shows a similar scene, but with an important difference: one of the combatants is on horseback. The horse, introduced to the Americas by the Spaniards, had gradually worked its way north to the western plains, where it reshaped the native nations that lived there. An even later rock painting shows another encounter, except this time dashes indicating the flight of arrows are accompanied by dotted lines representing bullets fired from rifles, another European import that, just as much as the horse, would irrevocably alter the native way of life. The ancient cultural form of rock painting remained the same over the centuries, but the changing subject matter revealed a new reality.

For centuries, aboriginal communities had interacted with each other—in war, but also in peaceful trading over extensive and well-developed trade routes. This contact meant that, along with the commodities that were being bartered, cultural influences moved back and forth as well. Styles of painting, carving, and music were exchanged so freely that it is difficult to find an aboriginal nation whose culture didn't show at least vague influences of its trading partners.

The arrival of the Europeans brought a very different dynamic, in large part because the missionaries charged with spreading the Christian gospel through the new world used culture as their primary tool. As a result, in addition to the same kind of creative borrowing that had marked relations between aboriginal societies for centuries, the meeting of native and European cultures came to have a corrosive effect on indigenous communities. The impact was not all one-sided to be sure—aboriginal influences would be seen in the culture that eventually flowered in North America. But in the short term, it was native culture that paid the heaviest price of contact.

———•◦•———

We know from the earliest exploration accounts that culture was one of the first things the Europeans off-loaded in North America. Before the gunpowder, the iron tools, the alcohol, the syphilis—before any other imports, the Europeans brought their culture. When Jacques Cartier anchored off the south coast of Labrador in June 1534, on the first of his three voyages of discovery to the so-called New World, he ordered that a mass be sung in celebration. The following year, upon reaching Hochelaga (on the site of present-day Montreal) in October 1535, he commanded that trumpets and other musical instruments be sounded to announce his arrival. Music, so central to European religion and courtly life, heralded the coming of a new culture to North America.

But Cartier and his men soon realized that they had little time for artistic endeavours—the struggle for survival consumed all their time

Lawrence R. Batchelor's watercolour of Jacques Cartier at Hochelaga, with his drums and horns in the rear, 1933.

and energy. It was the same for the Sieur de Roberval's little band of émigrés who vainly tried to found a colony at Cap Rouge, Quebec, in 1542; for the convicts who were settled on Sable Island, off the coast of Nova Scotia, in 1598; and for the handful of settlers who established themselves at Tadoussac on the Saguenay River in 1600. Samuel de Champlain was more aware of the need for entertainment, his Order of Good Cheer giving the inhabitants of Port-Royal, in present-day Nova Scotia, something to do beyond working, but that initiative was little more than a supper club. His only concession to culture was the reading aloud from historical accounts or *The Lives of the Saints*. Unlike the Innu woman encountered by Hearne, the first French settlers found artistic expression to be a luxury they could little afford. In short, exploration and culture apparently did not mix.

C.W. Jeffery's 1925 rendering of Champlain's Order of Good Cheer in 1606.

But religion and culture did mix, and the establishment of the Company of New France as the *seigneur* of all French territory in North America changed the equation. A consortium of private investors (the group was more commonly known as the Company of One Hundred Associates), its goal was to develop in the colony a viable trade system and self-supporting agricultural settlement. But the company's other objective was the conversion of natives to Christianity. Mindful of the failure of the Récollets, who had come to New France as proselytizers early in the seventeenth century but had been utterly defeated by the wilderness and the hostility of native tribes, the Company was determined to do things right. It despatched its first settlers to New France in May 1628; a revived missionary effort was not far behind.

This time, the Company gave the Society of Jesus exclusive control over relations with the aboriginal peoples of Huronia, a region in what is now southern Ontario that seemed to offer the most fertile ground for missionary work. This included responsibility for managing both the proselytizing campaign and the fur trade. In some ways this was a bad bargain for both sides. The Jesuits were not particularly interested in trade, but went along with it because of their fanatical pursuit of conversions; the Hurons were not especially keen to be converted, but humoured the Jesuits to retain the all-important trade connections. Within this often uneasy partnership, European culture quickly assumed a utilitarian value and, as a tool of the missionaries, slowly worked its way into the interior.

Europeans may have regarded the aboriginals as a people with no culture, but the Jesuits quickly realized that native society was strongly musical. They sent home long descriptions of native singing styles, often giving high praise to their vocal talents and the instruments they used for accompaniment. One newcomer who tried to render some Mi'kmaq songs into European notation went so far as to suggest that their musical vocabulary included the word 'alleluia.' Those missionaries who dismissed indigenous music as cacophonous or crude still realized that it might be possible to capitalize on the aboriginals' inherent musicality to aid in their conversion. The first step was to translate the lyrics of French hymns into native languages, and then adapt the original tunes to the new lyrics. If the end product proved to be unsingable, the missionaries were perfectly willing to write new music using either native rhythms or French folk tunes or drinking songs as templates. The best known example of this is the *Huron Carol*, probably written between 1634 and 1648 by the Jesuit missionary Jean de Brébeuf to music based on a sixteenth-century French folk song called *Une Jeune Poucelle* ("A Young Maiden"). Accompaniment might be provided by a violin or transverse flute, but more often it was simply the human voice raised in praise. For the Jesuits, who seem not to have considered that the natives might have been animated by a love of singing rather than an interest in the Christian gospel, this made all of their efforts worthwhile. The Jesuit *Relations*, the reports that described the work of the missionaries to their superiors in Europe, are effusive in their praise of music as a means of encouraging the natives to embrace Christianity. Through the 1740s, even allowing for a certain amount of exaggeration of the success of their efforts, they devoted more and more space to descriptions of natives rapturously singing hymns. As Father Louis Davaugour wrote earnestly, if condescendingly, from the mission at Lorette, west of Quebec, in 1710, 'they sing sacred hymns written in the vernacular tongue, and adapted to the feasts which are then being celebrated,—with a harmony truly beautiful, and not at all barbarous.'[25]

As a result, musical ability came to be emphasized as an ever more important trait in prospective missionaries. All priests likely had some rudimentary musical education, but with the apparent success of the conversion campaign, the religious orders became more cognizant of dispatching missionaries with higher levels of musical training. Father Paul Le Jeune, who arrived in New France in 1632 as superior of the Jesuits at Quebec, was the first missionary to promote music instruction actively, teaching Gregorian chants and musical notation to his charges; seven years later, the nuns of the Ursuline order arrived and began providing musical instruction to native girls.

The French had also concluded that art could be a powerful tool in conversion. Although it lacked the participatory element of music, it did allow for the use of graphic images to overcome language barriers and ensure that the messages were clear. Indeed, missionaries noted that pictures had a striking effect on aboriginals. The Récollet priest Gabriel Sagard reported that some of his converts 'were indeed so simple that they believed these images were alive, feared them, and begged us to speak to them.'[26] The Récollets and Jesuits requested specific kinds of images from France to assist them in their work, usually in the form of cheap engravings: full-face portraits of Mary or Jesus were preferred to profiles, because natives were apparently quite taken with faces that seemed to look back at them; and prints with reds and blues were more effective than those with yellows and greens, likely because of the powers that natives associated with certain colours. Aside from engravings by the hundreds, the missionary orders also sent artists to New France. Canada's first non-aboriginal artist was apparently Abbé Pommier, who volunteered to go to New France after reading of the martyrdom of the Jesuit fathers when the Iroquois swept through Huronia in the 1640s and destroyed the communities that the Jesuits had been carefully cultivating for a decade and a half. It appears that Pommier was not a particularly effective missionary (contemporary accounts suggest that he was rather lazy), but he had a strong interest in art and was the first of a long line of priests who turned a hobby into a means of conversion. One can picture a missionary like Pommier doing small oil or watercolour sketches and using them to teach scriptural lessons to natives he encountered in his work.

———•◦•———

But what did this cultural interaction mean for the natives who learned Christian hymns or studied the pictures painted by missionaries like Abbé Pommier? We know that, over the long term, the Christian message that the missionaries were preaching was tremendously damaging to native communities, but what about the medium used to convey the message? In some ways, the cultural dynamic that was emerging was similar to what native nations had been accustomed to for centuries; the arrival of European culture simply brought new opportunities for creative borrowing.

And, as in the pre-contact era, it is sometimes difficult to determine where one cultural influence ended and another began. Over a number of decades in the early twentieth century, for example, anthropologist Frank Speck, ethnographer Marius Barbeau, and historian Alfred Goldsworthy Bailey carried on a debate over the relationship between the geometric patterns and double-curve motif that dominated early Algonkian art, and the realistic floral patterns that seemed to evolve later. Speck believed that the geometrics and the double-curve were pre-contact forms, the latter related to the patterns of bitten birchbark; floral designs, he argued, were a natural outgrowth of the curve motif, and not necessarily related to European influence. Barbeau, on the other hand, argued that almost all such motifs were European in derivation,

originating with the French nuns who taught embroidery and needlework to aboriginal women. What Speck judged to be an ancient aboriginal form was, in Barbeau's view, adopted from French Renaissance
design. Goldsworthy, for his part, took a middle position, suggesting that
the double-curve was a pre-contact design, while floral patterns were
borrowed from the Europeans. According to his research, the Algonkian
tribe that was deepest in the interior, the Naskapi (Innu), used virtually
nothing in the way of floral ornamentation; the closer a tribe lived
to the St. Lawrence Valley, in other words the closer it was to European influences, the more prominent floral designs were in their art.[27]

The relationship between European and native culture is much
clearer in other contexts. In music, for example, the Mi'kmaq of New
Brunswick and the Hurons of Lorette took elements of Gregorian
chants and French folk music that they learned from the missionaries
and incorporated them into their own music. As a result, the music
that nineteenth-century ethnographers studied as being authentically
native was in fact quite different from what the first missionaries heard,
because the interaction of the native and the European tradition had
altered both. In west coast art, the introduction of commercial paints
changed the palette that was available to native craftsmen. Vermilion,
brought from China by fur traders, was available in the late eighteenth
century and within fifty years manufactured ultramarine and Prus-
sian blue were common in British Columbia. By the end of the nineteenth century, commercial oil paints were in widespread use, either in
conjunction with or instead of traditional pigments. But anthropologist
Erna Gunther is reluctant to see the adoption of new colours as evidence
of cultural decline, preferring to regard it as a sign of continued vitality
and search for novelty among native artists. In short, it was a classic case
of benign creative borrowing.

By the same token, the native women who learned musical styles
from the Ursulines also learned European techniques of embroidery.
They may have preferred to use moose hair and birchbark instead of
thread and fabric, but they clearly embraced the European technique as
well as the imported scissors and needles that made their work much
easier. This, in turn, was related to the broader acceptance of European clothing, a process that had an impact on aboriginal culture in
many ways. The intricate ornamentation using natural materials like

In George Heriot's etching, we see the impact of European fashion on native dress. Undated.

porcupine quills eventually gave way to decorative work with ribbon and glass beads obtained through trade with European merchants; the dangling shells and animal hooves that gave a musicality to their clothing were replaced by different objects such as keys and pulleys. The clothing itself came to be made of cloth or wool rather than fur or leather, validating Bailey's conclusion about the penetration of the floral motif: the closer a tribe was to European settlements, the more complete was the transformation. By the nineteenth century, for example, the Mi'kmaq of eastern Canada had largely discarded their traditional clothing in favour of woollen jackets and skirts, and robes made from woollen blankets. In the interior, the Naskapi retained their caribou-skin coats; but even they were influenced by European styles, and their clothing began to resemble military uniforms. The Ojibwa, who had rarely used black in their dress, developed a fondness for black velveteen, and increasingly used that European fabric in making their clothing. The tools of the trade changed as well; women became more accustomed to using metal awls and needles traded from the Europeans instead of the bone tools their ancestors had used.

In other contexts, native artists simply adjusted their traditional techniques to accommodate the new relationship. On the west coast the Haida, so adept at basketry, began to weave trade goods that resembled European trinkets like teapots and sugar bowls. The Nuu-chah-nulth,

The commodification of native culture: two women from Nootka Sound, British Columbia, weaving baskets at the St. Louis World's Fair, 1904.

who for generations had created utilitarian plaited or twined baskets with little in the way of decoration, began making more ornate objects, like basket-covered bottles or lidded baskets, items that were not part of their own craft tradition and were made specifically for the curio trade. The Mi'kmaq turned their skill at working with birchbark and porcupine quill to make lidded boxes—a form unknown in pre-contact Mi'kmaq society—apparently solely to trade with Europeans. In some areas, missionaries encouraged native women to collect rags to be woven into mats for their dwellings; here again, they used a native craft technique to produce a European commodity.

A similar process occurred in pictography, which served as the written language of native societies. The fact that the Europeans brought with them so many new objects and concepts meant that pictography had to change as the visual vocabulary expanded. The addition of horses and guns to rock paintings is just one example of a process that was occurring across the continent as native expression was transformed by the addition of new elements of vocabulary. Was this process positive or negative? In one sense, it is little different from the addition of words like 'internet' and 'cellphone' to the English language;

European literacy reaches native society: a missionary preaches to Cree families at Lac La Ronge (now in Saskatchewan) in the late 1840s.

all languages evolve, and the fact that native pictography a century after contact was no longer the same language that it had once been is not necessarily negative.

However, over time, contact involved more than simply the addition of new concepts and objects to the artistic vocabulary. Native pictography was eventually obliterated by the spread of the written word and European-style literacy in the same way that other native cultural practices were damaged, or even destroyed, by influences that may have seemed benign at first. The advent of European metal tools is a case in point. On one level, the sharper points and cutting blades gave native carvers much more versatility than they had ever enjoyed in the past. The Haida, for example, had long carved from argillite, a dense, black shale from the Queen Charlotte Islands. But the coming of iron tools enabled them to take their work to new levels, with larger pieces, finer detail, and more intricate designs. It was the same in Canada's north. The soapstone carving for which the Inuit are now so well known would never have been possible with the stone tools they used before contact with the Europeans; soapstone could only be carved with metal tools obtained from trade.

Indigenous talent meets European subject matter: natives performing a passion play at St. Mary's Mission, British Columbia, 1894.

But on a deeper level, the coming of metal tools was profoundly damaging. In aboriginal societies, culture was inseparable from religion; everything in the human world, even tools, was affected by spiritual factors. As Bailey put it, 'the efficacy of an implement, for example, was determined by factors which operated from beyond the material world.'[28] A stone knife was good, but it could be made better with the addition of carved designs or incisions to give it mystical power. But what happened to this philosophy when a plain European iron knife could be used much more effectively than the richly decorated stone knife? Logically, to the native mind, it worked better because it had a more concentrated supply of mystical power; by extension, the European who brought it must have had supernatural abilities that exceeded those of the native craftsman who carved and decorated the stone knife.

Something as simple as a metal tool, then, could call into question the very basis of aboriginal beliefs. Similarly, European cultural practices had the potential to undermine the authority of the spiritual leaders of the community. In this context, the arrival of the written word in native communities was a profound shock. In their initiation rituals, natives had become accustomed to seeing their young men repeat stories passed down by shamans or community elders; but the notion that different people could reproduce the same phrases verbatim, simply by reading from a text, struck them as verging on the mystical. When epidemics swept through Huron villages in the mid-seventeenth century, this perception was heightened as the natives came to believe that writing, and everything else imported by the Jesuits for that matter, possessed the power of sorcery. It was the same with art. Among the Anishnabe people before the arrival of the Europeans, painting and drawing was the prerogative of the shaman; painting was a spiritual act, because he used art to record his philosophical worldview and to teach new initiates the sacred beliefs of their people. But when the European missionaries arrived and casually passed around cheap engravings of Biblical scenes or sat down and sketched parables for native children, the very position of the shaman was called into question. Were the black robes challenging the spiritual authority of the shaman? Were they, in fact, the true vessels of mystical power?

Equally important was the fact that the Europeans introduced new dimensions to the barter economy. At first, the traders seemed only interested in furs, but eventually they developed a taste for certain native arts and crafts. With this, the relationship between culture and religion was further compromised. The disintegration of the Thule whale-hunting culture in the sixteenth and seventeenth centuries was parallelled by a decline in the quality of their art and craftsmanship, a fact that was probably directly related to increased trade with Europeans. As the whites became interested in trading their goods for carved objects, the Thule began to produce art for the sole purpose of trading with Europeans. Carving, once a spiritual activity, became a commercial activity, and as the Thule lost the spiritual dimension to their culture, their entire society became more vulnerable to outside influences. The poet William Kirby detected this transformation among the Huron people, and described it ruefully in his poem *The U.E.*: 'The Huron's once proud hand,/That shook the hatchet o'er the trembling land,/Bears venal trinkets round.'[29]

The same process occurred much later on the west coast. At first, the advent of new tools and paints, and the fact that trade with the Europeans brought great prosperity to some communities, caused west coast art to flourish. Native leaders with new wealth demanded larger and more elaborate works of art to demonstrate their affluence, and craftsmen now had better tools to meet the increased demand. Indeed, the abundance of totem poles dating from the late nineteenth century can be directly related to the new wealth generated by trade with the Europeans. But the bubble quickly burst. The sea otters so coveted by European traders were driven away by aggressive native hunting, and aboriginal nations had to find something else to barter. One of the things they turned to was their art, which they quickly realized was highly prized by Canadian, American, and European tourists, and by museum curators and ethnographers, who began to commission works directly from native artists. In a fairly short span of time, the craftsmen were transformed from artists creating works with important social and ceremonial functions to the manufacturers of commodities. By the 1830s, argillite carvings, increasingly depicting European-style people or boats, became standard trade items, and in time natives began to migrate to Fort Victoria, which the Hudson's Bay Company [HBC] had opened as a trading post in 1843. There, they could be closer to white buyers and, incidentally, could find work carving wooden moulds for wrought iron, which was becoming fashionable as decorative elements in the homes of the growing white population. But in 1862, the Haida encampments around the fort were decimated by smallpox, which eventually spread through the entire nation. The population plummeted from some 7,000 to around 800, and the survivors eventually gathered in two villages, abandoning all the others and leaving the wealth of carved and painted objects to rot. In the process, the region's cultural diversity, once strengthened by the number of flourishing villages scattered around the Haida homeland, began to disappear.

This, in turn, had broad ramifications for native culture. With the population so reduced, the need for ceremonies dropped correspondingly, as did the opportunities for artists to practice their crafts in the traditional way. The apprenticeship system—in which carvers had been trained by respected elders, acquiring not only technical proficiency but a high degree of social status in the process—deteriorated. Carvers with little or no formal training, and more importantly no social role, became more numerous. The gendered division of art was also altered, as women moved from crafts like weaving into traditionally male-dominated work like carving and painting. Even their architecture changed.

For generations, extended families had lived in large houses made from huge split cedar planks and decorated with ornately painted screens that featured the family's crests and expressed its lineage and status. But within decades of the arrival of white traders and missionaries, the distinctive dwellings had all but disappeared, replaced by single-family houses made from milled lumber — they were not named (as pre-contact houses had been, as another mark of respect) and were devoid of decoration, their plainness symbolizing the erasure of much of native expression in the years after contact.

At the same time, the missionaries on the west coast were doing their part to obliterate other aspects of the indigenous culture. At Port Simpson on the northern coast of British Columbia, the resident minister convinced the natives to take down and destroy the totem poles that had once been so central to their culture and communal life. The Anglican Reverend William Henry Collison, who set up shop at Old Masset, one of the two reconstituted Haida villages, made it his business to stamp out native dancing, which offended his Protestant sensibilities. He and other missionaries tolerated the carving of argillite souvenirs because it seemed harmless, but they waged an all-out war against the potlatch, a ritual that had already been dramatically affected by contact. Historically, the ceremony—which involved the display of hereditary possessions like songs, dances, and masks, the recitation of a clan's history and lineages, and the distribution of gifts to guests, all according to strict codes of hierarchy—had been most common in the nations of the northern and central regions of the west coast. Even then, potlatches were held infrequently, because they demanded considerable wealth and were regarded as the preserve of only the most important chiefs. But contact changed the entire socio-economic basis of life among the First Nations of British Columbia. The fur trade could be the source of immense wealth, and soon there were many people without noble status who nevertheless had the material resources to hold a potlatch. It was still uneven—by the mid-nineteenth century, the practice had all but died out in some communities, while elsewhere it was occurring more and more frequently—but it was common enough to become a target of missionaries and government officials.

But as historians Douglas Cole and Ira Chaikin have shown, it was not simply a case of whites attacking a native cultural practice that

A potlatch at Quamichan, British Columbia, in the late nineteenth century, where the four children standing represent the deceased in a 'death dance' (Swy-whee).

they little understood. Certainly there were some missionaries whose zeal seemed fanatical—the Reverend William Henry Pierce, who worked among the natives of northern British Columbia, dismissed potlatching as 'the root of all evil and the big mountain of sin...[it] is ruination to the progress of the Indian and is leading the young people on to destruction.'[30] But many others in the anti-potlatch camp were long-time Indian Agents who were intimately familiar with native communities and believed that the potlatch was injurious to aboriginal health (infant and elder mortality did seem to rise during potlatches, as did the incidence of communicable diseases). They also saw it as undermining the economic well-being of communities, because it kept aboriginals from fishing and farming and forced many of them to the brink of ruin—they gave away literally everything they had in an effort to demonstrate their status. And, although many natives fought the missionaries and government over their right to potlatch (some argued, quite logically, that it was little different from Christmas), others petitioned Ottawa to legislate an end to the practice. In the end, the federal government did. An amendment to the Indian Act came into effect on

1 January 1885, making it an offense to engage in a potlatch, a Sun Dance, a tamananawas dance (another ceremonial that particularly appalled Europeans because it involved the mutilation of live dogs, the use of human corpses, and ritual cannibalism), and a number of other native ceremonies. In the case of the potlatch, it is important to note that what was banned was not the pre-contact ritual, but the ceremony that had been transformed by trading relationships with whites. Nevertheless, few would deny that, when the amendment came into effect, a critical element of aboriginal cultural identity was lost.

Equally tragic was the fact that some native arts were lost altogether, because of a growing reliance on European consumer goods. For centuries, west coast artists had made their own paints from natural materials, but in 1921 anthropologist Harlan Smith reported that natives were willing to pay high prices for small quantities of paint, because they no longer knew how to make it in the traditional manner. The fate of the ancient Blackfoot art of ceramic-making is also instructive. The Blackfoot had been making pottery with consummate skill for two thousand years before the Europeans arrived. When smuggler-turned-trader Anthony Henday led a Hudson's Bay Company trade mission into Blackfoot country in 1754–55, he left the natives with a number of iron pots, but they much preferred their traditional clayware. This was confirmed by another HBC employee, Matthew Cocking, who followed Henday in 1772 and found that the Blackfoot were still using their old ceramics. But as trading posts pushed farther into the interior, the Blackfoot gained easier access to European trade goods; with the construction of the trading post known as Manchester House, north of present-day Battleford, Saskatchewan, in 1786, European goods were now right on their doorstep. A short time later, when explorer David Thompson wintered in the region, he made no mention of seeing any ceramics; apparently, iron pots had been almost universally adopted. It took time, but the Blackfoot had finally abandoned their ancient art form in favour of European goods.

At the time, few voices of concern were raised about the disintegration of aboriginal culture. Many missionaries were only too happy to see the end of it, and to do what they could to hasten that end, while traders were more interested in creating a demand for their goods than in preserving native culture. In truth, the loss of native cultural practices was probably of little concern to most newcomers. For them, native culture was hardly more than a curiosity, and the fact that contact had altered it irrevocably would have occasioned only passing interest. In any case, as historian Olive Dickason has pointed out, Europeans were unable to imagine that a painting done on an animal hide was the equal of one done on canvas, or that anyone could possibly prefer a clay pot to an iron one, or that natives would want to preserve their unique singing styles when they could be taught melodies and harmonies. What mattered to them was not the possibility that a new, hybrid culture could be created in North America, but that the continent offered a new field for the spread of European culture.

Chapter 3

Colonial Societies

On 26 September 1819, HMS *Hecla* and HMS *Griper* dropped anchor in Winter Harbour, off Melville Island, some 600 miles north of the Arctic Circle. For the first time, an expedition in search of the northwest passage would intentionally winter in the Arctic. Under no illusions as to the magnitude of this challenge, the crew got to work immediately, pulling down the ships' masts and draping sheets of heavy canvas over the yardarms, to create a tent over the main decks. Under *Hecla*'s canopy, they rigged up a bread oven and cobbled together a kind of central heating system that piped warm air to almost every corner of the ship. The sailors were in the most inhospitable environment imaginable, but at least they had a few of the comforts of home.

Had we been able to observe the *Hecla* on the afternoon of 5 November, we would have witnessed a strange scene under the canvas canopy. There, far north of the Arctic Circle, the crew mounted a performance of David Garrick's *Miss in Her Teens*, a saucy farce that had swept the London stage seventy years earlier. With the expedition's commander, Lieutenant Edward Parry, in one of the lead roles, the cast strode the makeshift stage in temperatures that dipped well below the freezing mark, despite the ingenious heating system. The cold even added a charming glow to the cheeks of Midshipman Ross, whose youth and slight figure made him a natural for one of the female roles. The performance was such a success that the crew immediately decided to continue the experiment. Parry and his fellow officers delved into the meagre library of books on board the two ships and every couple of weeks mounted another production. When they had used all the material on board the ship, Parry decided to write a new play, wishfully entitled *The North-West Passage, or Voyage Finished* and featuring five crew members, an Innu hunter, and a polar bear. The documents don't record precisely how the bear took part in the production.[31]

The upper crust replicates European polite culture at the Château St. Louis, Quebec, 1801.

For the crew of the *Hecla* and *Griper*, theatricals were primarily about diversion; as Parry realized, play-acting was a way to pass the long weeks of darkness that interrupted their quest for the northwest passage. But there was another element to it that stemmed from a desire to affirm their cultural heritage in a strange land. Performing Garrick in a world that was entirely foreign to these sailors confirmed both their Europeanness and their civilization; it reminded them that, however far they went from home, they could take their culture with them.

The European presence in the new world was all about extending dominion across the globe. Europeans brought to North America their religion, their politics, their economy, their social structure—it would be strange if they had not brought their culture as well. We have seen that the first newcomers focused on its utilitarian value in converting the indigenous peoples to Christianity; like military expeditions or native alliances, culture became a policy option, another way to achieve their goals. But as the settlements grew, culture became something more than just a weapon for missionaries to wield. It became an expression of values and ideals, a way to convey what the society was trying to achieve philosophically. As the years passed and the settlements grew larger and more established, it became increasingly clear that the new world was more than just an outpost of the old. It was possible to replicate Europe in North America to some extent, but the specifics of place became more and more critical in shaping the forms of artistic expression that evolved.

Given the church's reliance on music and painting to convert natives, it is hardly surprising that the distinction of being Canada's first great arts patron falls to a cleric, François de Laval, who became the first Bishop of Quebec in 1674. Aside from his support of the proselytising campaign, Laval was behind the establishment of New France's first arts and crafts school, which opened at Cap Tourmente, east of Quebec, in 1668. Craftsmen there taught cabinetry, painting, gilding, sculpture, masonry, and carpentry, and offered students a practical training regime that included assignments in which students decorated churches. The experiment lasted until practices changed and carvers and sculptors came to be trained as apprentices rather than in schools; by 1706, the school was teaching nothing but agricultural techniques. A private school, modelled after Cap Tourmente, operated in Montreal from 1694 to 1706 under the auspices of the Hospitallers of St. Joseph of the Cross. Connected to their hospice for orphans, the elderly, and indigents, it closed shortly after its sculpture and painting teachers died within two years of each other.

Laval's influence, however, went far beyond the training of artists. As the founder of the first parishes in the colony, he was also behind the erection of its first parish churches, a building campaign that fostered the development not just of architecture, but of painting, carving, and sculpting as well. Architecturally, Laval's churches tended to follow European models, with due allowance for local conditions. The Jesuit Church in Quebec (1666–76) was probably designed in France, to reflect the character of the large Jesuit churches there, but the French Baroque elements were simplified and modified to compensate for the harsher climate, the different range of materials available, and the limited artisanal skill. Many of the parish churches were patterned after Notre-Dame-de-la-Paix in Quebec. Similar to the secular architecture of the upper classes, this was a kind of ecclesiastical imperialism, a way to use architectural forms to project power over outlying communities.

In the 1928 photograph, Quebec wood carver Edmond Patrie works alongside examples of the craft from centuries past.

But it was inside the churches where the skills of local artists really shone. There, in the ornately carved decorations, the masterfully sculpted figures, and the intricate altar screens and tabernacles, we see the skill that moved art historian Russell Harper to call woodcarving 'Quebec's highest form of artistic expression and the real glory of the eighteenth century.'[32] At first, the work was done by craftsmen from France who came to Canada on contract, completed their assignment, and then returned home. But by the late seventeenth century, artisans had begun to take up residence in New France, either working on their own or as part of a workshop. The most prominent of these was operated by the Levasseur family, which dominated church decoration in New France from 1651 to 1782. Over four generations, the family included twenty-two artisans—sculptors, ornamentalists, carriage-makers, carpenters—and became essentially artistic contractors. The patriarch would enter into a contract with a parish council, and then sub-contract the work to his relatives or other sculptors, painters, and craftsmen. It might take as long as a decade to complete the decoration of a single church, but the end result was a building that blended European styles with Canadian materials and craftsmanship.

The rich decoration of a typical Quebec parish church. Undated.

Clerics, however, realized that the church had to walk a fine line—culture could be a powerful weapon for the good, but it could also be a tool of the devil. Art, for example, was clearly effective in conversions, but there was always the possibility that religious paintings could become objects of veneration themselves, the very graven images that the Ten Commandments warned against. Indeed, in the painting *La*

France apportant la foi aux Indiens de la Nouvelle-France by the Récollet missionary Frère Luc, who in 1670 became the first trained artist to come to Canada, the figure of France warns against becoming preoccupied by the beautiful images on the canvas she holds; she points languidly towards heaven, a reminder of where to find the true objects of veneration.

Literature could also be suspect. In fact, the Jesuits had been in New France just a few months before performing Canada's first book-burning, in 1625, when they hunted out and consigned to the flames a copy of the controversial pamphlet known as the *Anti-Coton*, directed at the former confessor to the French King Henry IV. There was no printing press in New France until 1751, despite petitions from administrators that it could be used to print laws; Swedish traveller Peter Kalm was told that the colony's rulers feared the power of the printed word in attacking the government. And while Laval's successor as Bishop of Quebec advised each family to own '*quelque bon livre*,' the church generally regarded lending libraries as a pernicious influence, and clerical suspicion of reading was strong. Baron de Lahontan, a minor nobleman who came to New France with the colonial regular troops, reported in 1685 that the clergy of Montreal 'prohibit and burn all the Books that treat of any Subject but Devotion,' and related an incident in which a local cleric, seized by what Lahontan called a fit of 'impertinent Zeal,' tore apart his volume by the Roman novelist Petronius. A friend had to restrain the outraged Lahontan from ripping the cleric's beard out at the roots.[33]

Nowhere was the conundrum clearer than in the church's attitude to drama. Not only was it a much more public art form than reading or painting, but in a society where literacy rates were low and books were costly, drama had the potential to be accessible and appealing to the mass of colonists. As early as 1584, the Jesuits had suggested using dramatic presentations as a way to make studies more interesting for novitiates, an innovation that the Ursulines eventually copied. The most common form was the *action*, a religious and pedagogic tragi-comedy, usually with a Biblical theme, that was soon established in the colony's rudimentary education system. Typical of this genre was a mystery play performed in 1640 as part of the festivities to mark the second birthday of the future king of France. It had been added to the bill to impress any natives who might be watching the performance and, if Father Le Jeune's description does it justice, it must have been quite a spectacle: 'the soul of an unbeliever pursued by two demons, who finally hurled it into a hell that vomited forth flames.'[34]

These presentations were usually for ceremonial or educational purposes rather than public consumption, but there was a tradition of civic drama in New France. In fact, the first play mounted in North America, Marc Lescarbot's *Théâtre du Neptune en la Nouvelle-France*, was performed on 14 November 1606 to celebrate the return of a party led by Champlain and Jean de Biencourt de Poutrincourt, a seigneur at Port-Royal, that had gone in search of a better site for the colony. *Théâtre du Neptune* was a variety of dramatic presentation known as a *réception*, the name given to the ritualized addresses and mixed dramatic dialogues that had long been used to mark important events in the French cultural tradition. On the calm waters of the Annapolis River, the play featured Neptune, drawn in a chariot boat, and his tritons giving a series of declarations that the settlement should be grateful for the blessings it enjoyed. A number of aboriginal warriors, also played by French settlers, then came forward to pledge allegiance and cooperation, and the entire production ended with a call to feast.

A ritualized ceremony was one thing; in the eyes of the church, however, secular drama was an entirely different story. A performance of Corneille's *Le Cid* in 1651, only four years after this masterpiece of French drama opened in Paris, drew little comment from clerics; but as the colony's political masters began to show a growing taste for more dubious forms of entertainment (the first ball in New France was held 1667, but twenty years earlier the Jesuit *Relations* had reported with alarm of a ballet performed in a warehouse owned by the Company of One Hundred Associates), the church became concerned. In an echo of what was occurring in France, where the court of Versailles was becoming increasingly pious and restrictive, prominent clerics began to speak out against all kinds of frivolous amusements—but particularly secular theatre. Father Pierre Nicole of Port-Royal referred to the playwright as 'a poisoner of the public,' but the great defender of the faith against theatre emerged in the person of Laval's successor, Bishop Saint-Vallier of Quebec, a narrow-minded and testy zealot who succeeded in making enemies of almost everyone he encountered in the colony.[35]

Even before arriving in New France in 1685, the bishop had informed the then-governor, the Marquis de Denonville, that theatre, dancing, and balls were injurious to Christian principles; he expected the governor and his wife to set a good example for the common people by avoiding all worldly diversions. Denonville, who arrived in New France at a time when native attacks and a terrible epidemic were threatening the very life of the colony, had more important concerns than theatre and dancing, but the next governor, the urbane and sophisticated Louis de Buade, Comte de Frontenac, was not above using the powers of his office to allow him to live in style. In the winter of 1693–94, he sponsored performances of Corneille's *Nicomède* and Racine's *Mithridate* in his home for a select audience of colonial elite. Saint-Vallier took no apparent notice until it was rumoured that the next play in the series would be Molière's *Tartuffe*. The comedy by one of the greatest dramatists of the age had already caused a storm of controversy in France, where leading churchmen accused it of subverting organized religion. The bishop would have known of the dispute and, when word of the proposed performance reached his ears, he could not sit idly by.

Saint-Vallier seemed to be as offended by the performance itself as he was by one Lieutenant Mareuil, the disreputable fellow who was to direct it, for he targeted both. He immediately issued a decree condemning theatre in general and forbidding any member of the diocese from attending the performance, and then charged Mareuil with blasphemy. But with this the bishop overstepped himself; blasphemy was a civil offence and Frontenac, who apparently relished any opportunity to annoy the bishop, protested strongly against the intrusion into his civil authority as governor. The dispute might have blown up into a nasty quarrel had Saint-Vallier not offered Frontenac 100 *pistoles* (over $9,400 in 2009) to cancel the play. Although the bishop insisted that it was simply a repayment of the expenses that Frontenac had already disbursed in preparing the play, it had all the hallmarks of a bribe. The governor, however, was neither offended nor insulted, and happily pocketed the money. The King's Council eventually decided that all sides should share both the blame (as historian Margaret Cameron put it so aptly, 'the council ruled that the bishop was in the wrong but that the governor was not in the right'[36]) and the embarrassment that resulted from the unseemly tiff.

And yet Saint-Vallier had the last laugh. His decree was reinforced in 1699 and remained on the books for two centuries. The records suggests that it was entirely effective, for there was little drama performed in the colony, except for the odd *réception* and some plays mounted by soldiers. There may have been other performances that have been lost to history, but at the very least it is clear that, thanks to the bishop's efforts, theatre ceased to be an important aspect of social life in New France.

———•◦•———

As the *Tartuffe* controversy reveals, not everyone shared the church's attitude towards culture. Frontenac was typical of the people who were reluctant to see it in simple utilitarian terms, as something that could be useful only in certain circumstances. For them, culture was part of the fabric of life and, as a result, it had a place in the colonizing impulse. They believed that the hinterland, whatever else it became, should be a reflection of the metropolis. More than simply an outpost of trade and commerce, it should be an outpost of European civilization and culture in the wilderness of North America.

The desire to replicate Europe in North America was evident in architecture from the earliest days. In Champlain's habitation at Île Ste. Croix, erected in 1604, the houses of notables had steep hipped roofs, similar to those that graced castles and stately homes in France, the very buildings that expressed in tangible terms the social hierarchy. The same was true of Champlain's second habitation at Quebec (1624–26), which resembled a medieval château of the Loire region, a form that Champlain would have seen as a symbol of feudal control, and the Château de Vaudreuil (1723–26), which had all the features of fine French houses of the day. As architectural historian Helmut Kallmann put it, the Château exemplified the architecture of the ruling class, 'formal, contrived, based on study, and consciously produced to express power, wealth and authority.'[37] Here, old world forms symbolized a kind of imperialism, a reminder that European civilization would be imposed on the new world.

The tendency to replicate European culture was strongest in the urban centres of New France, where roughly a third of the colony's population lived, including the wealthy and powerful who had the leisure time and the financial resources to enjoy and sponsor the arts. Over

Champlain's *Habitation du Port Royal*, 1614–15, showing European architectural styles in a North American setting.

time, they fostered a lively cultural life, even with the church's stifling influence. Elements of the Enlightenment could be found, although in a weaker form because of the remoteness of New France and the small size of the bourgeois group. Despite clerical attitudes towards books, there was a strong demand for reading that was satisfied by imports from France. Although there was little in the way of a retail book trade, and even that rarely extended beyond liturgical and prayer books, leading citizens had libraries running into the thousands of books imported from France, ranging from religion and Latin classics to professional books and contemporary French literature. By the mid-1760s there were probably some 60,000 books in New France, mostly in private hands, and the library of the Jesuit College in Quebec rivalled that of Harvard, the greatest university in North America at the time.

Secular painting also took hold early in the eighteenth century, as military officers, merchants, and government officials increasingly had the means and the inclination to commission portraits. One of the first professional painters in the colony was Jean Berger, a former soldier who established a studio in Montreal after being released from prison for counterfeiting money. Only a handful of works from the period still exist, but those that survive show a shift in style away from the clearly French-

influenced work of earlier painters like Frère Luc. If they are generally simpler, less ostentatious, and indeed less accomplished than their
predecessors' work, they can be seen as the beginnings of a Canadian
style. Russell Harper admits that these works continue to show the influences of French art, but argues that they nevertheless represent the 'first
attempts by local artists to paint the local scene as they personally felt it.'[38]

Through the first half of the eighteenth century, then, New France
experienced a kind of cultural flowering, even with the stultifying influence of the church. The same could not be said of England's North
American colonies, which were regarded much more as economic
outposts of empire and therefore not places where culture should
flourish. Literary activity there before the mid-eighteenth century was
sparse. *Quodlibets*, a verse cycle written by Robert Hayman, the English
governor of Harbour Grace, Newfoundland, in 1628, Donnachadh
Ruadh MacConmara's clever poetry that both praised and criticized
Newfoundland, a few verses written by naval officers passing through the
colonies, and the odd travel account—these represent the literary output
of more than a century of English presence in North America. Despite
the fact that the earliest surviving paintings done on Canadian territory
were by Englishman John White, who executed a series of watercolours
of Inuit he encountered on a voyage in 1577, art also lagged behind
New France. This was in part because of the influence of Puritanism,
which feared any kind of religious art and demanded that English colonial churches be austere and devoid of the decoration that had been so
important in fostering artistic activity in New France. Nor was there
much in the way of secular art—wealthy Nova Scotians patronized the
American portraitist John Singleton Copley because there was no good
painter in the colony. The city of Halifax, founded in 1749, could sustain
neither a dancing academy nor a bookseller. Henry Meriton placed an
advertisement as a dancing teacher in 1752, but the failure of his enterprise is suggested by a notice in the newspaper a year later, in which
Meriton offered his services as a man-midwife, surgeon, and apothecary.
In 1761, James Rivington advertised his intention to begin selling books,
but the venture only lasted a short time before Rivington departed Nova
Scotia for the greener commercial pastures of New England. There are
few mentions of music in surviving letters and diaries of the period, and
it seems likely that it was confined to churches and military bands. But if

QVODLIBETS,

LATELY COME OVER

FROM NEW BRITANIOLA,
OLD NEWFOVND-LAND.

Epigrams and other fmall parcels, both
Morall and Diuine.

The firft foure Bookes being the Authors owne: the
reft tranflated out of that Excellent Epigrammatift,
Mr. *Iohn Owen,* and other rare Authors:

With two Epiftles of that excellently wittie Doctor,
Francis Rablais : Tranflated out of his French at large.

All of them
Compofed and done at *Harbor-Grace* in
Britaniola, anciently called *New found-Land.*

─────────────────────

By *R. H.*

Sometimes Gouernour of the Plantation there.

─────────────────────

LONDON,
Printed by *Elizabeth All-de,* for *Roger
Michell,* dwelling in *Pauls* Church-yard,
at the figne of the Bulls-head. 1628.

Title page of Robert Hayman's *Quodlibets,* which was Newfoundland's first book of
English poetry, originally published in London in 1628.

the English colonies seemed to be a cultural desert, they would not long
remain so; war was about to re-shape their very essence.

───── ·•·• ─────

Like so many other aspects of their history, the paths of New France
and the English colonies were dramatically altered by conflict. The

declaration of the Seven Years' War in 1756, when a struggle between the imperial powers of Europe spilled over into their colonial possessions, began a period of turmoil that would continue until the end of the American Revolution in 1783. Those decades would mark a watershed in the political, economic, and social life of North America, but also in its cultural life. Not for the first time, war would be both the destroyer and the creator of art.

For the cultural life of New France, the most immediate conse-quences of the Seven Years' War were disastrous. Many of the colony's architectural gems were destroyed by British cannons, and the program of church building ended abruptly as resources were poured into defence. There was little demand for portraits as the colony's survival hung in the balance, and soldiers who had once turned their leisure hours to play-acting found their time consumed by military duties. The religious orders, once prominent sponsors of culture, stopped sending people to New France, and few young people could travel to the metropolis to study. The supply of French books slowly dried up as space in ships' holds was taken up by the tools of war.

But after the Treaty of Paris of 1763 returned peace to Quebec, the colony's cultural life was reborn. A program of church building that dwarfed Laval's was begun, and by 1791 thirty-nine new churches had been built and thirteen more repaired. The Levasseurs stopped working in 1782, but there were other workshops, like the Baillairgés', ready to fill the void. Jean Baillairgé was an architect, and in the 1770s he sent his son François to France to train as an artist. Upon his return to Quebec, François, and later his own son Thomas, took over the family workshop, winning contracts with some of the wealthiest parishes in the colony. The Baillairgés' workshop was active well into the 1830s, bringing into the nineteenth century the golden age of Canadian carving that the Levasseurs had begun in the seventeenth.

French-Canadian secular painting, too, came of age in the years after the conquest. Most artists still got the bulk of their commissions from the church, but the market for non-religious art was expanding, something that became clear when François Beaucourt became the first painter to advertise his services as a portraitist and art teacher in 1792. In this context, the isolation from France—not only during the Seven Years' War, but also during the French Revolution and the Napoleonic

Quebec's Récollet Church in 1761, showing the damage done by British cannons during the conquest of New France.

Wars as well—proved to be an asset. At the very time when there was growing demand for their work, French-Canadian artists were cut off from European trends and had to find their own way stylistically, developing an artistic vocabulary that combined the bright and playful elements of the rococo with the passion and power of neo-classicism.

There is little indication that the evolution of a French-Canadian style of painting was anything more than an accident of the times, but in literature there were concerted efforts to forge a distinct French-Canadian voice as an antidote to the English influences that cultural elites feared would sweep Quebec. Part of the concern stemmed from the fact that French-Canadian literature, unlike art, went into the doldrums after 1760; literary historian Gérard Tougas suggests that it was almost non-existent in the decades after the conquest. Only in newspapers was French-Canadian literature fostered. The first publisher, Fleury Mesplet, concluded that the best way to preserve the French language under the new order was to maintain every possible tie with France, so his *Le Gazette du commerce et littérature* relied heavily on verse and prose imported from France. Unfortunately, it also included generous doses of criticism of the educational system, the government, and the judiciary, commentaries that offended both the church and the governor, Sir Frederick Haldimand. After only a year, the paper was suppressed and Mesplet tossed in jail. Shortly after his release, he started a new paper, the *Montreal Gazette* (a direct ancestor of today's newspaper of the same name). This tamer venture was rather more successful; perhaps not financially, but at least it kept Mesplet out of jail. In 1817, Michel Bibaud established the journal *L'Aurore* in Montreal, using material taken from a Bordeaux magazine—thereby affirming his desire to keep his readers informed of French culture. Bibaud was also responsible for publishing the first volume of verse in French Canada, in 1830. Canadian in content but inspired by the satire of French writer Nicholas Boileau, the verses may have been weak, but at least they affirmed the desire of French Canadians to foster what Tougas called 'an autonomous life of the spirit.'[39]

The post-conquest years were less happy for the theatre in French Canada; despite the changing of the guard, it continued to draw the ire of the church. A company calling itself the Young French-Canadian Gentlemen performed Molière's *Fourbières de Scapin* after the conquest, but at least one actor complained about having to delete all the female roles because the church frowned upon the mixing of the sexes on stage. When the Théâtre du Société opened its first season in Montreal in the winter of 1789–90, a parish priest publicly denounced the plays, largely because they featured males performing in female roles. He threatened to withhold the sacrament from anyone who attended, but when the public and even his superiors chafed against this heavy-handed approach, the priest turned to the confessional to discourage theatre-going. This evidently had the desired effect, for the company survived only a single season. Clerics in Quebec adopted the same tactics, refusing absolution 'to all those performing, aiding, or abetting these sorts of performances.' Again, the effect was considerable: not a single play is known to have been performed in French in Lower Canada between 1797 and 1804. That year, an amateur group called Theatre Paragon, drawn from Quebec's social elites, appeared on the scene only to fall victim to Joseph-Octave Plessis, soon to be Bishop of Quebec. As concerned as Saint-Vallier had been about moral decay in the colony, Plessis demanded that church painting show more decorum, frowned on dancing, cowed writers and newspaper editors into toning down their criticism, and perhaps most importantly, denounced the theatre as being 'against the principles of God.'[40] For another decade, the pattern was repeated; a group of enthusiastic amateurs would come together to mount plays, only to find that they were unable to withstand the considerable pressure of the church. Perhaps the only milestone in the period was the completion in 1788 of *Colas et Colinette* by Joseph Quesnel, a Frenchman who became a Canadian when his ship was captured off Nova Scotia in 1779. The first play to be written and published in Canada, it was revived almost two centuries later and was performed widely, in French and English, in the 1960s and 1970s.

The heavy hand of the church concerned not only budding thespians, but the nascent arts community in general, especially cultural nationalists like Mesplet and Bibaud. Their fears that French Canada's culture would be swamped by the English occupiers were entirely justified, and they objected to clerical interference in their campaign for *la survivance*. The conquerors of New France brought with them not only their merchants, their administrators, and their soldiers, but also a cultural life that had been booming in New England through the Seven Years' War. Unlike New France, the English colonies had not themselves been under direct threat, so the lively arts scene of the region continued to blossom, stimulated by the energies of conflict. When that conflict ended, it was only natural that the energy would overflow into the new possession, Quebec, and also into the older English colonies as well.

There's nothing like a great military victory to inspire creativity in the songwriter and the poet, and the conquest brought a minor boom in celebratory music and poetry. John Worgan's 'I Fill Not the Glass—A Song on the Taking of Mont-Real by General Amherst' and Thomas Smart's 'General Wolfe' are typical of the patriotic songs dating from the period, while Valentine Neville's poem 'The Reduction of Louisbourg' (1759) describes the capture of the French stronghold on Cape Breton Island; Thomas Cary's *Abram's Plains* (1789) does the same for the battle at Quebec. Still, with lines like Cary's 'on the green-sward oft encamped they lay,/Seen by the rising and the setting ray./Here, in life's vigour, *Wolfe* resign'd his breath,/And, conqu'ring sunk to the dark shades of death,' few such works will ever be considered timeless classics of Canadian music or literature.[41]

The situation was a little brighter in painting. The arrival of British military units in Quebec brought a wave of activity in art that was every bit as important as the one that swept French Canada. In the days before photography, the only way to make accurate records of terrain or defensive positions was by sketching. Consequently, a number of British officers were also topographical artists who had been taught to draw landforms, cityscapes, and fortifications. They were not trained *as* artists, but they were trained *by* artists, indeed by some of the leading watercolourists of the day, and the best of them soaked up an artistic sensibility that tempered the severe pragmatism of their military training. This proclivity, combined with a growing demand in Europe for pictures of far-off places and the fact that garrison duty typically left soldiers with plenty of time on their hands, impelled British military artists to produce a large and vibrant body of work that captured the new colonies in all their many moods.

Thomas Davies's 'Chaudière Falls near Quebec,' 1792.

Typical of these artists was Thomas Davies, who entered the Royal Military Academy at Woolwich as a gentleman cadet of artillery in 1755, at the age of eighteen. His drawing master was the French artist Gamaliel Massiot, who saw enough potential in the young Davies to recommend him for further training in sketching. In 1757, Davies was posted to Halifax for the first of four tours of duty in North America. Over the next thirty-three years, he would travel widely on the conti-nent, primarily as attaché to British general Sir Jeffrey Amherst. He took part in Amherst's successful expedition against Louisbourg in 1758, and was probably the officer who raised the first British flag over Montreal in September 1760. He served in some of the most significant battles of the American Revolution, and finally left Quebec for the last time in November 1790, devoting his retirement to the study and drawing of birds.

Davies was first and foremost a military draughtsman whose training was directed at the near-photographic reproduction of what he saw. But he was an artist by inclination, and his work shows clear influences of the picturesque style that was popular in Europe in the eighteenth century. Both of these tendencies come through in his views of Canada. There is the delicate and detailed drawing of the best military topographers (something that makes it possible to identify, even two and a half centuries later, the precise location of many of his works), but there is also the skilful rendering of light and water, the assured use of colour, and, not incidentally, the wonderful human touches—a native hunter shooting a porcupine, an elegant couple reclining across the river from Montreal, an artist calmly sketching the scene—to give the watercolours a warmth and immediacy that makes them more than mere topographical sketches.

The conquerors brought artists and musicians (the military bands that became fixtures at public concerts and society balls, and whose conductors often did double duty as private music teachers), but they also brought another innovation that the church in New France had frowned upon: the public library. When it became apparent that a good number of Montreal's new militia captains were unable to read the Laws and Orders, the governor suggested a lending library as a way to improve the literacy of the upper classes. Accordingly, the Quebec Library was announced in 1779 and eventually opened for business in 1783 with roughly a thousand volumes. At £5 to join and a £2 annual subscription, it was beyond the means of all but the wealthiest in the colony. Even so, it was successful enough that Montreal followed with its own subscription library in 1796.

The library movement undoubtedly did its part in creating a climate that was receptive to reading, but it had little to do with the publication of Frances Brooke's *The History of Emily Montague*, usually considered to be Canada's first novel. Brooke came to Canada in 1763 while her husband was chaplain to the military garrison, and spent much of her time lobbying for his continued employment in the colony. When that seemed unlikely, she turned to writing as a source of income. She had published one successful novel (as well as an equally successful transla-tion) while in England, and in 1766 began writing *Emily Montague*. The four-volume novel had slow but steady sales over succeeding decades, and became a kind of travel guide for Europeans embarking on a journey to Canada. But was it really Canadian? It is entirely in the tradi-tion of eighteenth-century English novels, but her vivid descriptions of the people, places, and events (many of which can be linked to real details from contemporary Quebec) make it unmistakeably Canadian. It was written in Canada, yet published in England. Frances Brooke spent only a few years in Quebec, although she clearly got to know the colony well enough to describe it with great accuracy and sensitivity. The epistolary format may have been English, but the subject matter was purely Canadian. On balance, then, it seems reasonable to conclude that the history of the Canadian novel begins with *The History of Emily Montague*.

———•◦•———

However important it was in Quebec, culture loomed even larger in the new Loyalist settlements that sprang up after the American Revolu-tion. The ideals of the rebels were by no means universally acclaimed throughout the Thirteen Colonies, but opponents of the new order had just two options: swallow their principles and find a way to live in the republic, or leave everything and flee. In what has been called the first mass movement of political refugees in modern history, over 40,000 Loyalists decided they could not live in the new United States, and decamped for other British possessions in North America. The wealthiest of them came away with what they could, even to the point of floating their houses on barges to what would soon become the new colony of New Brunswick. The majority, however, left with only what they could carry. For Loyalists who had worked for generations to build up their positions, it was a huge sacrifice.

It was no surprise, then, that they felt a powerful impulse to rebuild what they had been forced to leave behind. They had fled a region with a well-developed culture—theatre, art, a lively book and magazine trade, music—and come to a place that had nothing. Reverend James Cuppidge Cochrane recalled growing up in Nova Scotia in the late 1790s with his Loyalist parents, and noted that it was a shock to his cultured family: 'we had no reading rooms—no lectures—no social gatherings for mental improvement—no performer to delight the ear and refine the taste by his admirable readings—no libraries except two filled with such things as Mrs. Radcliffe's romances...We had nothing in short to elevate and improve.' The first task for people like the Cochranes was to set this right, in literary scholar Gwendolyn Davies' words 'to re-establish in this "wilderness" the educational and cultural institutions left behind in America.'[42]

And so Loyalist émigrés such as Jacob Bailey and Jonathan Odell picked up right where they had left off, putting their talents to good use in their new land. As well as being a pleasant diversion, writing poetry and prose was also one of the social graces that characterized a truly civilized society. It might be entertaining and amusing—and in the work of someone like Bailey we see the roots of satiric literature in Canada—but more importantly it was integral to rebuilding in British North America a cultured community that was worthy of its heritage.

Another manifestation of this impulse is the fact that amateur theatrical performances were mounted in Saint John in 1789, only six years after the earliest settlers arrived. The first professional actors to reach Saint John were probably the Marriotts, a husband and wife team who came north to try their luck with less sophisticated audiences after a disappointing experience in the United States. In February 1799 they performed *Douglas*, a tragedy by Scottish playwright John Home, and Mrs. Marriott became the first woman to act on stage in Saint John, ironically cast in the role of a boy. But the Marriotts picked a bad time to come to New Brunswick. The city's theatre-going elites were hit hard by an economic downturn, and the couple did not have the legion of local friends and relatives who filled the seats for amateurs. We can follow the decline of Marriott's fortunes through advertisements in the local newspaper, as he tried his hand at being a restauranteur, butcher, wine shop owner, barber, school teacher, and hotelier before eventually giving up and leaving Saint John. But the situation would improve, and New Brunswick would soon boast a thriving theatrical scene. Saint

John's original venue, Mallard's Long Room—an empty hall that the actors shared with the Common Council and the Legislative Assembly—hosted a wide range of professional and amateur performances in the early nineteenth century before the city's first purpose-built theatre, the Drury Lane, opened in 1809. There, in 1816, citizens witnessed a performance of the first locally written play, a two-act farce called *The Sailor's Return, or Jack's Cure for the Hystericks*. Even when the Drury Lane fell into disuse, troupes continued to visit Saint John, performing in any converted hall that happened to be available.

Sometimes one wonders why they bothered, given the incredibly harsh judgements offered by budding theatre critics. A performance at Halifax's New Grand Theatre in 1796 led one critic to throw up his hands in despair: 'In the name of all the Gods at once, what can induce you to act operas? Is it to convince us what dismal singers you are?... [we] invariably have seen more to be disgusted with, than pleased at; for instead of sterling Sense, we receive Grimace and wretched Buffoonery.' Describing a performance of *Kate and Petruchio* in Montreal in 1806, the British traveller and writer John Lambert reported that the actors' talents 'were nearly eclipsed by the vulgarity and mistakes of the drunken Katherine, who walked the stage with devious steps and convulsed the audience with laughter, which was all the entertainment

Garrison Theatre in Halifax, Nova Scotia, where military officers are putting on a show, 1872.

we experienced in witnessing the mangled drama of our immortal bard.' He did not find the next season much better, observing that 'the performers are as bad as the worst lot of our strolling actors…I have seen none except Col. Pye and Capt Clark, of the 49th, who did not murder the best scenes of our dead poets.'[43]

Some people were less concerned with the quality of the theatre than its morality, and the debate that had bedevilled New France for two hundred years was reignited in Saint John. Critics continued to insist that the theatre's only purposes were to separate the gullible from their money and to provide training for thieves and other 'persons of professionally evil life' who were attracted by the proceedings. The profession of acting had never produced 'any practical and positive good,' they wrote, and was nothing more than 'a blank in creation.' Supporters, however, believed the theatre offered 'public benefit to our improving community' by teaching lessons of virtue and advocating the cause of religion.[44] Eventually, the tussle was brought to the attention of the mayor, who felt the theatre was beyond his jurisdiction and referred the matter to the Grand Jury. Seventeen of the twenty-one jurors accepted free tickets to see this nuisance first-hand; they must have liked what they saw because they failed to present a report and declined to suppress the theatre.

Clearly, the Grand Jury was grappling with more than simply a form of entertainment. Loyalist families had faced a very painful choice in deciding to leave everything they had built to start over as homesteaders. But they remained utterly convinced that their choice had been right, and were determined to demonstrate this at every opportunity. Creating a theatrical community in their new home was one way to convince themselves that they had made the right choice, and to dispel the sadness associated with having left behind all they had built. As one newcomer to Saint John wrote in a 1795 poem entitled 'On Opening a Little Theatre in the City,' culture could serve as 'consolation to distress.'[45]

It was also a way to convince others that they had made the right choice, and that they were every bit the equal of, and perhaps even a little superior to, the Yankees who had remained behind in the new United States. In this respect, culture was a means to affirm the values that the Loyalists held dear. They saw the world as a hierarchy ordained by God; every person had a place in that order, and a set of responsibilities to go

along with it. In New England, the order had been challenged and ultimately destroyed by the rebels, but in the Loyalist colonies it would be
preserved, thanks to the stewardship of the Anglican Church, which gave
the society its moral compass, and the wisdom of the ruling classes—
whose passion for rationality saved their world from disintegrating into
chaos. This belief would find expression in the work of people such as
Bailey and Odell, whose writing, even when it wasn't overtly political (as
it had often been when they were still in the Thirteen Colonies), implicitly served the purpose, as Gwendolyn Davies put it, of 'reaffirming for
Loyalists the rightness of their social vision.'[46]

A typical manifestation of this worldview was *The Nova-Scotia
Magazine and Comprehensive Review of Literature, Politics, and News*,
founded in 1789 by William Cochran and John Howe to provide a
monthly digest of current literature, news, poetry, and natural science.
It was all in the name of sharpening the cultural sensitivities of readers,
and imbuing in them the 'good taste and sound sense' that underpinned
the Loyalist version of toryism. Much of its content was imported, but
Cochran and Howe encouraged local writers wherever possible and
looked forward to the time when the journal would be 'enriched with the
exertions of *native genius*.'[47] Its mailing list was not large, reaching only
276 at its peak (including 172 in Halifax); but it did have subscribers in
almost every township and brought culture to a wide range of people,
from leading clerics and military officers to carpenters and farmers, at a
time when there were no public libraries. In 1826, the *Acadian Magazine
or Literary Mirror* was established to carry on this tradition and, in so
doing, to correct the impression that the people of the Loyalist colonies
'were comparatively ignorant and barbarous.' John Graves Simcoe, the
lieutenant-governor of Upper Canada, had precisely the same thing
in mind when he advocated the establishment of a lending library for
Upper Canada in 1791. He saw it as part of the process of making the
colony a legitimate 'Rival, for public Estimation and preference, of the
American Governments near to which it is situated.'[48]

In seeking to rival the United States by cultivating an appreciation for
the arts, Simcoe made an implicit assumption about the uniqueness of
Canadian culture. The very fact that elites were interested in replicating
European culture in North America would seem to militate against any

sort of cultural distinctiveness, but it is possible to discern in this period the first glimmerings of a perspective that was different from the European models it replicated, or the aboriginal practices on which it was sometimes grafted. Perhaps without even knowing it, these artists were creating something that was distinct: a hybrid of European and North American culture, which took the principles of the former and adapted them to the milieu of the latter. It may have been derivative or rough around the edges, but the quality of the product was less important than the artistic impulse itself and the realization that culture was an essential part of life. As Gérard Tougas later wrote in a comment that could apply equally well to painters, musicians, and architects, 'the humble efforts of these pen-wielders have contributed to the spread, if not the acceptance of the idea that a writer, far from belonging to the ranks of the unproductive, is one of the most indispensable elements of a society.'[49] Whether a matter of la survivance or to demonstrate the rectitude of the Loyalist cause, culture was regarded as essential to building a better community. Without a vibrant cultural life, these people reasoned, a civilized society could not be said to exist. Theatre promoter Charles Powell had this in mind when he opened a reading academy in Halifax in 1802. In part he was motivated by a need to supplement his income through a lean period of the theatre, but he was also mindful of culture's ability to provide moral and spiritual uplift; studying classical literature was essential, he wrote, 'not only to point out the most distinguished beauties of each author, but to explain to the young reader the moral contained in the several respective passages, which may not be so clearly understood in general, so as to form the judgement and give them a taste for cultivating their minds with polite literature.'[50]

Powell's reading academy was not a success, and the difficulties that he experienced in trying to introduce Haligonians to this kind of intellectual stimulation suggest that not everyone shared his views. Indeed, in Canada's growing cities, there was an increasing divergence of opinion as to the proper role of culture. For Powell and his ilk, it was all about moral improvement; one of the foundations of an enlightened society was a vibrant cultural life to provide moral and spiritual uplift. But for others, culture was something very different. It was entertainment, pure and simple, a diversion from the drudgery of the workaday world.

Chapter 4

Common Showmen and Mountebanks

In June 1841, the legendary Junius Brutus Booth was playing *Hamlet* in Saint John. He was widely regarded as the greatest American actor of the age, and within three decades would find fame of another sort when his actor-son, John Wilkes Booth, went down in history as the assassin of American president Abraham Lincoln. Junius was also completely mad, as most people who knew him agreed, and his mental stability could not have been improved by that evening's performance in New Brunswick. As he thundered the Prince of Denmark's soliloquy, he gazed down from the stage at rows of empty seats and came face to face with a sobering reality: the circus was in town (just down the street, in fact) and the great tragedian couldn't compete.

In short, the kind of culture that Booth was proffering could only appeal to the elites, who, in simple numerical terms, were in the minority. The bulk of any city's population—the carters, spinners, washers, dockworkers, sailors, teamsters, mill hands, manual labourers—had neither the level of literacy nor the financial wherewithal for serious culture to be accessible to them. But more importantly, *Hamlet* did not provide the kind of evening out that they were looking for. After a long day of hard labour, heavy tragedy or a comedy of manners held little appeal. They were not looking for mental exercise, and there was little demand among the working classes for the spiritual or moral uplift that Charles Powell saw in high culture. They wanted entertainment, pure and simple, a diversion from their working day, and the kind of evening that would allow them to blow off a little steam.

Here, we see what later cultural commentators would characterize as the great divide between high and low culture. It would be particularly disturbing to cultural nationalists in the twentieth century, but in the pre-Confederation era the issues were not quite so clear as they would later appear to be. In the late eighteenth and early nineteenth centuries, the divide—to the degree that it existed in reality—involved little more than differing interpretations of the purpose of culture.

———•◦•———

The first Europeans to come to North America were not all drawn from the same class, so it should be no surprise that they did not all possess the same understanding of culture. New France may have been different from the metropolis in some respects; but in others, it was in fact simply France in America. The social hierarchy was replicated—the *seigneurs* came from the land-holding classes of France, the labourers came from the French labouring classes—and so too were the class-based assumptions regarding culture. We can see this in any of the towns of New France, but because of its isolation from the other colonial cities, Louisbourg offers a particularly good microcosm.

As much as they could, the economic, political, and military elites of the city made life on Île Royale (Cape Breton Island) resemble the life they had left behind in France. This meant bringing with them their musicians and instruments, their books and works of art, their decorative housewares and fine furniture, their dancing masters—in short, all the trappings of European polite culture. But none of those things, not the fancy masked balls, the books of philosophy, the courtly music, were found in the culture of the labouring classes. They brought their own artistic life with them to the new world, and centred it in the environment in which they moved.

Taverns were among the first businesses to be established in Canada, and quickly became among the most numerous. They ran the gamut from urban hotels offering a full range of accommodation, meals, drink, and entertainment, to tiny rooms, often in private homes, that provided basic food, strong drink, and a place to stay warm. There were several large inns in Louisbourg that catered to the wealthy traveller, but most working people frequented one of the many informal taverns, often just a few tables and benches crammed into the kitchen of a private home. They offered a standard fare of sausage and coarse bread, strong rum, and a chance to forget the travails of the day. The taverns became *de facto* gambling dens—the people of Louisbourg were inveterate gamblers and would lay a bet on virtually anything, from the sex of an unborn child to the arrival date of the first ship of the season—but they were also music halls. Patrons paying for room and board came to expect entertainment as part of the deal, and it was usually provided by the owner, a family member, or an employee. In common drinking rooms, a waiter might play a few tunes on the fiddle or flute, then pass around a box to collect donations from the customers. Often the performances were participatory—patrons would sing along to the folk songs imported from France, and occasionally to lewd, satirical songs that poked fun at colonial administrators (and, more than likely, at the courtly culture that they valued so highly). Officials may not have liked this combination of strong drink and subversive songs, but they recognized that working-class culture provided an important safety valve. Hence the fact that some ninety drinking establishments were allowed to operate in Louisbourg between 1713 and 1758.

The situation in Louisbourg was replicated in every other city in New France and British North America in the eighteenth and nineteenth centuries—a sharp demarcation between the kind of culture consumed by the educated elites, and the kind enjoyed by the greater mass of the population. The reasons for this divergence are not hard to find. In the first place, to enjoy what might have been called polite culture was an expensive proposition, whether it was the theatre, music, or reading. When a group from Albany, New York, performed the Restoration comedy *She Stoops to Conquer* in Montreal on 27 February 1786, the best seats cost eight shillings at a time when the average worker was lucky to earn that in a week. In 1809, a box seat in Saint John's new Drury Lane Theatre went for five shillings. In Quebec, the average cheap seat for an English-language play cost a full day's pay for an established teacher; the same seat for a French-language play cost twice that amount.

By the same token, the worker who wanted to keep up with the latest news and literature would have to spend two and a half Spanish dollars for a year's subscription to Mesplet's *Gazette du commerce et littérature*, $3.00 to get the *Quebec Magazine*, and $4.00 for *The Nova-Scotia Magazine*; at least one culturally sophisticated farmer offered, in verse, his thoughts on paying for the magazine:

I went home, and have been three days a-contriving
Which way I could pay, for I've thoughts of subscribing:

As cash in the country is quite out of use,
The only way left is to pay in produce.[51]

It was not until the 1830s, when the number of newspapers increased, that they became more affordable (although many, including Cape Breton's *The Spirit of the Times*, continued to accept produce in lieu of cash for subscriptions). There were still many four-page broadsheets that cost an average of twenty shillings a year, but smaller, cheaper papers were coming onto the market and, for the first time, publishers began to sell their newspapers by the single issue, using street pedlars who targeted the educated working class.

An even bigger hurdle was not income, but literacy. In the seventeenth century, the literacy rate in New France was actually higher than in France, at around twenty-five percent. It declined dramatically over the next century, however, because education was in the hands of the church, which had no interest in creating a literate public, and because the religious orders that ran many of the colony's schools were restricted in their ability to import teachers after the conquest. By 1800, the literacy rate in Lower Canada had dropped to around fifteen percent of the population, most of them urban, Anglo-Protestant males. Some scholars estimate that as little as 4 percent of Lower Canada's French-speaking population was literate. In Upper Canada and the Maritimes, literacy rates varied dramatically, although by 1840 probably less than half of the population of all the British North American colonies could read and write, and rates were everywhere lowest amongst the working classes and the labouring poor.[52] Even admitting that there was likely a significant amount of public reading of newspapers and journals in taverns, it must be conceded that literature remained largely irrelevant to the lives of workers.

Fortunately, the cultural menu in any city offered more than literary magazines, serious theatre, and chamber music; there were many other diversions more suited to the budget, and the sensibilities, of the working classes. Promoters with wagonloads of European paintings travelled the colonies, setting up exhibitions in churches or town halls and charging a few pennies for admission; but much more popular than this was the panorama painting, a phenomenon that swept North America in the mid-nineteenth century. These immense canvases, occasionally enlivened by ingenious lighting, allowed the onlooker to be visually overwhelmed by some of the great events of history—the battles of Waterloo or Trafalgar, the destruction of Babylon, the funeral of Napoleon, the Indian Mutiny (Robert Whale's panorama of the uprising was especially popular when it toured western Ontario with its graphic depictions of British soldiers enduring all manner of agonies). In 1848, American William Burr came to Montreal to display a huge panorama painting of the Great Lakes and the St. Lawrence River; the price of admission included a narrator describing the important historical and geographical features, and a folk singer who performed local songs from the regions shown in the painting. Three years later, a panorama of the Mississippi River (billed as 'La Plus Grande Peinture Dans Le Monde') came to Quebec, enabling people to travel vicariously from St. Louis ('avant le grand incendie') to the falls of St. Anthony. On the thousand-mile trip, they could inspect the Battle of Bad Axe, the last engagement of the Black Hawk Wars; and the departure of the Winnebago people from the Wabash prairie, a scene that alone featured over two thousand figures. And it was all available for the admission price of just thirty *sous*, well within the budget of the average worker.[53]

The tavern milieu probably changed very little over time, although as Canada urbanized and city inns became larger, they started to attract more elaborate forms of entertainment for their customers. Still, there is little indication that the nature of that entertainment changed substantially. The innkeepers and their employees probably still provided music for their patrons, but increasingly the larger taverns were visited by migrating troupes of entertainers, mostly from the United States. But what did this kind of popular culture look like in the colonial era? Fortunately, two itinerant performers, John Durang and Horton Rhys, have left detailed accounts of their travels through Canada, and they provide a fascinating window into the kind of mainstream cultural activities that were available in the British North American colonies.

One of the most famous travelling shows of the eighteenth century was Ricketts' Equestrian and Comedy Company from Philadelphia, starring John Ricketts, the greatest trick horseback rider of the time, and John Durang, a Pennsylvania-born showman who was likely the first person to perform Shakespeare in Pennsylvania German. But Ricketts and Durang were not best known for Shakespeare; their forte was the kind of variety-show extravaganza that had become all the rage in the post-Revolution United States. In the summer of 1797, Ricketts and Durang decided to take their company north, reaching Montreal with their six trained horses on 28 August 1797. They immediately rented a field from the military authorities and hired local carpenters to build their circus ring. Within two weeks they were ready to open, and from the 5th of September they performed every day at four o'clock in the afternoon, accompanied by the band of the 60th Regiment, Royal American Grenadiers (Ricketts and Durang paid the musicians half a crown a day, the same wage they paid their labourers, most of whom were off-duty soldiers).

The show was a mixture of tricks on horseback, clowning, pyrotechnics, and other stunts with mechanical contrivances. Ricketts, the more talented horseman, was known for being able to dance a hornpipe on the back of a horse as it raced at full speed around the ring. Durang, on the other hand, was the comedian. He rode around the ring on horseback, pretending to be a drunk. Then, wearing men's clothing, he climbed into a burlap sack and stood on two horses as they trotted around the ring; when he climbed down and emerged from the sack, he was dressed in women's clothing. He detonated fireworks and performed 'other mechanical exhibitions in machinery and transparencies,' and was also the technical brains behind the show; as he put it, 'I was performer, machinist, painter, designer, music compiler, the bill maker, and treasurer.'

What was most remarkable was the show's popularity. After four full weeks of performances, the officers of the garrison and the local merchants pleaded with them to stay on, so Durang commissioned the construction of a more permanent circus, made of stone and with a domed roof that Durang himself painted in sky blue and decorated with cupids bearing bundles of roses. The new building was ready at the end of December, and performances continued until the last show on 3 May 1798. For that, Durang pulled out all the stops. He had visited a number of native settlements around Montreal and had become interested in native dance, so he used the occasion of the last performance (which also featured Colonel McIntosh's regimental band and a two-act farce called *The Ghost*, from the work of a much-loved but now entirely forgotten playwright named Mrs. Centlivre) to showcase his

John Durang, dancing the hornpipe. Undated.

new repertoire. Wearing authentic native clothing ('which I purchased from an Indian for rum,' he wrote in his memoirs), Durang performed what he called a Pipe Dance, an Eagle Tail Dance, and a War Dance. The last was his *pièce de resistance*, and involved 'throwing myself in different postures with firm steps with hatchet and knife, representing the manner they kill and scalp and take prisoners with the yells and the war whoops.' As a grand finale, he jumped through a barrel of fire and shot off a huge display of fireworks. Shakespeare it was not, but it drew a large enough crowd that Ricketts and Durang took in $800 on that one night, a huge sum in those days.

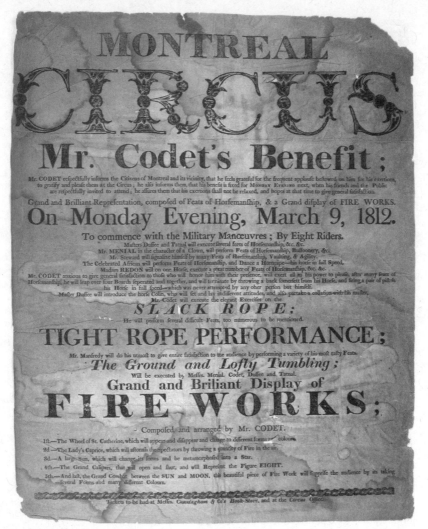

The advertisement for a Montreal circus *Mr. Codet's Benefit* in 1812 describes all the usual acts.

From there, the pair took their show to Quebec, where they built another circus ring inside the walled city and performed for two months in the summer of 1798. A British artillery officer even loaned them several of his men to help with the fireworks, and Durang was delighted to learn some new tricks with explosives from them. After dozens of profitable shows, they returned to Montreal for two more weeks of performances at a temporary circus on the corner of St. Paul and Bonsecour streets. Their time in Canada, however, ended on a sour note. One of the grooms fired a pea gun at some unruly young men, hitting one in the head and putting his eye out. The unfortunate groom had to hide from the mob to save his life, and Ricketts eventually paid $800 in damages to the injured patron.[54]

Sixty years later, a different kind of itinerant performer toured Canada. In 1859, British writer and actor Horton Rhys (who used the stage name Morton Price) made a wager with two friends: with an unknown actress of his own choosing, he would mount a theatrical tour in another country and, by selling admission tickets, sheet music of his own compositions, and copies of his own writing, would earn £500 over and above all expenses. If he succeeded, Rhys would win the pot of £1,000; if he failed, it would be divided between his friends. He promptly found an actress, Catherine Lucette, and on 23 April 1859, embarked at Liverpool for North America, where he had decided to mount his assault on the theatre-going public. On the Cunard steamer *Niagara*, he collected a Captain Bayly, a British officer who was transferring to a regiment in Canada and who, judging by his performances in some impromptu concerts held on board, was clearly a talented singer. Rhys persuaded him to join their tour, and the three-strong company was ready.

They landed in Boston but, finding an uncongenial atmosphere both there and in New York, decided to throw themselves on the tender mercies of Canadian audiences. On 25 July 1859, at the St. Louis Street Music Hall in Quebec, they began their tour. The program from that first show reveals that while it certainly wasn't clowns and pyrotechnics, neither was it *She Stoops to Conquer*. The feature was a short sketch entitled *A Country Manager's Perplexities* (Rhys had written it in a rush, because his other plays had not yet arrived from his Boston publisher), and it could have been either a slapstick or a comedy of manners— characters like Professor Hopskotch ('a high-low comedian and rising young Acrobat, pretending to do everything') and The Manager ('slightly deranged, from ill management') make it difficult to determine. Lucette sang operatic selections and popular folk songs, but there was also, cour- tesy of Bayly, 'a Daring Feat of Equestrianism, Never before attempted in this Country!!!' In short, the show seems to have been typical of the contemporary music hall, offering a little something for every taste.

They had a good run in Quebec, then moved on to Montreal where Rhys, as he had done at their first stop, asked one of the city's military commanders, Colonel Gordon, for the use of his regimental band. Gordon was obviously disturbed to learn that Rhys was a professional actor ('*Actors* in Canada are a little too much of the Fly-by-night order, to hold a *high* social status,' Rhys noted), but agreed to lend his patronage, and his band, to the performance. Montreal was followed by three nights in Kingston, five in Port Hope, four in Peterborough, and then a disappointing experience in Toronto. As another indication of the low esteem in which professional actors were held, Rhys learned that the printers had refused to print the advertising posters he had ordered in advance; he was told that they had been bilked by 'the travelling profession' so often that they would not extend credit to itinerant performers. The trio stayed in Toronto only long enough to perform a single show—Rhys found in the city 'too much assumption of exclusiveness,' another indication that he viewed his work as, if not low-brow, then perhaps middle-brow. However, their stops in Hamilton, St. Catharines, and Belleville were successful, and then they made a triumphant return to Kingston, just in time to play for crowds attending the provincial exhibition. They packed the house for a few nights, but made the mistake of scheduling their final performance for the night after the exhibition ended. Rhys faced the embarrassment of peeking out from behind the curtain to see the cavernous hall empty, save for two girls who worked there and a farmer who had driven twelve miles into town to see the show. They followed the Kingston debacle with two shows in a converted chapel in Ottawa, a venue Rhys remembered for its temperature (he wrote of Lucette's 'chattering teeth doing the castanets'), and then return engagements in Montreal and Quebec. There, where they had begun their tour, Rhys calculated that they had easily cleared £500 in only six months and all in Canada. The pot was his.[55]

Durang and Rhys have left the most complete accounts of popular culture in pre-Confederation Canada. Most of the other evidence is fragmentary—advertisements and newspaper articles, brief references in letters and diaries, the occasional court case involving a performer or audience member—but those fragments confirm that the kind of entertainments offered by Durang and Rhys were entirely typical of the period.

We know, for example, that Rickett's Equestrian and Comedy Company was not the only circus to visit Canada in those decades,

The name of this character, Betsy Prig, from a play performed in New Brunswick in the 1850s, suggests that it was not quite serious theatre.

and that similar troupes often came north from the United States. In November 1811, an American performer known as Mr. Cayetano arrived in Montreal, built a temporary circus, and held a number of performances between February and April 1812. One show featured Mrs. Redon (the first woman trick rider in the United States), Cayetano doing a scene called *The Canadian Peasant*, Mr. Codet acting *The Tailor's Journey to Brentford*, and something that was billed as a Drunken Soldier Tight Rope Performance. But Cayetano's time in Canada was brief; he left a few months before the War of 1812 broke out and, shortly thereafter, the entire company was lost at sea between New Orleans and

Havana. Susanna Moodie described the visit of a travelling American circus to Belleville, beginning with the arrival of large posters 'containing coarse woodcuts of the most exciting scenes in the performance.' Then, on the day of the show, a large tent was erected, with tiers of seats for as many as a thousand spectators, and a large chandelier of tallow candles 'that in the close crowded place emit a very disagreeable odour.' There were two shows a day, one at 2 PM that drew people from outside the city and families with young children, and another at 7:30 PM, preferred by the townspeople because the tent was cooler and less crowded. The show itself was very much like what Ricketts and Durang performed: 'feats of horsemanship, gymnastics, dancing on the tight and slack rope, and wonderful feats of agility and strength…it is provided with good performers, and an excellent brass band.'[56]

It also seems clear that the more popular entertainments focused on spectacle and action, something that even the promoters of serious theatre had to understand if they were to fill their seats. In Saint John, a new performance hall had been built in 1824 (ironically, to host the visit of another travelling circus), and it changed over to theatrical performances in 1828. But it was located in a part of town that the better class of citizens would never have dreamed of frequenting. As a result, wrote theatre historian Mary Elizabeth Smith, 'a larger, less educated and generally less prosperous group, liberally sprinkled with Irishman, formed the bulk of the audience.'[57] The character of performances changed to suit the new crowd; dialogue-heavy comedies and tragedies were replaced by romantic plays with little in the way of a plot but lots of opportunity for garish scenery, fantastic spectacle, and on-stage action. It was the same in Halifax, where promoter Charles Powell found that crowds at the New Grand Theatre demanded impressive shows with spectacular sets, big props, and lots of action. In 1798, he bent to the popular will by advertising 'A Representation of the Savages Landing in their Canoes, with the original March from their Landing, and an exact Performance of the War Hoop Dance and Martial Exercises.' The New Grand later booked a showman who was billed as the Antipodean Whirligig—he spun around on his head with crackers and other fireworks attached to his heels. Susanna Moodie recalled the kind of circus sideshow acts that came to Belleville: 'Barnham's travelling menagerie of wild animals, and of tame darkie melodists,' General

Tom Thumb (Charles Sherwood Stratton, the forty-inch-tall son of a Connecticut carpenter who was widely exhibited by the American circus *impresario* P.T. Barnum), and Signor Blitz, the great conjurer. Contemporary newspapers, letters, and diaries are filled with references to strange performances staged in Canadian halls—what can we make of an advertised performance by the Ethiopian Warblers, who visited the British-American Hotel in Kingston in September 1851?—but mostly they were scaled-down versions of the ambitious shows mounted by Ricketts and Durang. In 1830, the politician and merchant Edward Ermatinger was staying at an inn in St. Thomas, Upper Canada, and acidly described a show put on by a touring troupe known only as Mr. Long's Company—slack-wire dancing; balancing tobacco pipes, swords, and plates; hatching chickens in a hat; tumbling. Ermatinger, who was very fond of music and compiled French-Canadian folk songs as a hobby, was not particularly impressed (in his view, Long was 'a slick man, and deserved to be flogged'), something which probably had as much to do with class bias as with the fact that he returned from a long day out to find that his room had been taken over by the players.[58] Still, despite complaints from affronted elites and serious actors that the Antipodean Whirligig, Signor Blitz, and Long's Company degraded the stage, there was no denying that they were a hit with audiences.

Nowhere does the contrast between high and low culture come out more clearly than in Victoria, where the cultural suppositions of the political, social, and economic elites clashed with those of the greater mass of residents. In the early days of the British presence on the west coast, the kind of shipboard theatricals that had long been a part of life in the Royal Navy were common. The military elites used them as a sort of reward—an invitation to a performance was a social honour—but also to provide a version of polite British culture in an outpost of the empire. Scholars often cite a performance called *Splendid Theatre on board the Frigate 'Trincomalee'* on 18 October 1853 as being the first play performed in what would become British Columbia, but there was probably a performance of Molière's *The Mock Doctor* on the hydrographic survey vessel HMS *Herald* off Vancouver Island in the late 1840s. Employees of the Hudson's Bay Company also mounted plays (such as Sheridan's *The Rivals* in January 1857) at the company's trading post Fort Victoria.

All of these productions would have been entirely proper, at least in the eyes of the military and economic elites who dominated life in the fledgling colony, but Victoria was about to be reshaped. The discovery of gold on the Fraser River in 1858 brought in a flood of prospectors, primarily from the United States, and in their wake came travelling troupes of performers looking to profit from entertaining the would-be gold miners. With this influx of people, the character of Victoria was fundamentally changed. As theatre historian Chad Evans put it, the city was 'besieged by a heterogenous mass of people whose theatrical taste was indiscriminate.'[59] From that point onwards, the city would have a double life in a cultural sense: one sort of amusement for the large floating population of hopeful miners, and another for the sophisticated and conservative circle of British settlers.

The latter kept going much as they had always done, by forming dramatic societies and building theatres to ensure the survival of their kind of culture. The owner of the Union Hotel, for example, built the Naval and Military Theatre next to his establishment, offering respectable and traditional plays as frequently as he could, many of them performed by idle naval officers. They did this, of course, for free, or at the very most collected money to be distributed to local charities; as Horton Rhys had discovered in Montreal, amateur theatricals for the benefit of others and of society as a whole were sharply distinguished from the dubious profession of play-acting for money.

The city also relied on travelling troupes of players to provide a dose of the classics, even if the quality left something to be desired. On one occasion, *Macbeth* was performed in the Victoria Theatre and the entire production had a kind of Monty Python-esque charm about it. The set was a cotton plantation being reused from a previous show, while Macbeth's royal throne was a shipping crate with the name of the ship painted clearly on the side. One actor, after appearing on stage as a witch, was reincarnated as Duncan and then later appeared again, this time as a doctor. Another witch was an actor who had not bothered to shave his beard for the show, nor to learn his lines; he went through the entire performance reading from a script in his hand. In a number of

Frontier theatre: the M&N Theatre Troupe pulls into Dawson City, Yukon, 1907.

scenes, actors delivered their lines from one side of the stage, crawled not so surreptitiously behind the backdrop to the other side of the stage, and popped up there as a different character, only occasionally bothering to change their costume.

While this version of *Macbeth* may have verged on the slapstick, it nevertheless represented an attempt to keep burning the fires of serious, respectable culture. Plays like this became, according to Evans, a bulwark against the commercialized American culture that came north with the gold rush. That kind of culture arrived within a year of the first strike, with the appearance in March 1859 of the George Chapman Pioneer Drama Company. Although it offered higher priced tickets for the 'better classes' and promised that its performances were 'suitable for ladies; Indians and such ilk will have a corner by themselves,' it probably bore less resemblance to the Naval and Military Theatre than to the Fashion Music Hall—a symbol of the new popular culture that billed itself as a 'first class gambling house and dancing hall...[with] varied entertainments.'[60] The shows likely involved the same repertoire that Ricketts and Durang gave to eager Montrealers: jugglers, magicians, gymnasts, acrobats, dialecticians, singers, dancers, monologuists, and

minstrel shows with blackface performers whose material parodied the
singing and dancing of slaves.

An establishment like the Fashion grew out of the combination of
the English tradition of the music hall, a working-class entertainment
room added to a tavern to provide a series of solo acts; the 'free and easy,'
a kind of saloon with entertainment that resembled busking; and the
American tradition of the melodeon, a more commercialized concert hall
that catered to all classes. In time, the commercialized brand of American theatre offered by the Fashion came to predominate in Victoria.
Child acts were very popular because they were a welcome reminder of
the domestic life that many of these men had left behind to seek their
fortune. Equally popular, though, were eroticized acts featuring well-
known leading ladies, whose performances in this overwhelmingly male
society never failed to draw large crowds.

Though it was derelict when this photograph was taken, one does not get the impression
that the Atlin Old Music Hall in Stikine, British Columbia, was much more impressive
in its heyday. c. 1920s.

But regardless of the specifics, the hallmark of this kind of theatre,
in Victoria and elsewhere, was its seediness. It was rough-and-ready
culture. The fact that travelling companies breezed in and out of town
meant there was little time for preparations, and the need to travel with
all their gear meant that sets and costumes were few and were reused

for any kind of performance. Furthermore, the venues were generally poor. Fires were not infrequent because the camphene lamps that most theatres used for stage lighting were much more dangerous than gaslight, which would come into use later in the nineteenth century. Since many theatres were connected to bars, drunkenness was as much of a problem among the actors as the spectators, and brawls were not uncommon. A concert in Halifax in 1828, as *The Novascotian* reported, was 'repeatedly interrupted by all kinds of discordant noises, and several persons effected an entrance to the Hall through the back windows, and others threw dirt and offal in.'[61] A performance by the Amateur Dramatic Association of Victoria broke up in disorder after a young man in the dress circle threw an apple at a performer. The low point came on 6 August 1830, when a theatre company was re-enacting the Battle of Waterloo, using as extras a group of soldiers from the local barracks. The soldiers became a little carried away and the performance was halted after one of them was killed when a ramrod was jammed into his forehead. Oddly enough, the show was a popular one in Canada; it had been mounted in Quebec as early as 1816, although without fatalities or serious injuries.

Another source of conflict was the American content of some travelling shows. Historians generally concur that the War of 1812 created a strong sense of distinctiveness amongst Canadians, and that sense of difference was often manifest in patrons' response to popular entertainments. Although few of the travelling actors likely realized it, nerves remained raw for decades in Toronto, a city that had been occupied and burned by American soldiers in 1813. In 1825, a play at Frank's Hotel—the venue for Toronto's first theatrical performance (the hall was a low-ceilinged room on the second floor, described by a twentieth-century critic as a firetrap that 'would be contemplated with horror by a modern building inspector'[62])—degenerated into a riot even before the actors took the stage, when a member of the company asked the crowds to remove their hats as a mark of respect as *Yankee Doodle Dandy* was played. A decade later, a newspaper in the city wrote disparagingly of 'strolling players from Yankee-land.' It didn't help any when the performances included elements that were sure to inflame passions—like a re-enactment of 'the glorious victory over the British at New Orleans,' advertised on the wall of a country tavern near Ancaster, Upper Canada.

Nowadays, we tend to see a night at the theatre as relatively risk-free; a century and a half ago, it might involve all sorts of adventure.

———•◦•———

Still, it would be a mistake to see these two varieties of culture as mutually exclusive, or to imagine that they existed in separate spheres. The elites, whatever their opinion of popular culture, had no desire to stamp it out. One of the few exceptions to this were fundamentalist sects such as the Quakers and Methodists, who frowned upon such ungodly pastimes, putting them on par with drinking, cursing, and card-playing. The fiddle, they thought, was a tool for sin because it was used for dancing; religious music was the only legitimate kind, in their view. But this level of intolerance was unusual, and elites were generally much more ambivalent towards popular culture. On the one hand, they drew a clear distinction between the amateur, the gentleman or gentlewoman who acted or sang in public out of love for the art (or, at most, to raise money for a very worthy cause), and the professional, a much lower form of life who tried to make a living from entertaining the public (a career path chosen, they probably suspected, because the individual was too shiftless to do anything respectable). At the same time, however, they saw the value in supporting and even patronizing popular culture. Colonel Gordon may have regarded Horton Rhys with vague distaste upon learning that he was a professional actor, but he did allow his regimental band to appear on Rhys's bill. Ricketts and Durang, with an even more low-brow form of entertainment than Rhys, still enjoyed the active support of military officers and leading merchants in Montreal and Quebec, who were fully aware that the circus busied idle minds on the one hand, and brought in business on the other.

Whether or not the elites attended these performances themselves is more difficult to determine. In the larger cities, where there were other entertainments on offer, it seems unlikely. But in some of the smaller towns that Rhys visited, towns where cultural opportunities were limited and the class barriers less impermeable, any kind of travelling show was likely to draw people from across the social spectrum. Indeed, Rhys observed that his spectators often consisted of people of all ranks—he distinguished in his audience between the better classes, and the people who 'came in crowds, and sat on each other's laps, and cracked nuts, and ate apples.' Susanna Moodie, too, saw people of all classes at the travelling circus in Belleville and found that 'the variety of faces and characters that nature exhibits gratis, are far more amusing to watch than the feats of the Athletes.'

Realizing that there was some benefit to be found in circuses and travelling theatricals, the elites were quite content merely to regulate them. In the mid-nineteenth century, as municipal institutions were coming into being throughout the British North American colonies, lawmakers gave to local authorities, either municipal councils or town police forces, the power 'to regulate and licence all theatres kept for profit; and persons exhibiting for gain or profit, any wild beasts, puppet-show, wire dance, circus riding, or any other idle acts or feats which common showmen, circus riders or mountebanks or jugglers usually practice or perform, and to limit the number, and to provide for the purpose of licensing the same.' Typically, obtaining a license involved paying a fee to municipal authorities. In 1848, the New Brunswick House of Assembly mandated a £5 levy on 'each Circus Company, Showman, or exhibitor of Wild Beasts.'[63] A decade later, Rhys paid two dollars a week for a license to perform in Hamilton. He called it an 'ugly custom' and complained bitterly to municipal authorities, but apparently to no avail.

Had Rhys taken his act a little farther off the beaten path, he could have escaped the licensing fee altogether. Outside of the cities, there were no municipal police to enforce the licensing regulations, no town clerks or bailiffs to collect fees from travelling performers. On the margins of settlement, culture was a very different thing. There were no amateur dramatic societies, no travelling theatrical troupes. Neither the high culture of Junius Brutus Booth nor the low culture of John Ricketts and John Durang made it into the backwoods of British North America. There, culture was no spectator sport, as it was in urban Canada. The arts were not something you watched or listened to; they were something you did.

Chapter 5

Culture on the Frontier

In 1878, an Englishwoman who was one of the first settlers in the Muskoka District of central Ontario (known to history only as 'Emigrant Lady') reflected on the process by which civilization was brought to the wilderness. First came the 'laborious efforts to raise the rude and coarse necessaries of daily life, then the struggles for convenience and comfort.' Once the essentials of life were provided for, pioneers experienced 'the gradual demand for the luxuries of a higher civilisation.' Such luxuries, she observed, 'can only be obtained by the growth and encouragement of the ornamental as well as useful arts.'[64]

On the frontiers of British North America, settlers faced the same reality that the earliest European newcomers had faced: that cultivating the ornamental arts came a distant second to the needs of day-to-day survival. As our Englishwoman in Muskoka realized, homesteading was an all-consuming experience. The work seemed never-ending, so there was rarely much leisure time; taking an hour to read or sing could mean neglecting the stumping, seeding, or harvesting. Clearing virgin land also provided little in the way of disposable income. If a pioneer family had to choose between books or a few panes of glass for the windows, which would they pick? Even if the will was there, the isolation of many farmsteads meant that musical instruments or painting supplies were difficult to obtain. At a time when everything came in by cart over barely broken roads, it might have seemed absurd to devote precious cargo space to the niceties of culture.

But the desire to replicate European culture in the wilderness was stronger than we might imagine, and the arts were gradually transplanted to the bush. Indeed, the character of the frontier helped create an environment that was conducive to the growth of the arts. Few touring professionals visited the remote regions to mount plays or offer concerts, so culture became a participatory activity that involved everyone; settlers who sought the joys of music or art were usually left to their own devices. And the dispersal of the population, with neighbours separated by miles of forest, meant that cultural activities were often confined to the family home, or at most a handful of families. When the work schedule permitted it, every pioneer became a singer or musician, every log cabin a theatre or concert hall. But the kind of music that was played, for example, depended very much on class, for the pioneer experience was not homogeneous. Immigrants from upper-class backgrounds often had the financial resources to ensure a greater level of comfort, but this was not true for the majority of settlers. They lived hardscrabble and precarious lives, and shared an experience with native families: most of the objects they needed to work and to live they had to make for themselves. So, craft work and folk art became a feature of life on the frontier—everything from basketry and weaving to furniture-making and wood-carving. And the music they made while they were working came from a different tradition. But there was at least one commonality between the two kinds of experience: on the frontier, culture developed, not so much to provide the moral improvement that urban elites so valued, but for purposes that would have struck a chord with the urban working class, as a diversion from the struggles of making a living.

When he was well into his sixties, Canniff Haight looked back on the pioneer days of his youth, spent near the Loyalist settlement of Adolphustown, in eastern Ontario. He recalled his parents fondly, and expressed no illusions about the life of unceasing toil they led. Their existence might have sounded romantic, he mused: 'Love in a cot; the smoke gracefully curling; the wood-pecker tapping, and all that; very pretty. But alas, in this work-a-day world, particularly the new one upon which my parents then entered, these silver linings were not observed. They had too much of the prose of life.' For his father, that prose meant building a one-room log cabin, then spending endless days turning the thick forest into fields, an acre one year, perhaps two the next. In the fall he harvested the year's crops—Haight recalled being plopped in a half-barrel on the floor of the barn, so his father could keep an eye on him while he threshed the grain—and in the winter they made maple syrup, his father bringing in the sap and chopping the wood, his mother tending the boiler while Canniff lay beside her in a sap trough they used as a crib. 'Work was the normal condition of their being,' he recalled. 'Everything seems to have been so arranged as to preclude the possibility of idle moments.'

As Haight's account shows, the life of a pioneer left little time and energy to devote to cultural pursuits. 'The time had not yet arrived,' he mused of his parents' era, 'for the people to feel the necessity of cultivating the mind as well as providing for the wants of the body.'[65] And then there was the expense. The middle-class Englishwoman, who had been used to dabbling in poetry before her family immigrated to the Canadian wilderness, quickly found that everything she had taken for granted in the old country was costly and difficult to obtain. Ink and paper had to come in by mail, a service that was expensive, slow, and uncertain. In 1820, it cost over $7 (in 2009 currency) to send a letter between England and Quebec, and even more to get it from the city to the frontier. Author Susanna Moodie, trying desperately to earn a little extra money to keep body and soul together on her homestead near Peterborough, Ontario, had to turn down lucrative commissions from American publishers because she simply could not afford to post her manuscripts to the United States. Even the candles that would allow her to write in the long winter evenings represented a small fortune—a month's worth of candles costing the equivalent of over $112. A torch made from rolled birchbark or a burning pine knot was a poor substitute.

But the same kind of settler accounts make clear that the will was certainly there. Frances Stewart, who immigrated to the Peterborough area with her family in 1822, lamented in 1836 that her 'mind has sadly degenerated for want of exercise…my old tastes and enjoyments are the same, but somewhat mouldy for want of brushing up and employment.' To avoid these mental cobwebs, many immigrants ignored the advice of Robert Mudie, whose how-to book for aspiring settlers warned that novels would be no more useful in the wilderness than 'Paganini, or even his fiddle,' and found ways to take a few books with them or acquire them locally.[66] Frances Beavan, an Irishwoman who lived in New Brunswick from 1836 to 1843, recalled that a typical house in the backwoods of the colony would have a small shelf of books, including the Bible, a new almanac, and Stephen Humbert's *Union Harmony*, a book of psalm tunes that went through four editions in the first half of the nineteenth century. On a trip down Lake Simcoe, Anna Jameson, another Irishwoman whose short stay in Canada in the 1830s spawned one of the most vivid accounts of life in the colony, stopped at a tiny village to rest in a cabin while the men were taking in wood. There, in the middle of nowhere, she was surprised to find a few books by William Shakespeare and Walter Scott, as well as 'a good guitar.'[67] What interested Jameson was not that English literature had made its way to Canada, but that it could be found in a rude cabin so far from civilization (Jameson did not consider Toronto to be especially civilized). She never found out whose cabin it was, but it may well have been someone like Frances Stewart, who fully appreciated the importance of these fragments of old world culture in the new world: 'The greatest pleasure was derived from the books—a wonderful comfort—not only enjoyed by us, but many of our friends in Cobourg borrowed and were glad to get our treasures. My mother's connection with the Edgeworths, Beauforts and Wallers ensured a good supply of most entertaining, useful and amusing reading…It would be impossible in these times to form an idea of the pleasure these yearly boxes were to the whole settlement.'[68]

But few settlers had the connections with literary luminaries like the prolific Anglo-Irish novelist Maria Edgeworth that Stewart enjoyed, and instead had to rely on the kindness of their neighbours. As Susanna Moodie's sister Catherine Parr Traill (who became a neighbour to Stewart when she immigrated to the Peterborough area in the early 1830s) put it, 'every settler's library may be called a circulating one, as their books are sure to pass from friend to friend in due rotation.' The Emigrant Lady in Muskoka frequently loaned books to an English neighbour who lived alone; he visited them only when it was time to change books, but on those occasions they had many good conversations about 'a particular reign in Cassell's "English History," or one of Shakespeare's plays, both of which voluminous works he was reading through.'[69] Some women even established lending libraries, of a more formal variety than the kind Traill described, for the benefit of local homesteaders. Mary Gapper, the daughter of a Somerset landowner who came to Canada on a visit in 1828 and married and settled near

Thornhill, north of York, rode on horseback from farm to farm, trying to recruit subscribers for a lending library that she called the Book Society; she found the experience as frustrating (according to her journal, she was only able to enroll eleven members) as having to wait ten months for the first parcel of books she had ordered to arrive from England—even then, the first book to arrive was a biography of Reginald Heber, the Bishop of Calcutta, hardly the kind of light reading her subscribers would have expected.[70] Ann Langton, who came to Canada with her family in 1837 and settled not far from the Stewarts, helped to form such a library in Bobcaygeon, in eastern Ontario, but found that the local school commissioner was the only member who would reliably remit his sixpence subscription each quarter. Almost everyone else in the neighbourhood either declined to subscribe, or were delinquent with their fees: 'others who are really thriving say they have never found themselves rich enough...John [her husband] says there seems no difficulty in producing sixpence for a glass of grog!...I think I shall be obliged to accept a pound of butter or a few eggs in payment.' For Frances Beavan in New Brunswick, the problem was not in getting her neighbours to contribute a load of potatoes or a barrel of buckwheat to buy books, but in selecting what books to buy: 'the grave and serious declaim against light reading, and regard a novel as the climax of human wickedness.'[71] They probably would have preferred the biography of Bishop Heber.

Where books were too expensive or too difficult to import, newspapers filled the gap, providing a welcome lifeline to the cultural world beyond the frontier. Furthermore, many newspapers were willing to accept goods—produce, firewood for the printing office stove, linen that could be turned into newsprint—in exchange for subscriptions, something that put them within reach in the notoriously cash-poor frontier society. Fifty or sixty pounds of beef or twenty-five pounds of butter might be enough to bring a four-page weekly paper into your farm for a year. Frances Beavan recalled that, in her early days in New Brunswick, they could not afford to buy books through the mail, but they could subscribe to newspapers: 'for our few yearly dollars the Albion's [the New York *Albion*] pearly paper and clear black type brought for society around our hearths the laughter-loving "Lorrequer," the pathos of the portrait painter, or the soul-winning Christopher

North, whose every word seems written in letters of gold, incrusted with precious jewels.' The papers were a blessing, she recalled, because they 'afforded plenty of food for the mind, and prevented it brooding too deeply over the realities of life.' Beavan's prose betrays her class, but it wasn't just the well-educated who came to appreciate the value of a newspaper on the frontier. As Thomas Priestman, a settler in the Niagara District, wrote to his brother in England in 1839,

> we have got an agraculturel paper published at Rochester in the State of New York once a month, which I think a good deal. It is both usefull and entertaining. It only costs half a dolar yearly, besides a little postage. It is printed in pamflet form and at the end of the year it makes a handsom book with a title page and index to it.[72]

We see the importance of reading, too, in the willingness of settlers to band together to establish rudimentary schools. Through the first decades of the nineteenth century, most of British North America's colonial governments enacted legislation to provide state support, usually in the form of teachers' subsidies, building grants, or both, for common or elementary schools (grammar schools for the more affluent were already well established). Education spread slowly through rural areas, with the main obstacles being poor pay for teachers (it was not uncommon for teachers to be paid in flour or sheep); the difficulty in finding qualified instructors (educational historian J.G. Althouse remarked that a teaching position 'was commonly regarded as the last refuge of the incompetent, the inept, the unreliable'); a lack of books; the inability of many settlers to pay the annual school fees (which averaged $10); and the fact that, during spring planting and fall harvest, young bodies could not be spared from farm work to improve their minds. But the will was certainly there and, as the administrative apparatus became more efficient, the number of rural schools grew. In Lower Canada, where there had been only thirty schools for a rural population of 128,000 in 1790, progressively more effective legislation meant that by 1832 over 102,000 children—one in three—received some kind of education. Even though the statistics cannot tell us how many children actually attended school regularly, as opposed to those who were simply enrolled, they are interesting, especially since most studies point to steadily rising literacy rates in settler areas after the 1840s.

As Anna Jameson noticed during her stopover on Lake Simcoe, some settlers also went to great lengths to make music available. In the summer of 1826, Stewart's family ordered a piano from Ireland, although it did not arrive until the following spring; even then, it only just made it, the team of horses that were pulling it having gone through the ice on Rice Lake. But it arrived safe and sound and, as Stewart wrote, became 'the wonder of everyone, it sounds so well, the poor thing, it goes in and out of tune of its own accord. I never allow any common tuners who come here to touch it, it had not been tuned for six years. Sometimes it gets a little asthmatic like myself in damp weather.'[73]

The journals of Lucy Peel, who spent three and a half years with her husband homesteading in the Eastern Townships of Lower Canada before returning to England, give an indication of the importance of music to that class of settlers. In 1833, she noted that two girls went to Sherbrooke to take music lessons from the wife of the local cobbler, who taught many of the young women in the vicinity. Lucy herself was an accomplished musician: 'I am considered quite a musical wonder here,' she wrote, for she had two guitars on which she composed and performed her own music. Her talents made her immensely popular as a performer, and her diaries record many evenings spent playing for her neighbours at spontaneous get-togethers. Interestingly, she makes it clear that there was no distinction between performer and spectator; everyone performed a song, a dance, or a piece of music to the best of their ability. In short, culture wasn't just something they watched; it was something they did. The result was a combination of back-breaking manual labour and genteel upper-class English amusements. The McGrath family immigrated to Upper Canada from Ireland 1827, eventually settling at Erindale where, as T.W. McGrath wrote to a relative in 1832, they could experience both the frontier and the city in the same day: 'My younger brother lends a hand at everything, from a duet on the piano-forte to the threshing of a sheaf of corn…we have frequently occupied the morning at work in a *potato field*, and passed the evening most agreeably in the *ball* room at York!!!'[74]

What was behind this desire to bring culture to the frontier? Pioneering, of course, was a profoundly disruptive experience, and even the immigrant from the tiniest village or remotest glen must have felt a sense of displacement at being transplanted to a wilderness that often seemed essentially hostile. Nova Scotia poet Oliver Goldsmith (a relative of the English poet of the same name) was not a settler himself, but could well imagine the emotions of an immigrant gazing at the forest that had to be turned into farmland:

> How sinks his heart in those deep solitudes,
> Where not a voice upon his ear intrudes;
> Where solemn silence all the waste pervades,
> Heightening the horror of its gloomy shades.[75]

Recreating a cultural life, even in its most basic form, became a way to ease the stress of facing such a potentially threatening environment, and to cope with the almost inevitable homesickness that ensued when immigrants pulled up roots and moved an ocean away. In such situations, reminders of old world culture were welcome. Thomas Radcliff, whose family emigrated from Ireland to Adelaide Township in the London district of Upper Canada in 1832, recorded with evident delight that 'a family, which had been attached to some choir in England, has arrived here, with capital voices and good instruments, so that even your practised ear would acknowledge the merit of the performance.' Lucy Peel wrote in September 1834 of playing the harp for a local woman, who cried through all of it; 'she said, hearing me made her think of England and former days,' Peel wrote.[76] Furthermore, for middle-class settlers like Frances Stewart and Frances Beavan, who had come from a society in which the arts were relatively accessible, it was second nature to surround themselves with culture at the earliest opportunity. So, as soon as circumstances allowed, Lucy Peel ordered a harp from England on which she composed a collection of songs that she called *Canadian Airs*. Such determination was likely combined with strong feelings of pride in the British way of life and all it entailed. British imperialism, after all, was based on a profound faith that the government, religion, society, and culture of the mother country represented the apogee of human achievement. Not everyone could take Protestantism to the darkest corners of the empire, but people like Peel and Stewart could do their part by spreading British culture. So, transplanting the arts to the Canadian wilderness served the same purpose as theatricals did for the crewman of the *Hecla* and *Griper*: it reminded them that, however far they were from civilization, they could remain civilized by taking their culture with them.

—————•◦•—————

Over a century later, literary critic Wilfred Eggleston wondered how long these impulses could have lasted under the ceaseless demands of pioneering life. Not very long, he thought, for he imagined 'the flame of transplanted "bookishness" and urbane culture fading under the engrossing exactions and ruthless demands of pioneer struggle.' It was 'not so much that the literary flame died out as that the intellectual and imaginative faculties were diverted into other channels, in the process of challenging the physical obstacles and of mastering the frontier environment.' Reflecting on the place of culture on the prairie frontier, he noted that,

> You could spend half a lifetime in that rangeland setting without ever seeing a play, hearing a lyric well read, meeting an author, browsing in a bookstore, seeing a publisher, attending a literary society, or talking to a literary critic. In a soil so barren of literary stimuli, should vigorous growth be looked for?[77]

Eggleston's comments said more about his class bias than about Canadian culture. On the margins of settlement, you probably would go for years without ever seeing a publisher, taking in a play, or talking to a literary critic. But how long could you go before dancing the night away in a neighbour's log cabin while someone played the fiddle, hearing a half-dozen-strong choir sing hymns in a clapboard church, listening to folk tales at the knee of an elderly relative, or enjoying some earnest if amateurish verse that a neighbour had composed in his head while pulling stumps? Probably not very long. The frontier may not always have been conducive to the growth of what Eggleston calls 'polite letters,' the kind of culture that well-bred settlers like Peel and Stewart tried to transplant, but we should also not imagine that it was a cultural desert. It was in the long winter nights in the wilderness that a new Canadian culture was being created to lighten the hearts and loosen the bodies after a day of labour. As historian Richard Saunders wrote, 'the elements of originality in this culture are rooted in the lives of the mass of the people.'[78]

It began with the houses themselves. If the homes of the elite expressed their social suppositions and their desire to imprint the old world on the new, the dwellings of everyone else represented a home-grown architectural style that used forms because they were appealing, regardless of their symbolic content, and tailored them to local conditions. For example, the *habitants* of Lower Canada tended to use the hipped roof, a style that was rarely seen in peasant houses in France, because it was best suited to cope with the weight of snow that it would have to bear. In doing so, they adopted a certain architectural feature, but stripped it of any class connotations. There was, therefore, no conscious reliance on design rules or architectural styles; settlers built homes in a certain way because they were easy to construct and suited the character of the place, particularly the weather. For this reason, architectural historian Harold Kallman has argued, it is a mistake to look to European models in assessing domestic architecture. The earlier notion, that houses around Quebec were stylistically linked to those in Normandy while Montreal-area houses were more closely connected to Brittany, has largely been replaced by the belief that differences in style were the result of local factors, rather than the *habitants'* roots in this or that region of France. By the same token, Kallman argues that Acadian houses bore more resemblance to those of English settlers in Nova Scotia than of French *habitants* in New France, for the simple reason that geography was a more important determinant than cultural origin. In Upper Canada, the log cabin eventually gave way to the style known as Ontario vernacular, a single-storey cottage with a centre gable. On such homes, the elaborately cut bargeboard, the decorative woodwork running under the eaves, allowed for a similar kind of freedom in design as craftsmen worked in motifs like thistles, lilies, roses, and vines—some because of their ethnic significance and some simply because they made a pleasing finished product.

But it was also inside the homes that a distinct culture was being created, in the arts that people did themselves for their own purposes, be they practical or aesthetic. It is usually referred to as folk art, although

The tools of the pioneer craftswoman. Undated.

the term requires some clarification. It does not necessarily mean work that is crudely rendered and more preoccupied with detail than design; some types of folk art, known as naive or primitive, certainly had these qualities, but other examples are extraordinarily well crafted and show great sophistication, suggesting that the practitioners had some training, or at least a basic familiarity with artistic principles. Nor was folk art the preserve of the amateur; it was also practised by professional craftspeople who made their living from it. And typically, two varieties of folk art are discernible: the personal, which is based in individual expression; and the ethnic, which relies on traditional techniques and motifs of a certain ethnic group. Linking them is the fact that both were practised extensively on Canada's frontiers, suggesting, in the words of folklore scholar Michael Bird, that the energies of pioneers 'were far from exhausted by the effort required for subsistence.'[79]

Some of this work was purely decorative, like *Fraktur*, the elaborate calligraphy in the Swiss-German tradition that Mennonite settlers brought with them to Canada in the nineteenth century. By contrast, the tradition of *ex voto*, or votive, paintings, imported from France to the new world, did have a religious purpose. Done out of gratitude for some narrow escape, they were executed by untrained painters in the naive style, with little thought for spatial depth or perspective. If poorly crafted, they were tremendously important to the life of the community,

Mary Sheepey's sampler, 1764; a fine example of early embroidery done in Quebec.

for they were normally displayed in the vestibule of the parish church for all to see. As a result, the locals who were familiar with the stories told in the paintings 'examined them with great interest on many, many occasions, retold the incidents with relish, and discussed and gossiped about the affair at length,' as art historian Russell Harper put it. He called them 'forceful living histories,' the most personal and vibrant works of art produced in New France.[80] At the same time, we should not underestimate the pride of a successful pioneer family whose prosperity might give them the means to record their good fortune by hiring a 'limner,' an itinerant painter who was often supplementing his income as a coach, sign, or house painter by doing small oils on a commission basis. It might be a tidy farmhouse, a prize bull, or a young child—what mattered was the indigenous subjects that made these folk art paintings the same kind of forceful living histories that Harper saw in the votive paintings of New France.

Other varieties of folk art, such as woodcarving—perhaps the most diffuse form of art among the *habitants* and pioneers—straddled the boundary between the decorative and the practical. Under the skilled hands of the carver, this most abundant of materials was turned into toys, religious objects, furniture, tools, and dozens of other things. Like the Dorset people of the Arctic, pioneers probably possessed a general level of carving proficiency, with a few craftsmen of exceptional ability whose work could stand with the best of the professional sculptors. And they probably were craft*smen*, because craft work was a gendered practice in pioneer communities, just as it was in aboriginal societies. Men worked in metal and wood, while women worked with fabric and straw, often beginning with the embroidered samplers that girls made to demonstrate their proficiency with needle and thread. The sampler was a practical demonstration of having achieved a level of competence, but it was also a charming decorative element that could brighten the walls of a pioneer cabin. Weaving, too, was both utilitarian and decorative. Just like generations of native women, the pioneer women relied on their ingenuity to find raw materials. The husks or straw of corn, oats, wheat, or rye could be woven into mats, while scraps of fabric could be turned into carpets, a pound and a half of rags producing a yard of carpet. Everything that could be used, would be used; one woman collected animal hair from the vats at a tannery, then cleaned, carded, and twisted it into thread to make a blanket. The land surrounding them yielded up the colours for dyeing: bright blue from logwood, purslain weed, and alum; yellow from onion skins, smartweed, horse-radish leaves, or waxwood; orange from copperas and the lye of wood ash; brown from sumach blossoms, walnut husks, and butternut bark; and black from logwood chips steeped in cider or vinegar and copperas in an iron pot. If the colour palette was not extensive, it was rich, strong, and infinitely variable.

And then there was the practice of embellishing utilitarian objects with folk art designs, something that recalls the native practice. As the farm became more prosperous and existence less tenuous, pioneers gradually realized that they no longer had to make do with house-hold objects that were distinctive for their plainness. Decorative

The Sarah and Peter Mitchell house in Waterdown, Ontario: a typical storey-and-a-half, centre-gable cottage, in the style known as 'Ontario vernacular.'

elements—even if it was only a scalloped edge or a turned leg—could be worked into the furniture they made. Painted motifs with traditional significance could be added to chests, coat racks, tables, and trunks: from the German tradition came the six-pointed compass star and the whirling-sun motif; from French Canada, the *coeur saignant*, or bleeding heart; from the Doukhobor heritage, compass stars and lilies. As Michael Bird put it, these techniques and motifs were the 'simple tools with which ordinary people gave their everyday life a modest beauty.'[81]

Many of these objects from the eighteenth and nineteenth centuries have survived, but other forms of culture were more transitory, despite the fact that they were probably just as important and widespread in the lives of the people. Singing was immensely popular because it didn't depend on literacy, it could be tailored to suit the time and place, and it could be done while working. Predictably, many of the folk songs were imported from Europe, although in the nineteenth century more and more came north from the United States, particularly to the Canadian west ('The Red River Valley', for example, refers not

An 1878 illustration, in which children learn folk tales at the knee of an elderly relative.

to the Red River in Manitoba, but to one in Texas). Often the lyrics were altered to Canadianize them—the Irish folk song *The Wexford Girl* became *The Lethbridge Girl*, while *The Lake of Pontchartrain* was transmuted into *The Banks of the Similkameen*—and a single folk song originating in Europe could exist in dozens of variants across North America. Thematically, there were regional as well as ethnic variations. Sea shanties were popular in the Maritimes and around the Great Lakes of central Canada, while the lumber camps of New Brunswick, Quebec, Ontario, and British Columbia produced a range of songs describing the travails of the woodsman. The miners of Nova Scotia, Ontario, and British Columbia created a similar variety of songs about their own experience. And because many of these workers tended to be seasonal, coming into the mines and lumber camps to work for a few months at a time, they would take songs back to their own villages, to mix with local folk songs. Even songs that were not rooted in labouring gangs were often connected with work. Ethnographer Marius Barbeau, one of the most important collectors of folk songs, writes that 'work in the past was made more attractive by an artistic refinement and a playfulness unfamiliar to the present generations. Work songs of all kinds sustained the rhythm of the hand in toil, while the mind escaped on the wing of romance.'[82] So workers sang songs with rhythms that corresponded to the rhythm of their work. Fulling, the process of cleaning and thickening cloth, usually involved a group of women seated along a trough holding the wet, soapy material. They would pound wooden stampers on the cloth, matching their strokes to the beat of an old French folk song such as *À la Fontaine*. George Head, a British soldier and travel writer who came to Canada in 1814, recalled hearing a 'genuine Canadian boat song,' whose rhythm matched that of the paddlers, as he was conveyed from Kingston to Montreal:

> in it there was a vast deal more noise than music, nor of all the others that I heard these men sing during the voyage, did the melodies bear the slightest resemblance to any I had heard before…they roared out without mercy, in full chorus, and one at a time sang the song itself, which treated of the hardihood of the Voyageurs, the troubles and difficulties they encounter, not forgetting their skill and bravery in surmounting them.[83]

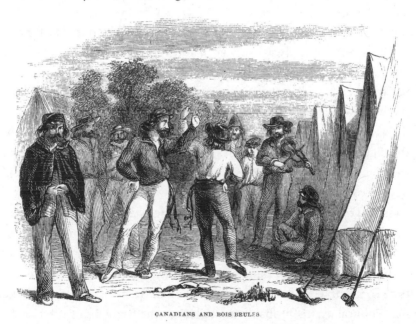

CANADIANS AND BOIS BRULÉS.

This illustration from *Harper's New Monthly Magazine* in 1859 shows the Métis of Red River enjoying their leisure.

There was a massive storehouse of songs—folklorists have catalogued some 10,000 folk songs in Quebec alone—retained within the collective memory of the supposedly uncultured labouring classes. Donald Ban (Fair Donald), the subject of Alexander McLachlan's poem

The Emigrant (1861), was probably representative of the typical settler who came to Canada, in this case from Scotland, with a large repertoire of songs at his disposal:

> The spirit of the mighty hills,
>   Within his breast he bore,
> And how he loved to sit and sing,
>   Their balladical lore;
> For he had treasured in his heart,
>   The legends and the lays,
> The loves, the joys, the smiles and tears,
>   The voice of other days.

Such settlers, as Barbeau put it, 'were their own libraries…In songs and ballads of this kind…there was much poetry and fine feeling, which we generally do not associate…with peasants who are uneducated in the remote country by-ways…we find that the instinct for fine arts, for real artistic expression…[was] very keen and very marked indeed.'[84]

So, for every tiny hamlet with genteel settlers who tried to replicate the best of English culture, there was another where the culture was a little more earthy. This was as true on the *seigneuries* of New France in the eighteenth century as it was a hundred years later on the western frontier, the very place that Wilfred Eggleston had lamented as being devoid of cultural inspiration. In 1884, when the city of Saskatoon consisted of fourteen log houses, the evenings were always enlivened by dances accompanied by a local man with a fiddle. 'What squeak was not inherent in the fiddle John scraped into it,' recalled one participant, 'but he had a tune for every dance and strangely, we had a dance for every tune so it worked out to the enjoyment of all.' In nearby Battleford, the first cultural events probably took place at the barracks of the North-West Mounted Police, where a minstrel group had been organized. One of their early concerts in 1879 boasted such enduring songs as 'Massa in de Cold', 'Cold Ground', 'Nigger on the Fence', and 'Mother Says I Mustn't'. In 1882 the settlement got its first piano, which came up the Saskatchewan River by steamboat after sitting in storage in Grand Rapids. Mice had eaten away the buffers, so the local minister made new

Although this photograph was taken in 1943, it depicts a timeless scene: loggers enjoying some fiddle music after a day's work.

ones out of an old felt hat; and two or three times a week a bunch of local men would gather around it with fiddles, flutes, piccolos, and tin whistles for an evening of singing.[85] It may not exactly have been what Wilfred Eggleston had in mind, but it was culture all the same.

But however much they fiddled and danced and sang as a respite from the incessant demands of work, that work had to be done, and it had to be done as efficiently as possible. Here, too, culture could play a role. In an interesting echo of the Jesuits' use of music and art to spread the Christian gospel, the new British rulers of Canada also believed that culture could have a utilitarian element: literature could spread the gospel of efficient farming.

Rural Dramatics
1912
Plum Ridge School,
Pleasant Home, Manitoba

The theatre comes to the Manitoba frontier, 1912.

The colonies' potential for agriculture emerged as a theme for writers in the early nineteenth century. A typical example was Cornwall Bayley's *Canada: A Descriptive Poem, Written at Quebec, 1805*, which invited prospective settlers to take advantage of 'All that Creation's rural sceptre yields,' while the editors of *The Nova-Scotia Magazine* frequently invited local contributors to submit articles on agricultural improvement.[86] Colonial administrators in the years after the War of 1812 were delighted at the influx of settlers who were keen to open new districts to agriculture, but dismayed by the backwardness of their farming techniques. The Earl of Dalhousie, the lieutenant-governor of Nova Scotia from 1816 to 1820, had tried to demonstrate the benefits of a scientific approach to farming on his estates in Scotland, and jumped at the opportunity to do the same in Nova Scotia. In 1818, he got his chance when a series of letters began appearing in the *Acadian Recorder*. Signed by Agricola, the pseudonym of Halifax merchant John Young, they contained a range of suggestions for agricultural improvement, all couched in a didactic yet accessible style. Dalhousie immediately endorsed the letters publicly, and in 1822 more than half of them were published in book form, under the title *The Letters of Agricola*. As one of the earliest books written in Canada and dealing with indigenous subject matter, it was a test case to determine if Nova Scotians were ready to read home-grown literature.

At about the same time, the *Acadian Recorder* began publishing a series of letters signed by Mephibosheth Stepsure, who was in reality Thomas McCulloch, a secessionist Presbyterian minister and founder of Pictou Academy, one of the great educational institutions of nineteenth-century Nova Scotia. More obviously literary than Young's rather utilitarian prose (indeed, literary critic Northrop Frye suggests that McCulloch should be considered the founder of Canadian humorous writing), it carried the same message: that sensible, progressive farmers like the lame but successful Stepsure and his neighbour Saunders Scantoscreesh prosper, while those who desert the land in hopes of finding an easy fortune elsewhere court disaster. And these were just the best known examples of literature with an agricultural message behind it. Oliver Goldsmith's *The Rising Village* (1834) describes the growing prosperity of one settlement, thanks to the hardy pioneer:

> While the poor peasant, whose laborious care
> Scarce from the soil could wring his scanty fare;
> Now in the peaceful arts of culture skilled,
> Sees his wide barn with ample treasures filled.[87]

Indeed, there are enough works related to this theme—from Bayley through Agricola and Stepsure to Joseph Howe's *Western and Eastern Rambles* (originally published in *The Novascotian* between 1828 and 1831) and Thomas Chandler Haliburton's *Recollections of Nova Scotia* (which first appeared in *The Novascotian* in 1835 and 1836)—to speak of a genre of literature that preached the gospel of agriculture's potential to enrich the energetic, progressive farmer.

The popularity of such work among local readers suggests that indigenous literature, particularly if it had practical utility behind it, was indeed valued. And this was not just the case in Nova Scotia. In 1819, when the newly created National History Society began to award literary prizes to stimulate writing in Canada, the first medal went not to a well-crafted novel or a fine collection of poetry, but to Joseph Abbott's essay on agriculture in Lower Canada. The Canadian sojourn of Scottish novelist John Galt, who lived in Upper Canada from 1826 to 1829, spawned the novel *Bogle Corbet* (1831), a literary prescription for the kind of agrarian emigrant who was most likely to succeed on the Canadian frontier. Galt might well have been offended to be compared to a Jesuit, but the comparison is an apt one. If the missionaries of New France regarded culture as the handmaiden of religion, the colonizers of British North America saw its potential as the handmaiden of agriculture.

In 1912, a Vancouver newspaper reflected on the difficulties faced by culture on the frontier: 'For many years it has been a reproach against Canada in general and Western Canada in particular that the fine arts are neglected…Art seemed stifled by Commerce, and the minds of our prominent men seemed to be so full of that pioneer spirit which has carved an empire out of virgin territory that there was no room for an appreciation of "les beaux arts."'[88] And yet one might argue that there were two frontiers, at least in terms of cultural development: the frontier of Lucy Peel, who had the resources and the inclination to import a harp to the Eastern Townships, to give music lessons to her neighbours, and to compose genteel airs to be performed in a civilized drawing-room environment; and the frontier of the countless and largely forgotten pioneer women and men, who expressed themselves through basketry, weaving, naive painting, and woodcarving. The same divide that characterized urban culture, then, was making itself felt elsewhere.

But the divide between the two was never absolute. In 1846, a local woman, imagining she was being helpful, offered the wife of the minister in the backwoods of eastern Ontario a copy of Brooke's doctrines for the church. 'Oh, I never have time for those kind of books,' she quickly replied to the crestfallen woman. 'I can only give my attention to light reading.'[89] In other circumstances, one would expect the minister's wife to prefer improving literature like Brooke's doctrines to frivolous reading, in the same way that she probably would have chosen Junius Brutus Booth over a touring circus company. But the demands of the frontier made her crave something different in the little time that was available to her for recreation. Perceptions of the value and meaning of culture, then, could be as dependent on place as they were on class. As the years passed and the frontier became the heartland, this fact would become clearer to the consumers of high and low culture alike.

Chapter 6

The Dream of Useful Knowledge

A decade before Confederation, the Quebec newspaper *Le Pays* mused about the fortunes of culture once settlement was firmly rooted in British North America:

> Now that the axe has pushed the forests back from the edges of our rivers and lakes; now that the way has been cleared for natural population growth and immigration, both by land and by sea— since rich, densely populated cities form many stops along the traveller's route—it is time to hope that the development of artistic tastes and needs, created through superfluity, will soon give impetus to the cultural arts.[90]

But what kind of cultural arts would flourish? Would it be 'polite letters'—the literature, music, theatre, and art that social elites patronized—or the more down-to-earth culture of circuses, tavern amusements, and folk songs? As settlement spread, elites became ever more concerned that things could not be left to chance. If Canada was to develop into the kind of society they wanted to see, they would have to take an active role in shaping it. They already controlled politics, the economy, and social life; it was time for them to use their influence to ensure the kind of cultural life that befitted a civilized nation.

More to the point, they realized that whatever other pleasures their brand of culture afforded them, it also had the potential to make better citizens. Of course, they always had some dim conception of this reality—why else would they have gone to such pains to recreate European polite culture in the Canadian wilderness? But now they saw that their way of thinking should be impressed more forcefully on the populace at large. Perhaps it was not enough simply to tolerate circuses and tavern entertainments; if the elites truly felt a sense of *noblesse oblige*, part of that obligation entailed using culture to help the lower orders improve themselves. For if the workers improved, so too would society as a whole. But if the labouring classes were left to find their own amusements, who could tell what disorder they might cause?

The first building block was, of course, education; literacy was a prerequisite to a civilized, progressive society. Beyond that, the situation demanded the creation of institutions that could provide workers with the right sort of cultural opportunities in their idle hours. Libraries, Mechanics' Institutes, reading societies, art clubs—if the working classes took advantage of such offerings, they would be morally, spiritually, and personally elevated; they would become better people, more financially secure, and, not incidentally, better attuned to their responsibilities as citizens. The larger beneficiary of this process of improvement, of course, would be the nation itself.

There were few members of the polite classes in British North America who didn't believe wholeheartedly in the nostrum that idle hands were the devil's workshop. They would have interpreted the old saying in the figurative sense, but also in the literal sense: the mill hand who had nothing to do in his idle hours away from the factory was bound to get into all sorts of trouble. Left to pick his own amusements, he would invariably choose the wrong ones. The British writer John Foster caustically described such people in *An Essay on the Evils of Popular Ignorance*. The lower orders, he wrote, 'had far more the character of a colony of some barbarian nation, than that of an enlightened and Christian state might have been expected to impart.' The situation could not be allowed to continue; the state had a responsibility to 'train them to sound sense; civilize them; promote the reformation of their morals; inculcate the principles of religion.' *The Novascotian* was less dismissive, pointing out that the joys of culture were never intended only for the elites: 'God, when he painted the rose, and breathed its mysterious perfume upon the violet, did not deny the mechanic the senses to enjoy—neither did he close his ear to the delights of harmony, nor strike music out from the fascinations of his humble fireside.'[91]

Across British North America in the mid-nineteenth century, clergymen, editors, politicians, and academics published similar warnings.

Artist Cornelius Krieghoff wrote to the Minister of Finance A.T. Galt (a son of the novelist John Galt) in 1859 to complain that the lack of art training in Canada's schools was turning 'our young men [into] drunkards, and our young girls flirts.' In New Westminster, British Columbia, the *North Pacific Times* warned in 1864 of the 'many unfortunates in the city condemned throughout the long months of winter to recreate themselves incessantly and unvaryingly by playing billiards from morning till night.'[92] Torontonian Richard Lewis wrote in 1876 of the city's need for some cultural institutions as an antidote to the tendency of working-class men to 'find their excitement and relief to their passions in the lawless disorder, intemperance and even violence…[or the] wild excitement of the whiskey saloon.' Even in the most remote trading posts, the potential for disaster was very real. As fur trader William Thorburn of the North West Company wrote, his predecessors in the post at Cross Lake, now in central Manitoba, lacked any respectable cultural diversions and instead 'passed their time in card playing, gambling and dancing; which brought on disputes, quarrels and all respect was lost.'[93]

This dissipation didn't just affect the individuals themselves, although the Chatham, Ontario Board of Trade took pains to point out that 'the more intelligent the mechanic or labourer, the higher his wages, and the more comfortable is his home.' The real loser was the nation. When large parts of a society remained ignorant of polite culture and divorced from the moral improvement it provided, they developed, as Robert Lachlan put it, a 'discreditable state of unaspiring ignorance, ending, not infrequently, in a feeling of apathetic distaste, if not contempt, for everything in the shape of acquired knowledge.'[94]

The other fact that became clear was that the lower classes were not about to take the initiative themselves. If things were to change, it was up to the social and political elites to provide the institutions that would improve the cultural sensibilities of the working class. As the politician and poet J.D. Edgar told the Ontario Literary Society in 1863, 'Literature, and the elegant Arts, must grow up side by side with the coarse plants of daily necessity, and must depend for their culture… on hours and seasons snatched from the pursuit of worldly interests by intelligent and public-spirited individuals.'[95]

One of the first things to which those individuals turned their attentions was the state of education. Common schooling was spreading, but despite the fact that literacy rates had risen slowly through the first half of the nineteenth century, there still remained some trouble spots. The 1861 census, for example, revealed that 28 percent of Nova Scotians and 31.3 percent of adults in the Northwest Territories could not read. Quebec was even farther behind, with a 36 percent illiteracy rate according to the 1871 census; and in Newfoundland, studies from 1874 revealed that less than half of the adult population on the south and west coasts could read and write. In one parish on the south coast of Newfoundland, geographer Allan Macpherson calculated a literacy rate among young married people of only 18 percent.[96] Other case studies reveal that, in urban areas in 1861, illiteracy was higher among women than men, while there was less of a gap in rural areas. Indeed, in some districts, men came to make up the majority of illiterates; historian Michel Verrette posits that, because female labour was less essential on the farm than male, girls had more opportunities to attend school. Even so, literacy rates remained of deep concern; if they could be improved, argued Richard Lancefield, the chief librarian of the Hamilton Public Library, in 1893, 'there is little doubt but that many grave social problems which now threaten us with disaster would be peaceably and speedily resolved.'[97] Ironically, Lancefield wasn't one to talk about grave social problems—in 1902 he destroyed the library's financial records and absconded with thousands of dollars.

Support for expanding basic education crossed political and class lines. Reformers such as Louis-Joseph Papineau and William Lyon Mackenzie supported it out of the belief that an educated public would be better able to act in its own political interests. Papineau and Mackenzie's arch-enemies, the elites who made up the Family Compact in Upper Canada and the Château Clique in Lower Canada, were more ambivalent. They were naturally suspicious of common schools: there were dangers inherent in educating the lower orders, who might start to think above their station, and in any case their own children were already well served by private schools. But they were receptive to the argument that an education system could inculcate in young Canadians values such as citizenship, loyalty, respect for property, and deference to authority. Farmers with large families began to realize that they might not have enough land to settle all of their children on farms and that those who had to seek work elsewhere would do well to have an

Cultivating the feminine arts: Mrs O'Neil plays in her parlour in Prescott, Ontario. c. 1898–1920.

education; even those who remained on the land could benefit from basic literacy, not to mention fundamental business and technical skills. And so, with broad support, schools spread across British North America; Prince Edward Island in 1852 became the first jurisdiction in the British Empire to require province-wide, free common schooling. Legislation did not necessarily mean attendance, but over the next few decades the literate population, which elites regarded as essential to a cultured society, slowly grew.

———◦—◦—◦———

The next logical steps were the institutes of higher education, the universities and colleges that emerged through the nineteenth century to instruct and improve those who could afford it. Until after the Second World War, this was never more than a tiny slice of the population, but their influence should not be underestimated. Typical of such institutions was Hellmuth Ladies' College, established in London, Ontario, in 1869 by the Anglican Dean of Huron to provide 'a thorough, liberal and useful Education for young ladies, adapted to their wants in life, and

Educational institutions in the Toronto area. Undated.

based upon the soundest PROTESTANT CHRISTIAN PRINCIPLES as
the only solid basis for the right formation of character.'[98] To achieve
that character, the school taught languages (interestingly, French was
the language used at Hellmuth), the domestic arts, history, geography,
and arithmetic, but placed particular emphasis on literature, reading,
drawing and painting, dancing, and vocal and instrumental music. That

the girls of Hellmuth devoted much of their time to these elevating pursuits is suggested by the fact that the year-end ceremonies of 1887 featured dozens of musical performances and an art exhibition of over a thousand pieces.

But at $254 a year (not including school supplies), the Hellmuth experience was available only to the select few. What about the great mass of the population who, for financial or practical reasons, did not go beyond elementary school? If learning ended once they left school, the years spent under the tutelage of the schoolmaster would soon be forgotten and people might slip back into their old, mentally unproductive ways. The solution was the library. By making the right kind of books available to the general population, all kinds of social ills could be avoided. The work of the common schools could be continued as education became a lifelong pursuit—they would give workers 'food for the mind...[thereby] raising them in the scale of moral intelligence.'[99] Libraries would provide, according to the *Western Herald and Farmer's Magazine*, 'one of the best preservatives against dissipation,' the spirit of inquiry and desire for knowledge that they fostered giving 'a death blow to all low grovelling and outwardly vicious habits.' In short, a city with full library facilities could avoid a host of social problems. As John Hallam, a leader of the free library movement in Toronto, said, such institutions 'must necessarily diminish the ranks of those two great armies which are constantly marching to gaols and penitentiaries...I want Toronto to pay for intelligence—for popular education in the free library sense. If she does so fairly and fully, her bill for poverty and depravity will be materially lessened.'[100]

As we have seen, the lending libraries created in the late eighteenth century were never intended to be for anyone but the upper classes. Governor Sir Frederick Haldimand had urged the establishment of Quebec's subscription library to combat 'the ignorance of the populations,' but the very people he would have considered ignorant could never have afforded the subscription fees. Even more exclusive was one of Kingston's first libraries, which charged an annual membership fee that was much higher than the yearly wage of even a skilled labourer, and also levied a hefty deposit on joining, to cover future loss of books. John Graves Simcoe finally saw his library open in Niagara-on-the-Lake in 1800, but the forty-one subscribers were primarily clergymen,

The public library in London, Ontario. Undated.

yeomen, officers, and government officials, for they were the only people who could afford the membership dues. Still, they all agreed that the influence of the institution could reach beyond its subscribers. As the first entry in the library's ledger says, 'we are at the loss in this new and remote country for every kind of useful knowledge, and convinced that nothing would be of more use to diffuse knowledge amongst us and our offspring than a library supported by this town.'[101] Unfortunately for subscribers, the library was badly damaged in the War of 1812 and, with too few subscribers to rebuild, it closed in 1820. Similar libraries cropped up across British North America—York in 1810, Saint John in 1811, Charlottetown in 1825—although their fortunes varied. A subscription library opened in St. John's in 1810, but declining membership forced it to sell its books to meet its debts in 1813; seven years later, it was succeeded by the St. John's Library Society with sixty-seven members, although by 1827 it was being supported by just fifteen members. Truro, Nova Scotia's library opened in 1812, and also soon withered for want of members.

Luckily, cheaper alternatives were available in the form of commercial lending libraries, such as Thomas Cary's in Quebec. Cary would loan any book for up to twelve months and had over 5,000 titles that could be sent anywhere in British North America, as long as the borrower paid the postal charges. His catalogue ran the gamut from highbrow material like the forty-five volumes of Alexander Chalmers' *The British Essayists* to one of the first penny dreadfuls, *The Terrific Register, or, Record of Crimes, Judgements, Providences and Calamities* (1825). There were also agricultural libraries to serve improving farmers, and church and Sunday School libraries for parishioners. People living near military garrisons could often take advantage of the libraries maintained for the local troops. The garrison library in Halifax, for example, was open to the public, and was one of the few institutions that encouraged women to subscribe; by 1835, there were thirty women on the membership rolls. Philanthropic organizations also became involved. By 1830, the Edinburgh Ladies Association had established three circulating libraries in Cape Breton, and in 1838 a branch of the Highland Society of Nova Scotia was established in Halifax. One of its primary goals was to promote education by importing books from Scotland for distribution to Scots settlements on Cape Breton Island, 'so as to diffuse more widely among Scotsmen and their descendants, whether Highlander or Lowlander, Catholic or Protestant, the blessings of a sound practical and moral education.' Its first library branch was set up at Margaree Forks in 1844.[102]

But just like education, this was a field in which governments could play an active role. The most important reformer in this regard was Egerton Ryerson, whose influence spread far beyond his own bailiwick in Canada West. Born on a farm north of Lake Erie, Ryerson dabbled in Methodism in his youth, an experiment that got him kicked out of the family home by his staunchly Anglican father. He was no friend of the Family Compact, thanks to his unwavering opposition to the Church of England's special privileges in Canada, but his great crusade was education, which became his life's work when he began a thirty-year term as Superintendent for Schools in Canada West in 1846. Even before his appointment, he had proclaimed his belief in the value of libraries for all who used them. They would allow people to become familiar 'with the greatest and wisest men of all ages, and countries and professions, on all subjects.' In such circumstances, 'the mind cannot be unhappy, nor will it become vitiated; its views will be expanded; its standard of manners and men and things will be elevated; its feeling will be refined.' Ryerson was fond of quoting from Henry Barnard, the American educational pioneer whose views accorded with his own:

Portrait of the Reverend Egerton Ryerson. c. 1850–51.

libraries, Barnard thought, would turn leisure time into useful time, thereby filling the void of idleness. They could teach all members of society to understand their 'relations and duties to society, themselves, and their Creator…All that is wanted to fill the community with diligent and profitable readers among all classes, is to gratify the natural curiosity of every child "to know," to convert that curiosity into a well regulated taste, and confirm that taste into a habit, by easy access to a library of appropriate books.'[103]

This, then, was the progression that colonial elites sought—from the natural curiosity of the child to the well regulated taste of the adult—and they were willing to use the power of the state to achieve it. In 1846, the legislature of Canada West enabled the creation of libraries for the province's common schools. As Ryerson said, 'the pupil should go from the schoolmaster to the library…Thus will the avenues to temptation be avoided, the circle of his knowledge be enlarged and he will be prepared to exercise his privileges with independence and discretion.'[104] Even more far-reaching was the Library Act of 1850, which enabled municipal councils to establish township libraries by purchasing, at cost, books from a roster of approved titles. Ryerson's first job was to acquire the books themselves, and a barrage of letters and a trip to England yielded about 4,000 volumes from English and American publishers. Department officials winnowed them down to a list of 2,776 potential titles, and then Ryerson himself began to categorize them and ensure that they were suitable for distribution.

In the summer of 1853, the chosen titles had been published in catalogue form for distribution to municipal councils. The list bore very clearly the stamp of Ryerson's conception of appropriate literature; as he put it, the books 'have been well-examined and contain nothing that is frivolous, or that could poison the morals of those who read them.' Despite the number of people who complained that the books on his list were too dull to appeal to general readers (even one of his own inspectors reported of 'the lighter and more amusing works being used the most: indeed scarcely any of the ethical, scientific, and more learned works, have been read at all'[105]), he hardly wavered from his position that anyone could derive pleasure from reading didactic tales, moral tracts, and illustrated works of natural history such as *Shells and Their Inmates*. Pleas, like the communication from the trustees of Section 13 of Howard Township, in southwestern Ontario, regretting 'that a little wider field for selections had not been permitted…we confess that the works stand in the front rank of Littery Merrit but in general reading the mind tires by a continual perusal of profound works be they ever so good of their kind,' often had little impact on Ryerson's theories of reading.[106] There were no popular novels by the likes of Sir Walter Scott or Eugene Sue (such work was deemed pernicious because it lacked any sense of moral inspiration), nor any works of imaginative fiction (the sole exception being *Uncle Tom's Cabin*, whose moralistic tone earned it a stamp of approval), but there was plenty of Shakespeare, Dryden, Milton, Byron, Burns, and Tennyson. Most of what was available in non-fiction would be considered 'useful knowledge': natural science, theology, biography, history, philosophy.

Many local councillors were clearly overwhelmed by the prospect of going through thousands of book titles to select a few hundred, and elected to leave the selection to Ryerson. Even so, some, like the reeve of Artemesia Township in central Ontario, were careful to provide him with some guidance as to the character of local readers: 'The great majority of very humble means and whose opportunities of information have been very restricted so that works of a highly scientific nature would not be appreciated[,] those of lower prices and adapted to Juvenile Capacities would be more acceptable.'[107]

Initially, the program was a great success. In the first year alone, the depository distributed over 100,000 books to more than 200 libraries, and received in return effusive reports from local officials. 'A great number of young men in this Township who in preceding winters have sought their amusement and recreation in the Ball Room and some even in the Bar Room,' wrote one councillor, 'during the past winter have been constant applicants for and readers of Books from the Public Library.'[108] In North Dumfries, near present-day Cambridge, Ontario, the impact was just as clear. In the immediate vicinity of the library, idleness had almost disappeared; when children read, reported a local official, 'parents [sat] and [listened] to them with interest and [drew] from the subject read, a theme for conversation next day.' But in parts of the township where libraries had not been established, nothing could be done to prevent children's 'minds being poisoned by the unhealthy publications which are being scattered broadcast, by speculators and designing infidels.'[109]

Elsewhere in British North America, the library movement was also picking up steam. The *Victoria Gazette* of 4 November 1858 advocated the establishment of a library as an antidote to the saloon, and within nine days W.F. Herre had opened the first of a number of subscription libraries to operate in the city. When the YMCA opened a reading room, it too drew the praise of the local press, perhaps making an oblique reference to places like the Fashion Music Hall: 'There are few evening amusements in Victoria, of an elevating character, that we have no doubt but that the Reading Room will prove a centre of attraction to all classes: and be a healthy check against dissipation which has made fearful sacrifices in countries like ours where a large portion of the young men were deprived of the society of home.' In Fort Hope, British Columbia, the Reverend A.D. Pringle pushed for the establishment of the Fort Hope Reading Room and Library in 1859, 'to offer mental recreation and enjoyment as a restorative to physical exertion and labour, not to the residents of Fort Hope only, but more especially to the large and important class of men engaged in gold mining, whose temporal success and moral and mental elevation, it is our interest as our ardent desire to further.'[110]

In what would eventually become Manitoba, the leaders of the tiny Red River Colony also saw the virtue of libraries. Most of the first settlers were illiterate, but they wanted their children to have a proper education, as did Lord Selkirk, the Scottish nobleman who made a hobby of settling landless highlanders in British North America. The first books arrived in the Red River a year after the first settlers, and by 1822 the settlement's library had 180 books. Two decades later, library boosters were advocating the amalgamation of a number of libraries, including a private subscription library started by a group of settlers, the collection of Hudson's Bay Company employee Peter Fidler (who spent the better part of his pay on books, eventually amassing a library of 500 volumes), and some books sent to the Red River by Selkirk, into a single institution. The Red River Library duly opened in 1848, and within six years had nearly 2,000 volumes.

Even remote trading posts boasted libraries. York Factory, on the western shore of Hudson's Bay, reportedly had a collection of 1,400 volumes in 1790, and the surgeon at Fort McLoughlin, at Bella Bella, British Columbia, suggested that books at Fort Vancouver be circulated to smaller posts and that a subscription plan be implemented. As Daniel Williams Harmon of the North West Company wrote from Fort St. James, on Stuart Lake in northern British Columbia, in 1813, 'there are few posts, which are not tolerably well supplied with books. These books, indeed, are not all of the best kind; but among them are many that are valuable. If I were deprived of these silent companions many a gloomy hour would pass over me.'[111] This is just the kind of sentiment that would have been music to the ears of Canadian elites.

———•·•———

The libraries, however, faced stiff competition from another institution that held great promise for bringing culture to the worker: the Mechanics' Institute. The first institutes were founded in Boston and Philadelphia in 1820 and London in 1823, after social reformers realized that the subscription fees being charged by many lending libraries were beyond the means of the vast majority of workers. In response, they envisioned an institution with modest fees that would provide instruction to working men, especially in the science underlying their work, through lectures, evening classes, and library facilities. Despite the goal of enrolling 'every man, who earned his living by the work of his hands' (and the gender division was clear—the target was the factory operative who worked with *his* hands, not the seamstress or washerwoman who worked with *her* hands), there was no great hope of attracting the mass of unskilled labourers. The Mechanics' Institutes reached out to what might be called the labour aristocracy: skilled workers and tradesmen such as carpenters, wheelwrights, toolmakers, masons, and boilermakers.

The idea appealed to some Canadian reformers, particularly William Lyon Mackenzie. In 1827, a decade before his rebellion against the elites of Upper Canada, Mackenzie imagined

> a society of 70 or 80 persons of all ages from 15 to 75, of all ranks, from the apprentice mechanic with his leather apron, up to the city bailie or parish minister with his powdered toupee, met together on an entire equality in a large hall full of books and papers, scientific apparatus, chemistry tests, models of machinery.[112]

For Mackenzie, it was a place where class distinctions would be obliterated by a common desire for knowledge, but others had rather different opinions of the utility of a mechanics' institute. The Napanee *Standard* called it 'a most interesting place, where our businessmen, mechanics,

The imposing quarters of the Montreal Mechanics' Institute Hall, 1854.

and young men may spend a leisure hour on an evening to advantage out of the way of temptation,' and thought it was 'well adapted to counteract any tendency towards unholy or profitless amusements…[and] to enable our youth to rise superior to the indulgences of vice.'[113] It was not necessarily a vehicle for social equality, but a place where idle hands could be given the right kind of cultural amusements to keep them out of trouble.

In 1827, the first Mechanics' Institute was founded in British North America in St. John's, followed by institutes in Montreal (1828) and Quebec, York, and Halifax (1830). Before long, institutes were springing up in every colony. In Upper Canada, where groups had to petition the legislature for grants in support of an institute, a consortium in Kingston drew attention to 'the great importance of improving the mental condition of the working classes, and thereby increasing the spirit of ascendancy enterprise, and exalting the moral character of the people.' In 1857, Benjamin Beddome spoke on the occasion of the opening of the reading room in the Belleville Mechanics' Institute, pointing out that the city had long needed a place where

young men may be able to read the newspapers and light literature of the day without the necessity of resorting to places in which pernicious habits and customs are imbibed or indulged in. Learning, knowledge, education (both secular and religious), will drive out, or, subdue, the desire for low, animal gratifications.[114]

In ideal circumstances, the typical Mechanics' Institute would provide a wide range of cultural activities. There should be a library stocked with 'improving' literature (Beddome mentioned Greek and Latin classics in translation, the writings of the early church fathers, Shakespeare, Milton, Byron, Scott, and James Fenimore Cooper; Dickens was acceptable, but only for young people), as well as respectable newspapers and magazines from Canada, Britain, and the United States. Fortunately, there were plenty of periodicals that believed in the ideal of useful knowledge. Richard Huntington, editor of *The Spirit of the Times and Cape Breton Free Press*, saw his newspaper as an instrument of public education:

May Learning flourish—Science here
The gloom of mental darkness cheer.
Our Press shall lend its tribute ray
O'er ignorance to pour the light,
As morning's beams dispel the night.[115]

In Canada West, Thomas Macqueen, the editor of the *Huron Signal*, agreed that the newspaper's duty lay in 'improving the tone of thought and action in a prosperous community.' Michel Bibaud, who edited a succession of periodicals from 1825 to 1843, evinced the same view in many columns, frequently referring to the notion of *plaire et instruire* ('please and instruct')[116]—precisely the kind of view that would be rewarded with space on the shelves of Mechanics' Institutes. At the same time, the institute should offer practical classes on such things as mechanical drawing, physics, elocution, and languages, but also in more aesthetic subjects like literary appreciation and music. Frequent lectures were encouraged on any topic that was both instructional and interesting, and diversions such as chess, musical performances, and theatricals were also available; many institutes also established museums to supplement their educational function. Institutes were empowered to charge membership fees, although the amounts varied widely, from a dollar a year (half price for boys under sixteen) for the Grenfell,

Saskatchewan Mechanics' and Literary Institute, to the $10 annual fee (half price for women) charged by the Victoria Mechanics' Institute.

However, in an attempt to keep subscription fees low, many institutes placed themselves in a precarious financial position, and went through a cycle of collapse, re-establishment, and collapse again. The Belleville institute went under in 1860 for financial reasons and was not revived until 1876, when future Prime Minister Mackenzie Bowell argued that 'men with means' should step forward and reform the institution 'where young men could spend their time profitably and pleasurably.'[117] In Grenfell, Saskatchewan, the Institute opened in 1892 with great promise and sixty-seven members, a number that climbed to 104 two years later. But in 1895, membership plummeted to just thirty-six, despite the librarian's efforts 'to make suitable arrangements as may seem best to him to induce the school boys to use the reading room.'

Ever-changing membership revenues meant that institutes had to rely more heavily on government support, which was also inconsistent and not especially generous. In 1851, the legislature of Canada West passed an act allowing for the incorporation and funding of Mechanics' Institutes, but abuses of the funding process and a general failure to provide instructional classes led to the grants being suspended from 1858 to 1868. In that year, legislation placed the institutes under the control of the Department of Agriculture and made available matching grants of $200 (increased to $400 in 1871). Nine years later, responsibility for the institutes was transferred to the Department of Education, and the number of institutions receiving provincial grants had risen from nine in 1871 to seventy-two a decade later. In British Columbia, there was no set grant; it varied from $500 to the Victoria Mechanics' Institute, to just $75 for the institute in Comox. In any event, there were only eight in the province in 1876, and some of them could be described as, at best, half-hearted. A businessman in Hastings Mill apparently applied for a grant to set up an institute on the sole grounds that a competitor in nearby Moodyville had established one. Grants were even meaner on the prairies. The Northwest Council passed its first act to create Mechanics' Institutes in 1890; no financial terms were stipulated, but in practice each institute was eligible for a grant of just $50.

Still, the Mechanics' Institute became an important presence in hundreds of Canadian communities (in 1895, there were 311 in Ontario alone). Whatever went on behind their doors—and their premises were frequently used by other cultural groups for art exhibitions, concerts, and theatrical performances—they expressed an ideal: that middle- and upper-class money and influence could combine with working- class drive and desire to build a society that was better educated, more cultured, and in all respects more civilized.

————— · ● · —————

Another child of the early nineteenth century that had an improving agenda was the literary society, or reading circle. The first of these organizations were probably informal clubs in which people pooled their money to buy books to share, but in 1820 the first official literary society was established in York. Its membership consisted of ten young men from the best families, who met every second Monday for 'mental improvement.' Similar was the Pictou Literature and Scientific Society, created in December 1834 by twenty-three local men 'for the material improvements of its members in the Sciences and General Literature and for the diffusion in the community of a taste for useful information.'[118] They met every second Wednesday from November to May, with the founding members paying dues of five shillings and all subsequent members paying 7/6, and were specifically prohibited from debating religion and politics. This rule was breached in a March 1850 meeting, when a paper entitled 'The Pleasures and Advantages of Literary Composition' degenerated into praise of republican principles and caused something that may have been either a heated argument or a fist fight, depending on how one interprets the newspaper report.

By mid-century, as Mechanics' Institutes were starting to prolif- erate, so too were literary societies. The fact that they were much more informal and didn't require incorporation or government regula- tion meant that they were well suited to smaller communities. And so contemporary newspapers report the meetings of, on Cape Breton Island, the Ship Harbour Young Men's Debating Society, the Mabou Literary and Scientific Society, the Literary Society of St Ann's, and the Scientific and Literary Society of Sydney. In British Columbia, there was the Nanaimo Literary Institute (1863–80), which included a Debating and Elocution Club, the Cariboo Church Institute in Barkerville

(1868–71), and the Methodist Library and Literary Society in Hedley. Perhaps the most famous reading club founder was Anna Leonowens, better known to the world for her memoir *The King and I*, who founded a club in Halifax.

Many of the early literary societies were created by and for elite young men as training grounds for their eventual ascendancy to the top of the social and political hierarchy, but others attempted to be more inclusive and bring education to people with limited opportunities to acquire it in other circumstances. In Amherstburg, in southwestern Ontario, the Western District Literary, Philosophical and Agricultural Association was open to men of all races and evolved into a moderately reformist club that tried to combine scholarly with practical knowledge. The African-Canadian people of the region, however, were more likely to join one of their own cultural organizations, which also tried to cater to a range of needs. Josiah Henson's Wilberforce Educational Institute, for example, stressed practical knowledge, while the Wilberforce Lyceum Educating Society (founded in 1850 as the first mixed-sex literary group in Upper Canada, and possibly in Canada) was more interested in promoting the appreciation of literature than practical education.

Women, not always welcome in libraries and often shut out of the early male-dominated literary societies, soon began to establish their own. The Windsor Ladies Club, founded by African-Canadian women in southwestern Ontario in 1854, may have been the first women's literary society in Canada. Its descendants ranged in size and influence from the powerful Toronto Women's Literary Club, which is known more for its promotion of suffrage than its literary interests, to the much more modest Griswold Reading Club in Manitoba. Established in 1900, its self-proclaimed aim was 'to study Authors and Books from the standpoint of the general reader,' and over the years the members discussed everything from Sir Walter Scott's *Kenilworth* to Stephen Leacock's *The Unsolved Riddle of Social Justice*.[119] The Griswold Reading Club's members had no formidable political or social influence, no powerful husbands to lend support, no connections in the press to provide sympathetic reports of their meetings. It was simply a group of local women animated by a desire to learn and a love of culture. In this, it was probably much more typical of hundreds of similar organizations than was the more well-known Toronto Women's Literary Club.

Such organizations were more about self-improvement than improving the working classes, but some did attempt to expand their class base so that their benefits could be felt more broadly. Some literary societies, for example, held Penny Readings (later 5¢ or 10¢ Readings) that were intended to attract people away from taverns to hear readings by trained elocutionists; to appeal to all tastes, classical literature might be combined with earthier fare like *Aunt Betsey's Bean* or *Jimmy Butler and the Owl*. Other groups kept their membership dues at a very low level, to ensure that even the poorest paid mechanic could join. The Congregational Mutual Improvement Society, established in Hamilton in 1873, for example, charged annual dues of only 25¢, an amount that would not deter a worker with a genuine interest in the organization's offerings.

Many literary societies were also involved in fostering art appreciation and, like the promoters of the Mechanics' Institute, regarded artistic training as especially important in cultivating a more enlightened society. For them, art meant everything from basic copywork that a mechanic might do, to complex designs of mechanical and technical drawings, to ornamental drawing for decorative arts, to fine art like landscapes, still life, and portraiture. In this regard, they joined nineteenth-century theorists in seeing a direct connection between industrial drawing and high art. The latter was regarded as the highest expression of good design, but an industrializing society depended just as much on practical artistic skills that could turn an idea into a steam engine or a cotton jenny. Even the charter of the National Gallery of Canada, written in 1882, referred to the industrial arts and the 'promotion and support of Education, leading to the production of beautiful and excellent work in manufactures.'[120]

As a result, Canada's earliest art organizations encouraged the development of artistic skills that were useful in the workplace, and the line between art and everything else was often non-existent. When the 1852 Upper Canada Provincial Exhibition was held in Toronto, the art section included not only paintings, but stuffed birds, wax flowers, boxes of cigars, fur caps, and dentures. Two decades later, London's Western School of Art and Design was founded and by 1880 had 457 students, including many men from the trades and professions who were trying to improve their position by taking mechanical drawing and

What better way to keep a man out of trouble than to enroll him in the local brass band? Undated.

modelling. The Toronto Mechanics' Institute also placed great emphasis on promoting art of various kinds. In 1848, it decided to inaugurate a permanent exhibition in Toronto to supplement the travelling agricultural fairs that had provided the main venues for budding artists. The arts section of the exhibition, which eventually became known as the Canadian National Exhibition, included not only painting and sculpture, but agricultural and mechanical implements.

But elites had even more lofty goals for artistic education and display. The promise that the mechanic or apprentice could better himself by developing his skills in industrial drawing was, in some ways, part of a bait-and-switch ploy. Once lured into the art societies and Mechanics' Institutes to study mechanical drawing, they could then be exposed to the higher arts, to develop an appreciation for the best painting and sculpture. In 1847, a catalogue from the Montreal Society of Artists quoted William Hazlitt, one of the most influential British cultural commentators of the nineteenth century: 'Useful Arts pave the way to Fine Arts. Men upon whom the former has bestowed every convenience turned their thoughts to the latter.'[121] This was the ultimate goal, for art had the power, in the words of the Lord Bishop of Montreal, the Right Reverend Francis Fulford, 'to refine men, to soften their manners, and

The St. Dunstan Dramatic Society, New Brunswick, 1909.

make them less of wild beasts.' A nation whose citizens had been refined by art would be a better nation. As *La Minerve* put it in 1849,

> Are not fine arts called upon to regenerate a country…They can awaken in the soul a host of mysterious impressions, evoke innocent emotions, foster in the heart of a man a million sympathies: in a word, slipping through all the chinks of his workaday existence, like those lilies of the field which are mixed with its painful harvest.[122]

All of these institutions had lofty aspirations to bring culture and education to the worker, thereby elevating the communal life of Canada, but did they achieve these goals? In fact, the general consensus is that they had little impact on the working classes. Labourers did not flock to libraries, the reading rooms of Mechanics' Institutes were not filled with tradesmen, and bricklayers and carpenters did not swell the membership rolls of literary and art societies. Too often, elite intervention was fatal to working-class cultural institutions. The Free and Easy Club had been thriving in Chatham, Ontario, with its regular evenings of singing, debating, and beer drinking at the British Hotel, but in 1839 Colonel Charles Chichester arrived with the 32nd Regiment. Concerned that the club was a little *too* free and easy, he transformed it into a mutual improvement society with a library, more formal debates, and serious lectures. Within two years, it had ceased to exist. No doubt Chichester had the best of intentions, and the efforts of people like him would have positive benefits for Canadian culture in the long term. But in the short term, the greatest beneficiaries of these middle-class institutions were the middle classes themselves.

In the first place, the elites overestimated the amount of time that workers had for amusements of any sort. As the *Hamilton Times* put it in 1885,

> the workingman, who has to be at his place in the shop at 7 o'clock in the morning, is not going to have much time to loaf in the evening after he has got his supper and read the daily paper. Professional and commercial men may make the library a place of resort, but mechanics and factory operatives, as a rule, will not.

This is entirely plausible, and the vision of a factory operative capping off his ten hours at the mill with a lecture on lobster habitats does seem fanciful; even the most enthusiastic Mechanics' Institute had to admit that 'there are a large class to whom any lengthened study after a hard day's manual labour is anything but enticing.'[123] But there were deeper reasons for the mixed fortunes of these institutions.

In the case of Mechanics' Institutes, their name simply did not live up to their character. Despite Mackenzie's lofty rhetoric of an organization that could bring together the apprentice and the clergyman, the Institutes were rarely more than middle-class clubs providing middle-class entertainments to middle-class Canadians. In the first place, they were organized and administered by elites, according to their own preconceptions of what such an institution should do. Legislators made efforts to avoid such a state of affairs—the charter of Kingston's Mechanics' Institute stipulated that two-thirds of the members of the Board of Managers should be mechanics, while the 1851 Canada West legislation providing for the incorporation of Mechanics' Institutes envisioned the establishment of a province-wide regulatory Board of Arts and Manufactures with delegates who were 'actual working mechanics and manufacturers'—but there is little evidence that these measures got off the ground. The Board of Arts and Manufacturers, for example, apparently never even met. Thirty years later, an 1881 Ontario special report on the Institutes admitted that they were still 'under the management of gentlemen of influence and wealth.'[124] In practice, this meant that a Mechanics' Institute was often run by the same people who ran the factories. For the average worker, there can have been little appeal in spending one's leisure hours in an establishment operated by one's employer.

As a result, Mechanics' Institutes took on a character that could not have attracted many workers. Instead of offering the kind of instruction that could have been materially useful to the ambitious mechanic, they tended to organize activities that the middle classes liked: vocal concerts, literary entertainment, musical events, dramatic presentations, billiards, elocutionists, and strawberry socials. Courses in practical mechanics were few and far between, and where they existed were not especially popular; in one institute, the course drew only a handful of students, as many, in fact, as the class on wax-flower making. The lectures were hardly more popular, probably because they covered topics like 'The Causes and Cures of Cahots,' 'Prison Discipline,' 'Lime Stones,' 'Aerial Currents,' 'Chlorine,' and 'The Turks in Europe'—and were often preceded by long, fulsome, and entirely irrelevant opening addresses. And the museums themselves were limited: Montreal's insti-tute museum, for example, contained nothing more than an old Roman coin, parts of a beaver, a stuffed hummingbird, and a petrified snail. And it is unlikely that later donations of a map of Quebec, a phre-nological chart, seven sea shells, and a stuffed crocodile significantly boosted its appeal.

The institutions also tended to enforce codes of respectable behav-iour, even to the point of discouraging free discussion of lectures, lest this lead to disorder. When the public gained greater access to the Pictou Literary and Scientific Society, the local newspaper, rather than celebrating the broadening of its appeal, complained that the institution had been overtaken by 'Boys and others not belonging to it, crowding in and occupying the room of the members and their regular guests.'[125] An

1875 committee criticized the fact that the average Institute's reading room had turned into a 'trysting place' for women; such a social function was not to be condoned, and the report suggests that absolute silence be enforced in the reading room. When the Halifax Mechanics' Institute put on a recreational day, the directors carefully stipulated that there was to be no alcohol or dancing.

Even architecturally, Mechanics' Institutes tended to be large and imposing structures that may well have put off the average worker. This was not the case in small towns, but in the big cities, where the concentration of mechanics was the greatest, the institute was more likely to resemble a bank or a gentleman's club than a worker-friendly organization. The 1840 institute in Saint John was an ornate, three-storey neo-classical temple, complete with Ionic columns. When the Montreal Mechanics' Institute opened the following year in a three-storey Italianate palace festooned with banners reading 'To Make a Man a Better Mechanic, and the Mechanic a Better Man,' directors noted that 'we should, however have preferred to see more mechanics' among the 500 attendees.' They might have, had the building looked less like a lyceum for the upper class and more like a workers' institute.

For all these reasons, the institutes rarely attracted the very people they targeted. The York Mechanics' Institute began with forty-five members, but only three of them could be identified as mechanics; fifty years later, of its 1,200 members, only forty-two could be considered manual workers. When the Goderich Mechanics' Institute was founded in 1851, the local newspaper listed the trustees, including 'John McDonald (carpenter)'; the fact that he was the only individual with an occupation listed suggested he was the only actual tradesman involved in the Institute. It was the same in Montreal, where the 1828 list of members' occupations included no mechanics or craftsmen; in 1840, of the 223 members, only six were listed as apprentices. In the absence of complete membership rolls, it is difficult to determine the membership characteristics of the average Mechanics' Institute, but there is little reason to doubt the opinion of Queen's University principal George Grant, who said in 1891 that 'if you want to go to a place where you are certain not to find mechanics, go to the Mechanics' Institute.'[126]

Libraries also had limited success drawing in the working classes. As one newspaper said of a proposed library in New Westminster,

British Columbia, 'we must be candid enough to tell them that they have sought to place the institution upon too narrow and exclusive a base to entitle it to that general support and that wide sphere of usefulness without which it could neither claim government aid nor hope for permanent success.' In this instance, the editor was referring not simply to the fact that the proposal had a distinctly middle-class flavour, but that the $10 initiation fee and $1 monthly fee was beyond the means of many workers.[127] Winnipeg's first public library also never escaped its 'narrow and exclusive' base. Initially established as a subscription library by the city's upper crust, it eventually became a free public library. However, it was housed in City Hall and retained the elitist tone of its predecessor, so few workers felt inclined to use an institution that, not so many years before, had discouraged their patronage. The fact that women could subscribe to libraries but were not permitted any role in their management, and that for decades children were not welcome in libraries, further restricted their potential clientele.

But nothing encapsulates the seemingly intractable issues involved in bringing culture to the working classes than the debate over novel-reading. In the view of most elites, all books were not created equal. Some, like the works of the great poets and playwrights, Greek and Roman classics, biographies of great men, dense historical accounts, informative works of natural science, theology, philosophy, and fiction with a moral purpose, were worthy of reading, for they had the potential to elevate the mind and the spirit. Other books were, if not downright dangerous, then simply wasteful—potboilers, penny dreadfuls, sensational accounts of contemporary events. All of these were referred to dismissively as novels (in this calculation, the moralistic fiction of Maria Edgeworth or the polite fiction of Jane Austen would not have been considered 'novels'), and they were not to be acquired, much less circulated, by a respectable library. Dr. S.P. May, the Ontario government official responsible for Mechanics' Institutes, described novel-reading as 'intellectual sham drinking, affording a temporary exhilaration, but ultimately emasculating both mind and character.' A person who read a novel was like a person who ate opium; both habits 'tend to produce that dizzy, dreamy, drowsy state of mind which unfits a man for all the active duties of life.' According to May, prominent physicians had proven that reading novels was 'a cause of evil to youth of both sexes, and disorders of nerve centres, which have so alarmingly increased in late years, have been caused by the enervating influences of the prevalent romantic literature.' May was far from a lone voice. The directors of the Berlin Mechanics' Institute expressed deep concern in 1873 that 'so depraved have the tastes of our people become by reading pernicious, trashy novels, that a book worth the perusal is scarcely touched.'[128]

In this regard, Egerton Ryerson cast a shadow far beyond the schools of Canada West, affecting Mechanics' Institutes, private libraries, and reading societies across the country. His list became the gatekeeper, warning librarians that 'useful and entertaining books of permanent value, adapted to popular reading,' were the only volumes worth acquiring. But what constituted 'useful and entertaining books of permanent value, adapted to popular reading'? In 1862, the directors of the Toronto Mechanics' Institute debated purchasing the works of English novelist Jonathan Swift for their collection, but eventually concluded that 'the matter in them is generally of an uninteresting character and of an immoral tendency; being filled with obscene language and should therefore not be placed on the shelves of the library.'[129] Even a Mechanics' Institute in the tiny village of Waterdown, Ontario, included in its 1843 constitution the stipulation that the library should contain 'only Philosophical, Historical, Biographical and Mechanical works, to the complete exclusion of novel reading of every description.'

Indeed, for the typical mid-century librarian, the number of novels on the shelves became a handy measure of their institution's success. A few years after missionary John Smithurst reported that the patrons of the Red River library consisted of two classes—those who read 'suitable' literature and another group 'whom I apprehend will be mainly novel readers'—John Ryerson reported with satisfaction that the trend had been halted by the purging of the collection, which now included 'a very small proportion of works of fiction.' Benjamin Beddome, speaking in the library of the Belleville Mechanics' Institute, regretted that 'there should be such a general demand for novels, in all libraries, and so little demand for works of a more useful, substantial, or instructive character,' and urged his colleagues to do something about it.[130] In this, the Ontario government was on Beddome's side, decreeing in 1880 that a Mechanics' Institute could spend no more than 20 percent of its book grant on works of fiction.

But the sustained opposition to novel-reading in favour of useful knowledge was taking a toll on the libraries themselves. Just six years after Ryerson's satisfied verdict on the Red River library, James Ross had to report that only eight people were using it out of a population of some 8,000. In Strathroy, Ontario, where the superintendent estimated the reading population was just over 1,500, only ninety-one people were borrowing books. Even Egerton Ryerson's flagship program had withered alarmingly, from a high of 100,000 books distributed in 1853 to just 13,701 three years later. Historian Bruce Curtis suggests that this was because Ryerson was unwilling to provide the kind of books that people actually wanted to read, and that librarians could choose from a much broader range of offerings from itinerant pedlars, book depots, or local merchants.

Even in successful libraries, the statistics were alarming. In 1880, the librarian at the Belleville Mechanics' Institute expressed concern that, on average, books on biography, history, literature, science, and art were taken out twice a year, while the average novel circulated thirteen times a year. This, thought the librarian, 'teaches a practical lesson as to the necessity of a strict supervision in the selection of works of this nature.' In Napanee, Ontario, the librarian tried mightily to 'cultivate a healthier public taste,' but still had to report that 76 percent of books signed out of his library were fiction.[131] It was the same in Toronto, where the librarian of the Mechanics' Institute reported that of the 30,000 books that circulated in 1880, 25,000 were fiction, and in Montreal, where 6,314 of the Mechanics' Institute library's 9,368 volumes were novels. The Institute library in Port Carling, Ontario, began its library collection with such classics as *Pre-History Man*, *Evidence of Man's Place in Nature*, *The Dawn of History*, and *The Story of Creation*. As a later historian wrote, 'judging by the good condition of these books today, they were not read a great deal.'

So, elites were forced to change with the times. In 1880, the Ontario Minister of Education finally gave in and conceded that the provision of some 'light reading' to libraries was necessary. Clergymen, too, eventually had to give ground; after years of opposing the popular fiction of authors like Dickens, Bulwer-Lytton, and Scott, they reluctantly allowed them into the category of 'acceptable fiction,' simply because the demand for them was so strong.[132] Part of their motivation came from the realization that people were obtaining their reading matter from other sources. Particularly worrying were things like the underground book club discovered at Port Hope Central School in 1861. A small group of students had collected subscriptions from their classmates and assembled a circulating library of what the headmaster decided was fiction of the most objectionable sort: 'Sylvanus Cobb with his love & murder, stories of highwaymen from Dick Turpin to Paul Clifford, lives of opera girls *et hoc genus omne* and the worst of Reynold's filthy & exciting publications.' The books were dirty and tattered, clearly a sign that they had passed through many hands, and the headmaster immediately set about separating, as he saw it, the filthy from the merely unclean. Of the seventy books the students had purchased, he decided that forty were fit only for the fire.[133]

This local scandal provides an exclamation point to the conclusion that the attempt to create a cultivated working class by giving them 'suitable literature' had largely failed. Ryerson never quite grasped the fact that his preferred medium wasn't suited to his message, and would have done well to heed the advice of newspaper editor Hiram Leavenworth, who admitted that a new magazine called *Youth's Monitor*, established in Toronto in January 1836, was 'calculated to afford instruction and amusement at the same time. We would suggest, in the most friendly spirit, that a style less grave and didactick, would make the lessons of wisdom more attractive to the imagination, and, of course, better adapted to improve the mind of youth.' Bruce Curtis noted that the elite's fondness for 'elevating' books may have created the very impression they wanted most to avoid: that reading was as dull and boring as the consumption of other forms of 'useful knowledge.'[134] This, for William Lyon Mackenzie, was a great tragedy, for there had been such promise in the notion that the working classes could be brought to a higher state of cultural awareness. The opportunity had been squandered, and he knew exactly where to put the blame:

> Instead of Mechanics' Institutes, Athenaeums, Public Reading Rooms, Apprentices' Libraries, Agricultural and Horticultural Societies, Forums, Literary Clubs, and other Institutions of a similar nature, to delight, instruct and elevate...we have a motley collection of upstart would-be gentlemen to set us the fashions—a race alike despised and despising the great body of the Canadian people.'[135]

But the need to create a culturally aware population was already taking on more urgency as ideas of nationalism spread from the United States and Europe to British North America. 'This is an age of unprecedented intellectual activity,' said Dr. A.R. Abbott in his inaugural address to the Chatham Literary Society in 1875, 'and any people who are content to slumber in mental inertia may expect to wake far behind in the race of life.'[136] The assumptions of Abbott and dozens of other educational reformers and library boosters about the working classes were now being applied to the nation as a whole. Just like the mechanic who did not improve his mind, a country that slumbered in mental inertia and failed to develop culturally would find itself rapidly outpaced.

On the other hand, a country that fostered its culture, whether it be through libraries, Mechanics' Institutes, reading societies, or art clubs, would create bonds of nationhood that could stand the test of time. In the words of John Davis Barnett, an engineer in Stratford, Ontario—reputed to have one of the largest private libraries in Canada at over 20,000 volumes—libraries provided the resources to educate 'our young, our various nationalities, foreign emigrants and social strata [into the] fibrous metal of a unified Canada.' George Ross, the Ontario minister of education, was even blunter at the opening of a library in London, Ontario:

> We hope, round the altar here, that young Canadians will worship with a pure heart loftier ideals of national life; that a broader patriotism will be quickened by higher conceptions of duty...there were Canadians made better and stronger men because it entered into the hearts of the citizens of London...to place at their disposal the treasure-house of knowledge.[137]

The relationship between culture and nationalism, hinted at vaguely in the eighteenth and early nineteenth centuries, was becoming the hottest topic of discussion in Canada's growing arts community.

Chapter 7

'Streaks on the Horizon'

From the earliest days of the European presence in North America, there had been vague signs that the culture that would develop here must necessarily be unique, because the place itself was unique. It is in Marc Lescarbot's poem *Adieu à la France*, composed on his departure for Acadia in 1606, which pictured the new world as a Garden of Eden (something that was especially appealing to the Parisian lawyer who was trying to escape corrupt European society, especially the courts that had just found against him in an important case), and in Pierre Boucher's 1664 travel guide, which was shot through with the notion that everything in New France was as good as or better than anything in France. It is in the Loyalists' desire to use culture as a way to show their superiority over the rebels, and in the determination of French-Canadian writers to make culture a key element of *la survivance*. It is in the emergence of folk cultures across the British North American colonies, and in the desire of elites to build a cultured working class as a prerequisite to a civilized, modern nation.

Of course, none of these people were really cultural nationalists, because a 'nation' did not yet exist; the most we can say is that they were proto-cultural nationalists. But they were all animated by a realization, however dim, that forms of expression in what would become Canada had to be different from those that existed in the old world or in the new republic to the south. In the middle decades of the nineteenth century, they began to give tangible form to that realization.

The Confederation of four of Britain's North American colonies in 1867 provided a further spur to the growth of cultural nationalism. If the British North America [BNA] Act itself didn't inspire poets and painters—a piece of legislation rarely moves the creative soul—it did usher in an era of boosterism. The generation that came to maturity in the wake of Confederation built on these foundations, seeing the

possibility, even the necessity, of going beyond the deal-making of politicians to give the new nation a distinct culture. In their work, we see the
first true glimmers, both good and bad, of cultural nationalism.

———•-•-•———

Through the nineteenth century, it had become a truism to assert that
the colonial milieu was inhospitable to the growth of an indigenous
culture, at least beyond the folk culture that flourished on the frontier.
There were many practical reasons for this—bookshops could make
more money selling American or British books than Canadian, it was
cheaper for a small church in Quebec to import a painting from Europe
than to commission a local artist, there was little demand for public art,
so sculptors had a hard time making a go of it—but perhaps the biggest
obstacle was psychological. As Canada's first poetry anthologist, Edward
Hartley Dewart, put it in a comment that could apply equally to French
or English Canadians, 'the majority of persons of taste and education
in Canada are emigrants from the Old Country, whose tenderest affec-
tions cling around the land they have left.'[138] Their first inclination was
to import old world culture rather than create a new culture for the
new world.

Still, a few people were willing to go against the prevailing tendencies
and do what they could to foster a Canadian culture. In Quebec, one
of the earliest beneficiaries of this was the artist Joseph Légaré. Almost
entirely self-taught, Légaré had honed his skills by doing reproductions
of European works, something that also earned him a fair living. A man
of diverse interests and talents, he helped decorate Quebec's new Théâtre
Royal in 1832; and he became the first art gallery owner in Lower Canada
when he built a large house to display his own collection. Légaré was later
involved in a number of schemes to establish art institutes in Quebec,
but their failure led him to pour his nationalism into his painting, something that the press appreciated. As the Quebec Gazette wrote, it was
cause for celebration that Légaré 'has devoted much of his time and art
to the charmfull and romantic scenery of his own beautiful forestland…
he has emerged from the dusty and prozing society of vigilworn Saints,
and other goodly canonized notables, to give his pencil a revel amid
the fair and fresh of nature's loveliness.'[139] Favourable press coverage

didn't pay the bills, but in this case it helped Légaré attract the attention of a growing number of art collectors in Lower Canada. In 1833, businessman Henry Atkinson traded a Carravaggio for some works by Légaré, and a decade later Archibald Campbell (a patron of poets, painters, and playwrights, the driving force behind the construction of the Quebec Music Hall, and a founder of the Literary and Historical Society of Quebec in 1831) bought Légaré's *The Engagement* and *The Despair of an Indian Woman* even before they were finished, because he saw in them the seeds of a Canadian school of art.

Habitant life, as depicted by Cornelius Krieghoff, 1848.

Cornelius Krieghoff was another artist who both created and benefited from the growing interest in Canadian subjects. He had established a home in Montreal around 1847, but didn't do well there; there are stories of Krieghoff going door-to-door, hawking paintings for $5 or $10 apiece. He would paint anything that paid—copies of European works, portraits, business signs, even, legend has it, a nude for a local barroom—and in the early 1850s, frustration at being unable to make a decent living sent him to Quebec. There, his work caught on as local military and social elites fell in love with the classic Krieghoff style: paintings full of narrative interest and amusing detail, and dramatic landscapes with a decidedly romantic feel to them. His work started to

Krieghoff's version of how the other half lived: Montreal's Place d'Armes, January 1856.

sell well—so well, in fact, that the quality varied because he often had to dash them off to keep up with the demand. There are over a thousand Krieghoffs currently in existence; many more have likely been lost.

Half a century after the appearance of the first music books published in Canada, *Le Graduel romain* (1800) and Stephen Humbert's *Union Harmony* (1801), Scottish emigré James Paton Clarke took seven poems from the literary magazine *The Maple Leaf*, set them to music, and published them as *Lays of the Maple Leaf, or Songs of Canada* (1853). They were fairly highbrow, but in 1865 Ernest Gagnon published the first collection of Canadian folk songs, *Chansons populaires du Canada*, giving Canadians the first glimpse at the music that had survived and evolved since being imported from Europe in the seventeenth and eighteenth century.

By the same token, literature boosters could celebrate the first novels written by native-born writers, Julia Beckwith's *St. Ursula's Convent* (1824) and Philippe Aubert de Gaspé's *L'influence d'un livre* (1837), and they also began to demonstrate a bullish pride that would have done the Loyalists proud. One editor complimented the *Literary Garland* for giving Upper Canada a 'monthly literary periodical…infinitely superior to much of what appears in some of the publications of the neighboring

Paul Cherré's monument to François-Xavier Garneau in Quebec City.

States.'[140] In Lower Canada, the foundation of the Institut canadien de Montréal in 1844 spawned the establishment of some sixty similar organizations over the next decade, all dedicated to nurturing French-Canadian culture. The parent branch soon embraced radical politics and literature, which drew the attention of clerical authorities. Its library was full of books the church had banned and, although it remained popular with Montreal readers (especially after it became a free library), it was under constant attack from the Catholic hierarchy; the Bishop of Montreal even issued a pastoral letter condemning the institution and threatening to excommunicate its members. The *institut* in Quebec was less controversial. Established in 1847 by Octave Crémazie (whose reputation as one of French Canada's national poets stands in contrast to his mostly mediocre verse), Théophile Hamel (best known as a portrait painter for the elites of Quebec), and François-Xavier Garneau (Canada's first great historian and a poet and essayist of no mean talent as well), it stayed much closer to its cultural mandate, publishing the works of its members and sponsoring concerts by local musicians. In 1860, Crémazie invited a number of writers—the poets Léon-Pamphile LeMay and Louis Fréchette, journalist and librarian Antoine Gérin-Lajoie, newspaper editor Joseph-Charles Taché, and Pierre-Joseph-Olivier Chauveau, the superintendent of education for Canada East—to meet in the back of his bookstore. Calling themselves the Mouvement littéraire du Québec, they aimed to create a distinctive school of French-Canadian literature and produced many of the most important early French-Canadian novels, as well as two literary magazines, *Les soirées canadiennes* (1861–65) and *Le foyer canadien* (1863–66).

In contrast, English-Canadian verse, as Professor Daniel Wilson wrote in 1858, tended to be 'less redolent of "the odors of the forest" than of the essences of the drawing room; and more frequently re-echoes the songs that are to be gathered amid the leaves of the library-shelf, than under those with which the wind sports among the branches'—a fancy way of saying that it copied European poetry rather than finding inspiration in Canada. Indeed, it became customary for English-Canadian writers to express some envy at the position of the poet in Quebec: French Canada 'not only honours her literary men,' observed G. Mercer Adam, 'but maintains and nourishes her national life on what they bring forth.'[141] At least English Canada got its first poetry anthology, thanks to E.H. Dewart's *Selections From Canadian Poets*. His stated aim was to preserve poetry that appeared in the daily and weekly press and that might otherwise be lost, but he was also a nation-builder at heart. For Dewart, 'a national literature is an essential element in the formation of a national character…[it is] the bond of national unity, and the guide of national energy.' He regretted the 'sectionalism and disintegration, which is the political weakness of Canada,' and lamented the fact that there was no literature to counterbalance it. In fact, he went on, there is no country 'where the claims of native literature are so little felt, and where every effort in poetry has been met with so much coldness and indifference.' This lack, for Dewart, was inexplicable, for the country's natural beauties are 'an inexhaustible mine of richest ore, worthy of the most exalted genius, and of the deepest human and spiritual knowledge.'[142]

But despite the efforts of these few pioneers, there were more failures than successes. A French émigré named Nicolas-Marie-Alexandre Vattemare (better known as the ventriloquist Mr. Alexandre) arrived in Montreal in 1840 to promote a scheme that would bring together the Mechanics' Institute, the Montreal library, and the Natural History Society into a single cultural institution. After receiving warm support from the Board of Trade and city council, Vattemare moved on to Quebec, where he pitched a similar scheme. It too was greeted enthusiastically by city council and the press, who saw it as a way to bring French and English culture together in a way that was mutually beneficial. In March 1841, Vattemare left Lower Canada for Boston, firmly convinced that his two institutions were on solid footings, but he had not reckoned on the ubiquity of politics in the Canadas. When Upper and Lower Canada were joined by the Act of Union in 1841, any talk of cultural institutions was forgotten (at least temporarily—the Institut canadien was modelled on Vattemare's scheme) as all energies were devoted to the political settlement. It would not be the first time that politics got in the way of the arts.

While in domestic architecture builders and artisans continued to adapt European styles to local conditions, producing uniquely Canadian forms like the Ontario cottage or the *habitant* dwelling, public buildings remained in the thrall of revivalism. Before 1867, like the rest of North America and Europe, Canada was gripped by the Gothic revival, which came first through church architecture in the 1820s. The most aggressive booster of the style was the Cambridge Camden Society and its campaign to promote thirteenth- and fourteenth-century Gothic styles for nineteenth-century churches. The first great structure built to this ideal was the Anglican cathedral in Fredericton (1846–53), but it soon spread to smaller churches, educational institutions, where the visual association with the great British universities was highly prized, and even commercial architecture. But beyond the translation of the style into wooden board-and-batten churches, there was very little distinctively Canadian about it. When university chancellor John Langton opined that Frederick William Cumberland's new University College in Toronto was done in what might be called 'the Canadian style,' he was commenting on politics rather than architecture. For him, the fact that University College represented a classic case of Victorian eclecticism, with motifs borrowed from Gothic, Italianate, Byzantine, Norman, and English architecture, parallelled the confusion of Canadian politics. Political deadlock was making everything a product of uneasy compromises, much like University College.[143]

Despite a boom that made York the third largest city on the Great Lakes by the 1830s, its artistic life remained tenuous. In 1834, when the town's name was changed to Toronto, a number of interested individuals came together to create the Society of Artists & Amateurs of Toronto. Its aim was to hold annual exhibitions, the first opening with great fanfare on 1 July 1834. Over 190 works were on display, most of them European landscapes and copies of Old Masters, but favourable press reports couldn't induce people to travel to the Parliament Building to view the exhibition. The fledgling society took a major financial loss and several of its key members decided to give up on Toronto. The Society of Artists & Amateurs failed to survive its first show and its successor, the Toronto Society of Artists (1847), did little better, holding two exhibitions before it too dissolved. Clearly, the Toronto *Patriot* had been right to wonder if 'there was sufficient taste among our citizens' to support even a small community of artists.[144]

Musical groups, too, faced an uphill struggle for survival, their most formidable enemy being public indifference. The *Société harmonique* in Quebec garnered rave reviews from the local press, but could not sell tickets and collapsed in 1857. An attempt to revive it in 1861 with sixty instrumentalists was no more successful. Toronto's St. James Cathedral imported organist John Carter from Britain to energize the city's musical life, but his Musical Union survived for just three years before being shut down due to lack of public interest. And musical ensembles were vulnerable to more than just financial disaster. Joseph-François-Xavier Perrault formed a band in 1831, only to see its players decimated by the Montreal cholera epidemic of 1832. In Saint John, the Harmonic Society built an enthusiastic base of supporters but folded after only three years following a dispute between its conductor and board of directors. The Toronto Philharmonic Society collapsed and reformed five times between 1846 and 1894, a boom-and-bust cycle that was duplicated in virtually every city in British North America: an orchestra or choir would be founded with great fanfare, perform for a season or two, and then vanish when its hall burned down, its conductor moved on, or it ran out of money.

Cultural journals, many of them with a vaguely nationalist bent, also came and went in great numbers in the 1850s and 1860s. Canada's first music journal, *L'Artiste* (1860) lasted only two issues; its successor, *Les Beaux Arts*, managed to survive for thirteen months before collapsing. The fate of the *Literary Garland*, the longest-surviving of these periodicals, is instructive. Founded in 1838 by Montreal publisher John Lovell and his brother-in-law John Gibson, it espoused a confident nationalism and published many of the greatest Canadian authors of the day, including John Richardson, Rosanna Leprohon, Susanna Moodie, and Charles Sangster. But despite its stated aim of becoming the vehicle for a distinctly Canadian literary expression, the *Garland* found that few of its potential contributors shared the same sense of mission. As the years passed, it became more and more like the American periodicals with which it competed, and in December 1851 published its last issue, a victim of the disinterest of writer and reader alike, and of competition with better funded American magazines. A successor never even got off the ground. The *Canadian National Magazine* was planned in 1863 as a monthly review of literature, science, and art, and included among its prospective contributors such established stars as Sangster, Leprohon, Louisa Murray, and Cornelius Krieghoff. Sadly, it was still-born, yet another casualty of a society in which politics was apparently more important that anything else.

The same year that Dewart's anthology was published, a group of Maritime politicians met in Charlottetown to discuss the possibility of political union. To their surprise, the leaders of Canada East and West

asked to come along—they were beset by their own political deadlock—
and there was enough common ground that they agreed to meet again
in Quebec two months later. Then came the arguments, in each of the
British North American colonies, for and against union, the political
manoeuvring, the carrots and sticks, the elections and the election-
eering. It all culminated in the passage of the British North America Act,
by which the Dominion of Canada came into being on 1 July 1867.

The Confederation Debates were published at the time, and
subsequently reprinted for later generations, but they make less-than-
scintillating reading. They are all about customs duties, railways, the
division of powers between different levels of government—nothing
about culture. The fact is that very few of the Fathers of Confederation cared much about the subject. George Brown was a publisher, but
took little interest in the cultural content of his newspaper, the Toronto
Globe. Sir Alexander Tilloch Galt was the son of novelist John Galt, but
his tastes ran more to essays on politics and economics than literature.
Hector-Louis Langevin had headed a branch of the Institut canadien
for two years, but as Confederation neared he found that he had to
champion French-Canadian rights generally, rather than just on the
cultural front. Almost the only politician with a passionate interest in
culture was Thomas D'Arcy McGee.

If he is remembered at all today, it is as the victim of the new dominion's first political assassination. But in the mid-nineteenth century,
McGee was as renowned for his interest in poetry as in politics, and
particularly in the relationship between literature and nationalism. He
had first come to North America in 1842, and was hired as a newspaper editor at the tender age of nineteen. But he returned to his native
Ireland three years later and became an ardent supporter of the Young
Ireland movement, which was fighting for self-government and believed
fervently that an Irish identity could be fostered through literature.
When McGee moved to Montreal in 1857, with a novel and a handful
of historical works to his credit, he began to apply the principles of
Young Ireland to his new home. 'Every country, every nationality,
every people, must create and foster a National Literature, if it is their
wish to preserve a distinct individuality from other nations,' he wrote
in his short-lived newspaper *The New Era* in 1857. 'Literature is the
vital atmosphere of nationality...No literature, no national life...let

us construct a national life for Canada, neither British nor French nor Yankeeish, but the offspring of the soil, borrowing lessons from all, but asserting its own title throughout.' For McGee, the 'offspring of the soil' was significant, because he had no doubt that a national literature must be based in the land and its glories: 'It must assume the gorgeous coloring and the gloomy grandeur of the forest. It must partake of the grave mysticism of the Red man, and the wild vivacity of the hunter of western prairies. Its lyrics must possess the ringing cadence of the waterfall, and its epics be as solemn and beautiful as our great rivers.'[145] In 1858, he published his first and only volume of poetry, *Canadian Ballads and Occasional Verses*, in which he elaborated upon his manifesto for a national literature:

> That we shall one day be a great northern nation, and develope [sic] within ourselves that best fruit of nationality, a new and lasting literature, is the firm belief, at least of those to whom this volume is mainly addressed…of all forms of patriotism, a wise, public-spirited patriotism in literature, is not the least admirable. It is, indeed, glorious to die in battle in defence of our homes or altars; but not less glorious is it to live to celebrate the virtues of our heroic countrymen, to adorn the history, or to preserve the traditions of our country.[146]

McGee had great hopes for the new nation, but, within a year of Confederation, he was felled by an assassin's bullet as he entered his Ottawa home. He had already decided to leave politics and devote his energy to the promotion of Canadian literature and historical writing; yet had he lived, he would likely have been disappointed by the post-Confederation era. In most respects, the jubilation of Dominion Day 1867 had little immediate impact on culture in the new Canada.

There were art shows that year, but most of the paintings on display were of English or continental European subjects. Some skilled British watercolourists were working here in the years after Confederation, but none of them inspired much in the way of indigenous artistic development. Many artists regarded painting as a profession rather than a form of expression; they were businesspeople, and the organizations they created were founded primarily to promote and sell their work.

George W. Hill's memorial to D'Arcy McGee on Parliament Hill in Ottawa.

The Society of Canadian Artists [SCA], established in 1867, sounds like it should have been a product of nationalist fervour, but in fact it was born out of frustration with the Art Association of Montreal. The AAM had been established in 1860 without any actual artists among its original members, and painters in Canada's largest art market soon realized that the association was little more than a forum for local collectors to display their collections of European masters. The SCA was intended not to foster a Canadian school of painting, but to sell Canadian art to wealthy buyers, both in North America and abroad.

Musical groups continued in the same boom-and-bust cycle that had plagued them before Confederation. Winnipeg, for example, saw the emergence of a succession of ensembles—the Philharmonic Society, Dr. P.R. McLagan's choir, the Apollo Club with its thirty-five instrumentalists—but none of them lasted for more than a few seasons. Confederation generated a mass of patriotic music, but scholars dismiss most of it as eminently forgettable. The best known product of 1867 was certainly Alexander Muir's 'The Maple Leaf Forever', which remained Canada's unofficial national anthem (and should have been its official one, in the hearts of many Anglo-Canadians) for decades, but most of the other patriotic songs of the era boasted stirring titles—J.D. Edgar's 'This Canada' (1867), C.P. Woodlawn's 'Our Old Canadian Home' (1868), Charles-Marie Panneton and Benjamin Sulte's 'Rallions-nous' (1874), Louis Fréchette's 'O mon pays, terre adorée' (1875)—and very little else to distinguish them. It was the same in poetry—lots of celebratory verses were published but few worth remembering a year later. Even the Mouvement littéraire du Quebec collapsed. Crémazie, chased out by fraudulent business transactions, decamped for France, where he showed flashes of brilliance in his prose writing that had been absent from his poetry; Taché and Gérin-Lajoie went to Ottawa to take jobs with the new federal government; Chauveau became the premier of Quebec; and Fréchette, disillusioned with the lack of regard for poets in Canada, moved to Chicago to live with his brother.

One of the few bright spots was the publication in 1867 of Henry Morgan's *Bibliotheca Canadensis*, a listing of everything that had been published in Canada up to that date. D'Arcy McGee, even while admitting that the few great Canadian books published were 'but streaks on the horizon,' lauded Morgan for his efforts.[147] Quoting Samuel Johnson's declaration that 'the chief glory of a nation lies in its authors,' Morgan offered a manifesto that would have done McGee proud. 'There is just now, and has been for some years past, a perceptible movement on the part of the two great branches, French and English, which compose our

New Nationality, and principally amongst the younger men, to aid in the cause of Canadian Literature by their own personal contribution to that Literature,' he wrote. This was entirely fitting, because the Dominion had entered 'an epoch which now sees us firmly implanted on the American continent as a vigorous and highly promising State, Federally constituted, full of brilliant hopes and fond yearnings for national greatness and renown…Now more than at any other time ought the literary life of the New Dominion develope [sic] itself unitedly.'[148]

<hr />

But the circumstances of the new dominion's birth did not exactly lend themselves to cultural flights of fancy—'We are what we are as a people by virtue of the struggle for responsible government, but what poet could read a tune into such refractory material?'[149] wondered Pelham Edgar—so the Confederation era was one of encouragement rather than production, of promoting a national culture rather than creating one. The first and most vocal of those promoters was a small group, inspired by the example of D'Arcy McGee, which would eventually be known as the Canada First movement.

It began very modestly in May 1868, with a meeting of five men in Henry Morgan's Ottawa hotel room: William A. Foster, George T. Denison, R.G. Haliburton, Charles Mair, and Morgan. In those early days, they simply called themselves the Corner Room; the name Canada First was not coined by Denison until 1870, and did not come into wide use until the following year, when Foster published a pamphlet entitled *Canada First; or, Our New Nationality*. After that, the movement loomed large in Canadian public life, although its bark was always worse than its bite.

Canada First was a collection of men with very different priorities. Haliburton, the son of the great satirist Thomas Chandler Haliburton and an amateur poet and ethnographer, was particularly interested in the tariff. Denison, a dyed-in-the-wool imperialist, was preoccupied with military matters; he wrote a very highly regarded book on cavalry operations but always considered himself a soldier, not a writer. Morgan was a civil servant and biographer, perhaps best known for reference works such as *The Canadian Parliamentary Companion* and *The Dominion Annual Register*. Foster, a Toronto lawyer, studied the economic aspects of Confederation and was the founder and first editor of the *Monetary Times*.

The most literary of them was Charles Mair, a native of Lanark, in the Ottawa valley, a town that was a cultural desert in the days of his youth; his only exposure to poetry came from his mother, who fostered in him a love of verse. Mair cared little for education—a schoolmate later said that 'he hated school with a perfect and undying hatred...the mental and scholastic attainments that he gained during that period were absolutely *nil*'[150]—and everything for the outdoors; he even detested being cooped up in the office of his father's lumber business. Poetry, however, was something he could do out of doors, and at a young age he began a quest to make a living from the pen. Indeed, when he went to Ottawa in 1868 it was not to meet with the future members of Canada First, but to enlist the aid of his acquaintance Henry Morgan in finding a publisher for his first volume of poetry.

But if they came to Canada First for different reasons, the five shared a number of views: if Canada was to be great, it had to be more than a political union of colonies, and its public life more than tendentious debates over legislative minutiae; a bitter disappointment that the factionalism and petty politicking of pre-Confederation Canada was continuing after 1867; the good of the new dominion should be placed ahead of any political or even personal considerations; and culture, especially literature, could be a powerful force in taking Canada to the next level of nationhood.

The members did practice what they preached about creating a national culture—Mair's *Dreamland and other Poems* was published in 1868, and the movement spawned a number of short-lived but influential periodicals, including its official organ *The Nation* (1874–76), *The Bystander* (1880–82, 1890–91), *The Canadian Monthly and National Review* (1872–82), and *The Week* (1883–96)—but there was always more preaching than practicing. Foster became the acknowledged prophet of the movement, using pamphlet and podium to urge others to rebel 'against the inanity, and worse than inanity, of what was offered to them as political discussion' and to work instead at building a national culture.[151] Canada First's mouthpiece echoed the call, *The Nation* remarking upon the 'rapid growth of culture and the increasing interest in intellectual life among the people. Knowledge is descending like the first and second rain and spreading with an uninterrupted flow over the land…in all directions bountifully irrigating the mental soil… to bear fruit, we trust, ere many days.'[152]

In the end, any fruit the movement might have borne directly was stunted by its diversion to other pursuits. Mair was forced to take a job on the Fort Garry Road shortly after his book was published, and his writing over the next couple of years was confined to articles for the Toronto *Globe*. After the Riel Rebellion, he settled in Portage la Prairie, and his cultural nationalism again took a back seat to the day-to-day needs of making a living. The other Canada Firsters also changed their orientation after the Riel Rebellion, expanding from the five originals to a larger group known as the Twelve Apostles and turning their efforts to establishing an Ontario empire in the west. Under Foster's leadership, they became increasingly involved in politics, something that proved to be the *coup de grâce* for the movement. Morgan, very conscious of his position as a civil servant, wanted to stay clear of politics and withdrew from the group; in time, it fell victim to the very factionalism it had so deplored in its early days.

The same pattern is discernible in the Canadian art world, where a certain amount of optimism had prevailed immediately after Confederation. The *Canadian Illustrated News* opined that the Society of Canadian Artists' 1870 show 'leads us to entertain great hopes of the speedy development of Canadian art,' while the Montreal *Journal* applauded the group for its planned Art Union (a fundraiser in which supporters purchased tickets to an exhibition, and received in return small works of art) in 1872, remarking that 'up to a late date those who had a wish to encourage Native Art had to fall back upon the multiplied crudities of Krieghoff.' In June 1872, John A. Fraser and six other artists took advantage of the spirit of optimism to establish the Ontario Society of Artists, consisting of both artists and patrons, with great plans to hold an annual exhibition, create an Art Union, and lobby for a permanent national gallery. The first show, which opened on 14 April 1873, was warmly received, *The Canadian Monthly* observing that 'we have a body of artists in our midst who only require adequate remuneration to beget a native School of Canadian Art; and to contribute in many ways to the refinement of taste and the development of education in the highest departments of aesthetic culture.'[153]

The Ontario Society of Artists' first exhibition in 1873 at Fraser's Gallery, King St. West, Toronto.

The problem for artists was not the lure of politics but the realities of the marketplace. In September 1873, Montreal's economy went into a nosedive. The AAM and SCA both collapsed, taking with them the major outlets for the work of Canada's most prominent artists. Then, in November 1873, the OSA executive discovered that its treasurer had been using the society's money to prop up his faltering coal business; later, another society official embezzled the money raised from Art Union ticket sales. Perhaps more important was the resignation of the Montreal members, which dashed hopes that the OSA could ever be anything but a regional organization. This would become a trend (in 1877, artists in the London area resigned to form the Western Art Union, and other local groups in Ottawa, Winnipeg, and Saint John would soon follow), the factionalism that ultimately destroyed Canada First weakening art organizations as well.

Individually, some artists continued to do well—Napoléon Bourassa, an extraordinarily versatile man who was, at various times, painter, novelist, architect, sculptor, and decorator, relied more and more on what he considered to be the distasteful task of 'doing ecclesiastical or historical canvases for mustard merchants or worthy curés who understood nothing about painting'—but many artists, particularly those who did primarily landscapes, found their sales drying up under the combined influence of economic depression and turmoil in the art organizations. Daniel Fowler, who painted on Amherst Island, near Kingston, Ontario, vowed that he would cast aside his brush and go back to farming unless prospects improved. They didn't. Fowler managed to eke out an existence, but Canadian landscape painting as a genre would take years to recover.

Of course, it would have been too much to expect for a national culture to burst forth fully formed while the ink on the BNA Act was still wet. Still, by the late 1870s, many of Canada's cultural elites concluded that the promise of Confederation, the optimism of the first decade after 1867, and the feverish activity of art and literary promoters had come to very little. Sara Jeannette Duncan, in an oft-quoted column in *The Week*, blamed the newspapers for not printing book reviews; an editor told her that readers did not like them and, in any case, they got in the way of the advertisements. 'The Province of Ontario is one great camp of the Philistines,' she huffed. Instead of fostering a lively literary milieu, the newspapers printed nothing but 'politics and vituperation, temperance and vituperation, religion and vituperation.' Her own hometown, Brantford, Ontario, certainly fit this description, at least as recreated in her novel *The Imperialist*: 'The town of Elgin thus knew two controlling interests—the interest of politics and the interest of religion.'[154] Some journalists agreed with Duncan—John Willison resigned his editorship of the *Globe* out of disgust at the ceaseless partyism of the newspaper world—but most editors and publishers were interested in topicality, and the favourite topics rarely extended beyond the ones Duncan had listed. Joseph Edmund Collins predicted wryly that 'If Shakespeare took his entire set of plays up and down Toronto to-morrow, he could not get a publisher to "touch them"; but if he induced his stage manager to write a book about the "Methodists" or the "Tories," or the "Episcopalians," or on "Irishmen," or could "get up" a good cookbook, there is not a publisher in Toronto who would not promptly enter with him into articles of publication.'[155] G. Mercer Adam lamented the apparent inertia that had overtaken Canadian culture at the very time when it should be booming: the consumers of culture were 'losing their poetic sensibilities and becoming indifferent to the claims of culture,' leading to 'the ebbing out of national spirit, a growing intellectual callousness, and a deadening of interest in the things that make for the nation's highest life. Native literature, with nothing to encourage it, is fast losing the power to arrest attention and is perceptibly dying of inanition.' After the collapse of the country's only true literary periodical, *The Canadian Monthly*, Charles Mair wondered 'what is the cause of the deadly blight which seems to rest upon and rust the public mind of Canada?' Were Canadians no more than a 'nation of intellectual eunuchs?'[156] The common denominator in all of these laments was obvious: Canada, despite the promise of Confederation, remained factional and parochial, and its culture was the poorer for it.

But all was not lost, for the generation born during the Confederation era was coming of age; it would create the kind of national culture that elites had hoped to see in the 1860s, and continued to demand and support. Two of the most influential promoters of a Canadian national art were the British governors-general, the 1st Marquess of Dufferin and Ava (1873–78) and the Marquess of Lorne (1878–83). Both were predisposed to culture—Dufferin was a descendant of the playwright Richard Sheridan and the son of a famous actor, while Lorne was an author and poet of some ability—and Dufferin set the trend by serving notice that he would use his influence to promote centralized cultural institutions: 'I believe the cultivation of art to be a most essential element of our national life,' he wrote.[157] He agreed to be the official patron of the OSA, and did much to preserve the architectural heritage of Quebec, which he feared was in danger of becoming the 'quadrangle monopoly of an American town.' When Dufferin's term ended, Lorne carried on his work, presenting a plan in September 1879 for the establishment of a Royal Canadian Academy that would convene annual exhibitions in the provincial capitals. With the cooperation of the OSA and the reconstituted AAM, the Academy came into being in 1880 with twenty-five charter members, including Napoléon Bourassa, landscape painter Lucius O'Brien, architect W.G. Storm, and a single woman, artist Charlotte Schreiber. Its first show was held that year in Ottawa, with the following year's moving to Halifax. In 1882, it was supposed to be held in Saint John, but the lack of suitable gallery space moved the show to Montreal; thereafter, it rotated between Toronto, Ottawa, and Montreal.

The National Art Gallery of Canada, as it appeared in 1900.

One of the Royal Canadian Academy's first goals, and another cause dear to Lorne's heart, was the establishment of a national art gallery. So, every artist who became a member of the academy had to present a diploma painting, to become the basis of the collection of the National Gallery of Canada, which formally opened on 27 May 1882. Reaction to the two new institutions was mixed—Lorne observed that the academy had been established in a 'marvellous amount of bitterness and bad language; half of the artists are ready just now to choke the other half with their paint brushes,'[158] and it didn't help that the gallery's first home was a small room on Parliament Hill that had once been a builders' workshop. Its move in 1888 to larger rooms above the government's fisheries exhibition on O'Connor Street was regarded as a step up, the *Ottawa Daily Free Press* observing that the very popular fish exhibit was likely to draw visitors to the decidedly less popular national gallery. Others were less certain, Sir John Bourinot writing that the National Gallery of Canada was 'not worthy of the name and place,' while Archibald Lampman wrote that the gallery mostly consisted of 'nondescript articles hardly to be considered or named. Of what use is such a collection in its present condition? What pleasure can it afford to anyone?'[159] Still, both the Academy and the Gallery, for all their failings, represented a significant step forward in federal patronage of Canadian culture.

Of course, by the 1880s the federal government was already deeply involved in adding to the country's architectural heritage; it might be said that the Department of Public Works was the new dominion's first government cultural patron. It could be no other way, because it was essential that the new country put its stamp on the landscape with an architectural program that expressed its values in stone. A building, after all, was much more than just a building. As Toronto mayor John Shaw later put it,

> great buildings symbolize a people's deeds and aspirations…wherever a nation had a conscience and a mind, it recorded the evidence of its being in the highest products of this greatest of all arts. Where no such monuments are to be found, the mental and moral features of the people have not been above the faculties of the beasts.[160]

At least the new nation started off on a solid footing, with a seat of government that was widely regarded as one of the finest in the world. The Parliament Buildings in Ottawa had been designed to house the legislature of the united Canadas, with construction beginning in December 1859. Like any government project, it was plagued by cost overruns and accusations of mismanagement, but the building was ready in time for the session of July 1866. The Centre Block, designed by Thomas Fuller and Chilion Jones, and the two flanking buildings, by Thomas Stent and Augustus Laver, were triumphs of the style known as High Victorian Gothic, with its emphasis on carved ornamentation, the use of multicoloured stone, and the free adoption of a wide range

The new dominion's first parliament buildings. c. 1880.

of architectural motifs. The architects' aim was not to copy any specific style, but to use the best elements from a number of styles to produce a set of buildings with striking visual interest—or, to use the contemporary term, a strong picturesque quality. In 1867, it became the seat of government for the new Dominion of Canada.

With a new federal government came new federal buildings, and an opportunity to cement a national style in the public consciousness. High Victorian Gothic in its purest form was not to be the model, for it was too closely tied to Canada's earlier colonial status. More popular was the Second Empire style, characterized by steep mansard roofs, projecting pavilions to break up flat wall surfaces, and classical decoration like superimposed columns and pilasters. Its adoption for Government House in Toronto, the residence of the Ontario lieutenant-governor (1868), the new Toronto Post Office (1870–71), and Montreal City Hall (1872) gave it the official stamp of approval, establishing a pattern for government architecture that would persist through the tenure of the first Chief Architect in the Department of Public Works, Montreal architect Thomas S. Scott. He used the same style for the federal buildings in Montreal, Toronto, and Victoria, and its echoes could be found in the other structures built by the Department, from immigration

Montreal City Hall. c. 1850–85.

stations and quarantine hospitals to penitentiaries and drill halls. The style could also be found in provincial public buildings like the Falcon-wood Asylum near Charlottetown, municipal buildings like the city hall in Belleville, Ontario (1872–73), and in commercial structures like the North Street Railway Terminal in Halifax. It was especially popular in Quebec, where Eugène-Étienne Taché, the deputy minister in the department of lands and forests and the man who coined the provincial motto 'Je me souviens,' used it in the new provincial legislature and Quebec City Hall. He was taken by its French roots and saw it as the perfect architectural vocabulary for his nascent nationalism, but in fact it was a style that enjoyed huge popularity across North America, from British Columbia to Florida, from Newfoundland to California.

Second Empire, however, quickly fell from fashion, enjoying barely two decades in the limelight. This was partly because it was expensive and was starting to be regarded as 'foreign,' but changes in the Department of Public Works certainly had something to do with it. Scott's successor was none other than Thomas Fuller, who had gone from the acclaim of the Ottawa parliament buildings to being dismissed from the contract to build the State Capitol in Albany, New York, because of cost overruns and disagreements over the design. But Fuller's star in

Canada remained on the ascendant, and his parliament buildings (not to mention the political influence marshalling behind him) overshadowed the Albany débâcle. Fuller started with the Department of Public Works in 1881, and created some of the most important government buildings erected in Canada in the nineteenth century.

Fuller was a true Victorian eclectic, borrowing elements from half a dozen different styles and combining them into a single building, just as he had done with the Centre Block on Parliament Hill. His first major creation, the Langevin Block in Ottawa (1883–89) brought together Second Empire, Romanesque, Flemish, and Queen Anne elements. His federal buildings in Brockville, Ontario, New Glasgow, Nova Scotia, Newcastle, New Brunswick, and Charlottetown added classical touches. But with the public building in Galt, Ontario, finished in 1887, Fuller built on the foundations laid by Scott to establish what would eventually become his 'federal style': rounded arches, rusticated stonework, prominent gables, and asymmetrical elements. Through the late 1880s and 1890s dozens of buildings, large and small, were erected in this style, creating what architectural historian Christopher Thomas has called the Dominion Image, to represent the new nation to its scattered citizens. Municipal governments, which came into being at mid-century thanks to legislation such as the Ontario Municipal Act of 1849, adopted the style, especially in the years after Confederation, when an increase in community social activities, the growth of municipal services, and civic pride demanded larger and better-equipped buildings. The result was the erection of splendid town halls across post-Confederation Canada, many of them in Fuller's Dominion Image and equipped with auditoria to accommodate cultural activities.

What distinguished much of this building was a recognition of the uniqueness of place. They were all revivals of one sort or another, but the styles were chosen for specific reasons and carefully adapted to suit Canadian conditions, particularly the climate. As Ontario architect G.F. Stalker put it, 'the only thing for us to do in this matter is not to ignore our climate…but to give it in our architecture that consideration and study which is its due and which shall give a certain amount at least, of national character to our building.'[161] Domestic architecture had always taken account of the climate—one need only look at the houses of Quebec, with their thick walls, small doors and windows set flush with the outer walls, and steeply pitched roofs that allowed snow to slide off—but modern innovations, particularly central heating and electric lighting, had made builders less captive to weather conditions. Still, many architects, like Charles Baillargé, a member of the family that dominated architecture and decorative work in Quebec for a century and a half, believed those very characteristics should remain the basis for a national architecture: 'let us improve and embellish them and adapt them to modern notions, that in the new production we shall have, if not a national, at least a local style of architecture.'[162] In fact, those characteristics would produce a national architecture, the forms used by Scott, Fuller, and their contemporaries constituting a style that, in its eclectic medievalism, seemed to symbolize Canada's heritage as a northern nation.

If a Canadian style of architecture evolved slowly and almost imperceptibly, literary commentators believed they could date the birth of a Canadian literature quite precisely: to 1880, with the publication of Charles G.D. Roberts' collection entitled *Orion and other Poems* (Roberts' pre-Confederation predecessors Charles Heavysege and Alexander McLachlan generally received short shrift—in 1914, T.G. Marquis would dismiss Heavysege as an English rather than a Canadian poet, while later critics argue that McLachlan had no desire to write distinctively Canadian verse, and was quite happy to be known as the Canadian Robert Burns). Roberts' background was not unlike Mair's. Born in rural New Brunswick in 1860, as a child he too showed far more interest in the outdoors than in things cultural. Painting lessons at Mount Allison Ladies College failed to hold his interest, and his father's attempts to teach him to play the piano and organ were mutually disappointing. Not until he moved to Fredericton in 1873 did he develop a love of poetry, thanks in large measure to his headmaster, George Parkin. His first published poem was written when he was only fifteen years old; he was just twenty and working as the principal of Chatham High School and Grammar School when *Orion* was published in Philadelphia.

The precocious Roberts sent copies of the book to every literary superstar he could think of, including Tennyson, Swinburne, Arnold, Longfellow, Whitman, and Wendell Holmes, but it was the response from critics in Canada that was most notable. *Rose-Belford's Canadian*

Monthly saw the book as a sign of 'the spread of a genuine literary spirit in Canada,' while Archibald Lampman, himself a budding poet, could scarcely contain his glee: '[it was] a wonderful thing that such a work could be done by a Canadian...*one of ourselves.*' He admitted to have been under 'the depressing conviction that we were situated hopelessly on the outskirts of civilization where no literature or art could be, and that it was useless to expect that anything great could be done by any of our companions, still more useless to expect that we could do it ourselves.'[163] But Roberts had shown him the light.

Soon, Roberts was at the centre of a group that became known as the Confederation Poets (although, like Canada First, the name did not come into wide usage until much later, when William Lighthall published a poem entitled 'To the Poets of Confederation, My Friends and Companions' in his 1922 collection *Old Measures*). Over time, other poets, such as Pauline Johnson, Isabella Valancy Crawford, and Alfred Durrant Watson, would flutter around the edges of the group, but at its core were six men: Roberts, Anglican ministers Wilfred Campbell and Frederick George Scott, Archibald Lampman and Duncan Campbell Scott, both civil servants, and Roberts' cousin Bliss Carman, an itinerant journalist. All were born in the decade of Confederation, and all were captivated by the ideology that had infused Canada First: that a new nation needed its own literature. And by common consent, they were the poets to give it that literature.

Their output was not large, but each successive volume of poetry was taken as proof that the nation was finding itself in a literary sense. Typical was the response elicited by Frederick George Scott's *The Soul's Quest*, published in 1888. William Lighthall gushed that

a Canadian literature, promising to be fine, conscious and powerful, is budding and blossoming, book after book, writer after writer. The nature of it shows that it is the result of Confederation. Its generation is that which has grown up under the influences of the united country.

Roberts added his own assessment in a column that he wrote for the *St. John Progress*: 'in all Canadian literary effort there is manifest a gain in culture in breadth, in insight, in facility...we are ripening...We are getting more self-reliant. We are beginning to work more in our own way…Such a beginning is rarely made till a people begins also to realize itself a nation.'[164]

Some of the highest praise, though, was reserved for the work of their predecessor, Charles Mair. His *Dreamland and other Poems* had not been universally acclaimed, his fellow Canada Firster R.G. Haliburton judging the poems to be too derivative of the verse of the old country. As he wrote in the Halifax *Daily Reporter*, 'we must bid goodbye to the literary grave-cloths of former years, and strive to create a new school that will interpret the fresh new life of a young nation.' Privately, he was even harsher: 'For God's sake drop the old style. You're living in a new world and you must write in the language of the living to living men.'[165] As Mair tried to provide for his young family, first in Portage la Prairie and later in Prince Albert, he must have mulled over Haliburton's critique. He began work on a verse drama about the native chief Tecumseh, who had died while defending Upper Canada against American invaders during the War of 1812. Through the 1880s he toiled away, convinced that the patriotism implicit in the story answered Haliburton's criticisms.

Finally, in early 1886, *Tecumseh* was published. Later scholars would conclude that Mair's nationalism had gotten the better of his poetic muse, but contemporaries were enthralled. More than one critic compared it to Shakespeare's *Henry V*, while others referred to it as 'purely Canadian.' It was the nation's greatest literary achievement, critics raved, and Mair its greatest national poet. But *Tecumseh* had no bigger booster than Mair's old friend George Denison. As one central Ontario newspaper wrote, 'you can't go within a mile of the National Club without being enquired of by Colonel G.T. Denison if you have read *Tecumseh*, and if not, why not.'[166]

But despite such accolades, all was not right in Canadian culture, as the later history of the Confederation Group of Poets reveals. The group, which Roberts held together for so many years with baling wire and glue, fell apart in the 1890s in an episode that has gone down in Canadian literary history as the War of the Poets. The gauntlet was thrown by American journalist Joseph Dana Miller, whose article 'The Singers of Canada,' published in New York's *Munsey's Magazine* in May 1895, ranked Canada's leading poets, praising Roberts, Lampman, and Carman but placing Campbell towards the bottom of the list as a rhetorician rather than a poet. The first response came in an anonymous article in the *Toronto Sunday World* that accused Carman of plagiarism, and cited passage after passage from his work, along with the lines from Rosetti, Longfellow, Kipling, and Stevenson they ostensibly copied. 'He has gone from poet to poet,' charged the article, provocatively entitled 'Poetry and Piracy,' and 'has stolen, in so far as he is capable, the ground work in style and rhythm of his vague lyrics.' A week later, the article's author owned up: it was Wilfred Campbell, who admitted that he had felt slighted by Miller's article, which he had learned was written with input from none other than Roberts, Lampman, and Carman.

Soon, newspapers, poets, critics, and academics had jumped into the fray, some taking Campbell's side, others accusing him of sour grapes. Carman confessed that he had unconsciously plagiarized a line from Lampman, but had amended the poem as soon as he was informed of his misstep. More importantly, the exchange revealed some interesting details about the Confederation Poets in particular, and Canadian litera-ture in general. In one letter, Carman admitted that he had only met Duncan Campbell Scott once and that he had never met Lampman, something that called into question whether the Confederation Group of Poets really constituted a group. The controversy also laid bare the prac-tice of 'log-rolling,' the tendency of certain poets to praise each others' work over-indulgently or to pass off their glowing comments as objective criticism. It even came out that one reviewer, who had savaged Camp-bell's *Mordred and Hildebrand*, had not even read the book but instead had relied upon the opinions of others who said they had read it. Finally, in August 1895, after two months of mudslinging, the *Globe* called for an end: the argument 'has ceased to be either amusing or instructive.'

But the damage had been done. The reading public, whose interest in poetry had been tenuous at best, turned away from their poets, perhaps accepting *The Week*'s judgement that the controversy had revealed little more than 'childish indiscretions.' Even worse, the Confederation Group was made fun of, most famously in A.C. Stewart's *Scribblers in the Service of Folly* (1896), which skewered each member of the group, from Roberts' 'tantramarian nonsense' to Campbell's 'mimicked Tennysonian rant.'[167] It would take years for Canadian poetry to recover from this embar-rassing public spat. Publishers shied away from it, and in 1901 Edward Caswell guessed that there were no more than 200 people in the entire country who were interested in buying a volume of Canadian verse. Six years later, Caswell reported that the collected poems of Isabella Valancy Crawford had sold fewer than 500 copies in its first sixteen months. It is impossible to say how much of this disinterest was because of the war of the poets, but the spat cannot have helped the situation any.

The War of the Poets was emblematic of deeper maladies affecting Canadian culture generally. In the first place, cultural elites were mired in a chicken-or-egg dilemma. Which came first: national culture, or national sentiment? For Sara Jeannette Duncan, it was pointless to hope for a distinct culture until there was a distinct national life: 'So long as Canada remains in political obscurity, content to thrive only at the roots, so long will the leaves and blossoms of art and literature be scanty and stunted products of our national energy...A national literature cannot be looked for as an outcome of anything less than a complete national existence.' Roberts agreed, saying that 'the literature of a people...is the effect, not the cause, of the national character.' Joseph Edmund Collins put it rather more colourfully, noting that one may as well 'hope for "roses in December, ice in June" as look for a literature without a nationality.'[168]

But others believed that it was the job of painters, composers, writers, and sculptors to build a national character by giving it cultural expression. For the editor of *The Nation*, it fell to the painters, by creating a native school of art, to build a national sentiment:

> We rejoice...at every genuine indication of the growth of a native school of art. Among our Canadian lakes and rivers may be found scenery equal to anything that the old world presents to the eye; and the evidence of the familiar study of nature, and a discernment of the poetry which lurks under its most homely aspects, are the truest evidence of that artistic feeling on which all genuine national progress must depend.

L.J. Burpee agreed, arguing that a 'strong and wholesome native literature' had to be in place to guide the new dominion to nationhood.[169]

As the *literati* debated this circular argument, they also warned of two other obstacles to the achievement of a national culture. The first, related to the practice of log-rolling, can be put down to over-enthusiasm: the tendency to over-praise a work for the simple fact that it was Canadian. In a sense, the first enemy of a national culture was, ironically, cultural nationalism. Even before Confederation, E.H. Dewart had warned against the trend towards indiscriminate praise simply on the basis of the creator's place of residence, but the fervent nationalism of the late nineteenth century seems to have exacerbated this tendency. In 1884, John E. Logan cautioned readers about the 'noxious mixture of colonialism and nationalism' that bred over-flattering reviews, many of which were as 'reliable as patent medicine advertisements, and probably as fostering to good literature.'[170] Wilfred Campbell was even harsher, warning that most literary criticism was 'mere senseless gush or brutal abuse or mean insinuation,' while Archibald Lampman wrote that literary critics 'greet every new production of whatever merit or demerit with the same ridiculous praises decked out in the same fulsome and meaningless phraseology.' Everything that was wrong with this tendency was summed up in Ernest Jackson Hathaway's reflection on Canadian novels. In his view, it mattered little whether these books were 'high enough in standard to constitute in themselves a literature'; so long as 'they interpret the Canadian spirit and…express the Canadian point of view,' their value could not be questioned.[171] Painters also had to take care. Harriet Ford warned in 1894 that a Canadian resident painting a Canadian subject did not constitute a Canadian school of art; critics should stop praising painters simply because they were Canadian, she wrote, and instead must demand more of them. As Sara Jeannette Duncan wrote, 'Gold is gold all over the world, and the literary standard should be equally unalterable. If not, the inferior metal we pretend to appraise at the same value because it was mined in our own country will be certain one day to be tried as by fire, with disastrous results.'[172]

Ironically, the second affliction was the direct opposite of the first: despite the fervent nationalism of the Confederation era, despite the glowing reviews of critics, despite the work of boosters and promoters from the Marquess of Dufferin to George Denison, the general public still demonstrated an inexplicable reluctance to buy Canadian products. Art collectors who would pay a premium for third-rate Dutch oils refused to pay enough for a Canadian painting to cover the cost of the framing. Newspapers rarely touched the best poetry of Fréchette or LeMay, but would happily print 'the most worthless fugitive French verse.'[173] Booksellers had little interest in stocking Canadian authors because there was more money to be made on cheap British or American reprints. 'For this indifference and denial of merited encouragement,' wrote one critic, 'there is no excuse, when so many foreign productions, inferior to Canadian works, receive liberal patronage.'[174]

This state of affairs certainly outraged Charles Mair, who had spent the best part of his life trying to encourage a Canadian literature, and with it a Canadian nationalism. On Dominion Day 1891, he poured out his frustrations in a letter to George Denison. He had staked his savings on the development of the town of Prince Albert, but its failure to get a railway link plunged him towards financial ruin, and into mental despair. Racial and cultural antagonisms in Canada had grown more bitter after the hanging of Louis Riel, he wrote, and everything was made worse by a depression that had gripped parts of the country for two decades. By all indications, Confederation had failed and the exuberance he felt when he visited Henry Morgan's hotel room in 1868 was crushed. But his greatest frustration was the failure of his cultural mission:

> To Canadian literature I have given more time and labour than it deserves. Canadians are mainly barbarians and consist, 99 out of 100, of backs and stomachs. To expect our polished boors to enjoy art in any of its developments is too much. I am done with the 'Canadian public' which consists of mere cattle, or worse…its true and only enjoyment (the heights of Canadian ambition in fact) are guzzling and drinking and rotten politics.[175]

We can surely forgive Mair for his outburst against the Canadian public. He was deeply hurt that thirty years of cajoling, promoting, and encouraging, while it produced some fine poetry, paintings, and buildings, had apparently done little to create any demand for a Canadian culture. He was the author of one of the most critically acclaimed works ever produced in Canada, yet he was unable to make a living from writing, and indeed was staring at financial ruin. And he knew why: Canadians preferred imported culture to the products of their own country. It was a reality that would change very little during his lifetime.

Chapter 8

Importing Culture

In June 1891, Sir John A. Macdonald, who had been Canada's prime minister for all but five of its first twenty-four years, died. He had captivated the nation with his brilliance and vision, and outraged it with his dissolution and corruption; with him, Canadian politics had never been boring. And now he had to be memorialized. The Marquess of Lorne made known his preference for a museum in Sir John's memory, but the campaign to commemorate the late, lamented prime minister in bronze and stone was already underway. Committees in five cities—Ottawa, Toronto, Montreal, Hamilton, and Kingston—announced that they would raise monuments, and all were in the market for a suitable sculptor. The contract for Ottawa's memorial went to Louis-Philippe Hébert, one of Canada's greatest sculptors, while Hamilton MacCarthy won the commission for the monument in Toronto, his native city. But the contracts for the monuments in Montreal, Hamilton, and Kingston went to a little known British sculptor named George Wade, who enjoyed the active support of Lorne and the Canadian High Commissioner in London, Sir Charles Tupper. Some memorial committees rationalized the employment of a British sculptor as a way to emphasize Canada's connection with the mother country, but Robert Carlyle saw only our colonialism in art. In the *Canadian Magazine*, he compared Wade's statue of Macdonald in Montreal to Hébert's fine monument to Ignace Bourget, the former Bishop of Montreal, which sat just across from Macdonald in Dominion Square. After looking at the two, Carlyle wondered, 'would any person care to say that Canadians must always go abroad to retain real art?'[176]

Charles Mair had certainly been right about literature, a field with which he was intimately familiar, but if he had been a sculptor, a painter, a musician, an architect, or a playwright, his concerns would have been equally valid. In each of those fields, Canadian creators faced stiff competition from Britain and the United States. It would be simple

Hébert's monument to Bishop Bourget, Montreal. c. 1902–12.

to say that Canadian culture was handicapped by a sentimental attachment to Mother Britain, or that it was the victim of a much bigger and wealthier society to the south that was able to extend economies of scale to the manufacture of cultural products. The reality was both of these, but it was also much more.

All cultures are, in some measure, derivative; they evolve by adopting and adapting influences from other societies. The Greeks called it creative borrowing and, for them, it had few negative connotations. But having invested so much emotional capital in creating a national culture, elites in Canada were leery of cultural imports. In some fields, like literature and drama, their concerns were justified; in others, imports filled a void that simply could not be filled by the native born. Either way, there was one painful reality that no one could deny: it was not easy for Canadian artists to make a living in their own country.

———————

The British North America Act may have created a Canadian nation but, as many cultural commentators knew, it had not created a Canadian nationality. Sentimental attachment to Britain remained strong, and not just because the majority of Canadians traced their roots to the British Isles. Anyone who went to school in English Canada was educated in a system that celebrated British culture, idealized British history, and inculcated British values, and people like Egerton Ryerson made sure that their school readers were filled with Sir Walter Scott and William Wordsworth rather than John Richardson and Charles Sangster. He also ensured that any art they were able to see came from the old world; in 1857, he established the Canadian Educational Museum, the only continuous public display of paintings in Canada West, but all were copies of European works that Ryerson had purchased or commissioned. The fruits of British culture were familiar and much loved—it is inconceivable that they would have been cast aside just because a piece of legislation changed the political status of the British North American colonies.

French Canada placed more emphasis on the development of an indigenous culture, but even then, the pull of the old world was strong. Ultramontanism, or the tendency of the Roman Catholic Church in Canada to look to the Vatican for inspiration and guidance, is usually understood in theological and political terms, but it had a cultural dimension as well. Ignace Bourget was avowedly ultramontanist, passionate about European art, and did everything he could to impose his views on the parishes he controlled. Each new church needed decoration, but Bourget saw no point in hiring a local artist to execute a devotional painting when a copy of an Old Master could be imported from Europe at half the cost. As a result, huge numbers of paintings and engravings were brought in from Europe—18,536 in 1855 alone—each of which represented a commission that might have gone to a Canadian artist. And those artists could make much more money copying European paintings for churches or social elites than doing their own compositions and evolving an indigenous style. Antoine-Sébastien Falardeau, who set up a studio in Florence and accepted commissions to reproduce Italian paintings for wealthy Canadians, built an enormous reputation, as well as a considerable fortune, as a painter; but, as art historian Russell Harper noted, he was really just a professional copyist.

Just as important as the sentimental element was the fact that the new dominion lacked many of the legislative tools that it needed to foster its own culture. As D'Arcy McGee wrote in 1858, in a comment that was relevant to much more than the book trade, 'Every facility is offered to the English or American publisher to inundate the country with their publications, whereas the Canadian publisher is obstructed by every possible means.'[177] Even something as simple as mailing costs disadvantaged Canadian printers. The postal agreement between Canada and the United States allowed magazines to enter Canada at a postage rate that seemed criminally cheap: an American firm could ship printed matter from New York City to Montreal for one cent a pound, but a Canadian publisher wanting to send magazines from Montreal to Toronto had to pay four cents a pound. British publishers were at an even greater disadvantage, for they had to pay twenty cents a pound to mail the same shipment. When this was combined with the already lower price of American publications, the price differential between American magazines on the one hand, and Canadian and British on the other, was enormous.

Most damaging, though, was the fact that Canadian authors, composers, artists, and playwrights enjoyed virtually no legal protection for their work, either before or after Confederation. The Literary Copyright Act of 1842 forbade the import into British North America of pirated reprints of British copyrighted works, including American works that had been copyrighted in Britain. This annoyed Canadian printers, who had been supplying reprinted British and American books and magazines since the 1820s, and booksellers, who had done well off the sale of these cheap, albeit illegal, editions, but it made no mention of Canadian creators, who were put at the mercy of printers in all three countries. As Goldwin Smith put it, 'a Canadian writes an important book in Canada and publishes it in England and the United States. He cannot afford to print a separate edition for the small market of Canada. But if he does not, he will be liable…to having his book pirated by any publisher in Canada who chooses to bring out a cheap and inferior edition.'[178] Most publishers were unapologetic; at least G.P. Putnam's in New York had the decency to send to Susanna Moodie ten copies of the pirated edition of *Roughing It in the Bush*, along with an apology for not being legally required to pay her. It was the same for a playwright, artist, or composer: any printer could copy and sell their work, pay them nothing in the way of royalties, and it was all perfectly legal. And it wasn't just printers and publishers who took advantage of the loopholes. In 1883, the Prince Edward Island artist Robert Harris was commissioned by the federal government to paint a portrait of the Fathers of Confederation, and he duly completed the assignment. But from that time until the portrait's destruction when the Parliament Buildings burned down in 1916, government departments made thousands of reproductions of the painting, some of very indifferent quality. Despite having been led to believe that he would share in the profits, Harris received not a penny in royalties from the reproductions of his work.

Long before that, however, a British government committee had concluded that the copyright law was failing. Most people in British North America were too poor to buy British books at British prices; in any case, the legislation had done nothing to curb the supply of cheap American reprints. They were still widely available, for booksellers happily and easily evaded the law. The response was the 1847 Colonial Copyright Act (also known as the Foreign Reprints Act), which allowed booksellers to import pirated reprints. Provincial customs officers would collect a duty of 12.5 percent on each volume, with the proceeds being turned over to the British copyright holder. But this act, too, was flawed, as far as the British were concerned. The customs agents were local appointees with little interest in putting themselves out to enforce regulations that benefited only English publishers and authors. Again, the legislation made no attempt to provide protection for Canadian creators.

Confederation did little to change the situation, for one of the things that British legislators kept to themselves when the BNA Act was drafted was control over copyright throughout the British Empire, and it was a power that they guarded jealously and used to their own advantage. For example, when negotiating with British authors, American publishers often insisted on having the Canadian rights included, giving them an additional market at a negligible cost and ensuring that Canadian publishers were unable to compete with them. The British government, anxious not to alienate the American book trade, showed no inclination to do anything about this inequity, even though the government in Ottawa passed half a dozen separate acts between 1872 and 1894 to protect the rights of Canadian authors and publishers. All of them were immediately disallowed by the British government. Slowly but surely, control of the Canadian domestic book market was falling into American hands.

A perfect example of this process involved William Kirby's novel of New France, *The Golden Dog*. It was first published in 1877 in the United States, where the firm was granted copyright, but when the publisher went bankrupt the copyright fell into the hands of the creditors. Kirby attempted to buy back the rights to his own book, but the creditors kept raising the price and he simply could not afford it. Eventually, another American publisher brought out a new edition of *The Golden Dog*, without the author's permission, so Kirby complained to the federal government. Its response was that they were powerless unless a Canadian edition or a French translation appeared. Kirby dutifully commissioned a French translation, which appeared in 1884, yet in 1896 another American publisher announced plans to publish a condensed version of *The Golden Dog*, with or without Kirby's authorization. In their eyes, and indeed under Canadian and British law, Kirby had no legal right to his book. On another occasion, a Canadian publishing house arranged with the British firm T. Fisher Unwin to secure exclusive Canadian rights to *The Raiders*, by best-selling British author S.R. Crockett. The Canadian edition was duly published, at considerable expense, and then Unwin appeared with its own cheap edition that it marketed aggressively in Canada. Though in violation of the agreement

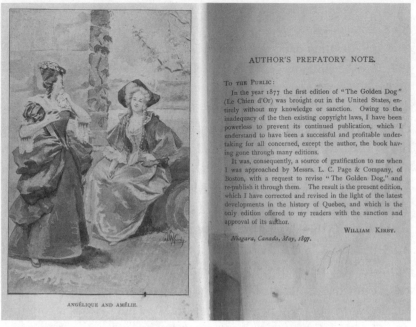

ANGÉLIQUE AND AMÉLIE.

William Kirby's *cri de coeur* over Canadian copyright laws, 1897.

between the two publishers, it was completely legal under the prevailing copyright regime.

But the lobbying by writers, publishers, and printers was incessant and in 1893, as the British government prepared 'to disallow for the sixth time Canadian copyright legislation, Ottawa slapped a tariff on American books entering Canada (the federal government did have the power to legislate customs duties). The response was immediate: Washington howled to the British government that it would retaliate against British authors and publishers unless Canada was forced back in line, and British delegations descended on Ottawa to cajole and bluster the federal government into backing down. But Ottawa held firm, even boosting the tariff on softcover books to 20 percent in 1897 as a way to force the imperial parliament to grant concessions. Finally, a victory of sorts was achieved with the Copyright Act of 1900, which allowed any author to sign a separate contract with a publisher for a Canadian edition. To safeguard the rights of Canadian publishers to sign similar deals with British or American authors, it also prohibited the import of any work published in the British Empire or the United States if the Canadian rights had been sold to a Canadian publisher. For the *Canadian Magazine*, this was a great victory, 'the first step towards making Canadian authorship a remunerative occupation by making the business of publishing itself more remunerative.'[179] The legislation would become even more author-friendly in 1906, when a suit launched in the Quebec Superior Court ruled that foreign authors should receive protection for their works in Canada. This was especially important for literature published in French, because literary piracy in Quebec persisted much longer than it did in the rest of Canada.

Before that success, though, there were a few alternatives open to the ambitious Canadian company wanting to get around the restrictive legislation. One was pioneered by the American-born Toronto publisher George Morang. In August 1897, he took advantage of the 1891 Anglo-American Copyright Agreement, which brought in agency publishing and allowed Canadian publishers to strike deals with British and American firms to issue the works of Canadian and non-Canadian authors. He sought out Hall Caine, the best-selling author of *The Christian*, and negotiated special Canadian rights to publish a seventy-five-cent paperback edition simultaneously with foreign publishers. It was the first time that a Canadian publisher had made such an arrangement and it was a great success, going through three printings and selling over 10,000 copies. Morang quickly looked for other authors to sign, and other Toronto publishers followed suit. By the time the 1900 Copyright Act came into effect, many of the era's best-selling authors, including Rudyard Kipling, Sir Arthur Conan Doyle, and Marie Corelli, were regularly arranging for separate Canadian editions.

Another solution was for a Canadian entrepreneur to partner with a British or American publisher and open a branch plant in Canada. One such firm was the Anglo-Canadian Music Publishers' Association, established in Toronto in 1885 to ensure that British composers and Canadian printers, rather than American pirates, reaped the rewards of selling the most popular sheet music of the day. The company did little to stem the flood of imported sheet music, the value of which climbed from $50,000 annually in the 1890s to over $300,000 in 1912, but it marked the beginning of a strategy that would catch on after the First World War. This trend was even stronger in book publishing, where Oxford University Press, Macmillan, Collins, and half a dozen other British publishers allied with local entrepreneurs to open Canadian subsidiaries so they could prevent the piracy of their work. Oxford University Press, which had previously used a travelling representative to sell books in Canada, opened a branch in Toronto in 1904. For years, its bread and butter was the Oxford Bible and prayer and hymn books, all of which were imported from Britain or the United States as plates or page blocks, but in 1913 the company published *The Oxford Book of Canadian Verse*, a sign of its determination to become an indigenous publisher rather than just a branch plant.

A third solution was to find and exploit a niche market. The Methodist Book and Publishing House grew out of an 1829 decision of the Conference of the Methodist Episcopal Church in Canada to print a weekly newspaper; by the 1870s, it had grown into an aggressive marketer of books to the church market and, under Book Steward William Briggs, became the largest publisher in nineteenth-century Canada. In 1885, it printed over 245,023 separate items, from hymn books to religious tracts, totalling over 31 million pages, and its revenue soared from nearly $24,000 in 1874 to over $103,000 in 1890. By that time, the firm had started to expand its contract printing, with revenues from that source increasing from $10,000 in 1874 to over $50,000 in 1890, but it was the virtual monopoly on church-related publishing that allowed it to go into other kinds of printing. It began with works that promoted what was known as Christian edification—'A thoroughly secular and often irreligious literature is being evidently diffused, and it is the duty of the Church to provide a literature surcharged with the vitalizing influence of an earnest Christianity,' observed an 1886 report—but soon branched out into a broader range of titles, including Catherine Parr Traill's *Pearls and Pebbles* (1893), Charles G.D. Roberts' *The Forge in the Forest* (1896), Ernest Thompson Seton's *Two Little Savages* (1903), and Nellie McClung's *Sowing Seeds in Danny* (1908), all of which were published with Briggs' name as the imprint. At the same time, the firm's directors looked for other business opportunities. In the 1880s, in cooperation with William Gage and Copp Clark, two other firms with strong Methodist connections, they established a stranglehold over textbook marketing with tactics that today would be regarded as price-fixing; in those days, it was simply good business sense. The Methodist Book and Publishing House also became a national leader in agency publishing, securing the Canadian rights for major British and

American firms such as Thomas Nelson, G.P. Putnam, and Cambridge University Press. It printed catalogues for Eaton's and Simpson's department stores, and in 1909 won a government contract to print and bind the sessional papers of the Ontario Legislative Assembly. What started as a modest venture to publish a church newspaper had become the largest printer-publisher in Canada.

The Methodist Book and Publishing House always operated within the law, but other companies found fortune through a less scrupulous regard for matters of copyright. The Montreal publisher John Lovell had counted on Canadian legislation to help his printing company, but when the 1872 Act was disallowed, turning him into a publishing pirate, Lovell was unfazed. He promptly expanded his new printing plant in Montreal and supplied both his New York and Montreal subsidiaries with growing numbers of pirated editions. John Ross Robertson was another publisher who decided to join the pirates rather than fight them. Using his newspaper, the Toronto *Evening Telegram*, as a springboard, he launched a book pirating business, beginning in February 1877 with a ten-cent edition (legal editions sold for fifty to seventy-five cents) of *Moody's Anecdotes*, a compendium of spiritual passages and thoughts. Popular American novelist Bret Harte's *Thankful Blossom* was next—it sold for three cents a copy, at a time when the *Telegram* sold for two cents. By the end of 1877, Robertson had announced twenty one new titles, including such classics as *That Husband of Mine*, *My Mother-in-Law*, and *The Rise and Fall of the Moustache*. That year alone, he probably sold 40,000 to 50,000 copies in total. In 1878, he came up with a new gimmick: four books in one cover for fifteen cents, an innovation that allowed him to add thirty-five new titles and eleven reprintings that year.

Robertson was a pirate plain and simple—as his source, he used current American journals that published novels in serial form, and could often get an illegal edition ready for sale within weeks of its publication in the United States—and he likely would have defended his actions by arguing that copyright legislation was unjust and that he had a right to fight that injustice to meet the public demand for books. But despite his financial success, Robertson was really part of the problem, as far as cultural elites were concerned. They always tried to patronize Canadian writers by purchasing their works, but the greater mass of book-buyers were not so conscientious. How many of them would seek out a Canadian book when the shops and newsstands were filled with cheap editions of American works? When faced with Bret Harte for three cents or Charles Mair for seventy-five cents, what would they choose? (The sad truth was that even if Mair was priced at three cents, readers probably would still have chosen Harte—as publishers well know, some books simply do not sell at any price.) Everyone who cared about such things knew the answer, and the best-seller lists analyzed by historian Mary Vipond provide the proof. In the fifteen years after the top-ten lists began to appear in the industry journal *Bookseller and Stationer* in 1899, only thirty-one of the 150 best-sellers were written by Canadian authors, and eight of those were by Sir Gilbert Parker and Basil King, who had long since left Canada for greener pastures elsewhere. As long as imports flooded the Canadian marketplace at a fraction of the cost of native works, writers and publishers would face an uphill battle for the attention of the reading public, and for the financial rewards that accompanied success.

If the legislative obstacles were substantial, the economic ones were even larger. The publishing industries in both Britain and the United States dwarfed Canada's, and were able to extend the economies of scale to the Canadian market. How could a Canadian magazine with a circulation of a few thousand, wondered Goldwin Smith, compete with an American magazine that printed 150,000 copies?[180] American publishing houses that printed editions running to tens of thousands of copies could afford higher production values, with glossy covers, better illustrations, and heavier paper stock than small-run Canadian publications. They also developed a warehousing system that allowed them to ship books quickly and cheaply to wholesalers in Canada, who then passed them on to shops or to itinerant book pedlars roaming the countryside. When catalogue shopping came into vogue in the late nineteenth century, it became even easier to purchase cheap American books. The consequences of this, to some minds, were dire. Rosanna Leprohon wondered very politely how 'our American neighbours should continue to inundate the country with reading-matter, intended to meet all wants and suit all tastes and sympathies, at prices which enable everyone to partake of this never-ending and ever-varying feast,' but others were blunter. 'Any one who has currently to appraise the imported literature of the time, or glances at it in its loud disarray in the news-stores, will be aware of the great deterioration in the mass,' wrote G. Mercer Adam in 1889, his eyes firmly fixed on the glut of American novels and periodicals filling the shelves of most book shops in Canada.[181]

Nowhere was the economic muscle of the American cultural industry more evident than in the theatre. 'There is no Canadian Drama,' wrote Jesse Edgar Middleton provocatively in 1914. 'It is merely a branch of the American Theatre, and, let it be said, a most profitable one.'[182] Here, the problem was partly due to the pernicious effects of copyright legislation, but more importantly to the concentration of the North American theatrical industry in the hands of producers and entrepreneurs in the United States.

Imported culture at its finest: Charlottetown thespians perform *H.M.S. Pinafore.* c. 1890s.

The roots of this went back many years, when the theatre was either frowned upon or actively discouraged, especially by religious authorities; to be a theatre promoter was only marginally more respectable than being an actor. 'Canadians cannot be called a nation of theatre lovers,' observed Frederic Robson in 1908. 'Religious sentiment which once placed the theatre as an accompaniment of the downward path is of too recent existence to be suddenly up-rooted.' Part of the blame, he thought, rested with the theatre-goer. Admittedly there were more of them than there had ever been in the past, but they were no more discriminating: 'You can draw a "house" with the *Broadway Maids*, which every man buying a ticket knows to be a fraud, when empty benches would greet Shakespeare, which every man in town knew before hand would prove a treat.' Only the ticket buyer had the power to improve Canadian theatre, 'but in nine cases out of ten, that man thinks so little of the quality of his amusement' that he was willing to watch any fluff advertised in the newspapers. 'The theatre-goer who remains away from the play of merit does as much to kill all merit on the stage as the one who turns out to the melodrama or frothy comic opera,' Robson concluded.[183]

Editors, too, were to blame, for printing effusive advance reviews written not by impartial critics but by theatre managers who gave free tickets to newspaper editors to ensure their continued support. Drama criticism in Canada was virtually non-existent—according to Robson, only three Canadian newspapers published drama columns that were worth reading—so the theatre-goer who wanted to learn discernment and taste had nowhere to go for guidance.

But most serious was the fact that US interests controlled Canadian theatre bookings. The copyright issue was a factor. It was the practice for playwrights to sell Canadian rights along with the American rights to producers in the United States; as a result, if the producer chose not to mount a certain production in Canada, there was no way for Canadians to see it. This affected many of the greatest British playwrights of the day—the works of John Galsworthy, Granville Barker, Arnold Bennett, Arthur Pinero, and J.M. Barrie were rarely performed by professional companies in Canada because the American producers who owned their rights weren't interested in mounting Canadian productions.

But performers as well as audiences were affected. Most of the large theatres in Canada were either owned or controlled by US compa-nies, like the Theatre Syndicate of New York, which were responsible for booking acts. They may have used local agents—C.P. Walker of Winnipeg booked acts for halls across the prairies, including the largest

theatre in the Canadian west, Winnipeg's 1,798-seat Walker Theatre—
but the ultimate decision about what and who appeared on stage in
Vancouver, Toronto, or Montreal was made in the United States. So,
as B.K. Sandwell wrote in 'The Annexation of Our Stage' in 1912, 'the
only road to the applause of a Toronto theatre audience is by way of
Broadway. The Montreal girl who wants to show her own people that
she can act must sign an agreement with a New York manager.' Canada,
he concluded, 'is the only nation in the world whose stage is entirely
controlled by aliens.'[184]

A typical Canadian theatrical offering of the late nineteenth century.

There were benefits to this, particularly in that Canada was visited by
the most popular international performers of the nineteenth century:
violinist Fritz Kreisler, the Hess English Opera Company, conductor/
composers Sergei Rachmaninoff, Artur Rubenstein, and Ignace Jan
Paderewski, Swedish opera sensation Jenny Lind, and legendary French
actress Sarah Bernhardt, who came to Canada seven times between
1880 and 1916 despite the church-sanctioned anti-Semitic demonstra-
tions that protested her visits. Still, the fact that Canada, unlike smaller
countries that had developed a national theatre tradition, was forced

'to take the crumbs from our masters' tables,'[185] as Robson put it, meant that there was little incentive for Canadians to try to make a living in the theatre world. There were amateur theatricals aplenty, but the world of professional theatre was largely closed to the aspiring youth who was unwilling to leave the country.

Here was the rub: there was an abundance of amateur theatre, art, and music, but for Canadian culture to evolve to the next level it required the kind of opportunities, especially in terms of formal training, that simply did not exist here. For example, there was virtually nothing in the way of musical education available, and what existed was largely confined to religious institutions. Few public schools taught music and when they did it was almost invariably vocal, because of the cost of instruments. For training in instrumental music (particularly the piano, which had become a symbol of middle-class status by the late nineteenth century), people had to rely on private teachers; many of them were experienced and accomplished, but there were also a good number of unqualified charlatans who adopted exotic names to make themselves sound more respectable. Not until 1874, with the founding of the Brantford Conservatory of Music, Canada's first, was there any mechanism to establish standards for musical accomplishment, either for teachers or students. Nor was there any music education at a higher level. The University of Trinity College in Toronto appointed a professor of music in 1856, but offered no courses or examinations in music until the 1880s. In such circumstances, if there was to be a musical life in Canada that went beyond folk music, it would have to be created by imported musicians.

Art education was a little more developed, thanks to the groundwork laid by the Mechanics' Institutes. Teaching was a way for established artists to earn extra income between commissions, either by tutoring individual pupils or opening private art schools. Napoléon Bourassa was lucky enough to win teaching contracts from a number of large schools in Montreal in the years before Confederation. After the founding of the Royal Canadian Academy, art instruction became more widely available due to the provision that, as a condition of membership, academicians had to provide a certain number of free lessons annually. This tutoring was done in private classes or in the new art schools that were starting to open across the country, such as the École des arts et manufactures

A women's violin quartet, Conservatory of Music, Toronto, 1888.

in Montreal (1871), the Ontario Society of Artists' school in Toronto (1876), and the Owens Art Institute in Saint John (1884).

But Canadian art had a lot of catching up to do, something that became apparent with the publication of the book *Picturesque Canada*. The brainchild of two American promoters, who patterned it after the immensely successful *Picturesque America* to satisfy growing middle-class demand for travel and scenery books, it was to consist of 500

The cover of *Picturesque Canada*, published in Toronto by James Clarke, 1883.

illustrations by members of the Royal Canadian Academy, working under art director Lucius O'Brien, and an accompanying text, edited by George Grant of Queen's University. Intended, in Grant's words, to 'stimulate national sentiment and contribute to the rightful development of the nation,'[186] it was published in 1883 to great critical acclaim, proving, according to *The Week*, 'that Canadians are ready enough to give a cordial reception to any home-production which proves itself equal in merit to what they can procure from abroad.' The *Globe* agreed, calling it 'a striking phase of national progress, and one that cannot fail to have far-reaching results in attracting attention to our material as well as our aesthetic achievement. Every patriotic Canadian will heartily wish it all success.'[187]

The only problem was that it was not really Canadian. Much to his chagrin, O'Brien had discovered that few of his chosen artists had mastered the technique of doing black and white sketches that could be used as the basis for wood-engravings. As a result, many of the works that had been commissioned from Canadian artists had to be done by American commercial illustrators before they were turned into engravings; of the 543 illustrations in the book, fully 452 were the work of American artists. Few had the nerve to point out what Ontario Society of Artists president John Fraser did: that *Picturesque Canada*, far from being 'a striking phase of national progress,' was almost entirely American, right down to the engravers and printers.

———•◦•———

One solution to this state of affairs was to send young Canadians out of the country for training. Ever since the days of the French Regime, it had been customary to send promising youths back to France for a couple of years to hone their skills in music, painting, or carving; in a sense, rather than importing the teachers (this happened in music, which was invigorated in nineteenth-century Canada by an influx of European conductors, bandmasters, choir leaders, and teachers), they would export the students, who would then return with new skills and techniques. Furthermore, it was widely accepted that part of the process of learning to paint was to study great works of art in European galleries. So, even if there had been a wider range of educational opportunities available in Canada, as there was in the United States, the exodus of hopeful young Canadian painters, sculptors, and architects to the capitals of Europe would likely still have occurred.

Typically, a youthful artist would work away in solitude, learning to draw by copying from books or sketching from life, until a mentor sensed a level of ability that could only be developed by instruction that was unavailable locally. For Robert Harris, whose first tutor had prohibited him from drawing for fear that it would spoil his penmanship, it was an artistically inclined sea captain who promised to take him to the galleries of England so he could study the works of the masters. After making his first visit to England in 1867, Harris painted portraits of local worthies in PEI for $25 each to save enough money to go to Boston to study. Quebec painter Wyatt Eaton was encouraged by a Montreal craftsman to study in New York; when he returned to the Eastern Townships, an art patron there provided the funds to allow him to study in Paris. Louis-Philippe Hébert had already made a name for himself by winning some important commissions when his mentor,

Louis-Philippe Hébert's memorial to Sir John A. Macdonald on Parliament Hill in Ottawa.

Napoléon Bourassa, advised him that the only way to become a sculptor of the first order was to spend some time studying in Paris.

Even after they were established, many artists and sculptors continued to make regular trips to Europe and the United States, to keep abreast of the latest styles and techniques and to meet and work with artists from other countries. Hébert spent as much time in Paris as he did in Canada, and many of his most famous sculptures were executed in France and shipped back to Canada. His figures for the Quebec legislative building, his monument to Paul de Chomedy de Maisonneuve, the founder of Montreal, his Boer War memorial in Calgary, his statues of Sir John A. Macdonald, Queen Victoria, Alexander Mackenzie (all in Ottawa), Ignace Bourget, Bishop Laval, Jeanne Mance, Madeleine de Verchères—all were sculpted and cast in France, and then shipped to Canada. George Reid, who had opened successful portrait studios in Wingham and Kincardine, Ontario, before going to Philadelphia to study, travelled frequently to Europe to visit galleries and the studios of other artists. He was among the more than two dozen Canadian artists who lived in Paris in the late nineteenth century; some stayed for only a few months, while others spent the better part of their professional careers in the French capital.

The danger, of course, was that they might absorb too much in their studies overseas. At the 1886 Colonial and Indian Exhibition in London, Sir Charles Tupper, the Canadian commissioner to the exhibition, asked a British art expert for a report on the display of Canadian art. The report was probably not what Tupper had bargained for. It 'has been rather a shock to me to observe in the Canadian pictures such evident traces of French influence,' wrote the expert, 'the influence, to speak plainly, of a school which is daily becoming more debased.' The wholesale migration of artists to France had done little for Canadian art, he concluded; he wanted to see 'Canadian art Canadian to the backbone.' Reid himself wrote in 1906 that 'we have no Canadian school; we have only influences.'[188] Later scholars, too, would observe that the tendency to make the pilgrimage to European galleries, schools, and *ateliers*, while a necessary part of an artist's education, was a mixed blessing; the exodus to Paris, according to art historian Dennis Reid, forced Canadian artists into a 'self-conscious orientation toward European art and European-trained artists' that would prevent them from developing an indigenous tradition in painting.[189]

——•—•——

But in many fields, there was no real alternative to importing teachers or exporting students, because of a lack of cultural development in the late nineteenth century. Apart from the buildings of the federal Department of Public Works that created the Dominion Image, Canadian architecture had fallen into a rut by the late 1870s, with little in the way of innovation in either materials or styles. But in the United States, architecture was going through a tremendously vibrant period in both respects. Increased use of iron and steel was opening up a whole new range of construction possibilities, most notably with the precursor to what would later be known as the skyscraper, and new styles, such as the Richardsonian Romanesque, were being used to great effect. American architects, in short, were creating the kind of buildings that captured the public imagination.

The big corporations were the first to embrace American architects: Richard Waite of Buffalo was commissioned to design the Standard Life Building in Montreal (1886), the Canada Life Assurance and Bank of Commerce buildings in Toronto (1889), and the Canada Life Assurance building in Montreal (1895); New York's Bruce Price was the architect of choice for the Canadian Pacific Railway (when he died, he was replaced by another American, Walter Painter), and also won the commission to design Montreal's Royal Victoria College (1895–99). The New York firm of McKim, Mead, and White, a legend in modern commercial architecture, took one of the most lucrative prizes of the early twentieth century, the contract for the head office of the Bank of Montreal (1901).

It didn't take long for Canadian architects to protest what they considered to be an unhealthy regard for their American competitors. The fact that the contracts to build the provincial legislatures in Ontario and Alberta both went to Americans raised a few eyebrows—Toronto architect M.B. Aylesworth said he couldn't imagine 'a more unpatriotic act by any government' than the awarding of the contract for the Ontario legislature to Richard Waite, over two Toronto firms[190]—although no one was so bothered by British architects winning plum contracts for the legislatures in British Columbia and Manitoba. When the contract for the Toronto Board of Trade building went to an American, Canadian architects were outraged; when the half-finished building collapsed during construction, they were even more convinced that American firms did not deserve the preferential treatment they were receiving. Tensions were even higher in Montreal, where the Board of Trade originally intended to invite only American firms to enter the design competition for its new office. The Board eventually bowed to pressure and allowed Canadian firms to compete, but even then the playing field was hardly level: American firms received a $300 stipend just for entering, while Canadian companies got nothing. In protest, most members of

the Ontario Association of Architects and the Province of Quebec Association of Architects' boycotted the competition, which was eventually
won by a Boston firm. This, of course, bothered Canadian architects
even more. 'Some businessmen have been very much disposed of late to
place a premium on American architects,' observed J.C.B. Horwood, a
Newfoundland-born architect who trained in New York before joining
a Toronto firm, in 1893. 'We need to be weaned of all such habits of
thought, and to awake to a consciousness of our position as a nation…
never till that is accomplished within us and it has become a habit of
our mind to think thus broadly, can we have work which will possess a
distinctively national mode of expression.'[191]

The fact was, however, that Canadian architects had failed, and they
knew it. Much of their work was either sub-standard or too derivative, and they had not kept pace with changing trends in architecture
internationally. A step in the right direction was the establishment in
1907 of the Royal Architectural Institute of Canada as a national body
to bring regulations and standards to the profession, and to act as a
lobby group to counter the tendency to rely on US firms. But more
importantly, Canadian architects had to change their way of thinking.
Rather than pioneering a new Canadian form of architecture, they had
simply recycled imported designs, with little attempt to adapt them to
the Canadian milieu. This had to change, thought Montreal architect
and founding member of the Royal Canadian Academy Alexander
Cowper Hutchison: 'the stamp of originality which we hope will be
placed on our buildings may prove that Canada is a nation…of which
we may all be proud.'[192]

The change began with the arrival in Canada of the Arts and Crafts
style in the late 1880s. An import from England, it sought to reunite
architecture with painting and sculpture, as it had been in the Middle
Ages. More importantly, it advocated the use of indigenous materials
and stressed the importance of 'naturalness,' the practice of ensuring
that a building blended into its surroundings; in contrast to other
imported architectural styles, Arts and Crafts demanded that it be
adapted to local conditions. Its most vocal proponent in Canada was
Percy Nobbs, a Scotsman who was recruited to take up the Macdonald
Chair in Architecture at McGill University in 1903. Nobbs believed
strongly in the relationship between nationality and architectural

development, and spent his first few weeks in Montreal studying the local architecture, declaring himself particularly impressed with some of the city's row houses and smaller dwellings. He became a passionate advocate of using vernacular forms as the basis for a national style of architecture, arguing that the old traditional styles were the kind of thing 'with which the architect must saturate himself if his work is to be indigenous at all.' The Arts and Crafts style, because of its reliance on place, was particularly well suited to this philosophy, while Nobbs had little time for the Beaux-Arts style, a favourite with US architects of the time, because he regarded it as impersonal and repetitious. 'Standard- ization is the vice of the Americans,' he wrote dismissively.[193]

Nobbs played a decisive role in bringing together the various archi- tectural concepts that were floating around Canada in the early years of the twentieth century: the Arts and Crafts style, the importance of climate in building design, the legitimacy of both English and French forms to the Canadian context, an interest in the vernacular architecture of Quebec and the Maritimes, and a new revival of classical forms. From those elements grew a Canadian architecture, as Ivan Macdonald, the editor of *Construction* magazine, realized in 1908. He complemented Canadian architects for their progress in 'applying themselves assidu- ously to the task of giving Canada an architecture suited to her tradi- tions, her climate, the habits, the tastes and the ideals of her people, and adapted to the use of the materials nature has given her.'[194]

Ironically, one of the American architects that so concerned Nobbs also played a role in the evolution of a distinctly Canadian style. New York architect Bruce Price had been retained by the Canadian Pacific Railway to design stations, but in 1886 he was put to the task of creating a luxury hotel in Banff, where work crews had discovered hot springs. Price drew from a number of sources—a Rhineland castle, a Tudor hall, a Swiss chalet, the châteaux of France's Loire Valley, and Scottish baronial architecture—to create an eclectic building with certain distinc- tive features: steeply pitched roofs, smooth wall surfaces, a profusion of dormer windows peeking out from the roof, towers and turrets sprinkled apparently at random around the building, and an asymmetrical and uneven roof line. The Banff Springs Hotel was such a success that when the CPR decided to build a new hotel in Quebec City, railway president William van Horne asked Price to create a landmark for the heights

Bruce Price's Château Frontenac in Quebec City. c. 1900–25.

of Quebec. When the Château Frontenac opened in 1893, it was clear by common consent that Price had succeeded beyond all expectations with a more elaborate, almost fairy-tale version of the Banff Springs. The Château style, characterized by high, steep roofs, round towers, dormer windows, and large, smooth wall faces, was quickly accepted as distinctly—if not uniquely—Canadian. Price and his successors built other château hotels for the CPR, and the style was later adopted by its competitors, by architects working on commercial buildings and private homes, and eventually by the federal government, which decided that the architectural vocabulary was particularly suited to a northern country, its elements in harmony with our environment and expressive of our character. Over time, the impression grew in the popular consciousness that the Château style was somehow naturally Canadian.

So the foreign dominance of Canadian architecture, once such a concern to professional associations, in fact played a crucial role in reinvigorating the field in Canada. Imported culture, in the persons of Scotsman Percy Nobbs and American Bruce Price, had been the catalyst to create an indigenous style. In some respects, such imports were essential. With no trained organists or choirmasters in town, a new cathedral had no choice but to bring one in from outside the country. A corporation that wanted the best and most innovative head office building that money could buy was often unable to find the necessary level of expertise in Canadian firms. A budding painter who wanted to learn about art could only do so by studying the work of the great masters, whether through copies imported to Canada or by going to Europe to study the originals.

Still, none of this changed the fact that, in the late Victorian era, it was still difficult to make a living in the cultural industries. Many creators who stayed in Canada battled poverty, or found alternative sources of income. Others saw that the secret to success was to become an exporter of culture, something they could do without leaving Canada. But just as frequently they had to go abroad to practice their art. In the post-Confederation era, the influx of foreign culture was matched by an outflow of Canadians who, if they wished to follow their muse, could no longer remain at home.

Chapter 9

Exporting Culture

In his autobiographical verse *Le dépit ridicule, ou le sonnet perdu* (1801), Joseph Quesnel summed up the tribulations of the poet: 'What is the good of the trouble I take for rhyming/If no one ever has time to listen to my verse?' As a last resort, he pondered inviting friends to dinner, locking the door, and forcing them to listen to his poetry.[195] Quesnel never did become rich from his poetry or plays, but his business dealings ensured that he could live out his days in relative comfort. Plenty of other artists, though, did not have that luxury to fall back on.

The stereotype of the starving artist is an international phenomenon; every culture is full of tragic figures whose genius went unrecognized during their lives and who died in poverty and obscurity. In Canada, the starving artist had a couple of easy scapegoats: Anglophiles could blame the US cultural megalith for robbing them of the means to make their livelihood, and others could blame the country's congenital preference for all things emanating from Mother Britain.

But not all Canadian artists found the challenge of making a living by their muse to be insurmountable. Because of our proximity to the United States and the ease of communications with Britain, it was quite possible to live in Canada and export work to the much larger marketplaces that were close at hand. Indeed, some of Canada's best loved and most successful artists were able to do quite well without emigrating. Others, however, found that they had to leave Canada. For many, it was simply a lack of financial opportunity, while others chafed at what they considered to be an uncongenial attitude towards the arts. Regardless of their motives, the verdict on these émigrés was mixed. Some people celebrated their success as proof that Canada could produce writers, painters, and composers who could stand with the best in the world. Other commentators, however, were deeply troubled by the exodus of talent; in their view, those who left were little better than traitors casting aside their homeland for financial gain.

———•◦•———

Like the cultural history of every other nation, Canada's is littered with people who spent their whole lives trying to scrape out an existence with their art. John Richardson probably received no royalties from a US reprint of his first successful novel, *Wacousta*, while his second novel, *The Canadian Brothers* (1840), brought him favourable reviews but no money. 'I published in Canada,' he wrote despairingly, '—I might as well have done so in Kamschatka.'[196] Richardson moved to New York in 1848 or 1849, after a decade as a failed journalist, to try his hand at fiction again, but he was no more successful. He died forgotten in New York, so poor that he was unable even to feed his dog. Catherine Parr Traill's *The Backwoods of Canada* (1846) sold well in North America and was translated into French and German, going through several reprints in the process, but she probably earned no more than £125 over her lifetime from the book. Her later book *Pearls and Pebbles* (1895) was only accepted by the Methodist Book and Publishing House when she agreed to pre-sell two hundred copies to friends and relatives, an industry practice in Canada that forced authors to bear the cost of publication, making it difficult for even the most talented writer to earn a living. Isabella Valancy Crawford, one of the greatest but least recognized Canadian poets of the late nineteenth century, spent much of her adult life sending out poems and short stories to newspapers and magazines. She died at age thirty-seven, worn out by poverty and never able to enjoy the critical acclaim that her work would later draw. The novelist Frederick Philip Grove died without leaving enough money to cover his funeral costs, while trying to make a living as an essayist cost Winnipeger C.W. Lloyd his wife, his home, his vision, and his dog before he finally killed himself. Even the great Charles G.D. Roberts, hailed as the father of the Confederation Poets, left at his death in 1943 nothing more than a $500 bond, a twelve-year-old Buick worth $400, and $600 in the bank—an estate worth under $18,000 in current values. The man once hailed as the father of Canadian literature went to his grave in a cheap coffin without the limousine that he would have considered his due. 'Everybody knows,' observed the trade journal *Books and Notions* in 1893, 'that Canadian literature has hitherto brought no profit either to publisher or author.'[197]

Just as numerous, though less well known, were those people who sacrificed mightily to promote culture, only to find their efforts were in vain; their experiences offer proof that the difficulties of trying to build a Canadian culture were not only felt by those who were creating it. We have seen how long it took for bookstores, music shops, and art galleries to become established in Canadian cities, and many small merchants could only sell cultural wares as adjuncts to other items. Typical was the Golden Mortar apothecary in Kingston, Upper Canada, operated by Dr. Z. Smally, where books shared the shelves with medicine, paints, oils, dyes, putty, nails, garden seeds, stationary, and ladies' bonnets. In 1823, Jean Chrysostome Brauneis received a license to sell musical instruments in Quebec, but the venture cannot have been a success because four years later he applied for a license to operate a billiard room on the same location. James Spooner, Toronto's leading dealer, operated a tobacco shop and a dog kennel along with his gallery, which never generated enough income to keep him afloat. The Nordheimer Brothers of Toronto manufactured pianos, but they also had a line of sewing machines as a safety net in case their musical instruments did not sell.

It was the experience of people like Richardson, Crawford, Brauneis, and Spooner that caused such frustration among cultural nationalists. But the alternative to lamenting the trials of earning a livelihood in the cultural industries in Canada was to do something about it, to take advantage of other opportunities. Canada was closely connected to two of the biggest markets in the world—for the go-getter who could tap into those markets, the rewards could be substantial.

At one end of the scale were the writers who were able to make tidy if not substantial sums selling stories and poems to American and British magazines. Indeed, it was the boom in the US popular culture market in the late nineteenth century, with new newspapers and magazines creating an almost insatiable demand for fiction and poetry, that allowed many Canadian writers to achieve the high profile, and income, that they did. The papers of Isabel Ecclestone Mackay, for example, contain many letters from publishers across North America that bought her work: $12 from *Youth's Companion* (Boston) for a poem; $20 from

The Red Book (Chicago) for a short story; $5 from *The Designer* (New York) for an article; $35 from *St. Nicholas Magazine* (New York) for two articles; $80 from *The Reader Magazine* (Indianapolis) for an article. In contrast, the *Canadian Magazine* bought the odd piece but was very disorganized compared to publications in the United States; it never seemed to know how much money was owing to her, and Mackay found it very difficult to get an accurate statement of her account. Marjorie Pickthall was another writer who proved to be a canny businessperson, employing agents in both London and New York to help sell her work. When the *Canadian Magazine* offered her $8 for a short story, she promptly refused and sold it to *Atlantic Monthly* for twice the amount or more; she only deigned to publish her work in miserly Canadian journals 'because I like to see my verse occasionally in a Canadian publication.'[198] In 1922, the year of her death, Pickthall earned some $8,000 (over $99,000 in current values) from her writing.

Mackay and Pickthall, despite their relative success selling to the English and American markets, could only dream of achieving the fame and fortune of the writers who were arguably Canada's greatest exporters of culture in the early twentieth century: Ralph Connor, Stephen Leacock, and L.M. Montgomery. In some ways, all were unlikely literary superstars. Connor came into the world as Charles Gordon, the son of a fiery Highland preacher and a cultured woman from the Eastern Townships of Quebec. He was ordained as a Presbyterian minister and, at the age of thirty, went west as secretary to the British Canadian North-West Mission. He was a reluctant novelist, turning from sermons to fiction only after a colleague asked him to write a short story for the church periodical *The Westminster Magazine*; Gordon agreed, not because he had any great interest in being a writer, but 'to awaken my church in Eastern Canada to the émigrés of the mighty religious adventure being attempted by the missionary pioneers in the Canada beyond the Great Lakes.' It doesn't sound like the stuff of a bestseller, but when Gordon's first stories were published as the novel *Black Rock: A Tale of the Selkirks* in 1898 (under the name Ralph Connor— Gordon had suggested the pseudonym Cannor, from the abbreviation for his position, and a well-meaning telegraph operator assumed it was an error and changed it to Connor, adding the Christian name Ralph for good measure), it was an instant success. He followed it up with a succession of novels—*The Sky Pilot* (1899), *The Man From Glengarry* (1901), *Glengarry School Days* (1902), and *Corporal Cameron* (1912) to name but a few—and attributed their popularity to the fact that they gave an 'authentic picture of life in the great and wonderful new country...rich in color and alive with movement...[and] presented a quality of religious life that "red-blooded" men could read and enjoy.'[199] And they certainly were read. Gordon wrote more best-sellers than any other native-born author, and from 1899 to 1924 he was a fixture on the Canadian best-seller lists—*The Prospector* (1904) sold more than 22,000 copies in just five months, and *Corporal Cameron* sold most of its first edition of 30,000 even before publication day. But these figures were a drop in the bucket compared to his sales in the United States and Britain. *Black Rock* sold 625,000 copies in the United States in 1898 alone, and *The Doctor* (1906), *The Major* (1917), and *The Sky Pilot in No Man's Land* (1919) also cracked the US best-seller lists. This success made Gordon, who travelled widely but always returned to Canada and his religious duties here, enormously wealthy; some estimates put his fortune in the mid-1910s at well over $1 million, or $18 million today.

Stephen Leacock could hardly have been more different from the Reverend Gordon. Born in England, he came to Canada as a young boy, only to be abandoned by his father, an alcoholic and failed farmer. But Agnes Leacock was made of stern stuff, and she worked hard to instill in her eleven children the qualities of character that her husband lacked. Stephen went through the prestigious Upper Canada College and eventually found himself, rather to his surprise, a lecturer in economics and political science at McGill University. He was extraordinarily prolific and wide-ranging in his writing: his best-selling book was a text, *Elements of Political Science* (1903), that became standard reading in many American universities and was eventually translated into eighteen languages, but he also wrote about Canadian history, imperial economics, Mark Twain, Charles Dickens, and social reform. Leacock, however, was best known as a humorist, a career he began in 1896 when he submitted perhaps his best short story, 'My Financial Career,' to *Life* magazine in the United States. In 1910, it opened his first collection, *Literary Lapses*, which he published with his own money—all 3,000 copies sold in Montreal, and it was promptly picked up by the British publisher John Lane. Leacock followed it up with more than

Stephen Leacock at work. c. 1947.

thirty collections of satirical short stories and acerbic commentaries, including the Canadian favourite *Sunshine Sketches of a Little Town* (1912), more popular in this country than anywhere else for the gentle but perfectly accurate way it pokes fun at small-town pretensions and foibles. By 1914, Leacock was in great demand as a public speaker, and the reading public in Canada, the United States, and Britain eagerly awaited each new collection, even if they became a trifle repetitious over the years. All of this meant that Leacock, like Gordon, became a very rich man. In 1923, his income was roughly $40,000, over $500,000 in current values and almost three times what the prime minister of the day earned. He was as famous outside Canada as he was at home, but he clung fiercely to his faculty position at McGill and regularly retreated to his lakeside cottage in Orillia, Ontario, where he fished, puttered around doing small renovations, and tried, not very successfully, to make extra money by growing vegetables.

Lucy Maud Montgomery fell somewhere between Gordon and Leacock—her work shows flashes of wit that the satirist would have appreciated, and elements of moral tone that would have done the minister proud. A native of Clifton, Prince Edward Island, she was raised by her grandparents and worked as a teacher and journalist before publishing her first novel, *Anne of Green Gables*, in 1908. Like *Black Rock*, this tale of a spunky, red-headed orphan was an immediate hit, although less so in Canada (where it was beaten on the best-seller list by Ralph Connor's *The Foreigner*) than in the United States, where it sold over 750,000 copies in the first year of publication alone. Montgomery was not as prolific as Gordon or Leacock—in 1911 she married a Presbyterian minister and her writing often had to take a back seat to her role as a minister's wife and as a mother—but her work has had considerably more staying power. Gordon's novels are now all but forgotten, while Leacock is known largely for *Sunshine Sketches* and the annual award for humorous writing that bears his name. In contrast, all of Montgomery's twenty novels remain in print, her millions of fans around the world, from North America to Poland to Japan, eagerly lapping up the reprints, movies, television series, plays, and cookbooks based on the experiences of the fictional Anne and Montgomery's other characters. Since 1908, she has been one of Canada's most popular and profitable cultural exports.

There were other Canadians who, though they may not have reached the dizzying heights of Gordon, Leacock, and Montogomery, still made international reputations with their work without being lured away from their homeland. Artist Robert Harris trained in Boston, Britain, and Paris, and then travelled frequently between Canada, the United States, and Europe, his reputation as a painter growing all the time. He could easily have set up his studio in New York, Philadelphia, or Boston, but opted instead for Toronto. The move was a success and, though Harris never stopped fretting about money (he was a bit of a worrier, always convinced, even after specialists assured him that it was not so, that his eyes were failing because of over-work), he started earning good money as a portrait painter. Some of the most influential industrialists in North America came to him for portraits, and between 1889 and 1896 he accepted fifty-five portrait commissions, beginning at $500 each (or around $10,000 in current values); it was a sizeable income for a man who, years earlier, had trouble prying $25 out of the Prince Edward Islanders he painted to hone his skills.

Equally successful was photographer William Notman, one of the few artists to prosper during the Montreal depression of the 1870s.

Inside William Notman's Ottawa studio. Undated.

Notman had arrived in Montreal in 1856, after fleeing from fraud charges that stemmed from the collapse of the family's cloth business in Scotland, and within a year had set himself up as a professional photographer, something he had dabbled in as a hobby. He was a shrewd entrepreneur, taking advantage of the public's interest in the new field of photography by selling pictures of prominent Montrealers; by 1860, he had to enlarge his staff by adding budding painters John A. Fraser and William Sandham. By that time, Notman had become one of the city's most successful artists—a founder of the Art Association of Montreal, 'Photographer to the Queen' (as his studios proclaimed in big, bold letters), president of the Montreal Camera Club—and over the next few years would open studios in Ottawa, Toronto, Halifax, and Saint John. Then, the ever ambitious Notman was ready to expand southwards. He got into the lucrative business of photographing university classes—one trade journal wrote that through the mid-1870s his company probably took more class photos than all of his rivals combined—but his first great success in the US came when he was named the official photographer for the Centennial Exhibition in Philadelphia in 1876. He took some 4,000 images of the fair, displayed his own work there (winning a gold medal in the process), and sold some $90,000 worth of photographs to fair-goers. Riding the crest of this triumph but facing the prospect of paying high tariffs on photographs he exported from Canada to the United States, Notman decided to set up shop south of the border, eventually opening nineteen studios in New England as branches of the Notman Photographic Company.

Pauline Johnson (Tekahionwake), the Mohawk writer and performer, followed a similar path. As it was for Notman, Johnson's art was also her vocation; she began writing to earn a living, but found little success until the 1890s, when she began to perform her own work. Over the next two decades, she embarked on a punishing touring schedule that included seven tours through western Canada, nine in the Maritimes, nine in the US, and two triumphant appearances in London. If she was not a poet of the first rank, she was a natural performer—beautiful, poised, dramatic, and with an intuitive sense of how to 'work' an audience. It all made her one of the most popular recitationists of the era and, were it not for the high cost of touring and her remarkable generosity, Pauline Johnson would have been a very wealthy woman.

Another great success story began with Joseph Casavant, a black-smith who gave up the hammer and anvil to study the craft of building organs. By working his way through a classic manual on pipe organs, he was able to complete his first instrument, an organ that had been left half-finished in the parish church of Saint-Thérèse. He built his first complete organ in 1840, and when the word of his skill spread, the orders started coming in. By the time he retired in 1866, he had built fifteen organs for Quebec parishes' churches and two for the Roman Catholic cathedrals in Ottawa and Kingston. But it would be up to his sons, Joseph-Claver and Samuel-Marie, to take the business to even greater heights. Joseph had turned his Saint-Hyacinthe factory over to a local builder when he retired, and the brothers worked there as boys before going to Europe to apprentice in the art of organ-building. In 1879, they returned to Saint-Hyacinthe and established Casavant Frères Limitée, installing their first instrument the following year, in the chapel of Notre-Dame-de-Lourdes in Montreal. Soon, orders were arriving not just from Quebec, but from around the world: Toronto, Boston, Manitoba, the Yukon, British Columbia, Paris, the West Indies, South America, South Africa, India, Japan. In 1914, they finished their

A Casavant organ being installed in Japan in 1927.

six hundredth instrument; by 1929, they had sold 1,355. Aside from fifty-four instruments built at a branch plant in South Haven, Michigan, all of them came from the factory in Saint-Hyacinthe.

The common denominator was that all of these producers made a conscious decision, for economic reasons, to expand into foreign markets. The Nordheimer Brothers found that their pianos sold better than their sewing machines, success that allowed them to branch out into music publishing, becoming the most prolific firm in Canada in the second half of the nineteenth century. In 1859, the company joined the American Board of Music Trade so that it could more easily expand into the American market. L.M. Montgomery, for her part, fully realized that there was much more money to be made from US publishers than Canadian. She 'wouldn't give [a] MS. to a Canadian firm,' she wrote. 'It is much better financially to have it published in the United States.'[200] The ledger that she carefully kept to record sales bore that out: in 1908, *Anne of Green Gables* sold twenty-three times more copies in the United States than in Canada, while the American sales of *Anne of Avonlea*, in its first three years of release, outstripped Canadian sales by a factor of ten.

But achieving success in other markets came with a cost. Susanna Moodie fully realized, in revising *Roughing It in the Bush* for English readers, that she would have to excise some of the earthier passages for the benefit of more sensitive readers. For readers in the United States, on the other hand, her publisher deleted 'certain passages of a purely personal or political character, which could have possessed no interest for the American reader.'[201] Marshall Saunders became the first Canadian author to sell a million copies and have an international best-seller, the 1894 novel *Beautiful Joe*, but much of her success was predicated on her decision to set her works in the United States. After hearing that the American Humane Education Society of Boston was offering a cash prize for the best story on domestic animals, she quickly made some altera-tions to the draft of *Beautiful Joe*, which was originally set in Halifax. As she wrote to W.A. Deacon, 'You know Nova Scotia and understand how much we are like our American cousins. It was no trouble to turn Halifax into Fairport, Maine, and Canadians into New Englanders.' And Charles Gordon must have been taken aback by a letter he received from Casper Whiteny, of *The Outing Magazine* in New York. Whiteny wanted something for a serial to be published in 1908; he had a story by a British author, but confided that 'I prefer to have an American—for literary purposes we may call a Canadian an American, mayn't we?'[202] Many writers were unhappy with such creative compromises. E.W. Thomson, a journalist and veteran of both the US Civil War and the Fenian Raids, left a job at the *Globe* to take an editorial position with the Boston-based *Youth's Companion*, one of North America's most popular periodicals with over 500,000 subscribers. On a financial level, the move was a success, but he was bothered by what the pull of the US market could do to Canadian culture. He complained that 'in appealing, by fiction, to foreign audiences we are required not only to drop out much racy of the soil and to refrain from merely allusive remarks that would instantly be understood in Canada, but also to place ourselves mentally in the place of the foreign reader. It is writing in hobbles.'[203] But Thomson also knew that not everyone could be a Montgomery or a Leacock—for many, the alternative to writing in hobbles was writing for pennies.

———•◦•———

Canada's great literary superstars tended to share one thing: even though they made thousands of dollars a year from their writing, they did not need to sell books to live. Montgomery was married to a clergyman (albeit a rather ineffective one), Gordon was a clergyman, and Leacock was a professor; if they had never sold a book, none of them would have starved. Even those outside the cultural firmament enjoyed a degree of security. Archibald Lampman and Duncan Campbell Scott had their civil service positions, the Nordheimer brothers their sewing machines, the Reverend Frederick George Scott his Quebec parish stipend, the painter Daniel Wilson his farm, Charles Mair his salary as an immigration agent, an appointment in 1898 that saved him from penury after a bookshop he had opened in Fort Steele, British Columbia, had failed— all of them had something to fall back on during the lean times. Mair had always said that writing was a better walking stick than a crutch, but the same could be said of all forms of culture.

But without the kind of royalty cheques that came to Montgomery and Leacock or another job to fall back on, the only alternative was to go where there was work available if they wanted to follow their muses. Ironically, this group of émigrés included some of the most bullish cultural nationalists of the post-Confederation era. In 1891, Archibald Lampman wrote to E.W. Thomson that 'I was not going to abandon the soil just yet, but that I had it securely in my mind to do so at as early a date as possible.'[204] Charles G.D. Roberts was never without a scheme to make money (he even contemplated dropping his middle initials so his name would be easier to remember, but instead people took to calling him God Damn, either as a term of endearment or as a criticism), although his prodigious output, including four books published in 1896 alone, didn't allow him to live in the style to which he wanted to become accustomed. In February 1897, the founder of the Confederation School left Nova Scotia to become an assistant editor at *Illustrated American* in New York. His cousin and fellow Confederation Poet Bliss Carman had already gone to New York, working as a literary editor for *The Independent*, *Cosmopolitan*, and *Atlantic Monthly*.

Another émigrée was Sara Jeannette Duncan, who saw an advertisement for the New Orleans Cotton Centennial and convinced the *Globe* and the *London Advertiser* to pay her $5 an article so she could go there. She continued working as a journalist, for the *Globe*, the *Washington Post*, and the *Montreal Star*, before marrying, moving to India, and becoming a best-selling novelist. Over her career, she would publish with some of the biggest firms in the world, earning an income that allowed her to live quite comfortably. Duncan was fully aware that her fortunes would have been much bleaker had she remained in Canada, for despite the nationalism of her earlier journalism she knew that her novels did not do well in her homeland. 'I have given up as hopeless any attempt to get my books on the market of my own country,' she wrote to John Willison, editor of the *Globe*. Her literary agent informed her American publisher that Duncan wanted Macmillan in Toronto to acquire the Canadian rights to *The Burnt Offering* (1909) because she thought 'if her book were published in Canada by a Canadian publisher, and the fact were emphasized that she herself is a Canadian, the results might be advantageous to all concerned.' However, the novel was not reviewed in any leading Canadian journals, and even *The Imperialist*, her only novel set in Canada, did not sell well here.[205]

G. Mercer Adam was one of the cadre of cultural nationalists who was especially bothered by the brain drain. In 1889, he wrote that public apathy, a small population, and a lack of wealth had led to the 'withdrawal of the native writer from Canada, and the carrying of good work to other and better markets...we talk with horror of political annexation yet we pay no heed to the annexation of another kind, which is drafting off across the line not only the brains and pens of the country, but the hopes and hearts of those who move and inspire them.' Adam was disturbed by the 'growing hopelessness of inducing Canadian publishers to take up literary enterprises which might bring honour as well as profit to the country' if all our best writers left the country.[206] But his protests rang hollow; a few weeks later, he left Canada to work in the United States himself.

Adam could comfort himself in the knowledge that at least some of these émigrés retained an interest in their native land. Robert Barr's family came to Canada West from Scotland in 1854, and his first articles for the Toronto satirical magazine *The Grip* spring-boarded him to a full-time job with the *Detroit Free Press*. From there he went to London to establish an English edition of the *Free Press*, but his greatest success there was in co-founding the legendary humour magazine *The Idler*. Aside from his journalism, he was a prolific novelist, publishing more than twenty novels, including *In the Midst of Alarms* (1893), a satire of the Fenian raids of 1866, and *The Measure of the Rule* (1907), a romance

Saskatchewan artist Gus Kenderdine and his fellow students at the Académie Julian in Paris, 1890.

drawn from his experiences at the Toronto Normal School. He never lived in Canada after leaving for Detroit, but retained a keen interest in Canadian literature and never ceased to do what he could to promote it from overseas. Niagara-born Clarence Lucas had a similar experience. He taught first at the Toronto College of Music from 1889 to 1891, before moving to New York, London, and finally Paris, where he died in 1947. Despite the fact that the bulk of his professional career was spent outside Canada, Lucas always considered himself, and was considered by others, to be a Canadian composer. Montreal-born painter James Wilson Morrice spent almost thirty-four of his fifty-eight years in Europe, mostly in Paris, where he moved in an exalted circle that included the painters Henri Matisse and Walter Sickert, the novelists Somerset Maugham and Arnold Bennett, and the occultist Aleister Crowley. Morrice exhibited in the most important art shows in Europe and the United States, but he never lost touch with the Canadian scene. He continued to exhibit in his homeland, although he rarely sent his best works (much to the dismay of his father, who wrote 'It would be distinctly in his interest to send out more of his important work to Canada, than he has been in the habit of doing'[207]), and played host to up-and-coming Canadian painters such as John Lyman, Clarence Gagnon, and Edwin Holgate, becoming a conduit between the Canadian and European art worlds.

Perhaps the most well-known émigré was Gilbert Parker, a professor of elocution at Queen's University whose first stab at literature was some not very good poetry about the 1885 North-West Rebellion. When his brother and a close friend both died in 1886, Parker coped with his grief by embarking on a tour of the south seas; he always intended to return, but for the rest of his life he would come to Canada infrequently, and then as a visitor rather than a local boy coming home. But if Parker never lived in Canada again, he never left Canadian subject matter. After settling in London, he wrote a short story called *The Patrol of the Cypress Hills*, a potboiler built around a number of stock elements—the frozen north, a Mountie, and a remittance man—that would become standard in the stories that made him famous. As his biographer put it, Parker was about to do for the Canadian northwest what Kipling did for India. He took the story to *The Independent* in New York, where Bliss Carman was an editor, and the magazine published it in 1891. He then returned to Britain to write his first novel, *The Chief Factor: A Tale of the Hudson's Bay Company* (1893). It was an instant success, selling 30,000 copies in the United States in three weeks, and Parker suddenly became a demon for work, publishing six successful novels in just three years. With *The Seats of the Mighty* and *The Pomp of the Lavilettes* (both 1896), Parker had pigeon-holed himself as a writer of the Canadian northwest or French Canada.

By now, success had given him a notoriety and affluence that he could never have achieved in Canada. In 1900, he entered British politics and was elected the Member of Parliament for Gravesend in Kent. His newest novel, *The Right of Way* (1901), was selling well, topping the US best-seller list and selling 25,000 copies in two weeks; one contemporary estimated his royalties at £7,000 a year. He became Sir Gilbert Parker at King Edward VII's coronation, and the *Montreal Herald* put him fourth on a list of the greatest living Canadians, after Prime Minister Wilfrid Laurier, railway baron Lord Strathcona, and former Prime Minister Sir Charles Tupper. It was quite an achievement for a man whose childhood had been spent in a succession of small Ontario towns as his unlucky father vainly sought ways to provide for his large family.

Despite having turned his back on his homeland, Parker never saw himself as anything but a Canadian novelist. The critics might have thought differently—the *Toronto Star* wrote that he gave the northwest 'a local color that existed largely in his own imagination...invidious people say that Parker's Northwest is as much like the real thing as a peacock is like a Moor hen'[208]—but Parker was satisfied that he had remained true to the land of his birth. When he received an honourary degree from Laval University in 1912, he took it as 'the seal of French Canada upon the work which I have tried to do for her and for the whole Dominion.' And George Grant, who was a scholar as well as a nationalist, complimented Parker for giving 'a profound and delicate insight into the facts of French-Canadian life that it would be well for our statesmen to understand.' Modern critics may pay little attention to his work, but contemporaries saw in Gilbert Parker proof of the old adage that you can take the writer out of Canada but you can never take Canada out of the writer.

———•◦•———

But there were just as many painters, writers, and composers who left Canada and lost anything that was distinctly Canadian about them. Sadly, the identities of most of them are unknown; they adopted American or British voices and blended into other cultural milieus, stepping back onto the stage of our history only if they returned home or consciously strove to maintain a Canadian identity. Some deserted their muse altogether—Charles H. Porter, the Halifax organist, choirmaster, and director of the Halifax Conservatory of Music, left Canada in 1900 to become a manager at the Equitable Assurance Company in New Haven, Connecticut—but more often they could follow their dream by deserting Canada.

Margaret Anglin has the distinction of being the first Canadian ever born in the Parliament Buildings (her father, Timothy Anglin, was the Speaker of House of Commons, and she was born in the family's apartment in Centre Block in 1879). Her mother Ellen was a theatre-lover, and found the money for her daughter to attend the Empire Dramatic School in New York. The investment paid off. Margaret got her first big break when she was cast in the US Civil War romance *Shenandoah*

Margaret Anglin as Medea, preparing to wring tears from a keg of nails. Undated.

in New York in 1894, and soon she was captivating audiences in the United States and around the world. Quite unlike her own vivacious, playful personality, she was renowned as one of the great tragedians of the contemporary stage, newspapers referring to her variously as the 'unchallenged first practitioner of anguish,' a 'tearologist,' and an actor who could 'wring emotion from a keg of nails.'[209] She frequently visited Canada, not only with shows and touring companies but also for special occasions; in 1927, she accepted Prime Minister Mackenzie

King's invitation to help mark Canada's Diamond Jubilee by reading Bliss Carman's poem 'Dominion Day 1927' to a crowd of 30,000 on Parliament Hill and many more over a live radio broadcast.

Margaret Anglin became an international superstar, although her father never quite reconciled himself to her chosen career path. Timothy Anglin had absorbed the anti-theatre mentality of the Catholic church, refused to allow the subject of her profession to be mentioned in his presence, and never saw her perform. Once, after Margaret had become an international celebrity, the governor-general, the Marquess of Dufferin, adjourned the House of Commons for a day so Timothy would have no excuse to miss her show in Ottawa; however, the seat of honour that Dufferin had saved for him remained unoccupied. On another occasion, Ellen dragged her husband to Buffalo to see Margaret perform; this time, he agreed to enter the theatre but sat through the entire performance with his eyes tightly shut. Her eldest brother, who later became the Chief Justice of Canada, never saw her act either. It is just possible that the male Anglins, who devoted their lives to the public service of Canada, were dismayed by her decision to abandon the country of her birth. Margaret lived in the United States from the age of eighteen until her death at seventy-four, became an American citizen by marriage, and, despite protestations to the contrary, frequently spoke as an American rather than a Canadian. For Timothy Anglin, this might have been just as painful as the fact that she had chosen, in his eyes, a less than honourable profession.

Margaret Anglin's counterpart in the world of opera was Emma Lajeunesse, whose ancestor, a soldier with the Carignan-Salières Regiment, came to Canada in 1665. The family had lived in Plattsburgh, New York, but in 1856 they moved back to Montreal when Emma's mother died. Her father was aware of her musical gift and determined to get the training that Emma needed to develop as a singer, but despite the fact that the newspaper La Minerve said she had 'a voice that seemed sent from heaven,' a subscription concert to raise money for her education failed. Disappointed with the public's indifference to his daughter's talent, Lajeunesse promptly moved the family back to the United States.

After studying in New York and Paris, Emma (who had adopted the more operatic surname Albani) made her debut at the Teatro Vittorio Emmanuel in Messina, Italy, in 1869. She was an overnight sensation

Emma Albani pictured near the peak of her fame, 1883.

and spent the rest of her career touring the great opera houses of the world, becoming most closely connected to the prestigious Royal Italian Opera at Covent Garden in London. The toast of monarchs and aristocrats, a favourite of Queen Victoria, widely regarded as one of the greatest opera singers of her age, Emma Albani was blessed with a voice of astonishing range and a warm personality quite in contrast with some of the other divas of the era. She also never forgot her Canadian roots 'I have married an Englishman, and have made my home in England, but I still remain at heart a French-Canadian,' she said. She toured the country a number of times, and when she came to Montreal in March 1883 one city alderman said she was proof that 'the most

brilliant artistic talent could flower amid the snows of Canada.' She
was even the subject of a verse tribute, 'When Albani Sang,' by the best-
selling dialect poet W.H. Drummond.

But there was little in Anglin or Albani's work to mark them out as
Canadian. This is hardly surprising—after all, opera was a European
art form and would remain so for decades, and it is difficult to conceive
of a distinctively Canadian style of acting. Other expatriates, however,
made a conscious decision to discard their Canadianness for the sake
of commercial success. One of the most successful Canadian authors of
the mid-nineteenth century was May Agnes Fleming, born in 1840 in
Saint John, the daughter of a ship's carpenter and an illiterate mother.
Her first published work appeared in a New York magazine in 1857, and
from then on she went from strength to strength, becoming a master
of sentimental romances with gothic touches. In 1868, Philadelphia's
Saturday Night, a weekly magazine with a circulation of 100,000, offered
her an exclusive contract to write three stories a year for $2,000. Four
years later, her talents were the subject of a bidding war that eventually
took her to the *New York Weekly*, which paid her $6,000 for three stories
a year. At the same time, she struck a deal with the *London Journal*
that earned £12 a week for serializations of her stories, and another to
publish her novels in book form after they had been serialized (she was
the personification of Leacock's adage that 'the sagacious author, after
having sold his material to magazines and been paid for it, [should] clap
it into book-covers and give it another squeeze'[210]). Her annual income
probably exceeded $10,000 (or over $200,000 in current values) and
later the *New York Weekly*, which by then had a circulation of 350,000,
the largest of any weekly in the world, reportedly offered her $15,000 for
two novels. By this time, Fleming had left New Brunswick and moved to
Brooklyn to be closer to her publisher, but she had long since expunged
any Canadian content from her work; readers would never have known
she was Canadian, and she has been all but forgotten by literary scholars
in this country. But when she died in 1880, she was one of the highest
paid authors in the United States.

Artist Paul Peel followed a slightly different path, although with the
same results. He studied in London, Ontario, then enrolled in the Pennsylvania Academy of Fine Arts in Philadelphia in 1877. From then on, he
would spend most of his time in London (England), Brittany, or Paris,

returning only occasionally to London to see his family and sketch. His fondness for his hometown soured a little, however, when a collection of paintings he sent back to London for auction drew disappointing bids. After that, he stopped sending paintings home; from then until his untimely death in 1892, he was essentially a French painter who just happened to have been born in Canada. Far from having any nationalist leanings, Peel revered European and especially French styles, favoured French subject matter, and consciously tried to emulate French practices.

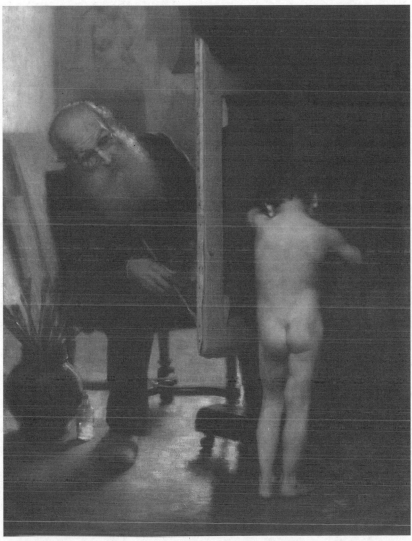

One of Paul Peel's most famous works, *The Modest Model*, 1889.

Paul Peel's experience demonstrates that it wasn't just money that sent people away; many were driven from Canada by an uncongenial attitude towards the arts. There was a certain amount of Victorian stuffiness that kept the arts conservative and unprogressive, and the heavy hand of the National Gallery and the Royal Canadian Academy provided little help. Sir Wyly Grier said in 1913 that if an artist was any good, he couldn't paint a picture that was acceptable to the Academy, and argued that all too many artists left Canada because they found it a stifling society that resisted innovation and placed little value on artistic creativity.

One such man was Calixa Lavallée. Born in Verchères in 1842, his father had worked in the Casavant organ shop, exposing the young Calixa to music from an early age. He studied in Montreal, but was possessed of a restless soul and at age fifteen went to seek his fortune in the United States. After a year as a musician in the Union Army during the US Civil War, in the early 1870s he was made director of the Grand Opera House in New York. But the first of a series of professional misfortunes came when the theatre owner was murdered just before the premiere of Lavallée's opera bouffe *Loulou* and the show was promptly shut down. His luck did not improve upon his return to Canada, but then he couldn't blame a common murderer; instead, it was an indifferent government that seemed to stand in his way. He put much effort into a proposal for a music conservatory, to be sponsored by the provincial government, but the politicians showed little interest in his idea. Then in 1879, on the invitation of the government, he composed and conducted a cantata for the visit of the governor general, the Marquess of Lorne, to Quebec City. It was a critical success but the government, despite having made the initial request to Lavallée, refused to reimburse him for his considerable expenses. This, for the composer, was the last straw. Discouraged by the indifference to his work, especially in official circles, and desperate to find a way to recoup his losses, he moved to the United States for good in 1881, settling in Boston.

But before leaving, he had one more great contribution to make to Canadian culture. In 1880, Lorne asked the British composer Sir Arthur Sullivan to write the music for his poem 'Dominion Hymn.' But Quebec's St. Jean Baptiste Society did not like the idea of a British composer, especially one so British as Sullivan (best known for his archetypally British operettas, written with Sir William S. Gilbert, such as *H.M.S. Pinafore* and *The Pirates of Penzance*), writing a Canadian anthem. At the same time, Quebec's lieutenant-governor asked Judge Adolphe-Basile Routhier and Lavallée if they could compose a suitable anthem. The result was *O Canada*, which premiered at the Pavillion des Patineurs on 24 June 1880. It was an instant hit with both French and English Canadians, although the official English lyrics were not adopted until a parliamentary committee revised Robert Weir's lyrics in 1980. But despite the success of *O Canada*, Lavallée had become, for all intents and purposes, an American composer. Although he occasionally expressed concern at the state of music in Canada, he was a self-proclaimed annexationist, declaring to anyone who would listen that Canada would be better off as part of the United States. The bitterness of his earlier days, it seems, died hard.

And what of those who left the country for the sake of their muses? How did they stand in the estimation of their peers? Many commentators, even the cultural nationalists, admitted the obvious, that there simply was not the market to sustain creators in Canada, and congratulated the émigrés on having the courage to pull up stakes and move. Gilbert Parker advised budding writers to follow his lead and go south, for 'Whatever hope Canadians have in a literary way is centred in the great cities of the United States.' Canada was not 'the Utopia of authors,' wrote Duncan Campbell Scott in 1893, 'and when a man feels that letters is his calling he must depart from our shores and be a sojourner in an alien land.'[211] Archibald Lampman thought Sara Jeannette Duncan had made the right choice in leaving the 'small prospect of advancement' in Canada for greener pastures elsewhere:

> it is quite natural that those who seek the widest field for their abilities should wander abroad. Let us find no fault with them on that account. They probably bring more honor to their country in the fields which they have chosen than they would if they had remained at home. Here their energies might have withered away in petty and fruitless occupations, and their talent have evaporated in the thin sluggishness of a colonial atmosphere.

G. Mercer Adam also defended her decision, writing that it was 'a matter of regret that a Canadian writer has…to ignore the native book market and even to assume the piquante guise of an American girl, to enable her to win the ear of an adequate and appreciative public.'[212] Even Prime Minister John A. Macdonald offered encouragement when speaking of the tendency of artists to leave Canada: 'We could not expect all those Canadians who distinguished themselves in this way to remain in Canada; the centres of art and civilization, like London and Paris, would certainly attract a great portion of this talent, but whether they were in Canada, in England, or in France, they were Canadians, and would do honour to Canadian genius and Canadian ability.'[213]

Others were not so forgiving. In their view, the great tragedy was that the émigrés had lost any distinctive Canadianness that their work possessed. One critic lamented poet Louis Fréchette's departure for Paris because 'he may soon lose the very charm which enriches his work to-day'; in this, he would follow the fate of Hector Fabre, once regarded as the best French-Canadian essayist of his age. After moving to France, wrote George Stewart in *The Week*, Fabre became 'the Frenchiest of Frenchmen, and he has lost completely those traces of Canadianism which gave him his fame.' The same criticism was made of artists who went to France. Commenting on a recent show of the Royal Canadian Academy, Archibald Lampman wrote scathingly that painter F.M. Bell-Smith, who trained in France in the academy tradition, 'appears to have been in Paris and to have filched some of the mannerisms of the French watercolorists.'[214] Paul Peel drew the same snide remarks. 'I am not aware that any of his work dealt with Canadian subjects,' wrote Duncan Campbell Scott dismissively (in fact, Peel had painted a good number of Canadian subjects); 'those pictures of his which I have seen seemed to show French ideals, and were painted from French subjects.' *The Week* was even more unkind, criticizing Peel for having all the faults of French school: 'I should prefer…one little Canadian sketch by L.R. O'Brien, to those dusky Moors, whom, surely, I have seen so often before in foreign and New York galleries.'[215] Sara Jeannette Duncan suffered the fate of being scorned by contemporaries—the *Canadian Magazine* wrote in 1899 that she 'has never done much for the literature of her native land…a desire to live in the hearts of her countrymen seems never to have moved her,' while another journal opined that her decision to leave Canada cost her 'the pre-eminence of being the leading Canadian female novelist' to the now-forgotten Alice Jones—and marginalized by modern critics such as Misao Dean and Michael Peterman, who suggest that she became a 'homeless writer' who lacked a national tradition.[216]

To add insult to injury, fame and fortune was all too often fleeting. As the taste for tragedians waned, Margaret Anglin eventually had to sell off her possessions to pay back taxes; before long, she was relying on her brother to cover her bills, and eventually he had to liquidate everything she owned to clear her debts, moving the once-great actress into his home on Long Island Sound to live out her years in dotty obscurity. Emma Albani, formerly the toast of Europe, was also hit hard by financial reverses and the high cost of keeping up appearances. She was forced to sing in music halls and give lessons to make money, and Mackenzie King even tried to get her a pension from the Quebec government. His apologetic letter to her hints at her standing in the Canadian consciousness: 'I appreciate of course that you belong to Canada rather than to a province; when I urged this point I met with the reprimand that you belonged also to the world and more particularly to the British Isles with which your professional life and present days are so intimately associated.' A benefit concert, organized by *La Presse* at King's request (he agreed to stand as the official patron of the event), was more successful, raising $4,000, including $50 from the prime minister–patron, but when the great singer died she was, like Anglin (whom King also tried to help in her declining years), all but forgotten in the land of her birth.[217]

Still, it would be a mistake to make too much of this haemorrhaging of talent from Canada, as the cultural nationalists of the era frequently did. The simple fact was that nineteenth-century North America was an extremely mobile society, and for every actor, painter, or writer who elected to leave the country, there were a thousand farmers, merchants, tradesmen, and students who made the same move. The fact was that, for many people, the border was largely theoretical—Charles Gordon, Stephen Leacock, and Marjorie Pickthall moved easily between Canada, Britain, and the United States, and were at home in all of them; just like the farmer who decided to leave England for Manitoba, then perhaps moved on to Iowa, and eventually migrated to Saskatchewan. Pulling up stakes for greener pastures in another country was part of the North

American experience—for the majority of Canadians, moving between Britain, Canada, and the United States was a natural migration pattern, rather than a trend to elicit lamentations and hand-wringing. But when the First World War began in August 1914, borders suddenly became vital. Once again, culture and nationalism would be thrown together in a way that they hadn't been since the era of the Confederation Poets and painters.

Chapter 10

The First World War

The coming of the First World War in August 1914 caught L.M. Montgomery at a difficult time. Pregnant with her second child (who would be still-born before the month was out), the news from Europe agitated her terribly. She professed to being 'weak and unnerved' by events; 'on some nights I cannot sleep…I have not had one decent *dinner* since the war began.' Creatively, she also felt at a loss. Although she was trying mightily to work on a new Anne book, she admitted that it was 'all but impossible to sit calmly down and write for schoolgirls and their little doings while the nations are locked in their death struggle.'[218]

On the other side of the ocean, Charles G.D. Roberts was wrestling with the same emotions. 'I have lost ten pounds in weight, and more than half my sleep, since war began,' he wrote to his son. The news from the front pushed all other thoughts from his mind. 'There's only the war, always the war, with the roar of it almost near enough to hear, & the bulletins coming in every hour, & the lists of the killed and wounded, till I almost cry in the street, & can't speak a word.'[219] Roberts (who would regain a measure of equilibrium by lying about his age and joining the army) and Montgomery both realized that the war was a threat to their craft; writing seemed so much less important when the fate of nations hung in the balance.

Before long, a different reality had become apparent: culture was incredibly important as a powerful propaganda weapon that could be mobilized for the cause. It could raise money for patriotic organizations, and sustain the morale of the stay-at-home and the fighting man alike. It could act as a record, capturing the story of the nation's struggle in paint, ink, and stone. Ultimately, it could stand as a symbol of everything that Canadians believed they were fighting for.

But even as culture was booming to an unprecedented degree, its weaknesses were also becoming painfully clear. There was much activity, to be sure, but little of it was distinctly Canadian. As the poems and novels and paintings and songs piled up, it was increasingly obvious that the nation had not yet found its voice. With the wave of patriotic fervour that swept the country during the war, this state of affairs could not be allowed to continue. Canada had become a nation on the battlefield; now, it needed its own distinct, indigenous culture to express that nationhood.

In those first few weeks of war, the country was a hive of activity. Thousands of young men converged on Valcartier, Quebec, to be turned into the First Division of the Canadian Expeditionary Force; they would sail overseas in December, and undergo their baptism of fire at the Second Battle of Ypres in April 1915. As the reports streamed back of Canadian soldiers fighting through the haze of poison gas to stem the German attack, clerics, academics, politicians, and business leaders filled the air with patriotic rhetoric, exhorting the people of Canada to gird themselves for the fight. It was a death struggle, and the very survival of Canada and the British Empire hung in the balance. As one newspaper later wrote, 'If we lose the war, nothing else matters.'

There were so many things that seemed more important than writing or painting, and Montgomery and Roberts were not alone in regarding the future of culture with a sense of gloom. A.Y. Jackson wrote that the war had 'a depressing effect on the arts' and admitted to being too disturbed by events in the spring of 1915 to do much painting (he would soon enlist in the infantry and serve in the trenches as a private). Royal Canadian Academy president William Brymner was saddened by the fact that people seemed to be 'thriving on munitions' instead of art.[220] Virtually every arts organization that enjoyed government support—including the National Gallery of Canada, the RCA, and the Ontario Society of Artists—saw its funding drastically reduced. It was the same in the private sector. Patrons who would have purchased art bought Victory Bonds instead; Robert Harris, accustomed to being busy with portrait commissions, now found he had idle time on his hands. Commercial galleries forsook artists' work for more profitable exhibitions of posters or patriotic art. Building projects that had been anticipated were shelved, particularly in the federal Department of Public Works, and the architects learned that their services were no longer required. The Calgary Symphony Orchestra collapsed when Max Weil, its German-born conductor, was forced to resign, and choirs and ensembles in Toronto, Regina, Halifax, and Victoria folded when their members enlisted or found other outlets for their energies. The *Toronto Daily Star* predicted nothing less than the end of good poetry: 'There is nothing poetic in killing men by machinery. Hence there is no more great war poetry…Modern wars are waged by machinery, according to the experts, and modern war poetry seems to be machine made too.'[221]

But the reports of culture's death were much exaggerated. It soon became apparent that almost every form of cultural expression would be energized and revitalized by war. The bustle of activity that touched every part of life was felt in the cultural realm as well. The arts joined the struggle, and culture became nothing less than the handmaiden of the nation. Even so, it would be a mistake to discount all of this activity as mere propaganda. Some of it certainly was, but culture was also a source of consolation and diversion, something that Canadians created and consumed first and foremost because it addressed their own needs, not the needs of the state.

Shortly after the war began, for example, culture emerged as an effective way of raising money for patriotic causes, and the musical, dramatic, or artistic fundraiser soon became a staple of Canadian life. There were so many causes to support—relief for Belgian civilians, the Canadian Patriotic Fund, the Red Cross Society, and dozens of other charities large and small. There was probably not a single one of them that didn't take advantage of local artistic talent to raise money. In December 1914, the RCA created its Patriotic Fund Exhibition Committee to organize exhibitions and sales of donated art. It toured the major cities from Halifax to Winnipeg, and by July 1915 had raised more than $10,000 for soldiers' dependents. The Men's Musical Club of Winnipeg, founded in December 1915 by forty businessmen interested in 'the promotion, extension or elevation of the art of music,' established the Male Voice Choir, which entertained the people of southern Manitoba with patriotic concerts through the war.[222] In Victoria, the Red Cross Stock Company was recruited from 'the best available theatrical talent in the Town' for the sole purpose of raising money for the Canadian Red Cross. All performers worked without remuneration, and their productions at the Royal Victoria Theatre, such as *The Caliph of Baghdad*, *King of the Cannibal Isles*, and *The Mandarin*, were popular with local theatre-goers for their lavish production values, talented cast, and sumptuous programs.[223]

But more important than money was morale, and in this respect culture could serve two contradictory purposes. Beyond filling the coffers of charitable organizations, it provided a diversion, from the desperate news that filled the daily papers, from the grief of friends and neighbours, from the seriousness that the war demanded. A night at the theatre or music hall was a break from the war, a reaffirmation that there was something beyond the needs of the conflict. But culture could just as easily boost morale by reaffirming what the war was all about, and by reminding people of the issues at stake. Music, literature, art, even vaudeville—they could all be vehicles for trumpeting the values represented by the Allied cause.

Poetry, for example, served this dual purpose. On the one hand, it offered refuge from a violent time. Writer and editor John Garvin noted that the war had brought a renaissance in poetry, because it moved people to turn 'instinctively from the terror and confusion of devastating human emotion, to the purity of a clearer and serener air' that was captured in the best verse. But as Carrie Holman recognized in her introduction to the verse anthology *In the Day of Battle*, war poetry could just as easily remind people of the values that were being defended: 'Repeatedly during the last year, when our courage may have become faint and our vision dimmed, there has come to us from the Front, insistent as a bugle call, the voice of the Soldier Poet, proclaiming, not so much the glories of war as a realization of the high spiritual significance of his task…many of these poems envisage for us the spirit and meaning of these tragic times.'[224]

Popular music also revealed these competing motives. Because the US entry into the war did not come until 1917, Canadian composers enjoyed a virtual North American monopoly on patriotic music for almost three years. They took full advantage of the opportunity, churning out hundreds of war-related songs between 1914 and 1918. Many came from professional songwriters such as Gordon V. Thompson and Morris Manley, already well known to Canadians, but amateurs also

Culture as diversion: the Queen's Sceptre dance of the King Edward Pageant, Saskatoon, June 1918.

found a ready audience for jaunty patriotic songs. Even classically trained composers like Alexis Contant and Healey Willan got into the action, Contant with the march 'Les Alliés' (1914) and Willan with 'In the Name of Our God We Will Set Up Our Banners' (1917), composed to mark the departure of Toronto's 169th Battalion. The demand appeared to be inexhaustible. Sheet music of the most popular songs sold remarkably well, Gordon Thompson estimating that his song 'When We Wind Up the Watch on the Rhine' sold 100,000 copies in Canada alone.

The themes were predictable—the imperial tie, lovers separated by war, the justice of the cause, the bond between soldier boy and mother—and the lyrics trite ('There's goin' to be some hollerin' from the House of Hohenzollern/Ere they finish with the khaki uniform'), all characterized by a mixture of escapism and utility. Some songs were clearly designed to lighten hearts by poking fun at the enemy (the cover of Harry Taylor's *You're Up a Tree, Old Bird, You're Up a Tree!* pictured the Kaiser as a vulture perched uncomfortably on a withered tree while a fat and not-so-fierce-looking German soldier stood beneath him), but others verged

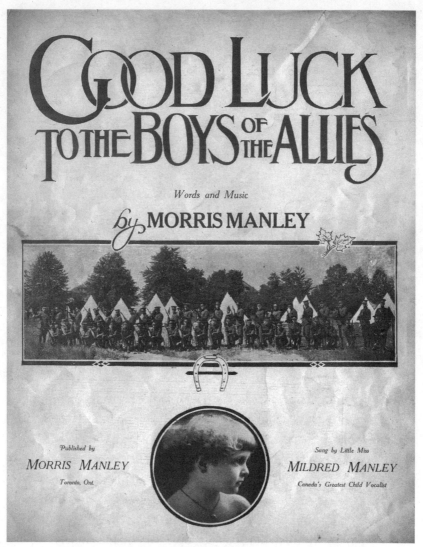

A product of the boom in patriotic sheet music during the First World War.

on the apocalyptic in their efforts to exhort Canadians to continue the struggle. Wyldes and McPhee's 'Arm Canadians! March to Glory!', for example, attempted to spur recruiting by conjuring up images of 'wailing babies and weeping mothers/tortured by the fiendish Hun.'

On another level, Canadians saw poetry and music as a kind of emotional release. In a time of great sorrow and great tragedy, great excitement and great triumph, people craved outlets for their feelings. Poetry was a part of most people's lives; they learned to read and write by studying poems in their school texts, so it was natural for them to turn to verse. It was the same with music. Most middle-class families of the time owned a piano, and the family singalong (and indeed the music lesson) was a feature of most households. Pouring one's heart out in verse or lyric—to mourn the death of a loved one, articulate the fears of the time, or celebrate a glorious victory on the battlefield—came naturally to Canadians. Poetry and music were part of the fabric of their lives, and they turned to them for comfort in times of trial.

The Canadian Corps String Band, 1916.

But it was not just the home front that required regular fillips of morale boosting. The need to entertain soldiers at the front ensured that the Canadian Expeditionary Force [CEF] quickly became a hothouse for the arts. Soldiers with literary aspirations took advantage of an eager public and gentle critics to publish volumes of verse. Others with less lofty goals submitted poetry and short stories to the dozens of unit newspapers published during the war, newspapers that were often illustrated with cartoons by soldier-artists. Actors, singers, and elocutionists also found a ready audience, once their commanders realized that entertaining the troops was essential to morale. Walter McRaye, the self-proclaimed 'apostle of Canadianism' who had spent the prewar years crossing the country doing public poetry readings, joined the little

Pierrot Troupe of the 126th Battalion, Canadian Forestry Corps, 1918.

concert party formed in his unit, #2 Canadian Field Ambulance. In his postwar memoirs he recalled standing on the steps of a ruined chateau in France reciting W.H. Drummond poems to his fellow soldiers; he was followed by a pal named Dick Kimberley who yodeled for the troops, and then a former Toronto actor did a recitation of Robert W. Service's 'The Shooting of Dan McGrew.'[225]

By war's end, all four divisions of the Canadian Corps, as well as a few brigades and battalions, had concert parties or unit bands. There were the Maple Leafs, which entertained the men of the 4th Division, and the Princess Patricia's Canadian Light Infantry Comedy Company, made up of members of Canada's first infantry battalion. But none of these troupes came close to achieving the success of the Dumbells. In 1917, Merton Plunkett of the YMCA combed the 3rd Division and drew the most talented performers he could find into a concert party that he named after the symbol on the divisional insignia. With their mix of sentimental ballads, slapstick, female impersonation, and rousing singalongs, the Dumbells quickly became the toast of the CEF and in 1918 Plunkett expanded the troupe to fifteen singers, actors, and musicians. Their four-week engagement at the London Coliseum outsold the shows by the famous Ballets Russes, but the men turned down offers of lucrative contracts from theatre promoters, preferring to return to

France to entertain the troops. By war's end, they were arguably the most famous members of the CEF.

———•—•••——

But in those momentous times, culture could serve a more enduring purpose than mere entertainment, even if the entertainment was in a good cause. History demanded that a record be kept of these formative years in Canada's history—what better job for writers, artists, and sculptors than to turn their talents to telling the nation's story? It was this realization, as much as the recognition that culture was a factor in maintaining morale, that was behind the unprecedented burst of artistic activity.

For the publishing industry, the first consequence of the war was a boom in business. People like L.M. Montgomery might have found it difficult to concentrate on writing, but the book-buying public was determined to keep reading. The Christmas 1914 season set new records for sales figures, and demand remained very strong throughout the war. This was particularly so in non-fiction publishing, which had shown some encouraging signs of life before the war but took off after August 1914. The trade periodical *Bookseller and Stationer* reported that the demand in Canada for 'serious' books had escalated dramatically, so much so that the magazine started publishing separate best-seller lists for fiction and non-fiction. For most of the war, books on current affairs and the military situation (many by British or American authors) dominated the lists; after 1915, there were never fewer than seven war books among the top ten best-sellers, and often the entire non-fiction list consisted of books about the war. It was the same in the nation's lending libraries. The Hamilton Public Library, for example, reported in 1916 that the circulation of light fiction had dropped by almost half, while there was 'frenzied demand' for non-fiction, primarily war books.[226]

The waning interest in fiction was only temporary and by mid-war, in what *Bookseller and Stationer* saw as welcome antidote to excessive wartime morbidity, the demand for fiction began to rise again. Canadians continued to prefer American or British authors, but there was a steady growth in the number of Canadian novels published, from twenty-six in 1917 to seventy just two years later. Some of these were written by new authors, but many came from the pens of the old standbys of Canadian literature. L.M. Montgomery and Charles G.D. Roberts, who had been so distracted by the coming of war, both soon rediscovered their muse. Montgomery would complete three novels, a collection of verse, and a brief autobiography during the war years, while Roberts would publish a best-selling account of Canadian soldiers in action and a handful of poems and short stories.

For the first-time novelist or perennial best-seller, the war offered the same opportunity to combine war-related plots and patriotic moralizing with traditional romantic or melodramatic formulae. 'The romantic side of this war will continue for generations to be valuable raw material for the weavers of literary fabric,' wrote Lindsay Crawford in *Canadian Magazine*. 'Thrilling tales of adventure that would delight the heart of any schoolboy devotee of Buffalo Bill may be found in the reports from the battle fronts in Europe.'[227] With this, contemporary events became the inspiration for literature, and the line between truth and fiction blurred; fictionalization came to be regarded as merely an artistic device that only accentuated a book's authenticity. Indeed, some of the most popular novels of the war, such as L.M. Montgomery's *Rilla of Ingleside*, were lauded for capturing the true essence of Canadian life.

It is not going too far to say that the war either rescued or made the careers of more than a few authors. Ontario-born but raised in Manitoba, Robert Stead had attained a certain stature before 1914 with patriotic poetry collections like *The Empire Builders* (1908) and his novels of prairie life, *The Bail Jumper* (1914) and *The Homesteaders* (1916). But it was the war that vaulted Stead (if only temporarily) into the top rank of Canadian writers. His 1916 poem *Kitchener*, mourning the death of Britain's Minister for War, was praised as one of the finest of the war and earned him the unofficial title of Canadian Poet Laureate. Two years later, Stead's novel *The Cow Puncher*, full of bracing patriotic rhetoric about duty, honour, and sacrifice, would become his best-selling book, with over 70,000 copies sold. He would follow that up in 1920 with another war-themed best-seller, *Dennison Grant*.

As Stead discovered, the public's thirst for war stories was unquenchable, and he and his fellow authors were only too happy to oblige. Indeed, the prodigious output of some war writers became a standing joke in literary circles. One reviewer reconstructed an imaginary conversation between a publisher and Eric Dawson, a member of the notoriously prolific Anglo-Canadian literary family, in which Dawson is cornered by the over-excited publisher: 'But haven't you another brother? What's he doing? Where's his manuscript? And what about your mother and sister in America, and your sister in Holland? Don't tell me they're not all writing?'[228] This apocryphal story carried with it more than a grain of truth for, as the print trade realized, virtually any book related to the war would find a ready audience. Macmillan of Canada head Hugh Eayrs reported in January 1919 that Canadian publishers had distributed over a thousand different war books since 1914, some of them selling as many as 40,000 copies. Before the war, a tenth of that was regarded as a very respectable sales record.

If the war was kind to authors, it was also kind to painters, offering opportunities that simply had not existed before. This was thanks in large part to Lord Beaverbrook, the transplanted New Brunswicker who had set up the Canadian War Records Office [CWRO] in London with responsibility for recording every aspect of Canada's war effort. The CWRO published a number of highly successful books, including the best-selling *Canada in Flanders* (1915), but Beaverbrook often complained of having trouble finding illustrations. He hired the first Canadian official war photographer and war cinematographer in 1916, but the art of combat photography was still in its infancy and so many pictures were faked that the medium began to lose its credibility. Beaverbrook also tried popular illustrators such as Richard Caton-Woodville, but their work looked contrived and artificial, and lacked the enduring qualities that he sought. Eventually, Beaverbrook began to lean towards using art as the means to capture history. Painting, as he later came to admit, was 'the most permanent and vital form in which the great deeds and sacrifices of the Canadian Nation could be enshrined for posterity.'[229]

It was his friend and fellow press baron Lord Rothermere who first suggested that official war artists, employed by the Canadian government, could record the story of Canada's war. Both Beaverbook and the government in Ottawa reacted warmly to the suggestion, and on 17 November 1916, the Canadian War Memorials Fund [CWMF] was established to provide 'suitable Memorials in the form of Tablets, Oil-Paintings, etc., to the Canadian Heroes and Heroines in the war.' The

program's title was revealing. It made no reference to art for, as Beaverbrook had implied, the motivation for the collection was not primarily
artistic. Ability was certainly necessary to get artists into the program,
but that was only a means to an end. As critic Barker Fairley noted, they
were being asked to produce not just art, but 'national records.'[230]

Despite the fact that they were national records, however, the first
appointment went to British artist Richard Jack. This annoyed painter
Ernest Fosbery (then recovering from wounds sustained in the Battle
of the Somme), who wrote indignantly to Beaverbrook that, because
'Canada is taking its place as a nation and Canadian art has more than

Arts patron Sir Edmund Walker. c. 1890.

kept pace with the developments of the country,' it was entirely appropriate that the program employ Canadian artists.[231] Suitably chastened,
Beaverbrook then appointed A.Y. Jackson (pulled from the trenches and
instructed to apply to the CWMF, Jackson prepared for his interview
with Beaverbrook by reading *Canada in Flanders*), Cecil Barraud, and
James Kerr-Lawson. More appointments, made possible by the success
of the CWRO's publishing ventures, soon followed. Eventually, the RCA
and the Ontario Society of Artists took a greater role in recommending
artists for the scheme, and advised the appointments of Maurice Cullen,
J.W. Beatty, Frederick Varley, and Charles Simpson, who left Halifax for
the front in March 1918. By war's end, well over a hundred Canadian,
British, and other Allied artists had been enrolled in the CWMF, their
work covering every conceivable aspect of the war, from battlefield to
munitions factory, air training base to convoy, hospital to cavalry depot.

The scheme did not sit well with everyone, however. Sir Edmund
Walker and Eric Brown were concerned that the Fund was engaged in
journalism rather than art, and advised that the artists confine themselves to making sketches; the finished canvases could be completed
after the war, when art advisors had been able to look at the material and make suggestions. But Beaverbrook was a man of action. The
artists were there, the money was there, the demand was there—now
was the time to get the job done. He realized, quite rightly, that once
any one of those elements disappeared (as they inevitably would), the
opportunity would be lost. Convinced by the obvious success of the
scheme, by the fact that no other war art program could compete with
the CWMF, and by Beaverbrook's cheques (which amounted to more
than the National Gallery of Canada's total annual budget), Walker
finally dropped his principled objections and became an enthusiastic
ally, despite his continued reluctance to become involved in the selection process, 'owing to the rather irritable minds of artists.'

What precisely did the war offer these artists? Not necessarily
money—the officer's rank and pay was welcome, but as the CWMF began
to run out of money late in 1918, artists found it increasingly difficult
to be reimbursed for supplies. Rather, the program offered rewards that
were far more valuable but much more difficult to quantify. There was
the opportunity to be shown in major exhibitions attended by thousands of people, including the most influential art patrons in the world.

There was participation in a high-profile art program that brought together some of the best artists in the Empire (British artists such as Augustus John, William Orpen, and C.R.W. Nevinson made no bones about the fact that the Canadian government was more generous than the British government, and was attracting the best painters). There was the realization that their work, which was to be hung in a massive, purpose-built war memorial museum in Ottawa after the war, would become an important part of the nation's cultural heritage. And, not incidentally, there was the chance to work on the big canvases that Beaverbrook saw as the focal points of the CWMF collection. Eric Brown knew this would be a real perk, so he played it up in his discussions with prospective artists. Robert Gagen agreed that artists rarely got the chance to work on really large canvases; they were difficult to sell and it was unwise to do them on spec, because one might never recoup the costs of canvas and paint. He believed that some artists would never again get another chance to work on so large a scale. Taking all these things into account, the CWMF was a once-in-a-lifetime opportunity for a painter, as Lawren Harris (who nevertheless declined to join the program) realized: 'It means so much to them—has benefited them in in [sic] every way and the enthusiasm the idea has engendered will, I am certain, be productive of the best work they have ever done. It is very gratifying in every way and a great pleasure to me to see them all so content and busy (young and old, particularly the old).'[232]

The CWMF was a kind of cultural funding program, giving dozens of artists a steady income, guaranteed sales, and a higher profile, but it was by no means the only one. It served to honour and record the war effort of the nation as a whole, but individual communities were determined to commemorate in bronze or stone their own contribution, particularly their sons and daughters who gave their lives. For the sculptors who did not enjoy CWMF patronage (only four, Frances Loring, Clare Sheridan, Derwent Wood, and Florence Wyle, did), the commemorative impulse was a ticket to creative fulfilment and financial security.

It was especially important because, despite the artistic vibrancy of the late Victorian era, sculpture was in the doldrums. The first *Year Book of Canadian Art* (1913) had included only one brief essay on a sculptor (Walter Allward); Hamilton MacCarthy had earlier complained that there was little interest in sculpture in Canada, and noted that

Toronto had surprisingly little public sculpture for a city of its size and political importance. A few prominent names, like Allward, MacCarthy, and Louis-Philippe Hébert, made a comfortable living, but most others were not so fortunate. It is an indication of the dire straits of the art that the RCA saw fit to waive its membership fees for sculptors for over twenty years before the First World War.

But the situation was about to change. As early as 1915, communities that proudly sent their youth to war began the sad task of commemorating those who would not return. Memorial scrolls came first (J.E.H. MacDonald was so busy decorating honour rolls that he had little time for 'the luxury of painting'), but monuments and memorial buildings were soon to follow. Despite a Vancouver MP's advice against 'turning to iron and stone to perpetuate flesh and blood,' most communities would do just that.[233] From 1919 to the mid-1930s, the demand for memorials was so strong that there was work for every sculptor who wanted it.

Frances Loring was just one beneficiary of this demand. Born in Idaho, Loring came to Canada shortly before the war and established a studio in Toronto with her life-long friend and fellow sculptor Florence Wyle. Thanks to glowing reviews of her work in an exhibition at the Art Museum of Toronto in late 1915, she and Margaret Scobie were commissioned to craft from staff (a mixture of plaster and straw) a twelve-foot-high figure of Miss Canada, to adorn the main entrance of the Toronto Eaton's store to mark the fiftieth anniversary of Confederation. She later received a commission from the Canadian National Exhibition to create a large allegorical figure (flanked by an imperial lion and cubs) representing the Spirit of Canada sending her sons off to war. It was just the kind of monumental work Loring relished; as Wyle put it, 'she doesn't like to do pieces unless she has to climb a ladder to get at them.'

After the war, having completed a half-dozen bronzes of women factory workers for the CWMF, Loring began to draw the attention of war memorial committees. Over the next decade, much of her time and creative energy would go into a series of fine commemorative works, including reliefs for the Toronto General Hospital memorial (1921), a plaque honouring Edith Cavell, a British nurse executed by the Germans in 1915, another at the University Avenue armouries in Toronto (1921) in honour of General Malcolm Mercer, who was killed in action in 1916, and reliefs in the Memorial Chamber in the Peace

Tower in Ottawa (1928); and larger memorials in St. Stephen, New Brunswick (1926), Osgoode Hall law school in Toronto (1928), and Galt, Ontario (1930). Her forms varied, from restrained, almost classical profiles to muscular and vibrant male figures, but the work is always recognizable as Loring's.

Robert Tait McKenzie's war memorial, entitled 'The Volunteer,' in Almonte, Ontario.

In this unprecedented wave of commemoration, virtually every sculptor with talent, and many without, secured contracts, with the most lucrative commissions going to the biggest names. Robert Tait McKenzie, a native of Almonte, Ontario, and widely regarded as one of the finest sculptors of the athletic figure, was asked to design the memorial in his hometown, a number of tributes to individual soldiers, including Colonel Harold Baker, the only Canadian Member of Parliament to be killed in action during the First World War, and major monuments in Britain and the United States. Walter Allward's memorials in Peterborough and Stratford, with their dynamic, allegorical bronze figures, foreshadowed the vision that would be fully realized in his finest work, the memorial on Vimy Ridge in northern France, unveiled in 1936. German-born sculptor Emanuel Hahn, a former assistant of Allward's and chief designer for the Thomson Monument Company, created one of the most popular memorials, a soldier gazing pensively down at a battlefield grave. Stone and bronze copies were sold to communities across Canada, and it remains the single most common sculptural memorial to emerge from the war. Elizabeth Wyn Wood, who married Hahn in 1926, was responsible for an equally striking memorial in Welland, Ontario. This powerful sculptural grouping, the last major war memorial to be completed in Canada in the interwar era, mixes stern, neo-realist figures with a traditional iconography. It is also one of the few to recognize explicitly the contribution of women to the war effort. In 1915, Fred Varley had predicted gloomily that undignified or amateurish war memorials would soon deface the streets of every Canadian town. Because of the sheer numbers involved, it was inevitable that many of them were undistinguished. But Varley was too pessimistic, for the sculptural legacy of the Great War is impressive. It took the art to a high level, and gave Canada some of its finest public monuments.

The common denominator in all of this cultural activity was that its primary considerations were practical rather than aesthetic. The war memorial movement certainly subordinated art to commemoration. A number of prominent artists and sculptors formed advisory committees to ensure that quality standards were maintained, but their efforts were for nought. The fact of the matter was that they were missing the point. Communities employed artists and architects not to create art, but to produce memory aids. Aesthetic judgements were irrelevant in

Emanuel Hahn's war memorial in Milton, Ontario.

assessing the success of a memorial; everything was about the feelings it inspired. If the proper emotions—reverence, pride, gratitude—were engendered, artistic merit was irrelevant. Great War monuments may run the gamut from the bizarre and the ham-fisted to the stunning and the sublime, but they are nothing if not sincere.

Elizabeth Wyn Wood's war memorial in Welland, Ontario.

The war in romantic mode: the death of Lieutenant-Colonel E.B. Birchall, as depicted in *Canada in Flanders*.

The CWMF was also frank about subordinating art to history. When one bureaucrat observed in 1928 that 'the collection contains actual battle scenes historically accurate and the pictures depict the type of warfare, materials and conditions of war fare and locations very correctly,' he was referring not to works of art but to historical documents.[234] As a result, contemporaries tended to value most highly those works with a clear narrative structure, such as the detailed battle scenes by Richard Jack that transformed the chaos and disorder of the Great War into rational and comprehensible events. Most observers, on the other hand, passed harsh judgement on those works (especially the Cubist or Futurist paintings) that, because they did not describe the war realistically, lacked the element of utility. Inevitably, such works were placed in a lower rank, often condemned as merely decorative.

This was true in literature as well. As literature became history, aesthetic standards grew less important; utility, not quality, became paramount. In some cases, this fact was made explicit. In 1918, for example, the Victory Loan committee invited Canadians 'with poetical talent' to submit entries to a verse contest. They were to be judged, however, not on their aesthetic quality but 'on their effectiveness as publicity designed to persuade Canadians to buy Victory bonds.' Indeed, Hugh Eayrs admitted after the war that quality often took a back seat to utility. 'In the decision to accept or refuse the average war book,' he recalled, 'the fact of usefulness from a propaganda standpoint had undoubtedly been a factor.'[235]

Not that this was a deep, dark secret of the publishing industry, for reviewers were not afraid to point out that many wartime books probably would not have been published during normal times. As J. Lewis Milligan observed wryly, the inspiration to write war poetry reached 'almost everybody who had ever written a rhyme, and that, of course, means everybody.' The result was a glut of poetry that had little merit. 'Under rigorous economic conditions,' observed a review of three volumes of poetry by Douglas Durkin, H.M. Thomas, and Owen McGillicuddy, 'books like these would scarcely come before the general public.' They were not bad or unworthy, just mediocre, he concluded.[236] Fred Jacobs, writing in *Saturday Night*, was a little less diplomatic. 'Pacifists tell us that war brings out all that is worst in man. The pacifists are evidently reading the war poetry in the daily press,' he quipped. He praised Alexander Muir's *The Maple Leaf Forever* because it covered the Battle of the Plains of Abraham in just four lines. All war poems should be four lines long, thought Jacobs; 'think what it would mean to the readers to have such a material curtailment to one of the chief horrors of war.'[237]

However, there was one very good reason why Jacobs' advice was never taken to heart, and why publishers continued to print books of poetry that, in other circumstances, would never see the light of day:

because the utility of the arts in raising morale and providing a historical narrative was based on the implicit assumption that the Allied cause was good, just, and right. Culture, therefore, became something of a war aim in its own right. It was the antidote to everything that Germany represented—Prussianism, frightfulness, *Kultur*. As artist Augustus Kenderdine said, the role of art in war was 'to nourish those cultural and spiritual forces for which we are fighting.'[238] This did not mean that the Allies were fighting to make the world safe for bad poets, but it did mean that the mediocrity of poets like Thomas and McGillicuddy could be overlooked if their work inspired the right emotions.

But if culture represented what the Allies were fighting for, how did Canada stack up? No one could deny that it had proven itself a nation on the battlefield, in the factory, and on the farm, but was it proving itself a nation in the theatre, the gallery, the library? Without question, some real masterpieces had emerged. Work for work, the Canadian War Memorials Fund was (and remains) the finest collection of war art in the world. Allward's Vimy Memorial is widely regarded as one of the most impressive achievements in commemorative sculpture and, while later critics have been less enthusiastic, contemporaries regarded John McCrae's 'In Flanders Fields' as the best poem to come out of the war. It was the same in virtually every form of artistic expression: the war inspired in Canadians work that could stand with the best in the world.

But how much of it was distinctly Canadian? Sadly, not very much. Arthur Stringer had earlier called Canadians 'mere suburbanites on the milk routes of international amusements,' and the cultural boom of the war years had, in many minds, merely set into high relief the realization that Canadian culture was lacking. Observers often pointed to the state of drama as being representative. There were playwrights in Canada ('I have personally met all of them—the whole three,' observed critic Harcourt Farmer), but none of them had produced anything that could truthfully be described as a Canadian play.[239] Many of Canada's best creative minds were immigrants from other countries, and they were content to reproduce European modes of expression without attempting anything distinctly Canadian. The result was a culture that was conservative, derivative, and imitative rather than original and unique. Traditionalism ruled the cultural roost.

Not surprisingly, this was partly due to the influence of the war. Many observers connected modernism with Germany; it was a fit of madness, a product of prewar excesses and wartime upheaval that would wither and die once peace and stability returned. J.J. Shallcross, speaking to the Island Arts and Crafts Club in Victoria in 1917, derided the Cubists and Futurists as 'the aftermath of a flood of Teutonic influence...[and the] unwholesome emanations of Prussianism.'[240] Estelle Kerr agreed, writing in *Canadian Magazine* that 'ultra-modern art which had its birth in Germany has been killed by the war.' Even artists from the Allied nations who practised these styles were condemned. The modernism of American poet Ezra Pound was full of 'vorticist banalities,' thought one critic, and could hardly compare to the 'exquisite verse' of Rupert Brooke.[241]

But modernism represented more than just a style that carried the taint of the enemy; it also represented a challenge to the existing order. And Canadians had quite enough other challenges to deal with during the war years. In this regard, Shallcross hit the nail on the head. The postwar dream was order and stability, a time when normalcy would return to life and Canadians could get back to their customary pursuits of nation-building. Modernism, with its unconventional metre, jagged edges, discordant rhythms, and brutal frankness, had no place in that ordered and stable world. Traditional modes of expression, on the other hand, were familiar, safe, comforting—everything that Canada wanted after four years of upheaval.

The persistence of tradition is evident in almost every branch of the arts. It is difficult to find a memorial sculpture, beyond Elizabeth Wyn Wood's in Welland, that is remotely modernist. On the contrary, memorial committees preferred the traditional Christian and imperial iconography of the prewar era—angels of victory, crowns of life, imperial lions, warlike soldiers in Victorian stances. For their part, viewers of CWMF exhibitions were generally puzzled by the Vorticist, Futurist, and modern artists represented, but reacted warmly to the Victorian battle pictures and nineteenth-century-style allegories. Literary anthologies, school texts, and 'top-ten' lists compiled by members of the *literati* provide a sense of the poetry that was most widely approved. Garvin's

Canadian Poets, which first appeared in 1916 and was republished in a new edition a decade later, is instructive in this regard. Garvin added over two dozen new poets to the revised edition, but could only bring himself to delete a handful of the old chestnuts; of the new poets represented only one, E.J. Pratt, had any kind of a modernist pedigree. The general taste in poetry, it appeared, remained solidly traditional.

The Canadian War Memorials Fund exhibition in Toronto, 1918.

Even the cityscapes of the period confirmed the dominance of traditional cultural forms. It was a great period of revivals, when everything from universities to government buildings to private homes adopted older styles. In domestic architecture, neo-Georgian re-emerged as the dominant form, its austerity, restraint, and symmetry lending a feeling of stability and calm to Canadian streets. The experimentation of the prewar era, inspired by the work of European architects, was largely cast aside, and all but disappeared even from the pages of architectural magazines. For private houses, the war and postwar years marked a period of architectural reaction. The same held true for public buildings. The most dominant style was the late Gothic revival, or modern Gothic as it was called at the time, which plucked forms and designs from medieval and renaissance English architecture. There were some fine examples in Canada—Toronto's Hart House, the College of Agriculture at the University of Saskatchewan, the Science Building at the University of British Columbia, Westmount City Hall—but they were all, to a greater or lesser degree, copies of landmarks from the old country.

The new parliament building, with Peace Tower under construction. c. 1900–39.

The high-water mark of revivalism, though, came in the nation's capital. A prewar plan for redeveloping the capital had been rejected on the grounds that its stern classicism would be 'foreign to Canadian sentiment.' Instead, the Holt Commission concluded in 1915 that the existing Parliament Building, a triumphant clutter of High Victorian architecture, and the nearby Château Laurier Hotel, in the Northern French Gothic style, were fine models for future government buildings. Another committee would eventually recommend that the government adopt the Northern French Gothic style for its building program, but the destruction of the Centre Block by fire in 1916 forced the government to act with despatch. With the Holt report in mind, the Chief Architects Branch was instructed to design a replacement for Centre Block without changing the general character and style of the building. This was done up to a point, but the High Victorianism was toned down to emphasize principles of order and simplicity. The result was an essay in Late Gothic Revivalism. The ornate design, colourful stone and roof treatments, and exuberant ornamentation were replaced by simpler, more restrained features. Solidity and simplicity took over where embellishment and intricacy had once held sway. At the very heart of the nation, it might be argued, the traditionalism of the Parliament Buildings offered a comforting sense of certainty in a turbulent era.

———•◦•———

The war, then, had proven two related propositions: that Canadians were enthusiastic consumers of culture; and that their culture was derivative rather than distinctly Canadian. But if the war revealed a problem, it also provided an unparalleled opportunity. Many observers saw the war as a blessing, for 'providing us thus early in our national life with a new and compelling purpose, which has brought the whole country together.' In the 1870s, the Confederation Poets had been inspired by a great event to celebrate the new nation in verse; this generation of creators would overshadow their predecessors, wrote W.D. Lighthall in 1918, because the Great War was far more momentous than Confederation. The poetry produced by the war would be unexcelled because 'none other proceeds specifically from our Canadian point of view, and so to speak courses directly in our national veins…the office of our war verse will be to apply the deep lessons of the struggle to the making of a better Canada.'[242]

This realization, that war both demanded and encouraged the creation of a distinct Canadian culture, coloured every aspect of the arts. Drama, for decades imported from Britain or the United States, would be nationalized. 'This war has made the Canadian National Theatre not only possible but imperative,' intoned A.B. Baxter; the country had to build its own dramatic tradition, so that Canadians would no longer look upon a theatre as little more than 'a slaughter house wherein to kill an evening.'[243] Magazines became more sensitive to the authorship of the articles they published, the new editor of Maclean's T.B. Costain realizing that readers would no longer be content with the literary cast-offs of other countries. Poet A.M. Pound agreed: 'every country with a spark of national pride must have a distinctive literature of its own,' he declared, and went on to quote Charles Mair: 'I have no dispute with those who advocate universality in poetry…but to my mind such poetry flies far and on feebler wing, than the muse inspired by love of country. This is the poetry that endures, for its home is in the heart of the people.' Painting styles, so long imported from Britain or the continent, would also have to be invented for the new nation: 'Canadian art will be distinguished by the fact that Canadian light is different, Canadian scenery is different, and Canadian temperament is different,' mused Augustus Kenderdine. 'It will be as distinctive as a Canadian prairie flower, which grows no place else.'[244]

This combination of cultural nationalism and confident patriotism comes out clearly in B.K. Sandwell's essay on Canadian culture, published in a 1916 volume entitled *Canada's Future*. The war, he reflected, had 'given Canadians a vastly enhanced consciousness of the values and meaning of their nationhood.' Having achieved that awareness, there was no going back; 'a nation with this experience behind it will never again consent to accept its artistic ideals, wholesale and unmodified, from another nation...Canada has new national experiences, understandings and aspirations, which will more than ever call for expression in a purely Canadian art and literature...If a finer culture and a prouder national consciousness are the first results of Canadian participation in the war, there need be no doubt that a stronger and purer national art and literature will follow closely after.'[245]

Many Canadians were ready, willing, and able to answer Sandwell's call, if we are to believe the lead editorials of the new journals that emerged in the wake of the war. The *Dalhousie Review* appeared in 1921 and espoused a mix of nationalism, self-improvement, and high-brow presumption. It had no desire to be just another journal 'of mere literary entertainment...superficial chatting about the transient occurrences of the hour,' observed the editor, playing on the distinction between high-brow and popular culture. Instead, it was aimed at that part of the public that is 'concerned about the things of the intellect and the spirit.'[246] The same belief animated *Canadian Forum*, which had published its first issue the year before. 'No country has reached its full stature, which makes its goods at home, but not its faith and its philosophy,' proclaimed its first editorial. To foster that faith and philosophy, the magazine promised 'to trace and value those developments of art and letters which are distinctly Canadian.'[247] In contrast to other publications of the time, *Canadian Forum* retained a discriminating loftiness, refusing to praise culture simply by virtue of the fact that it was Canadian.

Another product of this burgeoning cultural nationalism was *Canadian Bookman*, first published in January 1919 through the efforts of a small group of Montreal writers. Edited by B.K. Sandwell, it bespoke a sublime faith in the power of culture to improve the national fabric. Its glossy pages covered weighty issues like the need for more bookishness in Canada, the character of the reading public, and the history of Canadian publishing houses, and its first editorial claimed that the magazine was a product of 'a new national self-consciousness, a new demand that ideas be judged…by the standards of our own country.'[248] But bullish rhetoric didn't pay the bills, and two years later the editor admitted that there were not enough people genuinely interested in the creative arts in Canada to support a magazine that cost fifty cents an issue or $1.50 for a year's subscription. The journal bounced from publisher to publisher (the one constant was that the reviews were frequently more fawning than critical), moves that saw the format and size change and the price drop by half in an effort to boost subscriptions.

Revenues slowly increased, but *Canadian Bookman* might still have disappeared were it not for the foundation of a society that would eventually become the pre-eminent voice of writers in Canada. On 12 March 1921, some one hundred authors met in Montreal on the invitation of Stephen Leacock, who used the occasion of a lunch honouring the writer and literature professor Pelham Edgar to complain bitterly about the federal government's record on copyright legislation. By the time the spleens were vented and the brandy and cigars finished, they had decided to establish the Canadian Authors' Association [CAA].

The CAA's principals looked back on the founding meeting with fondness and good humour. Writer and folklorist J. Murray Gibbon recalled that the first constitution was modelled on that of the Isaak Walton League of America, an organization of Chicago-area sport anglers concerned about water pollution (Gibbon happened to have a copy of the League's constitution in his study), and mused that he was likely chosen as the association's first president because he had a pass from the Canadian Pacific Railway that gave him free travel across the country. But despite Gibbon's self-deprecatory tone, the CAA represented a significant advance for Canadian writers. It was to consist of a branch in each province, as well as a separate, self-governing wing, *la section française*, for French-Canadian writers (*nationaliste* journalist

Olivar Asselin had demanded a wholly separate group for French-language writers, but was unable to secure sufficient support for his proposal). It was, however, resolutely male and central Canadian. Even though as many as half of the authors at the founding meeting were women, only two, Nellie McClung and Isabel Ecclestone Mackay, were among the eight vice-presidents; only seven of the twenty-two council members were women. Furthermore, a regional bias existed as well. The CAA's head office was to rotate between Montreal, Ottawa, Toronto, and Winnipeg, even though the Maritime provinces and western Canada had produced some of the nation's best-selling and most popular authors of the day.

The organization acted as part lobby group, part writers' club. It carried on a long and often bitter battle to secure more favourable copyright legislation for Canadian writers, but it was also relentless in its campaigns to encourage people to buy Canadian books. Taking up Robert Stead's axiom that buying a Canadian book was 'fundamental nation-building,'[249] it mounted a series of high-profile public relations events, from a trail ride to the unveiling of a memorial to explorer David Thompson (the image of Bliss Carman, J. Murray Gibbon, and a host of other literary luminaries clip-clopping across the prairie on horseback is priceless) to its most ambitious event, the inaugural Canadian Book Week, held in November 1921. For seven days, booksellers, publishers, and writers bombarded the reading public with 'buy Canadian' advertising. The resulting sales may not have been robust (many publishers declined to take part, because there was still more money in printing foreign books than Canadian), but the week demonstrated that Canadian authors were becoming as open to self-promotion as their counterparts in the United States and Britain.

The CAA was part of a wider cultural renaissance that swept the nation around the time of the Great War. It was championed by people such as Gordon Thompson, who founded the Authors and Composers Association of Canada in 1918, to protect and promote the rights of songwriters. In book publishing, there were boosters like Hugh Eayrs, a charismatic Englishman who became president of Macmillan of Canada at the tender age of twenty-six and almost immediately changed the company's policy of doing only textbooks in Canada. Eayrs diverted some of the profits from educational sales to publish some of Canada's most important authors, such as Frederick Philip Grove, Raymond Knister, Mazo de la Roche, and E.J. Pratt; and Lorne Pierce of Ryerson Press (formerly the Methodist Book and Publishing House), more retiring than Eayrs but just as passionate about promoting Canadian culture and aiding up-and-coming writers. At the National Gallery of Canada, Eric Brown was buying Canadian art and encouraging Canadian painters, all part of his campaign to create a national school of art; 'no nation can be truly great until it has a great art,' he wrote.[250]

It was an exciting time to be involved in Canadian culture, for there was a vibrancy present that had not been seen in decades. In 1919 the Men's Musical Club of Winnipeg held its first annual music competition, drawing over 250 entries in thirty-eight classes.[251] Writers, even if their sales were not climbing dramatically, were at least obtaining new respect. Canadian literature was beginning to make its way into university curricula, and literary history was coming into its own, with publications such as Archibald MacMechan's *Headwaters of Canadian Literature* (1924) and J.D. Logan and Donald G. French's *Highways of Canadian Literature* (1924). For the more affluent reader, Lorne Pierce hatched a plan for a magisterial, forty-one volume series entitled the Makers of Canadian Literature. Not to be outdone, the Radisson Society launched the twenty-volume Master Works of Canadian Authors, a series of luxurious tomes selling for $100 (nearly $1,200 today) each. Both series petered out before completion, but the confidence they embodied were representative of the times. Not since the Confederation era had culture seemed so healthy in Canada.

———•◦•———

When Duncan Campbell Scott gave his presidential address to the Royal Society of Canada on 17 May 1922, he offered a commentary on the state of culture that was much broader than his title, 'Poetry and Progress,' suggested. He spoke with tremendous optimism, surveying the great leaps that had been made in every academic field, from literature to science to history, since the Society's inception in 1882. In poetry, he had only to look at the fortunes of Archibald Lampman (whose gifts had not been recognized in Canada until he had been praised by American critics) and Marjorie Pickthall (who was hailed immediately

in Canada as a poet of merit) to see that the nation was developing
an appreciation for the arts, and for its own distinctive contribution
to international letters. Scott's choice of poets to discuss betrayed his
own traditional sympathies; his talk was sprinkled with reverence for
the great writers of previous centuries—Shakespeare, Donne, Keats,
Milton, Wordsworth—'who made clear the paths of life and adorned
them with beauty.' But he could not ignore the fact that the ground
appeared to be shifting. In contrast to the grace and harmony he so
loved in the classics, modernism, he observed, was characterized by a
critical spirit based on irritation; its purpose was 'to insult older ideas of
beauty...to shock with unwholesome audacities...with the mere mali-
cious design of awakening protest, the more violent the better.' Scott
likened modernism to a virus that was infecting the arts, but he spoke
more in resignation than indignation, a tacit admission that he could
do nothing to stem the tide. It went against his own preferences, but
he had to allow that there was something very positive in the change
he was witnessing. 'It is the mission of new theories in the arts,' he told
the academicians, 'to force us to re-examine the grounds of our preferences, and to retest our accepted dogmas.' There was something to be
said for an artistic spirit that challenged and confronted the world: 'we
require more rage of our poets.'[252] As Scott knew full well, the signs of
that growing rage were already evident.

Chapter 11

The New Parliament of Art

Scott had spoken of rage, but he was also implicitly referring to age. There was a sense that the First World War constituted a great divide between generations, and that the beginning of the postwar era was the natural opportunity for the new generation to take the lead. As Bliss Carman wrote in April 1917, 'only new men, young men, or those who have taken part in the struggle will be entitled to take part in the new parliament of art. The Victorian days belong to history. I believe the new days will be better, but I doubt if any of the men who came to maturity before the great war will be able to find the new key, the new mode, the new tune.'[253]

Carman realized that the world would be different after the war, and that a new culture would be needed to express the new reality. This meant a changing of the guard—the generation of 1914 would champion new ways of doing things, and the cultural landscape would be reshaped in the process. But the burst of nationalism fostered by the war brought into focus a whole series of questions. How did Canadian culture stack up against the products of other countries? What should be the characteristics of a new Canadian mode of expression? How would the struggle between the old art and the new play out? And how would the general public react to the shift that was underway? In grappling with these questions, both generations of artists groped their way towards a new culture.

What had seemed so clear during and immediately after the war, that Canada needed to forge its own distinct forms of cultural expression, did not remain clear for long. Soon, all of the activity was overshadowed by the same old conundrum: was cultural nationalism its own worst enemy? When did art or literature become too self-consciously nationalist, and did that compromise its value as art? Although nine-teenth-century commentators had raised these concerns, they had been largely drowned out by the rhetoric of Charles G.D. Roberts, *Picturesque Canada*, and the Château style. But much had changed since then—had the nation matured to the point where an explicitly nationalist culture was parochial and self-defeating?

There was still some consensus that, because Canada represented a distinct geographical entity, it needed a distinct culture based on that geography; this, of course, was nothing new to those who had followed the rhetoric of Canada First and the Confederation Poets, but there was now a greater emphasis on the regional. 'The physical features, and the climate of a land, where work of true literary character is produced,' wrote A.M. Pound, 'may very often so determine the tone and colour of a writer's output as to make it *geographically* distinguishable... there may be a literature which is *distinctively of British Columbia*.'[254] Professor G.W. Snelgrove thought it was the duty of the Saskatchewan artist to paint the beauties of that province, because if they were not going to celebrate those beauties, no one else would. An Alberta jour-nalist agreed, arguing that the province 'inspires poetic effort' because of a unique, undefinable characteristic. 'There is something about the climate of Alberta which stimulates poetic fervour,' and this could not be found anywhere else in Canada, especially not (in a dig at the other prairie provinces) in Saskatchewan or Manitoba.[255]

But others argued that this fixation on regional and national culture constituted a parochialism that would ultimately hobble the arts. While admitting that Canada needed to break free of the American entertain-ment industry and make its own drama, Vincent Massey warned that 'the struggle to discover a Canadian point of view...creates the artificial Canadianism that is an offence against honest art...no arbitrary set of rules can be applied to a play to make it Canadian, and no standard set of virtues can be made to personify Canada.' Fernand Préfontaine, writing in *Le Nigog*, said that 'Art, like science, is universal. We wouldn't dare suggest that a philosophy or a branch of physics or chemistry is purely Canadian. It wouldn't make sense. Yet we expect our art to limit itself to depicting Canadian scenes.'[256] A.J.M. Smith, a Montreal-born poet who was beginning to make a name for himself as one of the standard-bearers of modernism, agreed that the preoccupation with nationalist literature was misplaced:

> If you write, apparently, of the far north and the wild west and the picturesque east, seasoning well with allusions to the canada goose, fir trees, maple leaves, snowshoes, northern lights, etc., the public grasp the fact that you are a canadian poet, whose works are to be bought from the same patriotic motive that prompts the purchaser of Eddy's matches or a Massey-Harris farm implement.

Even Pound, who had written so feelingly of a distinctive British Columbia literature, was torn: 'Literature which is too obviously national is not so much literature as it is propaganda…any attempt to *force the growth of a distinctly Canadian literature* would result in *sheer smears of publicity*; more likely to be appreciated by the railway and shipping companies, than by true lovers of literature.'[257] At the root of these concerns was the belief that cultural nationalism was one of the pernicious forces that had pushed the world to war in 1914; in its place, European cultural elites were now embracing internationalism and cosmopolitanism. As Smith put it, the times were changing; modern poetry is written by people 'whose emotional and intellectual heritage is not a national one.'[258] The nationalist poet, he thought, was rapidly becoming a thing of the past. The old ways were not suited to a country that had come into its own in the fires of battle; they were stale and ossified, and had little to offer the postwar world.

There was some justification to such criticism. For example, architect Percy Nobbs, Canada's leading practitioner in the field before 1914, believed in evolutionary change, not the kind of rapid innovation that characterized his profession in the immediate postwar period. His conviction that architecture needed a nationalist basis and his sympathy for British traditions predisposed him against modernism, and particularly against the International Style—a term coined in 1932 to refer to a style that relied on regularity rather than symmetry and eschewed surface decoration in favour of emphasizing the inherent aesthetic qualities of the building materials. Taken to its fullest extent, the style produced buildings that were precisely as the name suggests: international, in that a structure from one country looked very much like a structure from any other. This was a notion that Nobbs found distasteful.

While a few architects were receptive to the modernist movement in architecture—John Lyle spoke in 1929 in favour of the 'revolt against archaeology in architecture' and advised his fellow architects that they could find much of value in it[259]—Nobbs and the majority of the profession were less open. They were more comfortable with the revivals that still dominated the field, the late Gothic, the mature Château style, the Tudor revival, modern classicism, all of which looked to the past for inspiration. Canada's evolving urban landscape was not totally devoid of new styles, but buildings in the International Style were few and far between. Percy Nobbs, for one, retreated to the tried and true formulae, and was unable to come to terms with the challenge of modernity.

—•◦•—

He wasn't the only one. Modernism is a nebulous concept to define at the best of times, for its most basic characteristics, its subjective and intuitive nature, mean that it is open to virtually limitless interpretations, depending on the art form and the artist. In art, it might be Cubism, expressionism, or Futurism; in sculpture, a move away from representation. Modern music was atonal, modern dance appeared primitive and unstructured, and modern poetry did not rhyme. To people like Percy Nobbs, it must have seemed terribly confusing. He at least tried to articulate a critique of modernism, but others responded more viscerally; for many people in the 1920s and 1930s, modernism could be defined as any kind of culture they disliked. Not surprisingly, this led to some bitter debates.

One emerged over the British Empire Exhibition, held at Wembley Stadium in London, England, in 1924 and again in 1925. There was a huge variety of wares on display, including selections from Canadian literature, both in English and French, chosen by a joint committee drawn from the Toronto Public Library and the Canadian Authors' Association. It was, for CAA president Robert J.C. Stead, an unparalleled opportunity to showcase the talents of Canadian writers, 'the first occasion upon which a Canadian Government has officially recognized Canadian literature as a product worthy of display before the nations of the world.'[260] But it was not the books, the wheat, the minerals, or even the immense sculpture of the Prince of Wales and his horse, crafted

Meeting of the Canadian Authors Association, 1925.

entirely from Canadian butter, that turned the heads of exhibition-goers and critics alike. It was the art exhibition, specifically work by the members of the now legendary Group of Seven. Among them were paintings that would become some of the Group's most famous and beloved: Varley's *Stormy Weather, Georgian Bay* and Lismer's *A September Gale*, both featuring the iconic lone pine tree, bent against the wind that blasts the rocky outcrop to which it clings; Harris' *Shacks*, a striking winter scene showing broken-down houses in Toronto; and Jackson's *The Northland* (also known as *Terre Sauvage*), depicting dark and spindly pine trees against a threatening sky daubed with thick clouds. Together, they bore all the hallmarks of the Group's work: the use of strong, contrasting colours, often applied very thickly; a fascination with what their critics called wasteland, whether it be in the northern wilderness or in downtown Toronto; a confident handling of light and shadow, frequently using Impressionist techniques like dappling; and a rough paint surface, in contrast to the flat, heavily varnished paintings of their predecessors.

The battle to get the Group's work to Wembley was long and bitter—some scholars see it as the old guard trying to hold the gates against the tide of modernism or the Montreal art community battling the upstarts from Toronto, but art historian Ann Davis mounts a convincing case that it was simply one more episode in a long power struggle between the Royal Canadian Academy and the National Gallery of Canada, which

The iconic portrait of the Group of Seven, taken in the Arts and Letters Club in Toronto. c. 1920.

had emerged as the Group's strongest institutional backer. Leading academicians were horrified to learn that the National Gallery would be responsible for selecting the works to be exhibited at Wembley, and a number of them threatened a boycott. Hector Charlesworth got himself into high dudgeon, warning of the consequences if the nation were to exhibit only 'crude cartoons of the Canadian wilds.' The only solution, thought Charlesworth, was for the federal government to step in 'to prevent such a catastrophe.'[261] In the end, in true Canadian fashion, a compromise jury was selected, which eventually chose 270 works by 108 artists; significantly, only twenty were by the Group of Seven and Tom Thomson.

The organizers had decided that all art (except native art) would be in the Palace of Arts rather than in individual pavilions, to demonstrate 'how the Daughter Nations have developed their art from the English school.' But that was not the lesson that English and American critics drew when they studied the work of the Group of Seven. 'The Canadian artists,' wrote London's *Saturday Review*, 'are more independent of prevailing fashions than the younger English, while they are as remote from the academic.' The New York *Art News* agreed that Canada had freed itself from its colonial past: 'Here are people with something vital to say, who say it well and with emphasis, and at the same time with a typical Canadian outlook.'[262]

The Wembley show may have represented the Group's international coming-out, but the members had long been a thorn under the artistic establishment's saddle. It began before the Great War when four Toronto commercial artists, J.E.H. MacDonald, Franz Johnson (who would resign from the Group after its first show, to be replaced in 1926 by A.J. Casson), Arthur Lismer, and Frederick Varley, took to spending their weekends and holidays sketching in the countryside. Later, they were joined by Frank Carmichael, another commercial artist, and Lawren Harris, the only one of the Group who was independently wealthy. The seventh member, A.Y. Jackson of Montreal, was invited to join after Harris saw one of his works at the 1910 exhibition of the Ontario Society of Artists. Disgusted with the state of Canadian art, Jackson was about to leave for the United States when the invitation came. An eighth painter, Tom Thomson, would become just as influential as the others, but he died when they were generally known simply as the Algonquin School; the name Group of Seven was not coined until 1920, after the painters had received permission to mount a show at the Art Gallery of Toronto. Uniting them was a belief in the inadequacy of Canadian art. In a 1944 reflection, Harris recalled the words of an English critic about an exhibition of Canadian paintings sent to England: 'At present the observation is strong, but the more immutable essence of each scene is crushed out by a foreign-begotten technique.'[263] It was the quest for an alternative to that 'foreign-begotten technique' that motivated them.

Their early work generally drew moderate approval or indifference; a few major publications, such as the Toronto *Evening Telegram*, *Saturday Night*, and the *Canadian Magazine*, declined even to notice their first show, in May 1920, and only 2,146 people turned up to see the twenty-four-day exhibition. But a handful of anti-Group critics were soon competing with each other for the most derisive metaphor. It was F.H. Gadsby in the *Toronto Star* who gave them their most lasting sobriquet, the Hot Mush School, in a 1913 article that was more tongue-in-cheek than critical—Gadsby was surely pulling a few legs when he likened their paintings to 'a Dutch headcheese having a quarrel with a chunk of French nougat' or 'a plesiosaurus in a fit as depicted by an industrious but misguided Japanese.' But Samuel Morgan-Powell was

The Ontario Society of Artists Hanging Committee, 1932.

being completely serious when he described the work of one modern painter in 1913: 'His drawing would shame a school boy. His composition would disgrace an artist of the stone age—the paving-stone age… They are not works of art. They are travesties, abortions, sensual and hideous malformations.'[264] When the Wembley exhibition came around, Hector Charlesworth, who had compared two of MacDonald's works to Hungarian goulash and the contents of a drunkard's stomach, entitled his review 'Canada and her Paint Slingers' and referred to the 'graceless and depressing formula of…a group of Toronto painters who hold that Canada is only truly interpreted through a single narrow and rigid formula of ugliness.'[265]

But the critics were also capable of more serious, albeit still negative, commentary on the work of the Group of Seven, often arguing that the work was repetitive. In 1922, Augustus Bridle, who came to Canada as an illegitimate orphan in 1878 and worked his way to become an arts critic for half a dozen major periodicals, the president of the Arts and Letters Club of Toronto, and a bass singer in that city's Mendelssohn Choir, believed that 'the Seven are into a sort of quest for the Holy Grail of Art,' but that along the way their work had taken on a disconcerting sameness: 'In their search for what lies beyond, the group are becoming rather more alike. Two years ago I could easily spot any of the painters by their pictures. Now there are times when I wonder at first glance which is a Jackson, or a Lismer, at odd times a Harris, and now and then a Macdonald.' Bertram Brooker, usually one of the Group's strongest supporters, observed in 1928 that 'the influence of their work shows signs of hardening into a formula which a good many painters are adopting as being, so to speak, the "fashionable" native school of painting.'[266] Charlesworth agreed, writing two years later that 'there can be little "originality" in a school…All it could mean was that a number of our painters had chosen to adopt a syndicated technique of sufficient novelty to attract attention…most of the pictures seemed to be essentially timid, as though each member were afraid of violating his fraternal oath.' The *Toronto Star*, after pointing out that 'Their exhibit of pictures was interesting and attracted attention, but so would a wheelbarrow in a drawing-room,' observed that it was a bit too much to believe that they had all seen the light at once: 'the method adopted by the group of seven could, if it were adopted by one man, be regarded as an evidence of genius or of insanity. But when seven break out all at once and together one feels that geniuses do not come in sevens.'[267]

Implicit in such critiques was the notion that the Group of Seven had become surrounded by myth. For all their complaints about the old way of painting, there was little new in their insistence that the Canadian landscape was unique and demanded a unique response from painters. After all, however strenuously they might have denied it, they were building on the landscape tradition of the post-Confederation era, when painters such as John A. Fraser and Lucius O'Brien used their work to forge a bond between the natural glories of Canada and an emerging sense of nationalism. And when Lawren Harris wrote that 'our art is founded on a long and growing love and understanding of the North…in an ever clearer experience with the informing spirit of the whole land and a strange brooding sense of Mother Nature fostering a new race and a new age,'[268] he sounded strangely like D'Arcy McGee. And his claim that the Group played a major role in creating 'an art expression which is as much a part of Canadian life as the grain elevator, the maple leaf, and the west wind' would have done the nineteenth-century members of the Ontario Society of Artists proud. Furthermore, many doubted whether the Group ever succeeded in making itself a national school of painting. As Frank Underhill wrote in 1936, 'Instead of using the North as an instrument through which to express their vision of Canadian life, they began to use it as a means to escape from Canadian life.'[269] And in 1941, André Biéler observed that the Group, for all its merits, was a regional rather than a national school of painting that, when transplanted to other parts of the country, 'loses all sense.'

In this regard, the painters, and more importantly their boosters, liked to present them as organically Canadian, untouched by the fashions of Europe that, in their eyes, their predecessors had embraced all too enthusiastically. F.B. Housser saw the Group as a movement that had turned its back on Europe. 'For Canada to find a true…expression of herself through art,' he wrote, 'a complete break with European traditions was necessary.' But Harris himself admitted that he and MacDonald had been deeply impressed and influenced by an exhibit of Scandinavian art they had seen at the Albright Art Gallery in Buffalo, New York; in his words, the Scandinavian painters had clarified their purpose and reinforced their conviction, something that Paul Peel could well have said thirty years earlier about the French art he so admired.[270]

It is also true that much of the opposition to their work, so important in raising their profile, was not spontaneous but carefully cultivated. The members of the Group knew that there was no such thing as bad press and became gifted propagandists, always ready to stir the pot to keep their names in the newspapers. Jackson believed that early success would have been fatal to the movement because they needed conflict to get their message across, while Harris admitted in 1950 that 'We became not only used to…excited opposition to the paintings but encouraged it. We goaded the reactionary and cocksure writers of the press of that day to give full rein to their breezy diatribes.' Four years later, he revealed that 'Sometimes we would reply to the tirades in the press to keep the excitement going. We would also advise our favourite critic whom we would occasionally meet in the arts and letters club, of better, more violent ways of condemning our work.'[271] Of course, their fiercest critics were quite happy to join the fray, because there was nothing like a public squabble to get people through the turnstiles of art galleries. In short, there is an argument to be made that the Group's success was as much due to their art as to their public relations skills and their talent for manipulating the media.

Perhaps most ironically, the Group became the old establishment with remarkable speed. In 1924, the *Toronto Star* warned the members that 'they will be old fellows themselves one day,'[272] and in the rapidly changing cultural milieu of the interwar era the old modernists found themselves being bypassed by the new modernists. Thoreau MacDonald, the Toronto artist and illustrator (because of colour-blindness, he worked mostly in black and white) whose father had been one of the Group's founders, observed that 'in their efforts to be modern and free [the Group] are in danger of becoming more conventional than older societies. They lack life that comes from keeping their feet planted on the ploughed ground and eyes on the face of nature.' He wondered if they were content to be 'a nursery for incompetent painters.' F.B. Housser immediately leapt to their defence, but as historian Margaret Davidson put it, he sounded 'suspiciously like the Royal Canadian Academy members who had protested against sending Group paintings to Britain in 1924.'[273] By the same token, when traditional Group ally *Canadian Forum* lamented the fascination with new forms of art like Cubism and complained about painters who made 'studies of rotten apples and anti-macassars and blue horses,' it could have been Gadsby or Charlesworth writing. John Lyman, born in Maine but active as a painter and critic in Montreal from 1931, mocked the fact that A.Y. Jackson's new experimentation consisted of going farther north to paint the Arctic; 'The real trail must be blazed towards a perception of universal relations that are present in every parcel of creation,' wrote Lyman, 'not towards the Arctic Circle.'[274] Others suggested that the days of 'granite and jack pines' were past, and that it was time to embrace pure abstraction.

Perhaps realizing that their movement had run its course, the Group decided to expand for its 1930 show by inviting thirteen other painters to exhibit, including Emily Carr and LeMoine Fitzgerald. The following year, the show had twenty-five invitees in addition to the Group members, and for supporters like Bertram Brooker and *Canadian Forum*, this represented the end. With unenthusiastic reviews and no sales, the members met at Harris' house and decided that the Group would no longer exist in its original form. They had done much to inspire a new generation of artists, wrote J.B. Salinger in a kind of obituary, but their work had weakened over the years and, of the original seven, only A.Y. Jackson still exercised his full artistic powers.

He also never lost his good humour. In February 1925, he and Wyly Grier, representing the old school of Canadian painters, were invited to speak to the Empire Club in Toronto. In a good-natured address, Jackson and Grier revealed just how much sympathy there was between the traditionalists and the modernists (they both poked fun at the fondness of Canadian art collectors for Dutch barnyard paintings). But the last word went to Jackson, who looked ahead to the day when he was viewed as one of the old guard. 'When the last cow is taken from the drawing room and the walls are alive with red maple, yellow birch, blue lakes and sparkling snow-scapes, I can hear the young modern painter up north say to his pal, "There's the trail that those old academic Johnnies, the Group of Seven, blazed."'[275]

Just as the members of the Group of Seven had begun to grope towards modernism before the First World War, writers in the same period were calling for new literary forms. In fiction, their ideal was summed up by the catch-all term 'realism,' an amorphous notion that Canadian critics had as much difficulty defining as they did finding. For Archibald MacMechan, realism in literature meant tackling modern problems directly and honestly, rather than the 'conventional, decent, unambitious, "bourgeois"' approach that had characterized Canadian literature before the 1920s. For Marcus Adeney, realism implied a degree of social criticism, while Francis Dickie saw in it a determination to present the sordidness, emptiness, and sadness of life along with its 'humor and little deeds of kindness.'[276]

In poetry, free verse (usually defined as unrhymed verse with lines of irregular length) emerged as the shining path of the modernists. Arthur Stringer, born in 1874 and so of the generation of the Confederation Poets, had made a case for free verse in 1914, but it was not until after the war that the debate really started in earnest. J. Murray Gibbon, also usually lumped with the old guard, wrote in 1919 that free verse wasn't really new, but a revival—rhyming poetry had not come into fashion until the days of Chaucer—and quoted approvingly from the guru of the modernists, the American poet Ezra Pound: 'no book words, no periphrases, no inversions. There must be no clichés, set phrases, stereotyped, journalese—no straddled adjectives (as "addled moss dank")—nothing that you couldn't in some circumstances, in the stress of emotion, say.' Gibbon thought that Canadian poets had failed the test because they had tried to capture a new country with old forms; 'How can the spirit of a half-tamed new continent be expressed in a courtly seventeenth century jingle?' he wondered. 'Metrical rhyming forms are only the shibboleth of imaginary rank, of imaginary finish and style, of imaginary caste. They are a fashion…which shows every sign of passing away, and being relegated like the harpsichord and the crinoline into the domain of the museum.'[277]

Stringer and Gibbon mounted reasoned defences of modernism, but the modernists themselves preferred to meet their critics with liberal doses of sarcasm. Their principal vehicle was *Canadian Forum*, but they also established the *McGill Fortnightly Review* (1925–27) and *Canadian Mercury*, launched in 1929 and in publication for only six months, patterned after H.L. Mencken's stinging journal *American Mercury*. Both were self-consciously contrary, *Canadian Mercury* hoping that by criticizing the 'amiable mediocrity' and 'inspidity' of Canadian literature, they would encourage 'as modern Canadian painting had begun to do, a unique experience of nature and life.'[278] The *Review*, for its part, was accused of having communist tendencies, but in reality it was rather tame. One of its editors recalled that much of the poetry submitted 'was of the nursery-rhyme kind: it limped,' so A.J.M. Smith filled the empty columns with poetry he wrote under pseudonyms (like Brian Tuke, which inevitably was lampooned as Trian Puke); even so, literary scholar David Arnason characterized much of the verse as the juvenalia of writers who would later become well known. And the rest of the content was not so different from any undergraduate newspaper in the early twenty-first century—satirizing popular tastes, skewering the establishment, and trying to bring the high and mighty down a peg or two.

And that, generally, was the tone of the modernist critique—more mocking than constructive. S.I. Hayakawa argued that all Canadian poetry could be divided into four genres—Victorian, neo-Victorian, quasi-Victorian, and pseudo-Victorian[279]—while A.J.M. Smith poked fun at the conventions of all four: 'The most popular experience is to be pained, hurt, stabbed or seared by Beauty—preferably by the yellow flame of a crocus in the spring or the red flame of a maple leaf in the autumn.' Poetry like that, he argued, left the impression that the Canadian poet was 'a half-baked, hyper-sensitive, poorly adjusted, and frequently neurotic individual that no one in his senses would trust to drive a car or light a furnace.' It hardly mattered that most of them knew nothing of the nineteenth century poets they savaged ('We despised them unbeknownst,' admitted Leo Kennedy, the English-born poet who was writing verse for the *Montreal Star* under the pseudonym Helen Lawrence when he joined the McGill group)—their attack grew out of the spirit of youthful rebellion, not because any of them knew enough about Victorian poetry to be able to criticize it on its merits.[280]

Such stinging barbs were bound to be met in kind, and the anti-modernists were up to the task. Novelist Watson Griffin put his response into the mouth of the heroine in *The Gulf of Years* (1927), who has just received a realist novel as a gift from an admirer. 'A rank weed is real, Jack,' she responds, 'but no more real than a violet or a rose, and when I am decorating my room I prefer to fill my vases with lovely flowers than with noxious weeds.'[281] For Griffin and those like him, literature should be about fine ideals, beauty, strength, romance, and moral fibre. Realism, on the other hand, was about all that was nasty in human nature—'the foetid breath of decadence...[and] the morbidly unwhole-some,' as BC novelist Hilda Glynn-Ward put it.[282]

Writers like Griffin and Glynn-Ward could afford to gloat, because modernism had not caught on in Canada—but why? As far as its prac-titioners were concerned, it was because of the ossified writers who still dominated the profession through the Canadian Authors' Asso-ciation. Depending on one's point of view, their critique of the CAA was either merited or mean-spirited; either way, it was carefully calcu-lated (as Kennedy wrote in 1929, 'We are out to break the C.A.A. Every month, commencing in April we [the *Canadian Mercury*] will present something-or-other—a poem, a diatribe—sniping at the C.A.A.'[283]) and characterized by unconcealed disdain. The best known attack was 'The Canadian Authors Meet,' by Frank Scott, whose aesthetic and political radicalism stood in stark contrast to the fact that he taught law at McGill University and was the son of Frederick George Scott, one of the leading lights of the Confederation Poets. But few modernist writers passed up the opportunity to jab their pens in the CAA and everything it did. Leo

Kennedy derided the association itself as 'that pillar of flim-flam…a stumbling block over which the aspiring younger Canadian writer must first climb before approaching his local Parnassus,' while A.J.M. Smith wrote that it should change its name to the Journalists' Branch of the Canadian Manufacturers' Association because of its determination to hoodwink Canadians into thinking that they had 'a moral obligation to buy poor canadian, rather than good foreign books.'[284]

Another characteristic of modernism that limited its appeal was the fact that it was generally inhospitable to women. It was not exactly misogynist, although Scott's 'The Canadian Authors Meet' chose to make fun of the women in the group, the 'Virgins of sixty who still write of passion,' rather than the men, who probably wrote just as much feeble poetry. More importantly, as literary scholar Carole Gerson has argued, modernism was a masculine aesthetic that favoured detached, hard, abstract writing. More personalized forms of poetry and prose, of the kind that women typically wrote, were generally viewed with disdain by the high priests of modernism. Dorothy Livesay, who published what were arguably the first thoroughly modern Canadian verse collections, *The Green Pitcher* (1928) and *Signpost* (1932), was not represented in *New Provinces*, the manifesto of modernist literature in Canada, because its self-referential and pessimistic tone had little in common with the social activism that motivated Livesay as a poet.

But unlike in the art world, the greatest enemy of the modernist writer was not the cultural establishment but the reading public, who remained strikingly conservative in their tastes. There were plenty of novels available that had distinctly realist elements, even if only in a partial or transitional sense—Louis Hémon's *Maria Chapdelaine* (1914), Douglas Durkin's *The Magpie* (1923), Martha Ostenso's *Wild Geese* (1925), Frederick Philip Grove's *Settlers of the Marsh* (1925), Robert Stead's *Grain* (1926), Morley Callaghan's *Strange Fugitive* (1928)—but Mary Vipond, in her analysis of best-selling books in Canada through the 1920s, concludes that the preferences of Canadian readers remained consistently traditional from the prewar period into the late 1920s. They preferred to read books on the same subjects by the same authors, or on the same subjects by new authors, and eschewed anything that could be considered even vaguely modernist or experimental. Robert J.C. Stead's

Grain, his only strongly realist novel, scarcely made an impression on the Canadian reading public, nor did the novels of Frederick Philip Grove (*Settlers of the Marsh* was even banned from some public libraries for being too racy). Indeed, the only modernist Canadian novel to achieve best-seller status was Martha Ostenso's *Wild Geese*, which also had the distinction of winning a major US literary prize. Everything else on the lists was resolutely traditional, whether it be Mazo de la Roche's hugely popular romance *Jalna*, the winner of another big American literary prize in 1927, the westerns of Zane Grey, probably the single most widely read novelist in Canada during the 1920s, or the postwar novels of prewar favourites such as Hugh Walpole, John Galsworthy, and Mary Roberts Rinehart. 'The Canadian literary scene,' wrote Leo Kennedy resignedly in 1928, 'is dominated by the Frank L. Packards, the Howard Angus Kennedys, the Ralph Connors; the Robertses and the Campbells.'[285] In contrast, the 1936 anthology *New Provinces* sold just eighty-two copies in the first eleven months of publication and fifteen the next year, ten to Frank Scott alone.

The country's magazines were, if anything, more resolutely traditional in rejecting the new, the experimental, and the provocative. As the lawyer-turned-essayist and critic W.A. Deacon wrote, editors 'lose circulation in great chunks if they publish anything carnal.'[286] In 1930, *Maclean's* editor H. Napier Moore told the CAA annual convention that he accepted only five of the 250 manuscripts submitted to him each week. Most were rejected because the authors did not appreciate the predilections of readers, particularly their ideas of the subjects that should be off limits in magazine fiction: 'My readers cannot accept women smoking or drinking,' Moore declared. 'I also have to be blind to certain biological facts. Babies have to be brought by the stork or in the doctor's bag.' One wonders if Moore was recalling the comments of Sara Jeannette Duncan, who accused the modernists of her generation of being preoccupied with details that offended the average reader: 'The modern school of fiction, if it is fairly subject to reproach, may bear the blame of dealing too exclusively in the corporealities of human life, to the utter and scornful neglect of its idealities.'[287] The passage of five decades and a world war had apparently done little to alter the essential conservatism of Canadians.

But there was one thing that realist writers and their boosters failed to grasp—that the notion of what constituted 'realism' was far from constant. Those commentators who demanded a new school of realist fiction in the 1920s either forgot or ignored the fact that the best-selling authors of the previous generation had been so popular in part because their work was perceived to be realist. As we have seen, L.M. Montgomery's *Rilla of Ingleside* was lauded for its authenticity, while Ralph Connor prided himself on the fact that his novels described real life. In his autobiography *Postscript to Adventure*, he frequently noted that his work gave an 'authentic picture of life' and that it was drawn from 'personal experience'; he had actually done the things he wrote about, and his readers could not get enough of the veracity that experience allowed him to bring to his characters.[288] If we are to take sales as an indication, the average Canadian reader much preferred the realism proffered by Ralph Connor than the realism of Frederick Philip Grove.

This fact was irritating enough to modernists, but what must have been even more galling was that the twentieth century's newest form of mass culture, cinema, would be dominated not by them, but by their literary foes. In 1894, two brothers from Ottawa, Andrew and George Holland, had opened the first movie house in the United States, called a kinetosocope parlour, grossing over $16,000 in the first year of operation alone; but it was a Frenchman, the improbably named Monsieur Lumière of Lyon, who brought the moving picture to Canada on 27 June 1896, to a building at 78 St. Laurent Street in Montreal. The images were a little prosaic—a train coming and going at Lyon-Perrache station, a series of cavalry charges, waves breaking on the shore, two priests gesturing—but the local press had no doubt that a new era had dawned. *La Presse* insisted that 'the results were truly amazing' and predicted that moving pictures in colour and with sound were not far away.[289]

Like most futurist predictions, these were over-optimistic, but by the early twentieth century cinema had established footholds across Canada. At that time, the industry was dominated by European producers, particularly the French company Pathé, which by 1906 was releasing six new titles a week, most of them one-reelers with five or six different subjects squeezed into twenty minutes of running time. There were enough films in circulation that Ernest Ouimet, a plumber and electrician-turned-entertainment mogul, could run his Ouimetoscope Theatre in Montreal from eight in the morning until midnight. But Ouimet aspired to operate more than what was known colloquially as a grind house. In 1907, he opened a second Ouimetoscope, this one with 1,200 upholstered seats, richly decorated plasterwork, a refreshment counter, and an orchestra. It was the first large moving-picture palace in North America, and brought a measure of respectability to an industry dominated by the seedy film houses that were springing up across Canada.

Production companies soon followed. Most of them were American or British, but they did provide Canadian content with films like *The Battle of Long Sault, Madeleine de Verchères*, and *Evangeline*, all released before the beginning of the First World War. Between 1914 and 1922, thirty-six production companies were founded in Canada, but fewer than half of them ever produced a film. Some were simply created to relieve gullible investors of their savings while others lacked the experience and the financial acumen to make a go of it. There were also systemic obstacles to the industry—contemporaries cited the small domestic market, the high cost of materials, the fact that US interests controlled most of the distribution and exhibition of films in Canada (especially after the Allen Theatres chain, the largest in the country, was taken over by the American-owned Famous Players Canadian Corporation in 1923), and the lack of talent (because there was no indigenous tradition of theatre, there was no pool of writing, acting, and technical expertise). Indeed, only one producer had any success: Ernest Shipman, a native of Hull, Quebec, who had already made a name for himself in Hollywood, more on the charms of his wife and star, Victoria-born Helen Barham (better known to movie-goers as Nell Shipman), than on his own talent. They had a hit in 1916 with a film adaptation of James Oliver Curwood's *God's Country and the Woman*, and on the strength of that the Shipmans moved home to Canada, established a production company in Calgary, and began making Canadian movies. Their first effort was *Back to God's Country* (1919), which gave Canadian cinema its first nude scene and played from North America and Europe to Japan and Australia. But Curwood disliked how Nell had changed his story and parted company with the Shipmans; then, in 1920, Nell and Ernie divorced, bringing the successful partnership to a close after only two

The love of a good woman, the love of a good horse: a scene from *Cameron of the Mounted*.

movies. Curwood went back to writing novels, Nell started making nature films in Idaho, and Ernie looked for other ways to capitalize on what he imagined was a demand for Canadian films.

He decided to follow the lead of American producers. With France devastated by four years of war, the epicentre of the motion-picture industry had moved to California; Hollywood would rule the new medium just as New York had ruled the North American stage, and studio moguls, eager to meet the public's apparently insatiable demand for films, would cast their nets wide in search of screenplays. When Ernie Shipman or Hollywood went looking for material they did not go to the Groves and the Ostensos, but to Canadian literature's old guard.

Arthur Stringer was the first to get the call when the All-Red Feather Company turned one of his stories into *The War Pigeon* (1914), a tale of the War of 1812. He married actress Jobyna Howland, the original Gibson Girl, and made a comfortable living optioning his work to major studios and profiting from a string of movies that featured A-list stars such as Jack Benny, George Brent, Norma Shearer, Barbara Stanwyck, and Gloria Swanson. Ralph Connor was courted by Ernie Shipman, whose Motion Pictures Canada Ltd. contracted in 1919 to bring some of his best-sellers to the screen. The general manager promised that

> We have a purely Canadian company…and at an early date we intend to undertake the production of a number of purely Canadian stories, which shall be made in Canada on the locations around which the stories have been written. It is our wish to exploit Canada for Canada's sake, through the medium of a Canadian company. Thus far all attempts on the part of American producers to make Canadian pictures, have been more or less of a burlesque.[290]

Their first effort was a screen adaptation of Connor's 1908 novel *The Foreigner*, followed by versions of *Corporal Cameron* as *Cameron of the Mounted* (1921), *The Man from Glengarry* (1922), and *Glengarry School Days* (1923), and Motion Pictures Canada prided itself on shooting on location, whether it be Winnipeg, the Alberta foothills, or the Ottawa Valley.

Connor was not always enthusiastic about Shipman's work, such as the scenario for a film version of *The Sky Pilot* (1921). In short, Connor hated it. The language was 'impossible,' some of the characters were 'misconceived,' and the entire story had been degraded: 'from being a unique, purely spiritual, non-sex idyll, it has become a commonplace, wild west, melodramatic, maudlin yarn which will takes its place in competition with a thousand other similar and superior yarns for public approval…the unique power of the book which has made it the one book most read in the English language of all books published within the last twenty-five years, is its peculiar spiritual appeal. There is not a touch of sex in it. It represents the triumph of the spiritual over the coarse and brutalizing influences surrounding the cow-boys.' Connor was not averse to a love story involving the title character, 'but there must be no sex sensation in the pilot. He must be absolutely above all that; serene, human, spiritual, beautiful, unspoiled by taint of selfishness.' He probably appreciated Shipman's deferential reply ('This is constructive criticism. That is what is wanted from all extremes. We will blend a perfect pilot.'), and surely approved of the slogan chosen for Ralph Connor Productions: 'Telling the truth in pictures.'[291] But Shipman's practice of creating a new company with new investors (including

The Capitol Theatre, Saskatoon, 1950.

everyone from Robert J.C. Stead to Duncan Campbell Scott) for each film doomed his efforts; unable to compete with the huge financial resources of the American studios, he eventually gave up on Canada and finished his career making not very successful movies in Florida.

But it was Sir Gilbert Parker, that most nineteenth-century of Canadian novelists, who became the darling of the twentieth century's new medium. No fluffy serials or privately funded ventures for Sir Gilbert. *The Seats of the Mighty* was produced by Hollywood's World Film Corporation as a big-budget costume drama, complete with one of the biggest stars of the day, Lionel Barrymore, a lavishly staged battle scene, and a posh opening-night party at the Astor Hotel in New York City. Many more film versions of his novels followed—*Jordan Is A Hard Road* (1915), *The Right of Way* (1915), *You Never Know Your Luck* (1919), *The Translation of a Savage* (1920), and a remake of *The Right of Way* (1920)—before Parker himself went to Hollywood to write screen adaptations of his work for Famous Players-Lasky, run by the legendary Cecil B. DeMille. Parker adapted well to the demands of screen-writing, and *A Wise Fool* (1921), *She of the Triple Chevron* (1922), and *The Lodge in the Wilderness* (1926) all made their way to the silver screen, not always to

Rather less luxurious advertising for the Strand Theatre in Ottawa, 1919.

critical acclaim but always to the financial benefit of Sir Gilbert. When he died in 1932, a third version of *The Right of Way* had been released and plans were underway for a remake of *The Translation of a Savage*, both taking advantage of the new technology of talking pictures.

The fact that the newest cultural form sought out old-fashioned writers for material was one of the supreme ironies of the interwar era; the other was that, in searching for a new Canadian art, people finally saw value in rediscovering the old. Indeed, modernists were heavily outnumbered by those who were determined to recover the nation's folk traditions, its handicrafts, and its wealth of traditional tales and songs. For many observers, before Canada could look forward in cultural terms, it had to look back.

One who held this view was Marius Barbeau, born in Ste-Marie-de-Beauce, Quebec, in 1883 to the least affluent branch of a prosperous family; scattered through his family tree were politicians, real estate promoters, industrialists, and successful entrepreneurs, but Barbeau's father was a simple farmer with little interest in things cultural. His mother, on the other hand, had left the Grey Nuns while a novice to marry, and she imbued in her son a love of culture. He went first to Laval University to study law, and was successful enough to win a Rhodes scholarship to continue his studies at Oxford University. But shortly after arriving there in 1907, his interests turned to anthropology and Barbeau wrote a thesis on the totemic system of the Pacific northwest coast First Nations. In 1911, he was appointed assistant ethnologist in the anthropology division of the Geological Survey of Canada, established the previous year in response to concerns about the apparent disappearance of the aboriginal way of life.

Barbeau's first assignment took him to the Huron community of Lorette, where he asked a Huron elder to sing traditional native songs so that he could record them in musical notation. To his great surprise, he recognized the tunes as old French-Canadian folk melodies, a fact that he mentioned to his mentor, the anthropologist Franz Boas. Boas was excited by Barbeau's discovery and encouraged him to continue his work, offering to publish his findings in the *Journal of American Folk-Lore* as a way to help anthropologists understand the impact of French culture on aboriginal forms of expression. Barbeau went back into the field, travelling through Quebec by boat or bicycle, usually with an Edison gramophone and wax cylinders in his backpack, so he could record the songs as they were sung, not just by natives but by elderly French Canadians as well. He was astonishingly determined, collecting over 1,300 songs in one season's work alone and amassing some 13,000 song texts and 7,000 recorded melodies over his career.

Barbeau, aware that he was recapturing a nearly lost culture, began to publish the results of his research in special French-Canadian issues of the *Journal of American Folk-Lore* in 1916. But that publication was directed at the specialist; Barbeau wanted to give these folk songs back to the people. They had not been published since Ernest Gagnon's *Chansons populaires du Canada* appeared in 1865, and Barbeau saw them as vital to the cultural life of the nation. They were, he wrote, 'representative of the true cultural essence of French Canada—a culture which was purer than modern culture because it was directly connected with popular life.'

His first effort, *Folk Songs of French Canada* (1925), was published with a grant from the Oliver Baty Cunningham Foundation, established in memory of a Canadian soldier who had been killed in the Great

War. He then contributed to a number of smaller publications, such as *Twelve Ancient French-Canadian Folk-Songs*, with Harold Bolton and Arthur Somerval (1927), *Vingt-et-un chansons canadiennes* (1928), and *Chansons canadiennes*, with Healey Willan and Paul England (1929). But Barbeau had his heart set on a much more ambitious project, *Romancero du Canada*, to be published in French as a multi-volume set. He believed passionately that it would be the first step in the revival of interest in folk songs, but had trouble convincing a publisher to take it on. Hugh Eayrs of Macmillan was sympathetic, but even he was put off by the anticipated costs of publication, which were so high that 1,000 sales would have to be guaranteed before he considered undertaking the expense. Co-sponsorships with the Quebec government, American publishers, and the Canadian Pacific Railway were all discussed and rejected, and eventually the first volume was jointly published by Macmillan and Beauchemin, a small Quebec publisher, in 1937. At $2.75 it was far from cheap (roughly $40 in current values), but advertisements reminded prospective buyers that Canada's folk culture was rapidly fading in the modern era, and that they had a moral duty to support it. Still, sales were weak and, as passionate as he was about the project, Barbeau never had the heart to press Eayrs to consider publishing more volumes in the series.

Barbeau was one of the world's leading collectors of folk songs and, as University of Toronto professor John Robins wrote, it was natural for others to be daunted 'by the unapproachable richness of our song heritage among French-speaking Canadians.'[292] But there was little that daunted Helen Creighton, born in Dartmouth in 1899 to an old Nova Scotia family. She survived the Halifax explosion in December 1917, served as a driver with the Royal Air Force at the end of the Great War, and then drove a Red Cross caravan around Nova Scotia for the provincial public health authority. In 1929, after turning her hand to journalism, she was at a loss for something to write about when Dr. Henry Munroe, of the provincial education department, showed her a copy of W. Roy Mackenzie's *Ballads and Sea Songs from Nova Scotia*, published the previous year. Mackenzie had covered the River John/Tatamagouche area, and Munroe suggested that Creighton pick another part of the province and become a folk song collector. She was intrigued by the idea, although she admitted that she had never heard a folk song sung in her home province, and took herself to the villages on the mainland of the Eastern Passage and eventually to Devil's Island, in the mouth of Halifax Harbour. It was an odd sort of place—some of Helen's friends later claimed to sense malevolent forces there—but it was a goldmine for a folk song collector. Every morning, Creighton would go down to the fishing shacks and record the songs of the fishermen as they worked; in the afternoon, local schoolchildren sung for her, and every evening locals would descend on her lodgings, the music often continuing to 3 AM. She began transcribing the music by ear, but then got hold of an old portable melodeon that allowed her to do transcriptions in musical notation.

A transcription from Helen Creighton's session with Enos Hartlan of South East Passage, Nova Scotia, her first folk singer. c. 1928.

The experience transformed Helen Creighton into a life-long lover of folklore. She also had more luck than Barbeau in taking her material to a wider audience. She had a knack for co-opting highly placed people   Archibald MacMechan, then head of the English Department at Dalhousie University, CAA president Dr. E.A. Hardy, W. Stewart Wallace, the librarian of the University of Toronto, Dr. Healy Willan of the Toronto Conservatory of Music, composer Sir Ernest MacMillan— and with their assistance, her collection *Songs and Ballads from Nova Scotia* was published in 1933. With songs like 'Twas in the Town of Parsboro', 'Canso Strait', 'Guysboro Song', and 'The Hanstead Boys' (Creighton had requested that its name be changed from 'The Hatfield Boys', because she feared that the reference to the boys combing their hair with herring bones might offend the family), it garnered warm reviews, enough to encourage Helen to continue collecting songs on Cape Breton Island and in the Lunenberg area and, more importantly,

Handicraft display, Hafford, Saskatchewan, 1930.

to go on lecture/song tours. In 1938, that turned into a ten-week radio program on which Helen and her friends performed Nova Scotia folk songs for a national audience. In the years that followed, Creighton would publish nearly a dozen collections of Maritime folk songs.

While Barbeau and Creighton were trying to rescue the folk song from extinction (with the help of other organizations, such as Vassar College, whose 1929 Folklore Project in Newfoundland culminated in the 1933 publication of *Ballads and Sea Songs of Newfoundland*, and Laval University, which established Canada's first Department of Folklore in 1944), another group was trying to keep alive the craft traditions of previous centuries. The Canadian Handicrafts Guild had been established in 1906, 'with the prime object of rescuing the homecrafts of Canadians from the dust heap of oblivion,' as one of its supporters put it. Its members and affiliated organizations, such as the Canadian Guild of Potters, Cape Breton Home Industries, the Spinners and Weavers of Ontario, and Charlotte County Cottage Crafts, toiled away in relative obscurity to preserve techniques in quilting, basketry, carving, and a dozen other crafts that were second nature to pioneers. But in the interwar period their work took on a greater sense of urgency. In the first place, mass-produced consumer goods, which had been available in urban areas for decades, were now reaching every part of the country, thanks to the miracle of catalogue shopping and the spread of rural mail delivery. Rural Canada had always been the repository of the old craft traditions; now, there was growing temptation to replace hand-made goods with manufactured ones. Georges Bouchard, a professor in the agricultural college at Ste-Anne-de-la-Pocatière, Quebec, was not alone in lamenting 'the widening breach that modern conditions have made between art and life, between the beautiful and the useful.'[293]

Many people believed that this breach was contributing to the growing exodus from the countryside, as people were drawn by the opportunities, comforts, and excitement that the cities seemed to offer. Reviving the pride in the old craft traditions was one way to stem that tide. There was more than a little nostalgia in the images conjured up by supporters of the handicraft movement—picture a pioneer cabin, a howling blizzard raging outside, while inside, by the warmth of the fire, father carved a wooden toy and mother worked the loom, all the while singing folk songs to the family—but they firmly believed that an atmosphere in which children were surrounded by objects crafted in the old ways would keep them 'from the lure of idle dreams, the seduction of the catalogues and the attraction of big centres.'[294] Folk art, then, was a way to preserve the rural way of life.

The value of preserving these practices became even more evident in the Depression. Suddenly, as crops failed and farm incomes plummeted, there was no money to buy mittens for the children or a rug for the floor. Once upon a time, the woman of the house had made such things herself, the way her mother and grandmother had, but how many young farm women knew how to card and dye wool or weave rugs? However, there were encouraging signs that they wanted to re-learn those skills. When the Alberta branch of the Canadian Handicrafts Guild began broadcasting a series of craft lessons over the radio in December 1937, they expected a few dozen people to register and pay twenty-five cents a week for the notes and patterns; by the time the fourth lesson, on creative embroidery, was aired, there were over 830 registrants.[295] It's impossible to know how many of them were interested in reviving craft traditions and how many were just looking for a welcome diversion. It is also likely that some were thinking of making a little money; for, as the Canadian Handicrafts Guild often reminded its members, there was a good market among tourists for hand-made souvenirs. Georges Bouchard related the story of Irma Menard, a teenager in St-Urbain, in Quebec's Charlevoix County, who learned at her mother's knee the art of rug-making; within a few years, her rugs were selling at a big Ottawa

Music as an antidote to the Depression: Melvin Crump's combo, Edmonton. c. 1936.

department store for $8 each (over $110 today) or more. Such art, wrote Madame H.P. Renouf of the Percé Handicraft Committee in Quebec in a comment that would have struck a chord with the Group of Seven, was uniquely Canadian, 'untouched by the outer world, unacquainted with any source of pattern material other than nature…many of the designs are "the pure impulse of a Canadian heart.'"[296]

In a broader sense, the folk art revival was also an implicit rebuke to the modernists (but not, significantly, the members of the Group of Seven, who championed folk art; Jackson and Lismer, for example, worked with the Women's Art Association of Canada to assist the weavers on the Ile d'Orléans, Baie-Saint-Paul, and Ile aux Coudres, and helped create a healthy tourist trade for local artisans). It was a reminder that Canadian culture before the 1910s was not only the product of a 'foreign-begotten technique.' On the contrary, there had been a vibrant indigenous craft tradition waiting to be reclaimed. Anyone who wanted to find a distinct Canadian culture need look no further than the needlework of a Saskatchewan farm woman, the tin weather vane on a Quebec barn, or the sea shanty that enlivened many an evening in Nova Scotia. The preservation of such crafts 'is first and foremost an effort to perpetuate a national tradition,' as Dr. C.F. Martin said at the opening of the Canadian Handicraft Exhibition in Montreal in October 1937, 'an occupation of those people whose skilled techniques in the arts and crafts of Canada contributes something distinctive to the work of the nation…It is not mere labour—it is art in its broadest sense.' Georges Bouchard was even more optimistic. 'Benefited by the rustic arts,' he told the Women's Institutes of New Brunswick in June 1931, 'the Canadian people will become more and more united and prosperous, and will grow greater and still greater among the nations of the world.'[297]

Marius Barbeau and the Canadian Handicrafts Guild worked on the assumption that culture was, first and foremost, an activity to be engaged in by everyone, not just a small group of intellectuals and arts promoters. In this, they were closer to the public mood than the modernists, because the most striking element of Canadian culture in the interwar period is not the emergence of the Group of Seven or realist writers, but the tremendous boom in grass-roots arts organizations. The improvement-through-culture ethos that elites had tried to foster in the nineteenth century finally started to take hold in the early twentieth century, as book clubs, art groups, musical societies, and little theatres sprang up across the country. In their activities, we see the same fondness for traditional culture and disinterest in modernism that characterized best-seller lists or cinema bills.

Book clubs had existed in Canada since the mid-nineteenth century, but in the 1920s access to literature improved dramatically with the emergence of mail-order book clubs and catalogue shopping. The Book-of-the-Month Club and the Literary Guild, both based in the United States, were founded in 1926, and together had some 4000 members in Canada. Soon there were Canadian competitors in the form of the

Eaton Book Club (1928), which offered 'only worthwhile books' selected by two English professors from the University of Toronto and a former editor of *Bookseller and Stationer*. The club's first recommendation was Grove's *Our Daily Bread*, but almost everything on subsequent lists was either American or British. More nationalist was the Carillon Book Club of Ottawa (1927), promising its members only Canadian books chosen by a committee of three journalists, three literature professors, and the Parliamentary librarian. Although some writers, publishers, and booksellers accused the clubs of anti-intellectualism in that they often encouraged people to buy books based on what would look good in their living rooms, they did give readers greater access to more books at cheaper prices.

For this reason, they probably helped in the rejuvenation of the book club as a social and cultural institution. The Searchlight Book Club had been founded by a group of women in Winnipeg in 1910; they met on the first Saturday of the month, and each time the members drew slips of paper from a bowl to determine who would present a paper at the following meeting. The first year's papers covered best-selling authors such as Nellie McClung, Charles G.D. Roberts, Robert W. Service, Rudyard Kipling, and Henry Wadsworth Longfellow, but by the 1920s the club had expanded its subject matter dramatically. Each year, the members chose a different theme for the year's meetings—it might be drama, classical literature, or the epic poem. In 1927, it was Canadian literature and crafts, and the papers presented give us a window into what interested women of the time: Lord Selkirk's work in Canada, Laura Goodman Salverson's novel *The Viking Heart*, pottery, Susanna Moodie's *Roughing It in the Bush*, a trek across the Canadian subarctic, quilts, native art and artists, the work of Duncan Campbell Scott, the revival of traditional arts and crafts, poet Marjorie Pickthall, William Kirby's novel *The Golden Dog*, rugs, Thomas Chandler Haliburton's character Sam Slick, Canadian legends, Roberts' *In the Morning of Time*, and Canadian furniture.[298]

As the history of the Searchlight Book Club confirms, these were very different from today's book clubs. The earlier generation of book club was intended as much for improvement as enjoyment, and participants were expected to work, and work hard. The members of the Hawthorne Women's Club, founded in East Kildonan, Manitoba, in 1923, took turns (according to alphabetical rotation) providing a brief synopsis of currents events at the beginning of each meeting, and then other women read papers they had prepared on topics that had been assigned to them.[299] And a report dashed off on the morning of the meeting was not good enough; certain standards were expected, and members were encouraged to engage in considerable research. Novelist Frederick John Niven even received a letter from Agnes Wells of Britannia Beach, British Columbia, with some searching questions about his new book *Mrs. Barry*, which had been assigned to her for a future meeting of her book club.[300]

Many of these organizations were much broader in scope than their names suggested. The Literary Dramatic Club, founded in Banff, Alberta, in 1924, began with great hopes of placing equal emphasis on both of its priorities—reading, one of the founders wrote, 'makes possible the re-creation in the reader's consciousness of all the pregnant episodes in the story of the world, of all the most glorious deeds in human history, of the collective wisdom and achievements of mankind'—but soon the dramatic overtook the literary. It produced two plays, W.B. Yeats' *The Land of Heart's Desire* and Lady Gregory's *The Workhouse Ward*, in its first six months in existence, and had a third, Lord Dunsany's *A Night at the Inn*, ready to go in a few weeks' time.[301] The Women's Art Club in Portage la Prairie, Manitoba, established in 1927, was not strictly about art, but about the arts generally. In the 1929 season, for example, members presented papers on Charles Dickens, Ludwig von Beethoven, famous English artists, and Canadian poetry.[302]

Little theatre companies began popping up, too. The Community Players of Winnipeg was founded in October 1921, putting on its first performance, a private presentation of two short plays, in March 1922. In time it became the Winnipeg Little Theatre, and adopted as its slogan 'The greatest art has always been communal.' Its agenda was nationalist, promising 'to lay the foundation for such a Canadian Theatre as will offer to Canadian playwrights the possibility of national recognition,' but it was also proudly regional; of the twenty-two Canadian plays it produced in its first few seasons, fourteen were written by Winnipeggers.[303] It could not, however, completely avoid the serious tone adopted by the cultural improvers of the nineteenth century, predicting in 1925 that one consequence of its work would be 'to people the land with enough men and women familiar with art as a serious pastime, even familiar with it as a grave concern of life.'[304]

In time, the Winnipeg Little Theatre would be joined by other, similar local troupes—in small towns such as Dauphin and Melita, Manitoba, but also in bigger centres such as Brandon, Edmonton, and Saskatoon. There was the Green Room Club in Calgary, the Montreal Repertory Theatre, the Vancouver and Ottawa Little Theatres, and the Medicine Hat Amateur Operatic Society, which produced 'operas, musical comedies, etc, thereby providing a means for the development of musical talent and histrionic ability, and generally to raise the musical standard and appreciation of good music within our city.'[305] Even if some of these groups were unstable—what began as the Victoria Amateur Society later became the Mimes and Masques Club, the Victoria Little Theatre Association, the Victoria Little Theatre and Dramatic School, and finally the Victoria Players Guild, all the while moving between venues, including a renovated garage with a leaky roof that forced audience members and actors to dodge strategically placed buckets[306]—they brought the arts right into local neighbourhoods, returning it to the days when culture was participatory, rather than something one just sat and watched.

One of the most striking characteristics of this activity was that it was virtually untouched by the struggle between traditionalism and modernism, between idealism and realism, between a nationalist culture and an internationalist one. Such dichotomies apparently held no interest for the people who joined groups such as the Halifax Choral Union (1922), the Saskatchewan Drama League (1933), the London Little Theatre (1933), and the Young Women's Musical Club of Winnipeg (1938). For the most part, they were avowedly nationalist, and unconcerned that cultural patriotism might be anachronistic in the postwar world. They read and performed the kind of culture they liked, and they tended to prefer traditionalism over modernism. They were less interested in blazing a trail than in the ability of culture to provide positive influences in the community, and to lift up the individual morally and spiritually. As such, they were much closer to the improvers of the nineteenth century than to the cultural elites of the early twentieth, for their ideas of the role of culture could be taken directly from the opening ceremonies of any Mechanics' Institute in the 1870s. When the school district of Medicine Hat, Alberta, held its first music and drama festival in May 1933, organizers were quick to draw attention to

> the commendable purpose, of creating knowledge and apprecia-
> tion of Music and Dramatic Art, amongst the boys and girls...in
> the consciousness of some, there may be born an inspiration and
> ambition, that may carry some youthful mind into a new sphere of
> mental vision, and plant the seed which may develop a composer,
> actor, or musical genius. It offers enrichment of mental culture,
> and encourages the study and possession of arts that make life
> happier.[307]

Shortly after the Banff School of Theatre became the Banff School of Fine Arts in 1933, its directors selected as its epigram 'the relation-ships between art and life are solemnly reciprocal. An art which has gone astray will corrupt our existence; a corrupt existence mortally endangers artistic creation...If the inner attitude is strong and true, the emanating from it will be strong and truthful.'[308] Egerton Ryerson would have approved.

Modernists, however, probably would have been unconvinced, because they shared the less positive element of the nineteenth-century ideology of improvement, a marked disdain for the cultural tastes of the general public. There is an undertone of high-brow snootiness in their attitudes towards Canadians for their reluctance to embrace modernism by purchasing the proper books or waxing rhapsodic over the proper paintings, something that may have been as damaging to their cause as anything. 'Nobody understands them [modern paintings],' complained J.W. Morrice. 'I have not the slightest desire to improve the taste of the Canadian public.' A.J.M. Smith wrote that the Canadian public 'in the realm of culture and intellect...is timid, eager to please, and stupid,' while Lawren Harris rarely missed an opportunity to point out how ill-informed most people were when it came to art. The power of art, he wrote in 1944, 'was something which the vast majority of our people, most if not all of our art lovers and critics, simply did not understand... Too often they confused mere prettiness with real beauty. They did not know their own country...They had no other idea than that of accepting the crumbs from the richly laden table of European art and culture.'[309] Again, it is striking how often the modernists sounded like the cultural improvers of the nineteenth century. If only they listened to us, Smith and Lismer were implying, we could show the great unwashed how the arts could enrich their material and spiritual lives.

So there were really two divides in Canadian culture in the interwar era. There was the generational divide that W.A. Deacon referred to in a letter to the up-and-coming novelist Morley Callaghan—'I am of the last pre-war crop, you of the first post-war; and inevitably there is a gulf'[310]—but there was also an intellectual divide, between the intelligentsia of the *McGill Fortnightly Review* and *Canadian Forum*, and the people who joined organizations such as the Calgary Light Opera Society, the Searchlight Book Club, and the St. Peter's Dramatic Club of Saint John. The young modernists would soon have their day, but for now the traditionalists enjoyed the support, not only of the general public, but of the few private patrons whose wealth and influence supported the arts in Canada.

Chapter 12

Patron Saints of Culture

Were it not for the patronage of a Toronto eye specialist, the artists who eventually became known as the Group of Seven might have toiled away in individual obscurity, scraping out a living from commercial illustration work and the odd private commission. But a series of lucky coincidences put them in touch with Dr. James MacCallum, who saw something of value in their work and was determined to put his money and influence at their disposal. From the early 1910s until his death in 1943, MacCallum would be, according to A.Y. Jackson, the Patron Saint of the Group of Seven.

James MacCallum was one of a small but important group of Canadians who had the wherewithal and the interest to fund the arts. Some were like the good doctor—professionals whose success afforded them a level of wealth, and whose personal inclinations moved them to use that wealth for the benefit of the artistic community. Others were captains of industry or men and women of private means, people who might be classed as members of the Canadian aristocracy. Within this group, MacCallum was unusual only in his openness to new styles. Most other private patrons were more traditional; wealth and cultural conservatism often went hand in hand, and Canada's blue-bloods often had little interest in the new or the experimental.

But it was not just wealthy citizens who used their resources to support the arts—private foundations were generous benefactors, and corporate Canada also saw a range of benefits in sponsoring cultural activity, although it was often unclear where helping the community ended and public relations and advertising began. But like the private patrons, corporations tended to shy away from modernism, preferring things that were familiar and safe. After all, what company wanted to be known for promoting a form of culture that Canadians disliked? So, if public taste was one factor standing in the way of the progress of modernism in Canada, the conservatism of private patrons was another.

———•◦•———

What the Europeans would call private patronage of culture existed in Canada long before the newcomers arrived. Affluent aboriginal leaders on the west coast were patrons in the European mold, for they put their wealth into the creation of art as a way to demonstrate their social stature. The rich and elaborate material culture of the region would not have developed as it did without influential community leaders seeing the value of artists and artisans in affirming the social hierarchy.

This kind of private patronage was also well developed in Europe, and the practice was easily exported to the new world. Louis de Buade, Comte de Frontenac, was a typical patron of the arts—although he held political office, the financial support he gave to the theatre in New France stemmed from his own fondness for drama, not from any official obligation to the colony as governor. Through the eighteenth and nineteenth centuries, artists, writers, sculptors, or composers came to rely on wealthy patrons to encourage them, both morally and financially. Given the market for culture in colonial Canada, the patronage of a local worthy might be the only thing standing between an artist and destitution.

That patronage could take many forms, beginning with simply buying a painting or commissioning a sculpture. Painter Joseph Légaré was most grateful for the financial support of Montreal antiquarian Jacques Viger, who in 1839 was in the market for a Canadian artist to help illustrate an album of historical miscellanea that he was assembling, but it took a different sort of patron altogether to fund an art academy, a dance school, or a concert hall. That required someone like Thomas McCulloch, better known as the author of *The Stepsure Letters*, who founded the Pictou Academy in Nova Scotia (one of the focal points of the region's cultural renaissance) in 1816; the school's library in 1819; and a subscription library in the town in 1822. It took someone like the Nova Scotian journalist and politician Joseph Howe, who helped finance the Halifax Mechanics' Institute because of his firm belief in the value of 'supplying useful knowledge, at a cheap rate to all who desire it.'[311]

A century later, there was Frank Meighen, president of the Lake of the Woods Milling Company and a man whose résumé included directorships of everything from the Bank of Toronto to the Phoenix Assurance Company of England, putting up the money to establish the Montreal Opera Company in 1910. Its first season, which included tours to Toronto, Ottawa, Rochester, New York, and Quebec City, was a critical success but left Meighen to meet the company's $80,000 (well over $1.4 million at current values) shortfall. The following year, the story was the same—excellent reviews but poor ticket sales—and in 1913 Meighen regretfully decided that his pockets were not deep enough to continue financing the company. More successful was the Ottawa Drama League, which enjoyed the support of its great patron, *Ottawa Citizen* owner H.S. Southam. In 1915, Southam helped to float a bond issue to convert the Eastern Methodist Church into a new, 500-seat theatre.

Goldwin Smith in his library at The Grange. c. 1910.

Perhaps because of their relative scarcity, the leading cultural patrons of the day enjoyed considerable notoriety. Among the first in the new Canadian nation were the Smiths, Harriet and Goldwyn. Harriet was the widow of wealthy manufacturer William Henry Boulton, and when in 1875 she married Goldwyn, an English-born journalist who would energize the intellectual life of Toronto for nearly four decades, she brought to the marriage a healthy fortune, including a Toronto estate known as The Grange. Her money allowed Smith to spend his days the way he liked—writing, reading, debating, arguing, and actively and very publicly supporting a wide range of cultural ventures. He was one of the sponsors of *The Nation* (1874), the organ of the Canada First movement, and invested in Toronto's first major newspaper of the post-Confederation era, *The Evening Telegram* (1876). He supported *The Week* (1883), the literary and political magazine edited by Charles G.D. Roberts, and took over the agricultural newspaper *The Canadian Farmers' Sun* in 1896. And three years later he was one of the co-founders of the Canadian Society of Authors. Smith was a man of acerbic views that he was not afraid to state publicly (he opposed free public lending libraries, saying that 'a novel library is to women mentally pretty much what the saloon is physically to men'), but he was never afraid to put Harriet's money where his mouth was when he came across a cultural venture he believed in. Fortunately for Goldwin Smith, and for Toronto's cultural community, Harriet fully supported him in his efforts, so much so that when she died, she willed The Grange to the city of Toronto to serve as its public art gallery. The Art Museum of Toronto officially opened in 1918 with three new gallery buildings, all linked to The Grange.

True to its roots, the gallery remained dependent on private benefactors. When the original complex became inadequate, R.Y. Eaton, the president of the T. Eaton Company, spearheaded an expansion scheme, securing financial support from the company's executives and from Vincent Massey, who took on the chairmanship of the building fund. The new gallery opened in January 1926, and with it came a more aggressive acquisitions policy, thanks to a $10,000 donation (over $120,000 today) for the purchase of Canadian art from Kate and Reuben Wells Leonard of St. Catharines, Ontario. In 1930, the gallery's acquisitions budget was further bolstered by a subscription fund established by the Friends of Canadian Art. Without the efforts of this handful of private patrons, the gallery (which became the Art Gallery of Ontario in 1966) might have remained in the gradually decaying Grange.

The man who convinced Harriet Smith to bequeath The Grange to the people of Toronto was another of the era's great cultural patrons, Byron Edmund Walker, the president of the Canadian Bank

Alberta little theatre group, 1933.

of Commerce. One of the most successful and influential financiers of late Victorian Canada, Walker and his wife became accustomed to the rich cultural life of New York City when they lived there in the 1880s. They were shocked upon returning to Toronto, which appeared to be a cultural black hole, and set about rectifying the situation. For thirty years, Walker would be one of the most important power-brokers in Canadian business and politics, but he would also become one of the country's most important arts patrons. The University of Toronto, the Royal Ontario Museum (he and his friend Edmund Boyd Osler shamed the provincial government into funding the museum by raising substantial money on their own, and then Walker donated large parts of his own collection to get it started), the Toronto Guild of Civic Art, the Champlain Society (founded in 1905 to publish historic documents), the National Gallery of Canada, the Canadian War Memorials Fund, the government-appointed Advisory Arts Council (when he became chair, he succeeded in having the Royal Canadian Academy's grant increased from $2,000 annually to $5,000, and the budget of the National Gallery doubled), the Toronto Conservatory of Music, the Toronto Mendelssohn Choir—these were just some of the cultural organizations that Walker supported, either financially, politically, or both. Significantly, he was also a man of catholic tastes. As Lawren Harris observed in a eulogy, Walker was also 'the first and only man of position to detect that in the modern movement in Canadian art the country had found the beginnings of a distinctive, significant, and bold expression.'[312]

Banking and culture seemed a natural fit, but farm implements and culture was a little more of a stretch. Nevertheless, Walker's generosity to the arts was matched by that of Hart Massey, the agricultural equipment magnate whose name was known, if not necessarily loved, by farmers around the world. Much of his attention went towards religious and social causes (such as the Methodist Social Union of Toronto, the Children's Aid Society, and the Salvation Army), but he also had a passion for music. He was known for his willingness to fund musical ensembles organized by and for the workers in his factories, and he and members of his family were fond of donating organs to Methodist churches. Hart donated a fine organ to the Methodist Assembly at Chautauqua, while his sister Susan gave one to the Central Methodist Church in Toronto in memory of her nephew Walter. Hart's wife Lillian was even more enthralled by organ music; she had a special telephone line connecting their home to the Metropolitan Church so she could listen in, and at her death in 1915, she bequeathed a $61,000 endowment (or over $1.1 million) to pay the salary of the church organist and to fund twenty free recitals every year.

But Hart Massey had grander things in mind than church organs. He became the vice-president of the Toronto Philharmonic Society when it was reconstituted in 1891, and got to know its leader, Frederick Herbert Torrington, the organist and choirmaster at Metropolitan Church. Torrington complained bitterly about the dreadful performance venues in Toronto (he particularly disliked playing at the Horticultural Pavilion at Allan Gardens, whose acoustical properties made it entirely unsuited for concerts), complaints that found a sympathetic ear in Massey; as early as 1888, he had brought Canadian architect Sydney Rose Badgley from Cleveland, Ohio, to consult with him about building a replica of that city's concert hall in Toronto. Massey and Torrington settled on a property at the corner of Shuter and Victoria Streets, and presented their proposal to what they assumed would be a grateful city council.

Council, however, was not impressed, particularly when someone like Hart Massey asked for municipal property tax exemptions for a music

The interior of Toronto's Massey Hall. c. 1890.

hall that would not be managed by the city. Others argued that the industrialist could find a better use for his money—like an agricultural hall,
a public bath, a winter garden, or even a poorhouse for downtrodden
Massey employees. But Hart would not be put off and on 14 June 1894
the Massey Music Hall (it became simply Massey Hall in 1933, by which
time the phrase 'music hall' had come to have less savoury connotations),
opened with a performance of Handel's *Messiah*. In all, the facility cost
$152,390.75, or over $2.9 million in current values, and came outfitted
with the most modern equipment available at the time.

Regrettably, the hall's early days were dogged by criticism, either on
architectural grounds—the *Canadian Architect and Builder* commented
drily that it was 'as aesthetical as the average grain elevator'—or because
of the reputation of its benefactor. *The Canadian Farmers' Sun* ridiculed
the motives behind Massey's generosity, writing after his death that
'Canada never knew the dead Massey, and it wants no public monuments erected in his name,' while the satirical magazine *Grip* poked fun
at the industrialist's 'ostentatious acts of public charity.'

Nevertheless, it quickly became an anchor of Toronto's cultural
community, drawing 375,000 patrons in the first year alone. In its first
three decades, it would play host to some of the world's most famous

performers. In 1903, the sixty-one-year-old opera singer Adelina Patti made her farewell performance at Massey Hall, setting records both for ticket prices ($5, or over $90 today) and for her fee ($10,000, or the equivalent of roughly $190,000). The following year it was the turn of ten-year-old Ernest MacMillan, who made his first appearance in the hall as part of the Festival of the Lilies; MacMillan would go on to serve for twenty-five years as the music director of the Toronto Symphony Orchestra. In 1908, Massey Hall hosted Robert Peary, lecturing on his trek to the South Pole, and the wedding of the great Onondaga marathon runner Tom Longboat. In 1910, the renowned ballerina Anna Pavlova and her troupe performed *Giselle*, and the following year Sir Edward Elgar visited with the Sheffield Choir. Massey Hall drew the cream of the crop in part because of its acoustics. In 1961, it was pronounced the second best concert hall in the world (ahead of the Vienna Opera House) by a renowned German acoustician, who visited with sophisticated sound measuring devices, a pistol, and a handful of blank cartridges. Hart Massey would have been proud—even if by the early 1920s the boxing and wrestling matches held in his hall were out-drawing all other events by a margin of three to one.

Hart's descendants continued the family tradition of supporting the arts, in their own right and through the foundation that was created in 1918 with the residue of Hart's estate. However, the younger genera-tion was more interested in modernism. Hart's collection of French, Dutch, and English academy paintings was sold off, and Vincent and Alice Massey became important patrons of contemporary Canadian art. When Vincent was posted to the Canadian Embassy in Washington, he decorated their Washington residence with Canadian moderns, and became even more active in collecting after their return to Canada in 1934. By then, they had amassed the largest private collection of contemporary Canadian art in the country.

But one did not have to be as wealthy as Walker or Massey to have a real impact on the cultural community—James MacCallum was proof of that. Born in Richmond Hill, Canada West, in 1860, his father was a Methodist minister who was assigned to a parish on Georgian Bay when James was young. He fell in love with the area, and when he became an ophthalmologist and joined the faculty at the University of Toronto, comfortably but not fabulously wealthy, he bought a cottage on Go-Home Bay. MacCallum had broad tastes in culture—he was as interested in Chinese art as he was in African-American music—and he also had a weakness for starving artists. For example, he was a close friend of painter Curtis Williamson, secured for him a good number of commissions, and even loaned him money when times were bad.

His inclinations drew MacCallum to Toronto's Arts and Letters Club, where he met Lawren Harris, probably in late 1909 or early 1910. Harris in turn introduced him to the painters who would later make up the Group of Seven, and MacCallum began inviting them to his cottage to paint. J.E.H. MacDonald visited Go-Home Bay in the summers of 1911 and 1912, while Arthur Lismer spent part of 1913 living and painting on MacCallum's houseboat. But MacCallum and Harris realized that what the artists really needed was decent studio space in Toronto, so they had somewhere to paint during the winter. The pair bought a parcel of land on Severn Street, and shared the expense of erecting what would be the first purpose-built structure in Canada designed specifically with the needs of artists in mind. Curtis Williamson was the first tenant, followed by J.W. Beatty; both had originally been devotees of Dutch painting before embracing Canadian subjects.

But MacCallum was more than just a host and landlord. In the summer of 1913, he met A.Y. Jackson and was sufficiently impressed with his work that he offered Jackson space in the new studio and promised to purchase enough of his paintings to keep him employed for a year; later, he made the same offer to Tom Thomson. During the First World War, MacCallum commissioned some of the artists to paint murals for his cottage, as much to decorate the building as to support them financially and emotionally; after the war, he and Lawren Harris arranged for the loan of a box-car from the Algoma Central Railway so that the artists could travel to Algoma country to paint.

MacCallum supported most of the members of the Group in one way or another, but Tom Thomson was his pet project. After the artist drowned in Algonquin Park in 1917, MacCallum took it upon himself to help the family by promoting Thomson's work. He convinced the Montreal Museum of Art to buy a major work in 1922, but had less luck with the Art Gallery of Toronto; it acquired *The West Wind* in 1926, but only as a gift from Canadian Club of Toronto. So perturbed was MacCallum with the Toronto gallery's disinterest that he contacted

Eric Brown at the National Gallery of Canada and offered him his entire collection, 134 works in all, including eighty-three by Tom Thomson. When MacCallum died in 1943, the paintings went to Ottawa, a memorial to the Group but also to the patron who made it possible for them to paint as much as they did.

Still, the demand for willing benefactors more than outstripped the supply. Canada needed as many Walkers and MacCallums as it could get, but there were simply too few to go around. In 1903, the Royal Canadian Academy petitioned Prime Minister Wilfrid Laurier for assistance to artists, observing that 'The patronage of Canadian Artists by their fellow countrymen is certainly not large…The more important the work,… the smaller the chance there is of its author being able to dispose of it in Canada.'[313] A few years later, the author of an article on the little theatre movement lamented the fact that the 'generosity of wealthy Canadians' had not yet 'been awakened.'[314] And it was not just wealthy Canadians who needed to be nudged into action; original art was well within the budget of the middle class, but they showed the same reluctance to buy Canadian. Lawyer Norman Mackenzie, who would become one of western Canada's leading arts benefactors, commiserated with painter Inglis Sheldon-Williams about the art buyer, 'the class who go around and look at your pictures and tell you not to sell them for less that five hundred or a thousand, but if you were to ask them to take one at a dollar and a half they would run like a bear…Stick to your own ideas of £70 or £75. A picture sold and on a wall is worth a great deal more than a masterpiece lying in the artist's studio with the dust on it.' However, that was easier said than done. Even with its promotional skill, the Group of Seven was unable to convince Canadians to purchase their work. Over two and a half years of exhibitions in more than forty towns and cities, Lismer had to admit that 'sales [were] practically nil.'[315]

But if there were not enough wealthy Canadians around who were interested in supporting culture, two of the richest men in the United States did their best to fill the void: the Scottish-born steel magnate Andrew Carnegie and John D. Rockefeller, who turned Standard Oil into one of the biggest corporations in the world. Critics claimed that they were only interested in public relations—giving back to the community might help modify their image as robber-barons—and there may have been an element of this to their giving. But the sheer amount of money they gave away (Rockefeller donated over $550 million to various causes during his lifetime) suggests something more. Indeed, Carnegie and Rockefeller shared with Hart Massey a philosophy of giving that Carnegie articulated in an 1889 essay entitled 'The Gospel of Wealth.' Surplus wealth, he wrote, should become 'the property of the many'; the rich man had a duty 'to consider all surplus revenues which come to him simply as trust funds, which he is called upon to administer…to produce the most beneficial results for the community.' But that did not mean handing out alms to anyone and everyone. Instead, 'great sums…spent for public purposes, from which the masses reap the principal benefit, are more valuable to them than if scattered among themselves in trifling amounts through the course of many years.' Those results could be achieved by providing 'the ladders upon which the aspiring can rise.'[316]

For the foundation established to disburse Rockefeller's fortune, universities were the cause of choice, receiving the vast majority of the $11.6 million doled out in Canada by 1950. Direct funding to cultural institutions was limited to generous support for the National Film Society of Canada, considerably less generous support for the Public Archives of Nova Scotia, and scholarships to individuals (the playwright Gwen Pharis Ringwood studied at the University of North Carolina for two years, thanks to Rockefeller money).

But Andrew Carnegie had different interests. He believed that 'the best gift' a wealthy man could give to the community was a free library, a legacy of his boyhood in Allegheny, Pennsylvania, where he haunted a private lending library. Over some twenty years, the Carnegie program funded 125 libraries in Canada, the vast majority in Ontario because it had more urban centres (Carnegie was reluctant to finance facilities in towns of fewer than 2,000 people) and the province had a longer tradition of public libraries. Interested communities had to submit applications to Carnegie's private secretary, James Bertram, who judged them on a number of factors, including the quality of the plan and the pledge of local politicians to support the library's operating costs once the building was erected. Even though Bertram had ties to Canada (his wife was born in Seaforth, Ontario, where Bertram was buried after his death in 1934), his committee was no pushover. They were quite prepared to demand architectural changes—'The floor plan is so inadequate that it seems hardly worth while to criticise it in detail,' they wrote regarding the application of Guelph, Ontario. 'There is no children's room, nor librarian's office, nor catalogue room. There are rooms however for the Board of Trustees and its secretary, neither of which is needed'[317]—and had no time for things they considered to be frills. Still, they approved far more requests than they rejected. From the opening of the first Carnegie library, in Chatham, Ontario, on 14 January 1903, until concerns that councils were not living up to their pledges to fund operating budgets led to the suspension of the programme in 1917 (although Carnegie money was behind the establishment of a regional library system in the Fraser Valley of British Columbia in the 1930s, and paid for Prince Edward Island's complete library system), the $2.5 million that Carnegie dispensed for the construction of libraries made an enormous difference in the cultural life of many communities.

Carnegie Library, Penetanguishene, Ontario. c. 1910.

Even more significant financially, but less evident to the general public, was the work of the Carnegie Foundation, established in 1911 to disburse some of the proceeds of the $500 million sale of the Carnegie Steel Company in 1901. The bulk of the grants between 1911 and 1949, nearly $6 million, went to educational institutions—among other things, it funded Canada's first Department of Fine Arts, at Acadia University, and the first artist-in-residence, Goodridge Roberts, who worked at Queen's University from 1933 to 1936—but during the same period it doled out another $1.35 million to cultural groups large and small. At first, this was done rather haphazardly, but after a 1932 study by two British experts reported that 'the Dominion provides little to cultivate the appreciation of fine art, and it is a deplorable fact that so many cities of considerable size have nothing to show,'[318] the foundation established a Canadian committee to advise on its benefactions in the country. Its members included Frank Kermode of the Provincial Museum of Victoria, R.W. Brock of the University of British Columbia, and J. Clarence Webster of Dalhousie University (significantly, there were no women or French Canadians on the committee), but the driving force behind it was Harry McCurry, who, with Eric Brown, represented the National Gallery of Canada. One cannot minimize the impact of the Canadian committee's work, for it helped the Edmonton Museum of Fine Arts survive the Depression, established the National Art Centre in Ottawa, funded children's art classes across the country, and financed travelling scholarships for arts administrators. But because of the difficulty in bringing the members together, McCurry made many of the decisions himself, and the committee's recommendations reflected his predilections. Institutions in central Canada got the lion's share of the funding (beginning with his own, which received the largest chunk of the Canadian grant), the Maritimes and Quebec being largely ignored, and amateur organizations suffered in comparison to organizations connected to universities or other educational institutions. Still, however unevenly it was distributed, the Canadian cultural community could not afford to look the gift horse in the mouth, and the Calgary Public Museum, the Canadian Bureau for the Advancement of Music, the Committee on Cultural Relations, the Art Gallery of Toronto, and dozens of other organizations and institutions enjoyed the largesse of the Carnegie Foundation. It was enough for art critic Graham McInnes to call the foundation 'the fairy godmother to art in Canada.'[319]

Still, not everyone was happy with the benefactions of great industrialists. In the late 1890s, some leading citizens of Winnipeg wrote directly to Andrew Carnegie and asked him to consider donating a library to the city; in 1902, he came forward with a gift of $75,000 (over $1.4 million today), and the library was duly built, opening on 11 October 1905. What should have been occasion for civic pride, however, failed to move some of the city's more vocal labour unions, which were angry at the deaths of workers during a violent strike at Carnegie's Homestead, Pennsylvania steel works in 1892. As far as the labour newspaper *The Voice* was concerned, the city should never have accepted the robber-baron's money:

> There's a scent from the books of dead men's bones,
> And a splatter of blood all over;
> There's a rough ragged hole in each leaf you turn,
> Like the wound from a rifleman's ball.

A citizen of Orillia, Ontario did not want a library that was 'burdened with the Carnegie name as a prefix' and preferred that local philanthropy come from 'native born Canadians, or men born under the folds of the flag to which we are proud to owe allegiance.'[320] The problem was that such men (or women) were extremely scarce.

If the Carnegie Corporation was the fairy godmother of the arts in Canada, the private sector represented the stern uncle, a potential source of great munificence but one whose largesse came with strings. As with individual donors, these benefactors ranged from small businesses or community organizations looking for skilled artists or artisans for short-term work, to major national corporations with ambitious and far-reaching programmes involving cultural products. In the grand scheme of things, corporate Canada was probably the major employer of Canadian artists for most of the twentieth century.

Just as there had always been the odd wealthy businessman looking for a portrait or a building design, there were always odd private commissions, of varying value, floating around. The members of the Group of Seven all supplemented their income as 'serious' painters with commissions from the private sector: J.E.H. MacDonald did a series of murals for St. Anne's Church and interior decorations for the Concourse Building and the Claridge Apartments, all in Toronto, while

Thomas Moss, a musician for the Empress Theatre in Edmonton, 1922.

Arthur Lismer received a commission to paint murals for Humberside Collegiate Institute, also in Toronto. Frank Carmichael and A.J. Casson both worked as commercial illustrators, and even A.Y. Jackson, the only member of the group who could support himself through art, did occasional freelance work for corporations such as the Ford Motor Company. Musicians could rely on cinemas to provide work—in Toronto in the 1920s, at least five cinemas had full orchestras, and many other had smaller ones—and hotels were also a significant employer of musicians. In 1913, Winnipeg's Fort Garry Hotel paid its violinists, cellists, clarinettists, bassists, and pianists $30 a week, at a time when the hotel chambermaids earned $15 a month.[321] Stephen Leacock (who scarcely needed the money) and dozens of artists (who probably did) received a nice commission from the Seagram distillery to write and illustrate *Canada: Foundations of Its Future*, a handsome volume that celebrated both the country and the company that made some of its finest spirits.

But the biggest corporate patrons of culture were those involved in the travel industry, particularly the steamship companies and the railways. Over the years, they developed a symbiotic relationship with writers, artists, photographers, musicians, and folklorists; the companies provided lucrative commissions, receiving in return advertising and promotional material that they put to great advantage.

Typical was Canada Steamship Lines, which operated tourist cruises on the Great Lakes and the St. Lawrence River. After the company financed a book on the Great Lakes as a way to generate tourist interest in its cruise packages, publisher Hugh Eayrs of Macmillan suggested to Marius Barbeau that the company might fund a similar volume on the St. Lawrence region. The company's general manager, T.R. Enderby, was keen on the idea, but as soon as they began negotiations it was clear who was in the driver's seat. Enderby expressed reservations about the original title (*In the Heart of the Laurentians*), which he thought sounded too much like skiing and not enough like cruising, so Barbeau had to look for an alternative, eventually settling on *The Kingdom of the Saguenay*. He also agreed to tailor the content of the book to the company's needs, going to great pains to include local colour about areas that were stopovers on cruise routes and periodically sending drafts of chapters for Enderby's approval. Barbeau was able to direct commissions to illustrate the book to his artist friends, such as André Biéler, Yvonne Housser, A.Y. Jackson, and Arthur Lismer; Enderby retained the original works to use in tourist brochures and to display in his flagship hotel, the Manoir Richelieu. The project was a welcome source of revenue for a half-dozen of Canada's foremost artists, even if it was not a great success for Macmillan or Canada Steamships; the book did not sell well, and was not reprinted when the original stock ran out.

The railways were even more active in supporting culture, albeit again for their own promotional purposes. The Intercolonial Railway may have been the first to recognize the potential of modern advertising when it commissioned Alexander Henderson in 1875 to travel along its route, 'making photographs of the principal structures and natural scenery.'[322] As early as 1914, the Canadian Northern Railway sent J.W. Beatty and A.Y. Jackson west to paint the mountains along its lines, and when its Jasper–Prince Rupert line began losing money the company came up with an innovative idea to generate traffic: in June 1924, it helped create the Totem Pole Preservation Committee, with Duncan Campbell Scott of the Department of Indian Affairs, National Parks commissioner J.B. Harkin, and anthropologists Edward Sapir and Marius Barbeau as the principals. Not that the CNR had any particular interest in native art for its own sake; it simply felt that if the poles were preserved, they might draw tourists to an underused stretch of line. But the railway was not always so pragmatic. In 1923, the general manager in Jasper proposed the construction of a cinema to offer 'reasonable and suitable recreation for Government and railway employees.' Completed in 1926 at a cost of $5,000, the Chaba Theatre (the name was taken from the Stoney Indian word for beaver) provided entertainment to the workers of Jasper for years.

But it was the Canadian Pacific Railway that emerged as the fore-most promoter of culture in the corporate world. By the time the last spike was hammered home in 1885, the railway's managers had already realized that they had an unparalleled opportunity on their hands. Their route was blessed with some of the most stunning scenery in the world, just the sort of thing that wealthy tourists were paying top dollar to experience in the Alps. The CPR was manufacturing luxury carriages of the kind the upper classes had come to expect, fine hotels were on the drawing board, and there was even a hot springs at Banff that boasted healing waters like the finest European spas. All that remained was to bring in the tourists and their money. That required advertising.

The railway began modestly enough by hiring photographers to travel its route and produce images that could be used for promotional purposes. Alexander Henderson and the Notmans (father and son) all earned commissions from the railway in the 1880s, and by the end of the decade the CPR had fitted out a carriage as a travelling darkroom, so the photographers could develop their prints as they travelled. The railway's managers selected the images they preferred, then despatched them to the American Bank Note Company to be turned into half-tones or engravings for reproduction. Not only would the prints be used for publicity purposes, but they would be sold in the company's hotels, stations, and even on the trains themselves.

The railway's directors were also some of the country's greatest art collectors, however, so it seemed natural that they would soon turn to painters to capture the grandeur that lay along its line. In October 1885, John A. Fraser inquired if the railway was interested in new illustrations for its next guidebook, and general manager William van Horne responded positively, inviting Fraser to travel west in 1886 to do paintings of the Rockies (or, as van Horne called them, 'our mountain scenery') that could be exhibited at that year's Colonial Exhibition in London. Van Horne further pledged that the railway would purchase any paintings that went unsold during the exhibition.

Apart from the illustrations, the CPR also needed text in its promotional materials. One early brochure, *The Canadian Pacific, The New Highway to the East Across the Mountains, Prairies and Rivers of Canada* (1887), took three years to produce, largely because van Horne wrote the text himself; as the publicity plans of the railway grew, it became clear that such tasks should be turned over to professional writers. Word travelled quickly through the cultural grapevine, and soon the company was being deluged with requests for passes from writers who promised articles highlighting the railway's charms (artists had been badgering the CPR for similar privileges since before the line was completed). Officially, the railway decided that it would not provide free passage, but that it would refund the full fare of any author who wrote about the railway in a publication that was 'of sufficiently good standing to ensure its favourable reception and respect.'[323]

But there was more to the company's cultural work than promotional brochures. The railway put up $200,000 to construct the Vancouver Opera House, which opened on 9 February 1891 with a performance of *Lohengrin* by the Emma Juch English Opera Company. It was a partial sponsor of Marius Barbeau's *The Kingdom of the Saguenay*, and later would commission another work from Barbeau, *Indian Days in the Canadian Rockies*. A firm believer in useful knowledge and the value of the educated worker, the CPR established a library in the mess-room adjacent to its Winnipeg railway shops that provided some 500 volumes for the workers of the city's largest employer. Decades later, it would produce the CPR Foundation Library, intended to encourage employees to improve their minds with a series of books 'bearing on factors on railway life, on speaking in public, on Canadian citizenship, on relations with the public and on such movements as tend to encourage community spirit.' Each set of ten volumes, including Herbert Heaton's *Economic History of Canada*, W.J. Karr's *Canadian History Through Biography*, and Gordon V. Thompson's *Canada Sings* ('ideal for the home or for those interested in formation of choral societies and glee clubs'), sold for $2, less than half of what it cost the railway to produce.[324] At one point, the CPR's president, Sir Edward Beatty, even offered a $3,000

The CPR-funded Vancouver Opera House. Undated.

prize, a princely sum in those days, for the best musical composition based on a French-Canadian melody.

—•◦•—

In the early twentieth century, this rather haphazard promotional effort was professionalized. While painters such as F.M. Bell-Smith, William Brymner, and G. Horne Russell still travelled west on special passes, producing enough work to constitute a Railway School of painting that featured the Canadian mountains, most of the illustrations were being done by commercial artists on the railway's payroll. And there was a new man in the company to put together a coherent program of cultural support, someone who would work as hard for Canadian culture as a whole as he would for the railway. J. Murray Gibbon had been born in Ceylon, the son of a Scottish tea-planter, and was hired by the CPR's London office in 1907 to work on railway publicity. He showed such promise that in 1913 company president Sir Thomas Shaughnessy brought him to Canada to manage the line's entire promotional effort. Gibbon, who was not only a railway agent but a best-selling novelist (his first effort, *Hearts and Faces*, was published in 1916), would eventually lead a campaign to foster Canadian culture in a broader sense,

Craftsman Pierre Guérin with traditional French-Canadian woodcarving at the Canadian Folk Song and Handicraft Festival at the Château Frontenac, 1928.

with initiatives that were many and varied. In 1920, he arranged for the company to publish *Chansons of Old French Canada* to be sold to tourists at the Château Frontenac in Quebec City. Four years later, Gibbon established the Trail Riders of the Canadian Rockies as a promotional vehicle and organized its first ride in July 1924; among the people to benefit from the event were sculptor Henri Hébert, who was commissioned to design and create a bronze plaque marking the occasion, and aspiring cowboy singer Wilf Carter, who provided the entertainment at the pow-wow held at the ride's conclusion.

But perhaps Gibbon's greatest contribution was in organizing cultural festivals for the railway's hotels. These became hugely successful promotional vehicles for the CPR, but they were also a boon to Canadian writers, performers, and folklorists, who looked to Gibbon for commissions and for high-profile events to showcase their work. It all began in 1926, when Gibbon was asked to come up with ideas to promote the opening of the Château Frontenac's new wing. He began by holding a series of dinners for newspaper editors across North America, bringing along Quebec folk singers as the entertainment. The dinners were such a hit that the songs were published in English translation as *Canadian Folksongs Old and New*, and the following year the program was expanded into what would become the annual Folksong and Handicraft Festival at the Château Frontenac, four days of folk songs, dancing, fiddling, weaving, and spinning. Also sponsored by the Canadian Handicrafts Guild, the clothing store Holt Renfrew, the Quebec government, and the National Museum of Canada, the event was enormously successful, so much so that it was immediately exported to the railway's other hotels.

For Labour Day 1927, the Banff Springs Hotel hosted a Highland Gathering and Scottish Music Festival, featuring folk singers, a Hebridean choir, a Highland dance competition, and a sermon by Ralph Connor. In June 1928, the Royal Alexandra Hotel in Winnipeg was the site of the New Canadian Folk Song and Handicraft Festival, with 400 performers representing fifteen ethnic groups; the following year the Hotel Saskatchewan in Regina and the Palliser Hotel in Calgary welcomed the Great Western Canadian Folksong, Folkdance, and Handicrafts Festival. The Sea Music Festival at the Hotel Vancouver featured music from both coasts (for this event, Gibbon bought six pirate songs from Helen Creighton for $60, over $700 in current values, a sale that foreshadowed the later realization that folk culture could indeed be a profitable enterprise), while the English Music Festival at the Royal York Hotel, then the largest in the British Commonwealth, brought to Toronto the sounds of the old country. There is no question that the railway's patronage was motivated largely by corporate interest, but Canadian culture as a whole benefited all the same. As B.K. Sandwell said on awarding Gibbon with the Lorne Pierce Gold Medal from the Royal Society of Canada, 'only those who can recall the manner in which these traditional arts were ignored by the "cultural" elements of the country before the First World War can realize the extent of the revolution which was started by Dr. Gibbon.'[325]

But with patronage came compromise, particularly when the patron had a company agenda. John Fraser was one of the first to experience the clash between the artistic and the corporate vision when he presented his first sketches to William van Horne. The railway baron pronounced himself unimpressed, 'the mountain not being sufficiently imposing'; with his reply, enclosed a sketch of what he had in mind. This was certainly an insult to an artist of Fraser's stature, but he could little afford to turn down a lucrative contract from such a wealthy client; he readily agreed to redo the sketches as van Horne wished.[326] J.M. Gibbon too, for all his commitment to the development of Canadian culture, could never forget who was paying his salary. So, he carefully deleted from Barbeau's *Indian Days in the Canadian Rockies* any negative references to missionaries, to avoid causing offence to devout tourists. When comments reached him that some patrons regarded the rough and unpolished folk singers on some of the CPR's festival programmes as comedy acts, he promptly added a selection of French troubadour music, performed by professionals, to ensure that guests did not complain about low artistic standards. And when Herman Voaden offered his play *Symphony* to the railway for the 1931 festival season, Gibbon had to decline. It may have had artistic merit and it was certainly innovative— made up of five movements set in a large eastern city, the northern wilderness, a fishing village on a northern lake, a prairie farm, and the mountains, Voaden described it as 'a Canadian rhythmic-dance-colour music-light pantomime drama, without need for dialogue or poetry or libretto'—but the bottom line was that the CPR was a business, and the festivals were business activities. 'I do not see how we can make use of it,' Gibbon wrote to Voaden, 'as it does not appear to have the slightest relation to the Canadian Pacific Railway.'[327]

Few people, however, can have received the kind of letter that crossed Ralph Connor's desk in 1902. The author was deluged with requests for stories from magazines and newspapers from around the world, but the proposal from the Massey-Harris Company must have left him scratching his head.

> We desire to obtain a love story or storiette with Canada for the background and Massey-Harris Farming Implements interwoven in the theme. The tale would require to appeal strongly to the farming

community, and to be of such interest that it will be eagerly read. As to whether the implements themselves should be a prominent feature in the plot itself, or merely a subsidiary part thereof is a matter which perhaps should be left to your own judgement...We do not, however, wish the implements to be relegated to the background by any means. The idea is, first to set the Canadian farms on fire with Ralph Connor's story, and, secondly, out of the fire to get considerable salvage in the shape of profitable advertising.

Connor's personal papers contain no reply to the inquiry.[328]

Canadians were never able to savour *The Sky Pilot on a Massey-Harris Tractor* or *Glengarry Ploughing Days*, but the request offers a revealing window into the character of private patronage in Canada in the early twentieth century. As Raleigh Parker, the brother-in-law of Vincent Massey, wrote, 'The individual giver...as often as not has his own pet interests and his own strong views of how to carry them out and is seldom subject to the influence of the sort of people who are interested in creative imaginative thinking.'[329] Parker's comment was as true for private patrons as it was for the corporate variety and in art, at least, patrons tended to indulge their own tastes when supporting culture. Canada's richest art collectors, people like William van Horne, railway baron and steel magnate James Ross, and E.B. Greenshields, director of the Grand Trunk Railway and a founder of Royal Trust, preferred dead European artists to live Canadian ones, drawing a scathing comment from A.Y. Jackson, who wrote that Greenshields' motto is 'The painting doesn't begin to mature until the artist begins to ferment.'[330] The *Canadian Bookman* reported in September 1924 that only 2 percent of paintings bought in Canada were by Canadian artists, a fact borne out by the experience of the Vancouver art gallery. In 1925, several businessmen got together and committed $100,000 to the building of a gallery for the city; when it opened in 1931, not a single Canadian painting had been purchased for the collection.

The Depression simply made things worse for Canadian creators. The patronage that existed up to the 1920s started to dry up, and modernists and traditionalists were goaded into new slagging matches as they jostled each other to pick up the crumbs. The winners, if there were any, were foreign artists. After all, as president of the Ontario College of Art F.S. Haines said, the traditionalists and modernists had been so vocal in their criticism of the other side that more modest collectors, who might have been receptive to calls to buy Canadian, started to believe both sides and opted to put their money into imported Dutch or English masters.[331]

The arts suffered from the economic blizzard in other ways, too. Neither the Eaton Book Club nor the Carillon Book Club survived the 1930s, and Ottawa's Graphic Publishing, founded in 1926 for the sole purpose of promoting Canadian writing, went bankrupt in May 1932. Many writers who had placed their faith, and their work, with Graphic ended up with little or nothing once the dust settled. One of the losers was Raymond Knister, a recent winner of Graphic's $2,500 prize for the best Canadian novel for *My Star Predicament* (1929). Needless to say, Knister never saw all of his prize money. Montreal publisher Louis Carrier went under in the fall of 1929 and *Musical Canada*, established in 1907 as *The Violin* and one of the longest running musical magazines in the country, folded in 1933, despite the best efforts of Gordon Thompson to keep it going. With each of these collapses, a few more opportunities for artists to reach potential patrons and consumers went with them.

But the Depression probably helped the spread of cultural activity in other respects. As an Alberta journalist wrote in the early 1930s, 'the chill penury of an economic depression cannot freeze the genial current of the soul. Poetic expression rises above such material things as low wheat prices and falling stock quotations.'[332] Joining a book club, a little theatre, the local branch of the Canadian Handicrafts Guild, or an art society became an inexpensive form of entertainment during the lean years; the arts could take one's mind off the realities of life, if only for a few hours.

And so, as the history of the Fort Garry Reading Club records, 'on a blustery, chilly day in March, in the year 1931, an idea was born, that made history. Not the earth shaking form of history, but a pleasant, constructive and friendly sort of history.' Four local women decided to form a reading club, a form of mental exercise and social activity that was 'constructive, inexpensive and within the limitations set by small fry, and school age children coming home at four.' It grew in size over the decade, the members looking forward to the regular meetings that offered a few hours when they didn't have to cope with the strains of keeping a family together as the economy went to pieces around them. It continued until 1982, when the club disbanded and used its remaining funds on hand to buy flowers for Christine Curry, one of its surviving founders.[333]

In some sense, people like the women of the Fort Garry Reading Club became important Depression-era cultural patrons, and the big cheques that had sustained arts groups in the boom years were replaced by nickels, dimes, and payment in kind. The experience of Calgary's Excelsior Glee Party was typical. Founded in 1928 by a number of the city's leading male soloists, it became much more active in the 1930s, when it started to tour towns in rural Alberta. Realizing that there was not much money in the countryside to pay for concerts—Lethbridge's amateur theatre troupe coped by charging subscribers a bushel of wheat per seat for the season, a form of patronage that would have appealed to Hart Massey—they typically performed for free, sometimes getting a handful of change to cover their expenses, sometimes performing in benefit concerts to raise money for communities that had been especially hard hit by the Depression. Not that the Glee Party itself was immune; at one time, a third of its members were unemployed, and performing for an appreciative audience might have been one of the few pleasures available to them.[334]

Pocket change and bushels of wheat may have kept small groups going, but there was no substitute for the kind of financial support that private or corporate patronage could provide to the arts. When two-thirds of Canadians had annual incomes under $1,000, observed MP Dorise Nielsen in the House of Commons in 1934, it was difficult to convince them to spend any of that money on cultural products. As a solution, a Torontonian helpfully drew the attention of the artistic community to a scheme in Denmark wherein artists held shows directed at small businesses, which would trade services for paintings. 'The artist is then asked if he will accept the item offered—a filled tooth or a bath tub—for one of his paintings which the dentist or plumber has selected,' he wrote.[335] It is a sign of the desperation that had descended upon the cultural community that painter André Biéler thought that exchanging a landscape painting for a bath tub was a rather good idea.

There was no question that the 1930s represented a difficult era for the artistic community. Harry McCurry's insistence that 'the artist has perhaps been tried more severely than almost any other member of the community'[336] is certainly overstating the case—one wonders whether McCurry had any contact with a Saskatchewan farmer who watched his soil blow away and then stood by while the bank foreclosed on his property, or with a young man whose only job since becoming an adult was in a work camp run by the Department of National Defence, or with the woman driven to prostitution because there was literally no other way for her to feed herself—but the evaporation of private and corporate patronage during the decade removed a source of income upon which many artists had become almost solely reliant. But help was just around the corner: the economy was about to rebound, and it would take with it the fortunes of Canadian culture.

Chapter 13

The Second World War

In September 1939, for the second time in thirty years, L.M. Montgomery and Charles G.D. Roberts were forced to contemplate the prospect of a world war. Hit by a succession of personal tragedies and battling a case of deepening clinical depression, Montgomery stopped keeping the diary (save for two tortured entries in 1941 and 1942) that she had faithfully maintained for most of her adult life. Aside from her own disappointments, she probably reflected on the bloodbath of 1914–18. 'It is not fair that we who went through all this before should have to go through it again,' she wrote to a friend, perhaps wondering if her own sons would find themselves in the line of fire. Roberts, on the other hand, seemed energized by the war. He wrote to publisher Lorne Pierce that he longed to be back in uniform—'How it galls me to feel that I'm out of it this time…what I would not give to get up to our "Front" again & reel exultantly to the cracking of the big guns. That always thrilled me'[337]—but he had to be content with writing poetry. And in the first years of the war, he produced some of his best work in decades: 'Epitaph for a Young Airman,' 'The Ravaged Lands,' 'Canada Speaks of Britain,' and others, all of which appeared in popular magazines and anthologies.

Neither Montgomery nor Roberts lived to see the Allied victory in 1945. Montgomery, whose novels had brought such joy to readers around the world, died bitter and in despair in 1942; Roberts followed her in 1943, his last years spent in genteel poverty. They never saw how the war transformed Canadian society in general, and culture in particular. They had nothing to do with a new medium, documentary film, that became so important during the war years, and they played no role in the arts community's campaign to create a new relationship between the artist and the state. Montgomery and Roberts belonged to the cultural milieu of an earlier time, and their passing in the

1940s—along with Stephen Leacock, Frederick Niven, Frederick George Scott (all in 1944), Hector Charlesworth (who died in 1945 from a heart attack after receiving an angry telephone call from Duke Ellington objecting to Charlesworth's description of the jazz bandleader's work as 'jungle music à la Harlem'), Ernest Thompson Seton (1946), Duncan Campbell Scott (1947), and many others of the old guard—coincided with the beginning of a new age for the arts, an age of government intervention.

———•◦•———

In 1936, in *The Yearbook of the Arts in Canada*, Bertram Brooker issued a manifesto for the cultural community at a time when prospects for the artist looked bleak. He advised them not to panic, but to hold firm to the core values of their muse. 'Art is not—and should not be—*useful* to society, *in any sense whatsoever*,' he wrote. The artist's 'first impulse is not to produce anything—it is to experience something,' and he (Brooker used the male pronoun to refer to the generic artist, a reflection of the gender presumptions that ran through even the supposedly progressive members of the cultural community) 'is never—except on his days off—a propagandist for something commonly held by the mass of people—for a collective point of view.' Propaganda, in short, was the antithesis of true culture: 'art should be exciting, not persuasive,' he proclaimed.[338]

After September 1939, many people took Brooker at his word. Just as in 1914, culture seemed a frivolity when the world was locked in war. As critic Robert Ayre wrote in 1940, some artists 'are too uneasy to work whole heartedly, as if painting doesn't matter in times like these.'[339] Culture did not seem to be useful to the war effort, so members of the arts community should put aside their paintbrushes, their pens, their instruments, and do something that *was* useful. The Wauchope Branch of the Canadian Handicrafts Guild discontinued its work as soon as the war began so its members could join the Canadian Red Cross Society. The Banff Literary-Dramatic Club had been working towards establishing a little theatre group, but its revised 1941 constitution stated that 'this aim [was] to be forgotten while the country needs our help for war activities.'[340] Historian Maria Tippett compiled a long list of arts groups that restricted their operations, either voluntarily or by government edict: the New Brunswick Museum in Saint John, the Theatre Arts Guild in Halifax, and the National Art Centre in Ottawa lost part or all of their buildings to the war effort; Vancouver's Bach Choir disbanded when most of its members enlisted; Acadia University's Department of Fine Arts folded, as did Herman Voaden's Play Workshop in Toronto; and the Carnegie Foundation cut back much of its Canadian funding. The lesson was clear: many people, both inside and outside the arts community, viewed culture as a non-essential commodity in time of war.

But not everyone was ready to run up the white flag just yet. In June 1941, over 150 artists, critics, and educators assembled at Queen's University in Kingston, Ontario, for the Conference of Canadian Artists (financed, in the absence of government support, by the Carnegies). Its long-term goal was to use the example of the United States, where artists had benefited enormously in the Depression years from the mural commissions of the Federal Works Agency's Section of Fine Arts, to map out a long-term relationship between culture and the state in Canada. But sculptor Frances Loring identified a more immediate problem early in the conference: how to counteract the view that patronizing the arts in wartime was wrong. Montreal artist and architect Frederic Taylor articulated what many at the conference had already sensed, a feeling that 'artists and art workers generally are suspect,' and there was agreement that something had to be done to ensure that choirs would not disband, galleries would not shut, and drama groups would not be turfed out of their quarters.[341]

But what to do? The Kingston conference eventually considered a number of resolutions, including urging the federal government to inaugurate a war art program analogous to the Canadian War Memorials Fund [CWMF] of the First World War, but this was dropped in favour of striking a committee charged with combatting the feeling 'amongst governing bodies, and the general public, that art should not be encouraged in war time.' But many people thought that committees did not go far enough. The arts community had to be seen to be playing an active role in the Allied victory. 'If you can contribute to that victory,' predicted Montreal commercial artist Albert Cloutier, 'you will create a place for yourselves in the scheme of better things.' Norman Wainwright, a civil servant with the Wartime Prices and Trade Board whose bailiwick was paper products and the publishing industry, was even blunter: 'Each of us is now regarded as a potential fighter or a potential producer. Unless we can contribute to the war effort through our services in the forces, through our work, through our money, or through our spirit, we have no economic justification for existence today.'[342] Loring, Cloutier, and Wainwright were quite right in arguing that the arts had to contribute to the war effort in some tangible way. Culture had to become exactly what Bertram Brooker deplored; it had to become useful.

Fortunately, for most people in the arts community, *useful* was not a pejorative term. In their view, culture could be useful in many ways, without compromising its value as art. In the first place, it could create historical documents, as it had during the First World War. The Kingston Conference may have decided against urging such a program on the federal government, but Prime Minister Mackenzie King's administration did it all the same, albeit only after considerable prodding.

The driving force this time was another anglophile Canadian, Vincent Massey, now serving as Canada's High Commissioner to Great Britain. He had been inspired by Beaverbrook's Canadian War Memorials Fund but also by Britain's war art program, which held its first exhibition in December 1939. For the first three years of the war, Canada's program was largely unofficial, finessed by Massey, Colonel A.F. Duguid, the head of the Department of National Defence's historical section, and Major C.P. Stacey, the Canadian Army's historical officer in London. Painters who had already enlisted in the forces were simply diverted, sometimes covertly, from their normal duties to make an artistic record of Canada's war effort. Finally, in January 1943, King agreed to put the program on an official footing, and thirty-one artists were eventually engaged as official war artists; the only woman was Molly Lamb, who was forced to remain in Canada until May 1945, when the fighting in Europe ended.

The 5,000-odd works created under the program are very different from those of the CWMF. There are no immense canvases that dwarf the onlooker; most are small paintings and sketches. Technology is much more prevalent, a hint that the artist, and society as a whole, had become reconciled to war by machine. But there is the same mixture of the heroic and the mundane: the Ruhr Valley in flames, seen through the nose of a Halifax heavy bomber, and a mechanic

Official war artist Molly Lamb painting in London, 1945.

taking apart bent propellers; infantrymen dashing across a surreally ruined airfield at Carpiquet in northern France, and a barmaid serving drinks to servicemen in a pub. And like its predecessor, this program was as much about history as art. As the instructions to artists read, 'The intention is that your productions shall be worthy of Canada's highest cultural traditions, doing justice to History, and as works of art, worthy of exhibition anywhere at any time.'[343]

Aside from providing a record of events, culture could also be a bulwark against the enemy. 'If freedom is to endure, the arts must flourish,' proclaimed Harry McCurry at the Kingston Conference. Few in the cultural community doubted that this was a war of ideas, and that the artist should be 'in the trenches' with the soldier, sailor, and airman. 'We have an enemy battering at our gates who seeks not only our land and our wealth but would enslave our very minds and soul,' wrote Great War flying ace Billy Bishop in the foreword to *For Freedom*, a poetry collection by fellow airman George Creed. '"For Freedom" contains a message none of us can afford to ignore.'[344] The same assumption lay behind a Dominion-wide poetry competition sponsored by the Toronto Branch of the Canadian Authors' Association. As the foreword to the published collection wrote, 'let the poetic genius of Canada and of the Canadian people sound a spiritual challenge to the brutality of enemy despots and tyrants. "*Where goes a song, goes a spirit that no power of darkness can enslave.*"' There was no getting around it, thought critic Raymond Davies; cultural producers were the 'opinion moulders' who could 'help rally the people for the offensive.'[345]

But not everyone saw things in such grandiose terms. For most people, the main purpose of culture during wartime was to boost morale when things were bad, to celebrate when things were good (one music journal wondered why Anglo-Saxons were so reluctant to celebrate, preferring to internalize joy as well as sorrow: 'what we need for greater enthusiasm and greater effort is not repression but spiritual warmth, release, the tonic thrill of an authentic success dancing in our souls and eyes and voices. Is it any wonder the Russians can sing better than us? We will never be a musical people until we are first a natural people, a free self-expressing people'[346]), and to provide a diversion from the war whenever possible. After all, as Sheila MacDonald, the sister of Britain's High Commissioner to Canada, told the Empire Club of Canada in 1942, one couldn't maintain a constant commitment to the war effort without some respite: 'We are living at a great pitch, at a great intensiveness and whenever possible we must try and relax so we can return to our posts and exert even great effort. And attention to cultural things helps us to relax…cultural activities should be maintained in order to give people something to turn their attention to in order to keep up our morale.'[347]

And so musicians, poets, painters, singers, and actors looked for any opportunity to provide diversions. After the initial closures and disbandments, many groups took up the challenge and began to engage in the same kind of activities that their predecessors had during the First World War. In Regina, the city council supported the creation of the Citizens' Victory Choir, to perform at important public events such as Victory Bond rallies. The Victoria YMCA sponsored a series of concerts entitled 'A Salute to our Allies,' showcasing selections of American,

Russian, and Chinese music. As a newsletter of the Saskatchewan Registered Music Teachers Association put it in 1944, these concerts had benefits beyond raising money for patriotic causes: 'music is playing an important role in these days of tension, bringing comfort, relief from strain, and stimulating morale.'[348]

But music was not the only tonic that could help pave the way to victory. Radio station CJRC in Manitoba broadcast an eight-part lecture

Why paint in wartime? The Saskatoon Art Association found enough reasons in 1943.

series called 'Consider the Play,' which began in 1940 with Francis Sladen-Smith's comedy *St. Simeon Stylites*, chosen not arbitrarily but because 'in the first year of war, comedy was felt to be a sort of rest-cure for the emotions.'[349] Poetry was another weapon, although the Second World War was not as poetic a war as the last one had been—there was nothing like John McCrae's 'In Flanders Fields' to become a clarion call for the Allied war effort, although E.J. Pratt's 'Dunkirk' and Earle Birney's 'On Going to the Wars' were warmly praised by later critics. Still, amateur versifiers did what they could to keep the tradition alive. A typical collection was Oliver Fletcher's *Songs of Our Empire's War and Praiseworthy Allies*, which 'hits at the Nazi and Fascist parties and the war mongers of Japan' and tried mightily to make verse from topical subjects, producing such poems as 'The Great Russian Victory at Stalingrad,' 'The Gallant Defenders of Malta,' 'Unconquerables of Yugoslavia,' and 'To Our Brave Men Who Fought for Hong Kong.' This was probably what Earle Birney had in mind when he called sarcastically for a Poetry Control Board.[350]

Cinemas did a booming trade during the war, even if few of the films were Canadian. Ernie Shipman's attempt to build a feature film industry in Canada had failed to generate any momentum, and the studios that followed churned out mostly low-budget (and low-quality) films of little enduring impact. But the practice of American studios making films in Canada continued during the war. Sometimes it was simply because the scenery was right. In 1942, Columbia Pictures chose to film *Commandos Strike at Dawn* in British Columbia, because Saanich Inlet served as a good stand-in for a Norwegian fjord. Producers and audiences must have been satisfied with the ruse, because in 1945 MGM picked BC to film *Son of Lassie*, in which the famous screen dog entered enemy-occupied Norway on a secret mission. Other Hollywood films focused directly on the Canadian war effort. *Captains of the Clouds* (1942) followed James Cagney as he joined the RCAF and worked his way through air training in Canada, while *Corvette K-225* (1943) put Randolph Scott, better known for his westerns, in command of a Canadian warship under German attack. Needless to say, both Cagney and Scott triumphed in the end. So, too, did Canada's cinema. Despite dramatist John Coulter's diatribe against popular movies as 'flashy buffooneries, the deliberate triviality and trickery, the craven pandering, the cynical exploitation of what the mountebank commer-carios of Hollywood believe to be the lowest common denominator of public sentimentality and lack of taste,' the trade was robust enough for industry groups to refer to the war years as 'very healthy' and 'buoyant,' and to look with some trepidation towards the coming of peace, when they feared the good times would end.[351]

Literature, too, was widely regarded as a 'rest-cure for the emotions' and the publishing industry, which had been in the doldrums during the Depression, rebounded dramatically. In 1938, Hugh Eayrs had complained that 'the average novel sells, with luck, 250 copies in Canada.' But with the war, 'down tumbled the walls of sales resis-tance...Nowadays, books are ridiculously easy to sell,' crowed one trade journal.[352] There was a huge demand for books on current events, such as Watson Kirkconnell's *Canada, Europe and Hitler* (1939) and Edgar McInnis' annual accounts of the war effort, both of which produced healthy sales returns for Oxford University Press' Canadian operation. And for fiction, Emily Carr's *Klee Wyck* (1941) and Alan Sullivan's *Three Came to Ville Marie* (1941) attracted buyers as well as critical acclaim, both winning the Governor-General's Award for fiction.

Indeed, the problem was not demand but supply; paper was an increasingly scarce commodity (thanks to the enlistment of many men from the lumbering industry), printing machinery became more difficult to maintain, and binderies found it hard to retain the skilled workers who assembled books. Later in the war, the Wartime Prices and Trade Board issued guidelines to conserve paper: publishers should use the lightest paper possible, and should buy only the quantity that was needed immediately; margins should be narrower and the size and style of the typeface should be chosen to conserve space; and fly leaves, paper linings, slip sheets, backing boards, and special covers should be dispensed with for the duration of the war. Then came a new directive to book publishers (there was a difference of opinion as to whether it was mandatory or voluntary): 75 percent of each publisher's output had to be school textbooks, leaving only 25 percent for all other kinds of books. Publishers protested and complained, but generally complied.

The war was a good time to be an author, but it could have been a much better time. Grace Campbell's novel *The Thorn-Apple Tree* (published in October 1942) sold nearly 20,000 copies in three months, making it the best-selling novel of the year. But sales of Campbell's second novel *The Higher Hill* suffered because publisher William Collins was unable to print enough copies to meet demand; the same problem beset Hugh MacLennan's *Two Solitudes*. Collins was hoping that W.H. Pugsley's *Saints, Devils and Ordinary Seamen* would be another big seller, not only with sailors but with the general public, and planned an initial print run of 10,000 copies; it could only scrape together enough material to print 4,000. Even more frustrating was the fact that Collins' projections were low: the first 4,000 copies sold out in only four days.

And then there was the war poster. During the First World War, it had been the preserve (with a few notable exceptions) of often anonymous commercial illustrators. Since then, with the advent of the modern advertising agency, they had all but taken over the field and 'serious' artists rarely benefited from commissions to work on the large advertising billboards that came to dominate the urban landscape. But the war opened new avenues. Sophisticated propaganda, using techniques honed during the last war, would be put to use in this one. Canada would be covered with war posters that represented 'a psychological combination of message and design, coordinated into a clear statement, which must be read by the public,' as Albert Cloutier put it;[353] the only question was who would design them.

The debate was encapsulated in an exchange between artist Arthur Lismer and advertising executive Clement Saila. Lismer fired the first shot, claiming that he held no high-brow notions of a distinction between commercial illustrators and professional painters; each had the skill to produce an effective poster. What mattered was the ideas: 'This war will be won by ideas, not good colour scheme or efficient printing, or accurate drawing.' But then Lismer showed his true colours. 'If we want better posters,' he argued, 'we need to commission them from young, thinking artists. Away with competitions, prizes and advertising methods! Choose half a dozen fine artists and say that this is what we need, and leave them to it. Associate with them, writers, poets, psychologists, and let them think it out.' Clearly, Lismer *was* making the distinction between the real artist and the mere illustrator. 'Posters, like fine works of art in any country and in any age,' he went on, 'should be expressions of how *people do, think and feel*, not how advertising thinks they ought to feel.'[354]

Getting the message out with art, 1944.

Saila was quick to respond to this attack against his industry. 'A skilled, experienced commercial artist has ten times the chance, ten times the possibility of creating an instantly appealing poster than a fine arts man would have,' he stated. He objected to Lismer's suggestion that

humorous posters represented 'art created for half-wits,' and argued that
the public responded favourably to posters with a light touch. 'Like most
academicians,' Saila wrote, with perhaps more than a grain of truth, 'Mr.
Lismer shows an unfortunate tendency toward humourlessness.' In the
final consideration, the advertising executive stood by the commercial
illustrator rather than the artist, who was too divorced from society as
a whole: 'I will take my chances on an intelligent, gifted corps of hard-
working commercial artists—simply because such men can be depended
upon to stay within mental hailing distance of the public.'[355]

As it happened, Saila carried the day. Competitions remained a
popular device—an early Victory Loan poster competition offered a
$1,000 bond as first prize, a $500 bond for second, and a $250 bond
for third—and commercial illustrators (again, sadly, often anonymous)
produced the bulk of Canada's war posters. It is impossible to predict
what might have emerged had Lismer's plan been put into operation,
but it must be admitted that commercial illustrators produced some
very fine posters. 'Let's Go…Canada!,' the work of Montreal freelance
graphic artist Henry Eveleigh, depicted a young Canadian soldier, rifle
at the ready and the flag behind him. Even more impressive was the
anonymous Futurist-inspired 'The Men Are Ready…Only YOU Can
Give Them Wings,' with a rank of identical airmen waiting to take their
turn in the cockpit. Lismer himself had high praise for '… and WE talk
about sacrifice,' by Montreal graphic artist Roger Couillard, showing a
Russian peasant woman in front of the smouldering ruins of her farmhouse. It's not that posters by professional artists were sub-standard, but
that designs by graphic artists were every bit as good—in this context,
the battle between high culture (represented by artists) and low culture
(represented by commercial illustrators) should probably be declared
a draw.

———•◦•———

Underlying the debate between Lismer and Saila was an even more
fundamental matter: the relationship between propaganda and art.
Fundamentally, advertising was propaganda, while in Lismer's view art
was almost antithetical to propaganda. Furthermore, as historian Len
Kuffert has shown, propaganda was considered to be something the

A staffer at the National Film Board office in Ottawa previews footage, 1943.

enemy did; in contrast, Allied governments provided information to their citizens, attempted to foster national unity, and worked to counter enemy propaganda. The distinction is a fine one, but important all the same: if the Canadian government was going to use culture to shape the minds of its citizens, it would have to ensure that it did not look like mere propagandizing. This guiding principle can be seen in the work of the two main government offices responsible for information management, the Bureau of Public Information and the Wartime Information Board, but it also influenced a relatively new form of media that had an enormous impact on how Canadians viewed the war: documentary film and its major producer, the National Film Board.

Canada's tradition of documentary film-making began before the First World War; British Columbia, for example, got into the business in 1908, when premier Richard McBride commissioned a cameraman to document the province's industrial and tourism potential. The government continued commissioning films on an ad hoc basis until the creation of the BC Government Travel Bureau in 1938, which assumed responsibility for the promotional films. Corporations such as the CPR, which had its own Montreal-based production company, also made films for publicity purposes, as did the federal government. As in BC, Ottawa's efforts were initially informal; during the First World War, for example, the Canadian War Records Office employed a number of cameramen to preserve the nation's war effort on film. But in general the emphasis was on promoting rather than recording, and the Exhibits and Publicity Bureau was created in 1919 with the explicit task of using film to showcase Canada to potential tourists and investors. Later renamed the Canadian Government Motion Picture Bureau [CGMPB], it produced a wide range of films, from travelogues to newsreels to industrial films, and had developed a considerable reputation; but by the mid 1930s it had lost its lustre. A dissatisfied government looked for ways to regain its supremacy in documentary film, and called in an expert from overseas to make a diagnosis.

John Grierson came from a long line of Scottish lighthouse keepers, a brilliant young man who studied film on a Rockefeller scholarship to the University of Chicago. He started as a director, but aspired to greater influence on the evolution of documentary film as an art form. In 1938, he brought his expertise to Canada to pronounce on the nation's film industry. Grierson's report was underpinned by his customary distinction between movies, Hollywood productions that 'reflect a silly inconsequential outlook on life…[and] a neurotic, meaningless society which is all dressed up and has nowhere to go,' and film, by which he meant documentary film, 'a deep and serious thing, simple, straight-forward, informative.' Quite apart from the fact that it was not economically feasible for Canada to have its own movie industry, Grierson was philosophically opposed to such a thing because it did not improve Canadians' sense of themselves. Instead, he advocated the centralization of all government film-making into a single agency that would produce documentaries with the power to 'describe Canada's place in the world…Canada's achievements in industry and agriculture…[and] the various problems of finance and housing and labor and nutrition and child welfare. They progressively cover the whole field of

John Grierson and Ralph Foster mull over posters produced by the National Film Board, 1944.

civic interest—what Canadians need to know and think about if they are going to do their best by Canada and by themselves.'[356]

Acting with unusual despatch, the King government accepted Grierson's advice and established the National Film Board [NFB] in May 1939. Grierson was not angling for a job when he submitted his report, but he got one all the same: in October 1939, he became the board's first commissioner. He was initially reluctant to take over, referring to

himself as 'an outsider with no intention in the whole world of operating it' (he felt so strongly that a Canadian should have the job that he
initially requested a six-month contract at most).[357] But Grierson was
won over by the opportunity to put into practice the ideas he had been
developing for more than a decade. By war's end, what the government
had envisioned as a purely advisory body had absorbed the CGMPB
and the film branch of the Wartime Information Board to become the
largest documentary film maker in the world with nearly 800 employees,
offices in London, Washington, New York City, Chicago, Mexico City,
and Sydney, and over 500 films to its credit.

Under Grierson's stewardship, the NFB developed an enviable
international reputation, in part because of the Scotsman's determination that it not be a propaganda arm of the government. Although he
directed no films himself, his influence was broad, both in the directors
he chose and in the aesthetic he brought to the board's work. Propagandizing was incompatible with his ideal of turning documentary
film into a bona fide art form and his own politics tended towards the
internationalist, both of which militated against the kind of patriotic
film that one might expect from a government agency. The NFB's first
major series, *Canada Carries On*, began in April 1940 and was relatively
conventional—films such as *Wings of Youth*, *Battle of the Harvests*, and
Fighting Sea Fleas offered theatre-goers inspiring glimpses into Canada's
war effort. They were heavy on narration (much of it by future television star Lorne Greene), and were generally created with a specific
purpose, whether it be to encourage recruiting, attract women into the
industrial work force, or promote recycling. The board's other series,
World in Action, debuted in January 1942 and presented a new film
every month, tackling broader, more controversial subjects and, in the
process, sometimes putting Grierson at loggerheads with his superiors.
The government disliked *Our Northern Neighbour* (1944) because it was
deemed to be too sympathetic to the Soviet Union's political system, or
Balkan Powderkeg (1945), with its veiled criticism of British policy in
the region. But the films enjoyed international popularity—*World in
Action* played in over twenty countries to thirty million people—and
critical acclaim. Under Grierson, the tradition of NFB films winning
Academy Awards began, with *Churchill's Island* being recognized as
the best documentary in 1941. The federal cabinet may have wanted

more propaganda from the film board that it funded, but Grierson held firm. When he resigned as commissioner in 1945, he left a legacy of film that bridged the gap between high and low culture, in the form of hundreds of documentaries that audiences anticipated and enjoyed as much as Hollywood's 'flashy buffooneries' that followed them on Canadian movie screens.

———•—•—

There was one place where philosophical debates between high and low culture held little interest: in the subject of so many of the National Film Board's documentaries, Canada's armed forces. The military developed a unique culture of its own, drawing elements from civilian society but generally existing as a world unto itself. Furthermore, it was everything that people like Brooker and Lismer did not want culture to be: strictly for entertainment (in that sense it was completely useful, to use Brooker's classification), self-consciously low-brow, earthy and often obscene, and focused on practicalities rather than enduring or transcendental values. It was also enormously popular.

In music, the classics finished a distant second to American big band music, already well established in Canada before the war. American trombonist, composer, and conductor Glenn Miller and his entire band were taken into the US military to become the American Band of the Allied Expeditionary Force, while Robert Farnon, formerly a star of the hit radio comedy *The Happy Gang*, led the Canadian Band. It played to thousands of servicemen and women in Britain and on the continent, relying on a repertoire of recent big band favourites such as 'My Blue Heaven,' 'Georgia on My Mind,' and 'Begin the Beguine.' At the same time, there were dozens of military bands, concert parties, and travelling shows to entertain the troops. From the band of the First Canadian Division (the first to be formed overseas) to concert parties such as The Eager Beavers and The Bluebell Bullets to shows such as *Meet the Navy* and *The Johnny Canuck Review*, Canadians overseas rarely wanted for entertainment.

The Canadian Band was not Robert Farnon's first contribution to troop morale, however. The United States had the United Services Organization (USO) to bring the best entertainers to members of the forces serving overseas, while Britain had the Entertainments National Service Organization, better known as ENSA (or, for the more discerning, Every Night Something Awful). Canada had the Canadian Army Show, which began in 1942 by touring military bases across the country and then was

Johnny Wayne and Frank Shuster in a CBC Radio broadcast of *The Canadian Army Show*, 1944.

broken up into smaller units to visit the various theatres of war. One group, led by the legendary comedy duo of Johnny Wayne and Frank Shuster, went to Normandy with *The Invasion Review*, while another group went to Italy, taking with it four members of the Canadian Women's Army Corps, the first members of the Corps to enter an active theatre of war.[358] By the time the Canadian Army Show disbanded, it had showcased the talents of dozens of people who would go on to successful careers in the entertainment industry: Denny Vaughan, later musical consultant for the Smothers Brothers and Glen Campbell television shows; satirist Eric Nicol; Roger Doucet, for decades the musical voice of the Montreal Forum; conductor and cellist Glenn Stewart Morley; Andrew MacMillan, later of the Canadian Opera Company; and Lois Maxwell (who gained fame for her portrayal of Miss Moneypenny in fourteen James Bond films).

Perhaps even closer to the soldiers' hearts were the songs they sang themselves, including some that their fathers had sung thirty years earlier. The YMCA's *C'mon and Sing!* included not just the patriotic songs of the last war, such as Robert Harkness' 'For King and Country' (1914) and Morris Manley's 'Good Luck to the Boys of the Allies' (1915), but some new (if not necessarily better) compositions as well: Harold Walker's 'To The Stars', a tribute to the men of the air force, the 'true patriot sons of Mars'; Sydney Bland's 'Over Again', which looked forward to another meeting with the Mademoiselle from Armentières;

Winning the war through song: the YMCA's songbook *C'Mon and Sing!* Undated.

and Dumbells founder Merton Plunkett's 'We're On Our Way' ('We're on our way to Berchtesgaden.../And there's only one thing you can betcha/Jerry boy we're goin' to getcha').[359]

The songs that filled the air in mess and barroom, however, were unlikely to find their way into a YMCA song book. Some, like 'Tavern in the Town' (which traced its roots back to an eighteenth-century drinking song) or 'Here's to Good Old Beer', could be heard on virtually any base throughout the Allied world, but others were peculiar to specific units. 'O'er the Hills of Old Sicily' (sung to the tune of the Australian song 'Waltzing Matilda') was written by officers of the Loyal Edmonton Regiment as they waited to attack across the Senio Canal in northern Italy in December 1944. The unofficial song of Escort Group C-5, a flotilla of Royal Canadian Navy vessels based in St. John's, Newfoundland, was 'Beneath the Barber Pole', with lyrics written by a naval surgeon as he waited for the group to leave Northern Ireland for the voyage home. The men of the 43rd Battery, 12th Field Regiment, Royal Canadian Artillery, were known to bellow their own song at every opportunity:

> Have you heard, have you heard,
> Of the fighting 43rd?
> As our limbers go rolling along.
> Shoot 'em high, shoot 'em low,
> Where the hell did that one go?
> As our limbers go rolling along.

And then there was the famous (or infamous) 'North Atlantic Squadron', a drinking song that consisted of dozens of verses ranging from the tasteless to the pornographic. It was probably the most famous Canadian military song of the Second World War, despite the fact that few people outside of the armed forces knew the lyrics.

There were also artists in the military, quite apart from those who participated in the war art program, and their work was regarded highly enough by the artistic establishment that in November 1942, Hart House at the University of Toronto hosted the Canadian Armed Forces Art Exhibition, the first show of work by largely amateur artists in the forces; subsequent exhibitions drew generous praise in the pages of *Canadian Art*. But the men in the front lines had their own favourite artists—Merle Tingley of the Royal Canadian Corps of Signals, whose cartoon 'Occupational Oscar and This Doggone Army' first appeared in the Canadian Army newspaper *The Maple Leaf* in 1945; Les Callan, a cartoonist with the *Toronto Daily Star* and famous with the troops for his series 'Monty and Johnny;' and especially William 'Bing' Coughlin.

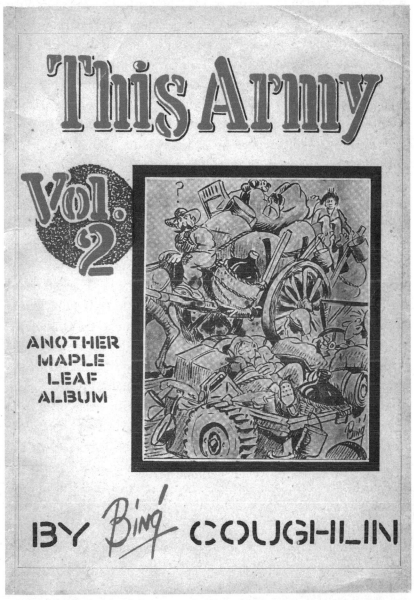

Bing Coughlin's Herbie, 1945.

The Ottawa-born Coughlin had moved to Philadelphia at a young age and studied at the Pennsylvania School of Art, returning to Canada in 1940 to work for an advertising agency. He enlisted with the Princess Louise's Dragoon Guards and took part in the invasion of Sicily in 1943, but his greatest contribution to the Canadian war effort was a chinless, pendulous-nosed fellow named Herbie. The hard-luck soldier debuted in *The Maple Leaf* in the spring of 1944, and soon became so popular that Canadian troops voted him Canada's Man of the Year. He was our equivalent of Old Bill, Bruce Bairnsfather's comic soldier-hero of the First World War, because the men at the front saw in everything about him a little of their own experience. As one of Coughlin's colleagues wrote, 'Herbie was thoroughly enjoyed because he caught the utter madness of what the fighting man was involved in—the hardships, the lack of logic—all wrapped up in a pixy humour that relieved the tension. Herbie was a tonic.' Despite the fact that he was hardly a model soldier and was constantly in trouble, the army command recognized Herbie's value to troop morale; he was 'the backbone of the army,' noted one official publication.[360]

Herbie and Occupational Oscar owed their existence to *The Maple Leaf*, one of the hundreds of magazines and newspapers that constituted the most prevalent cultural medium in the military. Just like in the First World War, the soldiers, sailors, and air force personnel of the Second produced an enormous range of publications, from no-frills unit newspapers to high-quality official publications with wide distribution. One of the largest was *The Maple Leaf*, published in a different edition for each theatre of war; the northwest Europe edition, for instance, began publishing in Caen, France, on 27 July 1944, then moved to Brussels in September, Amsterdam a year later, and Delmenhorst, Germany (where it catered to Canadian troops in occupation) in November 1945. The Royal Canadian Air Force had a number of equivalents, including the *Air Force Review*, *Canadian Air Cadet*, *The Observer*, *Wings*, and, of most relevance to those on active service, *Wings Abroad*, directed at Canadian units overseas.

At the other end of the scale were magazines and news sheets published by individual units, often on an occasional basis and frequently with low production values, such as *Flap* (39 Reconnaissance Wing, RCAF), *The Airman's Post* (#2 Manning Depot, RCAF), *FLAK* (6th Canadian Light

Anti-Aircraft Regiment), *The Tank* (Canadian Armoured Corps), and *The Column Courier* (1st Canadian Army Transport Column). Regardless of the unit, however, the content was basically the same: news of interest to personnel, cartoons and jokes (often salacious in nature), humorous poetry, and amusing short stories, most of it contributed by members of the unit with little or no experience as writers or artists. There was little in them that could be considered high-brow or elevating—although *The Blitz*, the monthly magazine of the Officers' Training Centre in Brockville, Ontario, reviewed serious literature and poetry, such as Earle Birney's verse collection *David*—and few of their readers would have considered them to be culture. But they were cultural products all the same, heirs to the material that their fathers had enjoyed during the First World War, and yet another manifestation of the popular culture that had existed in Canada through the centuries: rough and ready, crude, participatory, and explicitly about entertainment rather than improvement.

Regardless of their popularity, there was little likelihood that the Canadian Army Show, the *North Atlantic Squadron*, or Herbie would become cornerstones of postwar Canadian culture, particularly if the country's arts elite had anything to say about it. Before the war was three months old, the federal government had already started to plan for that postwar period. Determined that the mistakes of post-1918 Canada not be repeated, the King administration appointed committee after committee to determine what the country would look like once the war was won: the Cabinet Committee on Demobilization and Re-establishment in December 1939; the General Advisory Committee on Demobilization and Rehabilitation in August 1940; the Cabinet Committee on Reconstruction, with its four sub-committees on agricultural policy, postwar employment, conservation and natural resources, and building projects; and all of the provincial reconstruction committees. They were charged with examining every aspect of Canadian life, in order to determine what was most important to the people. From their deliberations, it was hoped, would emerge a blueprint for postwar Canada.

Every imaginable interest group wanted a say in this process, and the cultural lobby was no exception. This was one of the underlying

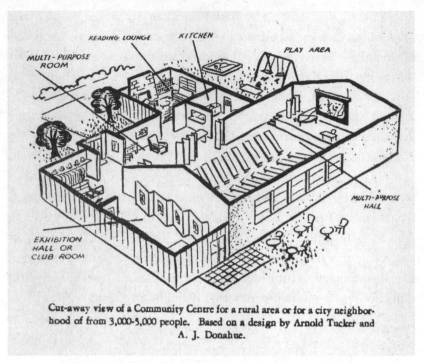

Cut-away view of a Community Centre for a rural area or for a city neighbor-
hood of from 3,000-5,000 people. Based on a design by Arnold Tucker and
A. J. Donahue.

Various plans for postwar cultural centres. Undated.

themes behind the Kingston Conference, and artists across the country
looked forward to carving out for themselves a better place in the new
Canada. But one thing, apparently, was not negotiable, and that was
the marginalization of women at the top of the cultural hierarchy.
Despite the fact that over a third of the participants in the Kingston
Conference were women, none of them were invited to address the
gathering. When Arthur Lismer announced the membership of the
resolutions committee, Paraskeva Clark, an artist born and trained in
Russia but resident in Canada since 1931 following her marriage to a
Canadian accountant, asked simply, 'No women?'; Lismer brushed her
off by saying that the matter could be dealt with later, but this did not
happen.[361] When nominations for a committee to discuss the creation
of a Canadian Federation of Artists were closed, there was just a single
woman, sculptor Frances Loring, on the ballot of nine names; she was
ultimately elected to the committee, along with André Biéler, Dr. Walter
Abell of Acadia University, A.Y. Jackson, and Lismer. If the arts were to
have a new place in postwar Canadian society, women would play little
part in the process.

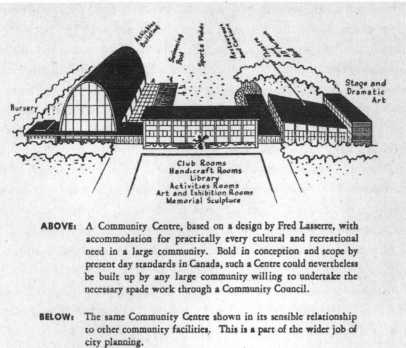

Athletic Building
Swimming Pool
Sports Fields
Restaurant and Cafeteria
Theatre
Stage and Dramatic Art
Nursery

Club Rooms
Handicraft Rooms
Library
Activities Rooms
Art and Exhibition Rooms
Memorial Sculpture

ABOVE: A Community Centre, based on a design by Fred Lasserre, with accommodation for practically every cultural and recreational need in a large community. Bold in conception and scope by present day standards in Canada, such a Centre could nevertheless be built up by any large community willing to undertake the necessary spade work through a Community Council.

BELOW: The same Community Centre shown in its sensible relationship to other community facilities. This is a part of the wider job of city planning.

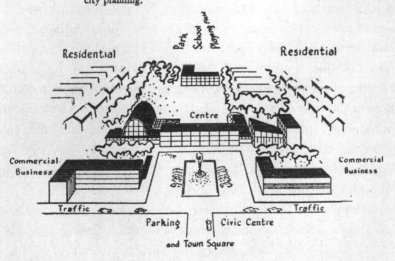

Park
School
Playing field
Residential   Residential

Centre

Commercial Business   Commercial Business

Traffic   Traffic
Parking   Civic Centre
and Town Square

The Federation of Canadian Artists was duly created, but it was dogged by disagreements over whether it should be inclusive (to create a broader base of support for art in Canada) or exclusive (made up of elected members), whether it should be a federation of existing arts groups or of individual painters, or whether it should be limited to painters and sculptors or open to all members of the cultural community. No more effective was the Artists-in-the-War Effort Petition, which tried to lay the groundwork for a new role for culture by urging the government that artists 'be enlisted in the war effort in the diverse, creative and constructive ways in which we are peculiarly best qualified to serve.' The petition, however, was long on philosophizing, short on practical suggestions; as Frederic Taylor wrote to Lismer, 'we're still miles up in the sky fluffing about in a deplorably impractical manner.'[362] Here again was the notion that Brooker had dismissed: practicality. Governments were not looking for vague plans or wish lists; they wanted concrete proposals with specific aims and, preferably, price tags attached. If the arts community was to have any impact on postwar reconstruction, it would have to get down to nuts and bolts.

Lawren Harris, serving as president of the Canadian Federation of Artists, understood this, and spearheaded 'a plan which would make the creative interplay of the arts and the life of our people widespread and fruitful.'[363] The aim may have been idealistic, but the means had been planned down to the last detail: twenty-five large cultural community centres in major cities and towns, each with a multi-purpose auditorium, art gallery, classrooms, library, and facilities for extending services to outlying regions; fifty smaller centres with a more limited but similar range of facilities; and as many as 500 buildings in villages and hamlets across the country. They would all be connected to the major national arts institutions, such as an expanded National Gallery of Canada with new outreach capabilities and the NFB, which would have an office and equipment in each centre. The price tag for the entire program was $10 million from the federal government, with matching funds coming from the provinces and municipalities.

The remarkable feat was that Harris, on very short notice, was able to get sixteen different organizations—the Canadian Authors' Association, the Royal Canadian Academy, the Royal Architectural Institute of Canada, the Société des écrivains Canadiens, the Sculptors' Society of Canada, the Dominion Drama Festival, the Canadian Handicrafts Guild, the Canadian Guild of Potters, the Music Committee, the Canadian Society of Graphic Artists, the Canadian Society of Painters in Water Colour, the Canadian Society of Painters-Etchers and Engravers, the Canadian Group of Painters, the Federation of Canadian Artists, the Canadian Society of Landscape Architects and Townplanners, and the Arts and Letters Club (not to mention the Canadian Trades and Labour Congress)—to back it. On 21 June 1944 their appointed representative, John Coulter, presented the plan to the House of Commons Special Committee on Reconstruction and Re-establishment. He began by focusing on the basic concern of the committee: the economy. 'The creative arts stand in a key position in the economy of the whole nation,' he stated; manufacturing was dependent on industrial design, and construction on architects. The publishing industry could not exist without writers and illustrators, while radio and everything that went with it, from research to retail, depended on musicians, dramatists, and actors. The bottom line—take away the artist and you take away tens of thousands of jobs. But culture wasn't just a make-work project; it had the potential to bring 'a better understanding between the different parts of Canada; between urban and rural areas; between west and east; between French and English sections of the country.' As a result, it was a matter of great significance to governments, but also to the 'millions of persons living in Canada [who] have never seen an original work of art, nor attended a symphony concert or a professionally produced play...[and] thousands of professional, creative minds [who] enjoy a field so limited that they are forced into activities unsuited to their talents.' Coulter then laid out an ambitious but carefully coordinated programme, consisting of elements that different groups had brought to the table: a federal ministry of culture (something that the Marquess of Lorne had raised as early as 1880); a state theatre, national library, and national orchestral training centre; an office to promote Canadian culture overseas; more effective copyright legislation; and, of course, Harris' community cultural centre plan.[364]

The response was overwhelmingly positive, both from parliamentarians (who were doubtless expecting pie-in-the-sky ideas from long-haired intellectuals) and from the press. North Battleford, Saskatchewan MP Dorise Neilsen, an Englishwoman who became the first member of the Communist Party of Canada (albeit on the Progressive Unity Party ticket) to be elected to the House of Commons, told the delegates that 'Ever since I have been a member of this committee I have been longing for something of this kind to come before us.' The *Toronto Daily Star* praised the 'Noble Vision for Canada' and argued that the plan 'would help complete the country's development and bring happiness to the people...[and] help promote national unity. Canada is a "melting pot" of races and nationalities. Spiritual harmony can more easily be attained when people spend time with each other enjoying music, books and drama.'[365] If the immediate reaction was any indication, a new day was about to dawn for the arts in Canada.

———————

The Second World War transformed the country in many ways, but one of its most significant legacies was to usher in the age of big government. Three large new departments were created (National Health and Welfare, Reconstruction, and Veterans Affairs), and the state assumed a role in the lives of its citizens that would have been unthinkable a generation earlier. To administer it all was a growing army of civil servants—116,000 by 1945, more than double the number of bureaucrats employed by Ottawa just six years earlier. Surely there would be room in this new interventionist state for Harris' community cultural centre plan, or for any of the other ambitious but practical programs that others had been urging: the *Canadian Review of Music and Art*'s 'ministère canadien des beaux-arts,' Elizabeth Wyn Wood's national theatre and government-subsidized non-profit publishing house, or W.A. Deacon's state pension for needy artists and generous awards for cultural achievement.[366] Surely, the arts community must have imagined, the end of the war would see the state take its rightful place as the chief patron of culture.

Chapter 14

Government Patronage

In her call for a national program for the arts in Canada, Elizabeth Wyn Wood described the artist as the nation builder *par excellence*: 'I do not think there was any greater single influence, political, economic or cultural, than the steady drive of the artists who, day in and day out, were saying, "This is Canada," "We are proud of Canada," "We are Canadians."' But, she lamented, governments did not appear to be interested: 'for the most part, those in authority have been remarkably unimaginative in all matters pertaining to culture.'[367]

There seems little question that governments were unimaginative when it came to supporting culture, but the bigger problems were twofold. In the first place, they were generally disinterested in the subject. When a project took the fancy of a politician or a civil servant, it might be lucky enough to secure financial support. Most of the time, however, culture was seen to be unrelated to the business of running a country. Just as pervasive was the notion that culture was a non-essential. When a legislative building had to be erected, it was time to call in an architect; when the country needed a national anthem, the government looked for a composer. But unless there were pressing practical reasons to become a patron of the arts, most governments (with a few notable exceptions) took the attitude that such activity was out of their purview. In many ways, they thought like the pioneers of earlier centuries—who had time or energy to devote to the arts when there was a country to build?

The mobilization of culture as a weapon during the Second World War had apparently confirmed the government's belief that it should only be patronized when it was needed. But Wyn Wood and others like her saw an opportunity at hand. By tying cultural development to employment and citizenship, they believed that governments could be convinced of the value of becoming patrons; by demonstrating that the arts fulfilled a valuable practical purpose by building national cohesion, they attempted to prove that cultural support had to be one of the core duties of government. Once this point was made, the diffuse, uncoordinated, and occasional nature of government patronage would be transformed into a cornerstone of public policy.

———•◦•———

Historically, architects were the only people who could count on official patronage in any substantial way: the one thing a government needs is a place to transact its business, and few legislators have been willing to conduct their affairs in shoddy quarters. So, the best source of patronage was public works, the civil servants charged with giving politicians the grand buildings that befitted their role as leaders of society, and the general public the rather less grand buildings in which to post their letters, pay their taxes, and have their day in court.

Even so, the opportunities were fewer than one might imagine. For the first fifty years after Confederation, the federal Department of Public Works relied on staff architects rather than freelancers, and used a few basic patterns for post offices, customs houses, and other government buildings across the country. These became plainer over the years as, for example, the clock towers that graced even the smallest federal buildings in the early twentieth century were replaced by squat pediments. At the same time, the other clients that Public Works had counted on—Militia and Defence, the Royal Canadian Mounted Police, Immigration and Colonization, the Quarantine Branch of the Department of Health— scaled back their own building programs, leaving the Chief Architect's Branch with little to do beyond routine maintenance.

But in the 1930s, this started to change. Growing criticism of Public Works' stale designs, combined with a realization that the architectural profession had been hit hard by the Depression, moved the government to start commissioning freelance architects, which in turn opened the Chief Architect's Branch to new trends from which it had carefully insulated itself. The turning point was the Public Works Construction Act of 1934, which committed Ottawa to spending $40 million on 185 new projects, many of them in urban areas where they could have the greatest impact on reducing unemployment. By November, more than

The Dominion Public Building, Amherst, NS, 1910.

two dozen projects had been contracted to private architects. They would give the federal government some of its most impressive buildings since the Château style had made its way across Canada.

There were the Dominion buildings in Hamilton, Winnipeg, Halifax, London, Regina, Vancouver, and a number of smaller cities, almost all of which were designed by private architectural firms. With their consistent style, a modernized Art Deco, they were instantly identifiable as part of a building program, just like the federal buildings of the nineteenth century. But in other respects, the use of freelancers gave federal architecture an eclecticism it had been lacking for decades. The Dominion Public Building in Amherst, Nova Scotia (1935–6), by Halifax architect Leslie Fairn, is a wonderful miniature interpretation of the classical Greek Doric style. Raoul Chénevert's Postal Terminal in Quebec City (1939–40) is pure Château, almost to the point of caricature, while Ernest Cormier's Supreme Court Building in Ottawa (1938–39) is a modernist version of the Château style, maintaining the steeply sloped roof but emphasizing clean lines and spare decoration. In Vancouver, the Shaughnessy Hospital (1940–41), by the local firm of Mercer and Mercer, is a more typical brand of modernism, simple and restrained in design, rational in its structure and planning. All of this construction was another consequence of the advent of big government. Public Works found itself busier than ever, and had no choice but to rely more heavily on freelancers. Between 1927 and 1939, the Chief Architect's Branch erected over 300 new buildings; by the 1950s, it might have 300 buildings under contract in a single year.

The provincial and municipal governments also became important patrons of architecture; not all of them employed full-time architects, for it was often more cost-effective to hold competitions or call for tenders as circumstances demanded. Not that they always felt obliged to hire Canadians for taxpayer-funded buildings. Of the seven provincial legislatures erected between Confederation and the Second World War, only three—in Fredericton, Quebec City, and Regina—were designed by Canadian architects. The legislature in Winnipeg is a veritable treasure-trove of non-Canadian craftsmanship. Designed by English architect Frank Simon, its most famous feature, the Golden Boy who stands atop the dome, was executed by Parisian sculptor Charles Gardet (who also created the figures of Moses and Solon in the Legislative Chamber and the two massive bronze bison flanking the grand staircase). Other distinguishing features of the building are the large First World War memorial mural (by English artist Frank Brangwyn), the caryatid figures on the third floor (by the Piccirilli brothers of New York), the allegorical grouping on the main pediment (by Englishman Albert Hodge), the murals depicting classical personifications of virtues in the legislative chamber (by American Augustus Tack), and the hand-woven carpet in the lieutenant-governor's reception room (from Donegal, in Ireland).

But more often, provincial and municipal governments decided that part of putting forth a good image in stone was ensuring that the work reflected native talent. As the role of municipal governments had grown through the nineteenth century, a fine town hall became a sign of civic pride. In smaller communities, they were usually designed by the contractors, carpenters, or stonemasons who erected them, and were typically small, functional buildings with a minimum of ornamenta-tion. But in larger towns and cities, the municipal building became a billboard to advertise quality, affluence, and, in some cases, superiority over nearby communities. So, the town of Cobourg, Ontario, erected Victoria Hall (1856–60), an edifice that was out of all proportion to the size or financial resources of the town, largely because it wanted to compete with the impressive municipal buildings in Toronto to the west and Kingston to the east. In response, Toronto's council eventually built

Toronto's Old City Hall. c. 1930s.

what would be the country's largest city hall of the era, an enormous Romanesque pile with a clock tower over twice the height of the main façade. Designed by Toronto-born and trained architect Edward James Lennox, it cost taxpayers more than ten times the original estimate, but mayor John Shaw had no doubt that it was money well spent. 'Great buildings symbolize a people's deeds and aspirations,' he proclaimed. 'Where no such monuments are to be found, the mental and moral natures of the people have not been above the faculties of beasts.'[368]

But there was more to be built than provincial legislatures and town halls, and where the contracts were smaller, local architects were more

likely to win commissions. Not all of their work was especially distinguished, but there were enough high-quality designs to confirm that the
architectural profession had shaken off the torpor of the post-Confederation years. Nova Scotia architect Henry Busch brought a restrained
and dignified version of the Second Empire style to the County Court
House in Lunenberg (1891–92), while Moses Edey designed Ottawa's
delightful Aberdeen Pavilion (1898) with enough Palladian windows,
turrets, and elements of Renaissance church architecture that it hardly
seemed suitable for cattle and pigs. The Land Titles Building in Saskatoon (1909), designed by Edgar Storey and William Van Egmond of
Regina, was a lovely example of Beaux-Arts classicism and the same
year, Arthur Nutter designed two fire stations for London, Ontario,
adapting the Italianate style and transforming the most distinctive
practical feature, the tall hose-drying tower, into something that might
have adorned a Tuscan villa.

Of course, it was not enough simply to erect the building; it had
to be suitably decorated, preferably with paintings and sculptures that
commemorated the figures and events of the past and pointed towards
the glories of the future. Here, again, Canadians could count on some
lucrative commissions, although governments were rarely as generous
or as visionary as the arts community desired. The Ontario government,
for example, ensured that most of the monuments dotting Queen's
Park were entrusted to Canadian sculptors. The only problem was that
there were few sculptors from which to choose. So, Walter Allward
(best known for his majestic memorial in France that commemorated
the Battle of Vimy Ridge) designed five of the eleven statues erected
near the legislative grounds by 1940. Hamilton MacCarthy, who was
responsible for two of the others, was also a favourite with various
levels of government. He, too, had many war memorials to his credit,
but he also won the commissions for the monument to one of the
founders of Acadia, Pierre du Gua de Monts, at Annapolis Royal, Nova
Scotia (1900), the splendid memorial to Samuel de Champlain (1915)
in Ottawa, on what is now known as Nepean Point, and the bronze
Anishinabe Scout (1918) in Major's Hill Park, also in Ottawa.

The federal government, too, was careful in the sculptors it chose
to decorate Parliament Hill with tributes to great Canadians. The first
commission, for a monument to Georges-Étienne Cartier (1885), went

to Quebec native Louis-Philippe Hébert, who would go on to win three more competitions for monuments—to Sir John A. Macdonald, Alexander Mackenzie, and Queen Victoria. Wilfrid Laurier's monument was executed by a fellow Quebecker, Joseph-Émile Brunet, who took the commission from over forty entries from around the world. Montrealer George William Hill was responsible for the memorials to D'Arcy McGee and George Brown (1913), and Walter Allward also benefited, the unanimous choice (in a competition limited to Canadian artists) for the memorial to Robert Baldwin and Louis-Hippolyte Lafontaine (1914). Not until 1957, when Frances Loring's monument to Sir Robert Borden was unveiled, did the work of a female sculptor make it to Parliament Hill.

Artists also benefited from government building projects, because decorative painting added dignity and stature to everything from a legislative chamber to a public-school classroom. And despite Walter Abell's complaint that Canada's civic buildings were 'bleakly bare of significant art,' there were a good many opportunities for the artist who was accomplished in mural or decorative painting.[369] The most sought-after commissions were for the provincial legislatures and other major public buildings, where governments were interested in a variety of themes. Sometimes they wanted simple narrative paintings with local historical significance, such as John Leman's *Before the White Man Came* (1933), in the rotunda of the Saskatchewan legislative building, or murals that used history as an object lesson. In 1935, British Columbia artist George Southwell did a series of four murals for the provincial legislature that used historical events to symbolize virtues he believed were essential in a civilized society: *Courage* (the meeting of Captains Vancouver and Quadra at Nootka Sound in 1792); *Enterprise* (future governor James Douglas' landing at Victoria in 1843); *Labour* (the building of Fort Victoria); and *Justice* (Sir Matthew Begbie, BC's first judge, holding court in Cariboo in the 1860s). Some governments preferred classical allegory, as in the series of figures that Toronto artist Gustav Hahn did for the chamber in the Ontario legislature: on the south wall, above the Speaker, Moderation and Justice; and on the north wall, above the members' desks, Power and Wisdom.

But there were many other kinds of government buildings whose walls could become canvases for the painter and again, the subjects.

chosen were often connected to the purpose of the building. So, when the federal government commissioned Augustus Kenderdine to execute a mural for the reception room at the World's Grain Exhibition and Conference in Regina in 1933, he chose to depict the rich agricultural lands of the Qu'Appelle Valley. Two of the winners of the Royal Canadian Academy's 1924 mural contest were intended for Montreal schools, and had an obviously didactic message: Donald Hill's *Time Pointing out the Opportunities to Acquire Education and its Rewards* for Strathearn High School, and Leslie Smith's *Education Extends an Open Hand to All Classes* for King Edward VII High School. In 1941, Pegi Nichol Macleod was commissioned to paint a mural for the Fisher Vocational School in Woodstock, New Brunswick, and chose to illustrate the crafts and trades that the school taught. It was the same in public libraries. At the Earlscourt Public Library in Toronto, for example, George Reid painted six panels of people in a variety of settings experiencing the joys of reading and conversation; in the children's room of the same library were paintings drawn from children's literature by Toronto artist Lorna Claire.

But governments were not always keen to part with their money for decorative painting, even if the alternative was 'bleakly bare' walls. George Reid tried to sell Toronto's council on a plan to decorate the new city hall with murals painted by some of the city's most prominent artists, including Wyly Grier, Frederick Challenor, William Cruickshank, and Reid himself. When the city balked at spending $8,000 to dress up a building that cost over $1 million, Reid agreed to do two murals, *The Arrival of the Pioneers* and *Staking a Pioneer Farm*, at his own expense, in the hopes of convincing the council to change its mind. The murals were duly painted, but the city was no more interested in Reid's modest proposal after seeing a sample of the work.

Faced with stingy governments, the alternative was for artists to lobby for other kinds of support. Paul Kane petitioned the legislature of Canada in 1850 for a grant to publish the illustrated journal of his journey through the western districts; instead, legislators voted to spend £500 to buy twelve of his paintings for display in the colony's public buildings. After Confederation, this became a common tactic of artists seeking government support. The Ontario government, for example, occasionally purchased work by local artists to display in public buildings, and in 1876 the government began making a $500 annual payment (later raised to $800) to the Ontario Society of Artists, intended for the purchase of members' works; the paintings would hang in the Toronto Normal School, and after 1912 were distributed to Normal Schools across the province. The same year saw the passage of a bill merging the Toronto Art School and the Central Ontario School of Art into the Ontario College of Art, with a $5000 annual grant and free premises in the Toronto Normal School. The college's council later convinced the provincial government to raise its funding to $25,000, and then secured a federal grant of $120,000 to build a new art school, which officially opened in September 1921.

Artists had less luck at the federal level, although in 1908 George Reid, then president of the Royal Canadian Academy, was a major player in the establishment of the Advisory Arts Council (consisting of Sir George Drummond, E. Arthur Boyer, and Sir Edmund Walker), which was allotted a $10,000 appropriation to purchase art, with most of the money earmarked for Canadian works. It was a bold step, but the gallery's purchasing policies eventually fell victim to the bitter struggle between the traditionalists and the modernists. In the long term, the struggle would hurt both sides, as money for purchases dried up in the late 1920s over accusations that gallery director Eric Brown was using his position to advance the fortunes of certain artists at the expense of others.

Architects, sculptors, and painters should have considered themselves lucky where government patronage was concerned, because few others in the arts community benefited from official support. Singers, actors, and dancers might find work in great public events like the Quebec Tercentenary celebrations of 1908, but such opportunities were few and far between. By the same token, there were only so many occasions when a government needed a composer to write a special piece of music. The National Film Board employed Canadian composers and musicians when possible, but ironically the only arm of the government that was a major patron of music was the Department of National Defence. Military bands, as they were in pre-Confederation Canadian cities, remained a part of the cultural life of their communities, leading Bernard Ostry to write that, for years, National Defence 'was alone among federal departments in developing a conscious, consistent and imaginative policy and providing the funds to make it work.'[370]

Writers were at the bottom of the heap; they were of little practical value to governments, so they and their boosters were reduced
to pleading for pensions or sinecures. When Archibald Lampman's
Among the Millet and other Poems (1888) garnered generous praise from
influential British and American publications, the Toronto *Globe* called
on Prime Minister Sir John A. Macdonald to get Lampman out of his
depressing job in the Post Office Department and into a position more
suited to his talents. In 1891, when W.W. Campbell enjoyed similar
reviews in the United States, there were calls that he be promoted out
of his temporary clerkship in the Department of Railways and Canals
to become the superintendent of the Library of Parliament; the federal
cabinet would only give Campbell a better position in the Department
of the Secretary of State, and later in the Dominion Archives. The
government was no more receptive to Pelham Edgar's lobbying for a
$2,500 annual pension for Sir Charles G.D. Roberts, so that he did not
have to live in poverty.

In the absence of such government subsidies, writers had to rely on
the occasional prize. Earl Grey, the Governor-General who gave Canada
its football trophy, also gave it the Grey Competition for Music and
Drama in 1907, open to any amateur group in Canada and Newfoundland. No money would change hands—Grey commissioned the winners'
trophies from Louis-Philippe Hébert and persuaded Margaret Anglin
to present a bracelet to the best actress—but it is worth noting that the
first drama trophy went to the only Canadian play entered, *The Release
of Allan Danvers*, put on by the Winnipeg Drama Club. The competition
ended with Grey's term in 1911, but the tradition was carried on by a
successor, the Marquess of Willingdon, who created the Willingdon
Arts Competition in 1928 'with the view of furthering the cultivation
of the arts and letters' by offering high school students prizes of up to
$200 in music, drama, painting, and sculpture.[371] In 1937, the Earl of
Tweedsmuir (formerly the best-selling novelist John Buchan) inaugurated the Governor General's Literary Awards, but not until 1951 did
they include an honorarium of $250. Such prizes were hardly sufficient
to compensate artists for their low earning potential. Hence Pelham's
approach to the Arts and Letters Club to establish a Canadian Authors'
Foundation, to assist authors in need, and W.A. Deacon's request for
pensions and prizes for deserving creators.

Author Kenneth Oppel receives the 2004 Governor General's Literary Award from Adrienne Clarkson.

Government-funded cultural institutions rarely came off any better. The anthropology division of the Geological Survey of Canada, created to study the arts of Canada's indigenous peoples, had done excellent work in trying to rescue what many people assumed was a dying culture, but other institutions had fewer fans. In 1918, British Columbia artist Harold Lamb complained that the National Gallery was national in name only, because the majority of Canadians could not afford to travel to visit it. In any case, its collection of 'a few fine things, and very many poor or indifferent ones' hardly made it worth the trip.[372] A government-commissioned report by two experts was equally gloomy, especially with respect to western Canada: 'comparatively little has been done by the provincial governments or the municipalities to provide a museum service, and in the matter of art the three provinces are even worse provided.' Even in major cities such as Montreal, Winnipeg, Hamilton, and London, there was no 'visible sign that the civic authorities are even aware of the importance of museums.'[373] The numbers told the story: the Canadian government spent only five cents annually per capita on museums and art galleries, while Britain and the United States spent almost three times that amount.

The only realm in which governments were recognizing, however dimly, the intrinsic importance of cultural patronage was in the provision of public libraries. The nineteenth-century ideology of the library as a positive influence on society had spread slowly, but by the mid-twentieth century, the library was recognized as being integral to a community's cultural life. The Ontario government acted first with the Free Libraries Act (1882), allowing any group of citizens to petition their council for a free library, which would be erected once the voters approved a by-law. In 1895, the province legislated the consolidation of the Mechanics' Institutes and existing free libraries under one act, the institutions to be known as public libraries; by 1901, there were 132, serving nearly a quarter of the province's population. Successive acts extended the reach of libraries, making it easier for communities to establish them and bringing more kinds of libraries under municipal control; by 1921, nearly two-thirds of Ontario's population had access to library facilities. The biggest growth period was between 1916 and 1929, when the number of citizens served increased by 30 percent, the circulation of books increased by 81 percent, and acquisitions budgets grew by 102 percent.

Ontario, however, was the exception to the general pattern. A 1930 study found that 80 percent of Canadians had no library service, and that six provinces gave 'a pious, theoretical approval to the principle that a library is an integral part of a people's welfare,' but did not actually value the principle enough to put money behind it.[374] Indeed, it was quite common for provinces to pass legislation providing for public libraries without any funding attached. Manitoba had only two tax-supported libraries in 1938 (in Winnipeg and Brandon), and the few rural dwellers with access to library services could thank the Manitoba Wheat Pool, which loaned books through its grain elevator system. In Newfoundland, despite the passage of a Public Libraries Act in 1935, the Commission of Government lacked the financial resources to do very much. There was a Travelling Library, established by the Bureau of Education in 1926 with a Carnegie grant, but other attempts to extend services ran into the harsh reality of Newfoundland's dismal economic situation. Finally, in March 1947, the Public Library Board succeeded in achieving its five-year plan of establishing twenty-five regional libraries; that the demand for reading material had long been present was confirmed by the fact that the system had 9,000 registered users and an annual circulation of 120,000 volumes.

The province that moved the most slowly was Quebec, where church control of education discouraged efforts to create a free secular library system. The province had legislation on the books to allow the establishment of public libraries but had provided no funding, and in 1944 the Dominion Bureau of Statistics reported that of the 275 parish libraries in the province, 118 had an annual book-buying budget of less than $5; the total acquisitions budget for the system was $12,700, or less than $50 per library annually. By the time the province passed An Act Respecting Public Libraries (1959), the situation had scarcely changed. Of the province's 233 institutions, 136 were declared to be '*moribondes ou condamnées à mourir*.'[375] It would be decades before Quebec's public library system was comparable to that in other provinces.

But if the government in Quebec City lagged behind in its support for public libraries, in other areas it led the country. Indeed, since Confederation, Quebec had been the most innovative and interventionist government in Canada when it came to patronage of the arts. The impetus for this dated back to the conquest, when French-Canadian intellectuals saw culture as one of the few things they could preserve in the face of the Anglo-American occupiers. Culture became a weapon in the battle for *la survivance*, something that was as true after 1867 as it had been before. Although it is difficult to find evidence of a coherent, concerted campaign to use government resources to bolster French-Canadian culture, legislators were more willing than anywhere else in Canada to offer support, both politically and financially. Little wonder that George Grant wrote in his famous *Lament for a Nation* that if French-Canadian culture was to be swamped by continentalism, at least it would go down 'with their flags flying, indeed with some guns blazing.'[376]

Examples of this are legion. In 1868, the Quebec government became the first jurisdiction in Canada to support the teaching of music at an advanced level when it provided funding for l'Académie de Musique de Québec. In 1877, it took the same proactive approach to art education, sending Napoléon Bourassa to Europe to report on the latest pedagogical trends in art education and how they might be applied in Quebec. In 1922, the provincial secretary, Athanase David, established the Prix David, which awarded a whopping $5,000 for achievement in literature and science (despite prodding by the CAA, Ontario declined to follow suit), and established a policy to purchase and distribute 30,000 volumes of Quebec books annually. When the Union Nationale came to power in 1936, it acted on a long-standing wish of Quebec authors by chartering the *Société des écrivains Canadiens* and achieving what many French-Canadian writers had wanted for years—their own organization that was distinct from the Canadian Authors' Association.

Furthermore, it was rare for a major commission for a public building in Quebec to go to an architect from outside the province. This was not just because of the obvious practical reasons—that the province had Canada's oldest and best architectural school, at McGill University, and a very capable architects' branch, under Sylva Frappier, in the Department of Public Works. Because a public building was a tangible expression of the community's spirit, it seemed self-evident that it had to be designed by a member of that community. To award a commission to a Briton or an American meant surrendering a little bit of French Canada.

This principle can be discerned in virtually every kind of public building: Quebec City's Prison des femmes (1929), Raoul Chénevert's gorgeous Château-style structure that looked more like a hotel than a penitentiary; the office of the Jardin zoologique de Québec (1932), for which Sylvio Brassard adapted the traditional habitant house, with its steep roofs, dormers, and stout chimneys at each end; Ludger Lemieux's Montreal Police and Fire Station #10 (1931), built, like so many public buildings of the era, in the Art Deco style; and Ernest Cormier's main pavilion of the Université de Montréal which, when it officially opened in June 1943, was the largest self-contained university in the world, stretching for six city blocks and capped by a graceful tower.

The clearest expression of the principle, however, is in the provincial legislature, completed in 1885. Its exterior façade is decorated by over twenty sculptures of important historical figures, each of them by a Quebec sculptor, including Louis-Philippe Hébert (who did over a dozen of them and, with his son Henri, created dozens of other monuments and memorials across the province), Raoul Hunter (who also won the commission for the monument to Prime Minister Mackenzie King on Parliament Hill), and Montreal-born Sylvia Daoust. It was the same inside. There was rich stained glass by Gauthier et frère, showing episodes in the journeys of Samuel de Champlain, and ornately carved

Exterior view of the Quebec legislative building. Undated.

wood and stone, in the finest tradition of the craft in Quebec. As for murals, premier John Jones Ross had declared that 'The interior offers a vast opportunity for wall decoration to which many of the various episodes in our national history lend themselves in all their magnificence.'[377] Napoléon Bourassa duly proposed an ambitious program of

Statues of Charles de Salaberry and Jean Talon at the Quebec legislative building.

murals, most of them depicting important events in the pre-conquest history of New France, such as Jacques Cartier landing at Hochelaga, the defence of Fort Verchères, and Dollard des Ormeaux at the Battle of Long Sault. Financial considerations prevented the government from accepting Bourassa's plan, and instead it commissioned Henri Beau to paint the much more modest *The Arrival of Champlain at Quebec* (1903). But concern over historical accuracy cost Beau further commissions and the government turned to Charles Huot to paint *Le Débat des Langues* (1910–13), a mural entitled *Je me Souviens* on the ceiling of the legislative chamber (1914–20), and *Sovereign Council* (1926–30), which replaced Beau's much maligned earlier work. The commitment of successive administrations to native talent was laudable, and made the Quebec Parliament Building as much a seat of government as a tribute to the culture of the province.

————◦————

The arts lobby never lost hope that other governments would take to heart the example set by Quebec. If the Second World War proved that the federal government was still inclined to base its decisions regarding cultural patronage largely on a medium's practical utility, it also brought some promising developments. In the first place, Ottawa was moving into fields that it had never before been involved in. The advent of unemployment insurance, family allowance benefits, the Veterans' Charter, and various other innovations that would constitute the social welfare state signalled a new, interventionist federal government; there seemed no reason why the intervention should not one day extend to the arts. Furthermore, the demands of the war had forced Ottawa to expand its patronage of culture. The war art program was not new, but there had been much more support for culture in the Canadian military. Furthermore, the federal government's willingness to fund the National Film Board as a serious producer of documentary films rather than as a generator of propaganda was encouraging, as was its support for another relatively new medium: radio.

In the control room of radio station CJVI in Victoria, British Columbia, 1945.

Radio had come to Canada at the end of the First World War, when the Marconi Telegraph Company established station WXA in Montreal. It received an official license in 1919 as CFCF, becoming the first regularly operated broadcasting station in the world; its French-language equivalent, CKAC, took to the air in 1922. Over the next few years, radio became the hottest thing around, with thirty-nine stations in Canada by 1922 (federal legislation in 1923 stipulated that only British subjects could apply for broadcasting licenses, to prevent Canadian radio from falling into the hands of US interests) and tens of thousands of Canadians tuning in on battery-powered receivers or crystal sets they could build themselves for next to nothing. Most stations were low wattage; because there were fewer sources of interference and no cellphones or police radios to compete for the airwaves, a 100-watt station could have a reach that might require 50,000 watts today. Many were back-room operations, such as Stewart Neill's CFNB in Fredericton, which he ran from his hardware store, or connected to related businesses. Edward Rogers, who would become one of Canada's radio pioneers, started CFRB in 1927, the first station in his twenty-one-station Rogers Majestic Network, as a vehicle to sell radio sets.

In those days, the twenty-four-hour radio station was a thing of the future—most stations were on the air fewer than twelve hours a day—but they provided a broad range of programming to suit a wide listenership. On a typical day in 1927, CHNS in Halifax signed on at 6:30 PM with business news, followed by thirty minutes of recorded music. At 8:00 PM, Helen Creighton hosted the station's children's program and then there was a remote broadcast of the Pierrot Orchestra from the Majestic Theatre. Rakwana Teatime, a local talent show, was next, with the Simpson Hour of Old-Time Music and thirty minutes of Dance and Popular Music to end the broadcast day at midnight.

Despite the fact that many of these stations were joined together into national networks, their programming was often unrepentantly local. Almost every station had an amateur hour, which turned over the microphone to aspiring local performers (ethnic musical groups were especially popular), and whenever possible, remote broadcasts from hotels provided live music; some had studio ensembles, often performing under the name of their sponsor (the A&P Gypsies or the Taystee Breadwinners), or the very least a pianist on stand-by who could fill dead air if a program ran short. Furthermore, most stations were mindful of the fact that, during the daytime hours, the majority of listeners were women, and tailored their programming accordingly. Some of Canada's pioneering women broadcasters developed a

Stars of Alberta radio: J.B. Ham and Sons of the South. c. 1940.

huge following: Susan Agar was known to listeners on the prairies as 'the Chatelaine of the Air' for twenty-five years, while Jane Gray, who began a weekly talk show on CFRB in 1927, was a fixture on Canadian radio until she made the leap to television in the 1960s. The smaller the operation, the more versatile the employee had to be. At CJWC in Saskatoon, located in the back of C.R. Wheaton's electrical equipment store, Saskatchewan's only woman on the airwaves—Ontario-born Martha Bowes—read the news, hosted broadcasts from Knox Church, presented a domestic science show, introduced concerts from the Zenith

Café, and spun dance records. She only spent six years at CJWC before marrying and moving to Ontario, but became one of Saskatoon's most popular radio voices in that time.

But it was becoming clear that all was not well with Canadian radio. The influence of the new medium was undeniable—one had only to look to Alberta, where William Aberhart was drawing tens of thousands of listeners to his broadcasts from the Calgary Prophetic Bible Institute, listeners who would soon help sweep Aberhart to power as premier. In Newfoundland, Joey Smallwood would also recognize the value of radio, using his alter ego The Barrelman on station VONF as a step towards the provincial premier's office. However, that power is precisely what made the rapid expansion of the industry in the US seem so dangerous. By 1930, Canadian stations together had a total of 35,000 watts, while American stations could marshal 675,000 watts. In practical terms, this meant that almost the entire settled portion of the country was within range of US transmitters, but only 60 percent of Canadians could pick up a Canadian station. The majority of these were in and around Toronto and Montreal, which together had half of Canada's transmitting power; the Maritimes had only 5 percent, and British Columbia (with ten trans-mitters but only 1,320 total watts) just 4 percent. To make matters worse, a bi-national agreement gave Canadian stations access to only six clear channels, in addition to eleven others shared with stations in the United States (all of which had the power to drown out Canadian signals). So, despite the fact that there were plenty of Canadian programs on the airwaves—from Edmonton's *Breakfast Brevities* to the dramatic serial *The Young Bloods of Beaver Bend*—80 percent of what Canadians listened to emanated from the United States.

At the same time, the federal government was drawing fire for its use of discretionary power in allotting channels. The flashpoint was in Toronto, where CFCA got its own clear channel, while its four competi-tors had to share channels with US stations. The deciding factor seems to have been that CFCA, though much smaller than the other stations, was owned by J.E. Atkinson of the *Toronto Daily Star*, a man with solid Liberal credentials. It was as much to forestall future charges of influence-peddling as to address the concerns of cultural nationalists that the government agreed to a royal commission to study the whole issue of radio broadcasting.

A blue-ribbon panel—chair Sir John Aird, president of the Bank of Commerce, *Ottawa Citizen* editor (and solid Liberal) Charles Bowman, and Dr. August Frigon, Quebec's Director of Technical Education—spent nine months studying the matter, issuing its report in September 1929. It was, in short, a blueprint for a nationalized radio system, patterned on the British Broadcasting Corporation. A public company capable of 'fostering a national spirit and interpreting national citizenship' would own and operate all stations in Canada, taking over existing stations and building seven 50,000-watt transmitters at points across the country as the basis of a national network. A combination of licence fees, government subsidies, and revenue from indirect advertising (sponsored programs rather than commercial advertisements) would pay for it all.

While all sides were pondering the potential impact of the Aird Report, Calgary millionaire R.B. Bennett swept to power in the 1930 general election. One of Canada's most successful business leaders and a man with close ties to the CPR (which owned a radio network that might be swallowed up by a new public broadcaster), Bennett was dead set against public ownership of anything. It looked as if the Aird Report would be a dead letter. Enter Graham Spry, a Manitoba-born Rhodes Scholar who, according to legend, once delivered newspapers to Bennett. Spry took it upon himself to found the Canadian Radio League, a lobby group with a gift for coming up with pithy slogans ('Britannia rules the waves—shall Columbia rule the wave-lengths?'). In short order, the League assembled a coalition of over fifty newspapers (most of them primarily were concerned that private radio stations were draining off their advertising revenue), women's, farm, and labour organizations representing nearly a million Canadians, twelve university presidents, six provincial education superintendents, the heads of Canada's major churches, and a good many French Canadians (who appreciated the fact that the Aird Report recommended significant provincial influence over radio). Against them stood some of Canada's biggest corporations and the stations they operated, including the CPR, Toronto distiller Gooderham and Worts (which ran the city's biggest station, CKGW), and *La Presse*, the newspaper that operated the most powerful transmitter in Quebec. As historian Michael Nolan has noted, they were unconvinced by the argument that, for the sake of the nation, Canada had to take control of its airwaves. They saw instead a nationalist lobby that deplored mass entertainment, American or Canadian, and wanted radio to become a state-controlled vehicle for cultural uplift.

In 1932, Bennett finally announced the establishment of a committee to advise the House of Commons on the issues raised by the Aird Commission. The committee's report was best known for a single phrase—'The question is the State or the United States?,' again the work of Graham Spry[378]—and it came down firmly on the side of the former. It unanimously advocated public ownership of the radio system in Canada, a recommendation that paved the way for the Broadcasting Act of 1932. The centrepiece of the act was a commission to control all broadcasting in Canada, with the power to purchase or expropriate any private station (although private stations would be allowed to exist, if it suited the commission's goals) and prohibit the establishment of private networks.

A broadcast of the CBC radio program *Citizen's Forum*, January 1949.

But the Canadian Radio Broadcasting Commission [CRBC] did not turn out to be the panacea that cultural nationalists were seeking. It began work during the depths of the Depression, when Ottawa was unable to provide the money to build the seven super-transmitters.

Purchasing the CNR system (which by 1929 had been reduced to just three hours of national programming a week) gave it stations in Ottawa, Vancouver, and Moncton, studios in Halifax and Montreal, and a technical facility in Winnipeg; a three-year lease on CKGW gave it a foothold in Toronto. However, it was still reduced to buying time on private stations to reach a national audience. Another House of Commons committee revisited the radio question in 1934, and two years later the CRBC was reorganized as the Canadian Broadcasting Corporation [CBC], a crown corporation with more secure funding and more freedom from political interference.

Even the new organization, however, failed to address many of the problems that the Aird Commission had identified. American content had continued to climb, and in some markets the public broadcaster was actually a more serious offender than private stations. In Vancouver, for example, American programming occupied about 17 percent of the broadcast schedules of all of the city's stations, but the CBC affiliate CBR had nearly 40 percent American content. To paraphrase Spry's mantra, the State appeared to be moving Canadian radio towards the United States.

With the Second World War, however, the CBC's fortunes took a turn for the better. The need for a united effort now manifestly clear, the government realized that its radio network could provide an invaluable service in wartime. The construction of new transmitters meant that the CBC was now available to 84 percent of Canadian homes, and even before 1939 a number of programs—*The Happy Gang*, its most popular variety show, *Hockey Night in Canada*, *Farm Radio Forum*— were starting to develop a strong following among listeners. But the war created an almost insatiable demand for news and public affairs programming, and the CBC took full advantage of the opportunity. Although the network's own news service wasn't officially created until 1 January 1941, it sent a small unit overseas with the First Canadian Infantry Division three months after the declaration of war. On 18 December 1939, the unit aired its first report, covering the division's journey across the Atlantic and arrival in England. After that historic broadcast, the CBC's correspondents, such as Matthew Halton, Marcel Ouimet, and Peter Stursberg, developed a reputation for compelling and objective news reporting, sometimes from the front lines on land, sea, and air. But the wartime CBC had more than just news: informational programming such as *Let's Face the Facts* and *Arsenal of Democracy*; musical shows such as *Victory Parade*; *Fighting Navy*, *Soldier's Wife*, and other dramas broadcast as *Canadian Theatre of the Air* and *Stage*; panel discussions such as *Things to Come: An Inquiry into the Postwar World*, hosted by novelist Morley Callaghan; and Radio-Collège in Quebec and its English-language equivalent, the National School Broadcasts. If Canadian radio listeners had been devotees of American radio in the 1930s, many of them switched their allegiance to the national broadcaster in the 1940s.

———————

There were many reasons, then, to be optimistic that the federal government would look favourably on the plan that John Coulter had presented to the Turgeon Committee. The community art centre idea seemed to be catching on because, as *Canadian Art* wrote, it represented 'the one great possibility of integrating all of the arts with the life of the people, of evoking the creative spirit in our people into a rewarding life.' During a Windsor, Ontario panel discussion on arts and community life, 'a picture was built up of a Canadian community aware of the value of the arts in daily life and of the national services necessary to provide exhibitions, concerts, and books for its citizens.' The Council of Women in Winnipeg held a day-long forum on the arts and the community, and at an army camp in Alberni, British Columbia, servicemen embraced the idea of community centres, even going to the extent of coming up with ideas for murals they would like to see in the centres.[379]

But the 1944 budget speech came, with a substantially larger appropriation for the National Gallery of Canada and no mention of the community cultural centres. It was the same the following year, and in 1946 the budget of the NGC was cut, the reduction coming from the acquisitions budget. In 1947, one Member of Parliament suggested that the community centre idea be combined with the desire to erect war memorials; instead of spending thousands of dollars on bronze soldiers, towns should be encouraged (with federal financial support) to erect war memorial community centres as a fitting way to honour the men and women who gave their lives in the Second World War. When these projects got underway, however, the arts lobby learned with dismay that many community centres had mysteriously transformed into hockey rinks. As the arenas went up, arts groups realized that the brief they had submitted to the Turgeon Committee, despite all the praise it had garnered, carried depressingly little weight in Ottawa. As Mark Kearley told arts leaders in Victoria, it seemed unlikely that the province or the city would provide significant financing either. In the BC capital, as in many other cities, it would be up to cultural groups to find the money needed to build a modest arts centre.[380]

But if the battle was lost, the war went on, this time with a new ally in Montrealer Brooke Claxton. His sense of nationalism had been forged by service with the Canadian Corps during the First World War, and Claxton threw himself into the nationalist organizations of the 1920s; he became one of the first people invited to join the Canadian Radio League. He entered politics in 1940, and by the end of the war had proven himself to be a shrewd and capable cabinet minister in the challenging new portfolio of national health and welfare. But Claxton never lost his interest in the promotion of Canadian culture, and when his Liberal party rejected a resolution from the Canadian University Liberal Federation calling for a government commission to study arts funding, Claxton decided to take up the case. In November 1948, he went directly to Prime Minister Louis St. Laurent with the terms of reference for a commission, a potential chair (Vincent Massey), and the support of two of the most influential civil servants in Ottawa—Lester Pearson and Jack Pickersgill. But St. Laurent wouldn't bite. The wily Quebec corporate lawyer disliked treading on provincial toes, and was sure that a commission on culture would raise a backlash in Quebec. Claxton responded by suggesting that the scope of the commission be broadened to include federal funding for universities and the state of Canadian broadcasting. Still somewhat leery, St. Laurent nevertheless agreed, and the Royal Commission on National Development in the Arts, Letters, and Sciences came into being in April 1949.

It would be known as the Massey Commission, after its chair, Vincent Massey, who served with four other experts: Norman Mackenzie, a university president and art patron from western Canada; Arthur Surveyor, a Montreal engineer who brought technical expertise in broadcasting and film; Hilda Neatby, an historian from the University of Saskatchewan; and Georges-Henri Lévesque, dean of the faculty of Social Sciences at l'Université de Laval. The commissioners would hold a month of meetings in Ottawa in the summer of 1949 before embarking on a cross-country tour to listen to Canadians. All told, they heard from nearly 500 groups and individuals, representing arts organizations, educational associations, service clubs, universities, government departments—everything from the Canadian Ballet Festival Association and la Fédération des mouvements de Jeunesse du Québec, to the Fiddlehead Poetry Society and the Newfoundland Public Libraries Board.

In June 1951, the Massey Commission published its long-awaited report, one of the most significant in Canadian history. It quoted chapter and verse on how Canada's culture was either crumbling through lack of support or slipping inexorably into foreign hands. The only truly national publication in Canada was *Reader's Digest*, published in the United States; more than twice as many US periodicals than Canadian were sold in Canada. Because of the American dominance in the textbook publishing industry, in one Grade 8 class more students knew the significance of the fourth of July than the first of July. Countless invaluable Canadian books could no longer be found inside the country; the largest collections of Canadiana in the world were held at the Library of Congress in Washington, the New York Public Library, and Harvard University. The American Museum of Natural History had more full-time researchers in its Insect and Spider Division than there were in the entire National Museum of Canada, in large part because the American institution's annual budget was more than ten times larger than that of the Canadian museum. It was the same at the National Gallery of Canada, which in the immediate postwar years had a permanent staff of four people and a purchase fund of a paltry $75,000. By contrast, the Toledo Museum of Art in Ohio had twenty-six full-time employees and an acquisitions budget of over $328,000. In 1948, there were over 1,800 works of fiction published in Great Britain and over 1,100 in the United States; in Canada, there were just fourteen.

To turn the tide, the commission set out 146 recommendations covering every conceivable aspect of culture. The National Film Board should receive extra funding to enable it to expand its staff and distribution networks. The National Gallery of Canada must put greater emphasis on outreach activities, like travelling exhibitions and lecturers and an expanded publication and reproduction programme. The CBC

The sorry state of cultural facilities in Canada encountered by the Massey Commission: the Canmore Opera House, Alberta, 1954.

should remain supreme over Canada's airwaves, with 'the privilege of radio broadcasting continu[ing] to be under the control of the National

Government.' Ottawa should provide money to establish new national museums of history, science, botany, and zoology, as well as a national aquarium. A national library should be established immediately. There should be greater resources available for the promotion of Canadian culture overseas. And, most ambitiously, the government should create a fifteen-member Canada Council for the Encouragement of the Arts, Letters, Humanities, and Social Sciences. In what must have been music to the ears of the cultural lobby, the council was explicitly intended as a funding agency; its work should be directed towards

> the strengthening, by money grants and in other ways, of certain of the Canadian voluntary organizations on whose active well-being the work of the Council will on large measure depend...[and] the encouragement of Canadian music, drama and ballet...by such means as the underwriting of tours, the commissioning of music for events of national importance, and the establishment of awards to young people of promise whose talents have been revealed in national festivals.[381]

The report generated enormous interest, and not just among the people who bought it in sufficient numbers that a second edition had to be printed before the end of the year. There were, of course, a good number of critics. Private broadcasters decried the report's support for the status quo, and the recommendations on radio became the most contentious element in English Canada. The CBC had become popular during the Second World War as a medium of home-grown mass culture; but instead of recognizing that success, the commission reverted to the elitism of the Canadian Radio League and portrayed the CBC as a bastion of uplifting national culture against the onslaught of American popular culture. This interpretation found few supporters in Canada, one Saskatchewan newspaper bemoaning the fact that Canadian listeners would be stuck with the high culture that the elites preferred, rather than the kind of programming they actually wanted to hear. This sentiment was sufficiently widespread to generate interest in Arthur Surveyor's minority report, which had proposed the creation of a separate regulatory body, so that the CBC, which competed with private stations, did not also serve as their regulator.

In Quebec, the major bone of contention was funding to universities, something that French-Canadian *nationalistes* regarded as a pre-emptive strike on Quebec's cultural distinctiveness. Many of the critiques were reasoned and rational, but there were also very nasty personal (and quite unwarranted) attacks on Lévesque, who was accused of being bribed by Ottawa to sell out the interests of French Canada. Opposition to the funding proposal was strong enough that, after accepting the initial grant in 1952, premier Maurice Duplessis declined the following year to take federal money for higher education unless provincial autonomy in the field was guaranteed.

Other criticims of the report were predictable. There was the old argument about forcing the average Canadian to pay for the culture of the long-hairs, one that E.C. Ertl put rather colourfully in the *Financial Times*: 'to shepherd a lot of people to galleries so that they may see the outpourings of tortured minds who should never have left the psychoanalyst's couch is not to encourage culture. It only makes phoneys out of people and encourages others to make a living out of being phoney.'[382] But generally, most commentators were willing to give the recommendations the benefit of the doubt. Government support for culture normally raised eyebrows of journalists, business leaders, and politicians, but the report was so successful in linking culture with nationalism that potential critics were willing to see government patronage, even of high culture, as a public good. The provincial rights lobby, by this time confined largely to Quebec, appreciated the fact that the report affirmed provincial jurisdiction over culture; in any case, the state of arts groups was such that few were willing to turn up their noses at federal money on a principle. Some editors expressed concern that the Canada Council was a Soviet-style cultural politburo, but most conceded that financial support did not necessarily mean control. All in all, for a report that advocated such sweeping changes in the way governments dealt with the arts, there was a surprising degree of positive consensus.

For optimists in the cultural community, it must have seemed as if the planets were aligning. The federal government had before it a blueprint that had generated enormous public interest and a considerable degree of support; the criticism had been, for most observers, entirely predictable. A booming economy meant that the public treasury had the resources to fund cultural initiatives, and the general public could afford to patronize them. Was Canada on the verge of the long-awaited cultural flowering, or would it simply be another case of raised expectations and dashed hopes?

Chapter 15

The Cultural Flowering

On 5 August 1955, in the dappled sunlight at his fishing camp at Cascapedia, Quebec, Isaak Walton Killam died. From a modest upbringing in Yarmouth, Nova Scotia, he had become, it was said, the richest Canadian of his day, with an empire that included hydro-electric companies throughout North and South America, the Toronto *Mail & Empire*, and a handful of pulp and paper operations. Austere and very private, he kept out of the spotlight during his lifetime, so much so that the *Globe* called him 'a mystery man to the public.' Five months later, on New Year's Day 1956, New Brunswick-born Sir James Dunn died, his greatest disappointment probably being his failure to reach the age of one hundred. Dunn was also enormously wealthy—a millionaire by the age of forty, he controlled, among other things, Algoma Steel and Canada Steamship Lines—but he was Killam's opposite in almost every other way. Flamboyant and blustery, he 'fought and browbeat his way through big industrial coups,' read his obituary. 'He lived the life of a prince, maintaining five homes on two continents and owning a fleet of cars and several planes…His private library was one of the world's finest, his art gallery the envy of many a museum and his private theatre air conditioned.'

Killam and Dunn shared two other characteristics. Both were deeply interested in the arts and together, because of the size of their estates, they presented the government with $100 million (over $800 million in current values) in inheritance duties that it was not expecting. The windfall would allow Ottawa to act on one of the key recommendations of the Massey Commission and, if the Canada Council lacked the immediate impact that its supporters hoped, it at least symbolized a decade of frenetic cultural activity. That's not to say that the postwar years had been stagnant, for there had been notable strides in art and theatre; but the decade that began with the establishment of the Canada Council and ended with the nation's Centennial celebrations in 1967 saw growing public interest in all forms of culture, a willingness at every level of government to fund the arts, and broad acceptance of the link between nationalism and culture. There were challenges—the cultural flowering of the 1960s meant something very different in French Canada than it did in the rest of the country, for example—but if the Confederation era generated high hopes for a distinct Canadian culture, the Centennial era saw the realization of many of those hopes.

The first few years after the release of the Massey Report had not been happy ones for the cultural lobby. On 19 June 1951, Louis St. Laurent announced interim funding for the CBC and outlined a program of grants to universities, but then there was silence. Ottawa initiated projects in dribs and drabs—the National Library Act was passed in 1952 and funding for a new National Film Board headquarters in Montreal was approved—but two years after the report was made public, only twelve of its 146 recommendations had been implemented. On the centrepiece, the Canada Council, there had been no action whatsoever, and St. Laurent kept pleading more pressing business as an excuse to avoid tackling the issue. First there was his tour of the Far East, and then the battle with Quebec premier Maurice Duplessis over taxation powers. In that climate, the prime minister would not touch anything that infringed on culture, a provincial area of jurisdiction.

But then came the deaths of Killam and Dunn, and the huge pot of money that the government would skim off their estates. The civil service mandarins in Ottawa debated amongst themselves about what to do with the windfall; the last thing they wanted was to see it frittered away in penny packets, and eventually they convinced St. Laurent to divide it between two major projects: $50 million more for universities; and $50 million to create the long-awaited Canada Council. The prime minister made the big announcement to the National Conference on Higher Education in November 1956, and early the following year the House of Commons passed the Canada Council Act, 'to foster and promote the study and enjoyment of, and the production of works in the arts, humanities and social sciences.' For the cultural lobby, it was cause for celebration.

In constituting the Council, the government faced the age-old Canadian conundrum of ensuring regional representation. Brooke Claxton, who had been behind the creation of the Massey Commission, was appointed chair, with the vice-chair going to Georges-Henri Lévesque, one of the commissioners. Other council members included Norman Mackenzie, composer and conductor Sir Ernest MacMillan, and Leonard Brockington of the CBC. Every province was represented among the twenty-one Council members, but only four were women and only one, distillery magnate Samuel Bronfman, was not of English or French descent.

It soon became apparent that achieving a measure of equal representation on the Council was much easier than ensuring that grants were spread out across the country. The Council could not be a meritocracy; the geographic origin of any funding request had to be considered along with its artistic value. Just a few months after the Council began work, Mackenzie raised a red flag: not a penny in grant money had found its way west of Winnipeg, and he warned of a public backlash if the Council funded only arts groups in central Canada. As historian J.L. Granatstein has shown, this dilemma was nowhere clearer than in the funding of ballet, a medium with unique financial and artistic problems. As the Massey Commission had pointed out, 'in the ballet, as in surgery, there can be no amateur status.'

Among the Council's first applicants were the country's three largest ballet companies: the National Ballet Guild of Canada, the Royal Winnipeg Ballet, and Montreal's Les Grands Ballets Canadiens. All were in desperate need of funding—their combined deficit in 1959 was over $250,000—but how should grants be allotted? If Canada was to have a company that performed to international standards, it made sense to direct the lion's share of the funding to the National. But what were the political consequences of telling Quebec and Manitoba that their companies were not worth supporting? On the other hand, if the pot was split, none of the three would have enough money to reach their full potential and Canada might be left with major ballet companies that were mediocre at best. After five years of giving the National the bulk of the available money, the Council decided to ask independent experts

Celia Franca as Giselle in the National Ballet's 1956–57 season.

to report on the state of ballet in Canada. They didn't mince words. Despite the differential funding of the past few years, the companies in Montreal and Winnipeg were judged to be strong and full of potential. The National was another matter. Even though it had drawn the bulk of the Council's ballet money, it was slammed for having 'atrocious' design standards, a lack of discipline, and an unimaginative repertoire. It may have been 'the largest Canadian company but mere numbers have neither contributed to elegance or flair...Its execution is undistinguished; its visual and musical tastes alarming...The artistic direction suffers as much from complacency as from ignorance.'[383]

With this damning verdict in hand, the Council altered its funding formula: the National saw its grant cut, with a stern warning to get its house in order, while the companies in Montreal and Winnipeg received higher levels of support. Ironically, the introduction of greater regional equity in funding was parallelled, probably coincidentally, by a marked improvement in quality. The Royal Winnipeg Ballet wowed the critics at a major dance festival in New England in 1964 and never looked back, while the National enjoyed glowing reviews, enthusiastic crowds, and increasingly generous donors through the 1960s. The Canada Council did not have the answers to the problems of every arts group; but for Canadian ballet companies, it clearly enabled them to get over the artistic and financial hump and, in doing so, may well have been the difference between survival and collapse.

But many arts groups were reluctant to wait for Ottawa to act on the recommendations of the Massey commissioners. Buoyed by the scope of the report and its generally favourable reception, assisted by a strong economy that created a potential audience with more leisure hours and disposable income, and in an environment that valued education and 'a recognition that there is more to life than acquiring material goods,'[384] they found new ways to take their work to the public that were profitable both financially and aesthetically.

One innovation was the art circuit, which emerged as a way to address concerns that reproductions, no matter how good, were no substitute for the real thing. In 1918, E.J. Lamb had complained that Canada's artistic heritage was inaccessible to most Canadians, simply because of the sheer size of the country, and a network of travelling art shows and lending services was a way to compensate for that deficiency. The first was the Southern Ontario Gallery Group (1948), a modest venture by four galleries to put together exhibitions to tour among the institutions. By 1952, the group had grown to nine galleries and transformed itself into the Art Institute of Ontario, which eventually secured Canada Council funding to organize lecture tours and travelling exhibitions of original works, slides, films, and reproductions, all 'to foster in the public a better appreciation of artistic beauty.' Although it was chronically underfunded, the Institute managed to offer 'a complete and personal service for art groups who themselves are not within reach of the material and information available only in the large centres.'[385] In the 1965–66 season, there were fifty exhibitions in circulation, together attracting over 450 bookings and 400,000 visitors. Clearly, the Institute had outgrown its resources; now servicing at least 100 Ontario communities, it decided to fold itself into the Art Gallery of Ontario, whose Extension Department would take over the program of travelling exhibitions.

The Art Institute of Ontario had counterparts in the Maritimes, where Lawren Harris became the driving force behind the establishment of the Atlantic Provinces Art Circuit, 'for the purpose of creating a cooperative effort in bringing exhibitions to or originating exhibitions in the Atlantic Provinces,'[386] and in the west, where the Western Canada Art Circuit [WCAC] was established in 1956 to make available a variety of exhibitions to galleries across western Canada. The WCAC divided institutions into three classes: large, established galleries like those in Vancouver and Winnipeg (Class A); newer urban galleries such as the Edmonton Art Museum and the Saskatoon Arts Centre (Class B); and smaller institutions with more limited space and facilities, such as the Prince Rupert Art Club and the Regina Public Library (Class C). Each year, the WCAC would send every gallery on its roster a list of available exhibitions, as well as the charges for borrowing them (the National Gallery of Canada provided a 50 percent subsidy to offset the cost of borrowing any show). In the 1966–67 season, for example, galleries could choose from British Columbia watercolours, the work of Montreal structuralists and constructivists, single-artist shows by Tony Tascona, Toni Onley, Ted Godwin, and Winston Leathers, photographs of space exploration, calligraphy, a UNESCO exhibition on the art of writing, northwest aboriginal masks, and English memorial brasses.

By that time, however, the circuit had already achieved many of its goals. A 1965 brief to the National Gallery reported that audiences in smaller centres had become increasingly sophisticated and were asking for different kinds of exhibitions: fewer 'introductory and didactic' shows, and more with original material. Tastes still ran to the conservative—as Mrs. E.S. Gregory of the Powell River Fine Arts Club wrote, 'I believe our public is nearly as conservative as our membership. I think it judges Art from the practical view point. Can it be displayed in the home?...I believe the nude is appreciated here as much as anywhere, but that the public feels the Italian Movie is the best medium for its expression. I believe our people out of their pragmatism would regard protest pictures as adolescent'—but 'their insistence of quality is no less definite than that of the larger centres.'[387] They were also more sensitive to the real value of art. The Vernon Art Association, for example, provided not only daytime security for the exhibitions it rented, but even had a member live in the gallery full-time during each show's run, to keep the work safe from harm. Furthermore, the directors of the WCAC recognized the need to reorganize, simply because it had outlived its usefulness in its current form. The larger public and university galleries no longer required assistance, while the smaller institutions still needed help but had become discerning and demanding enough that they could no longer be served by an organization that was largely amateur.

Other art organizations were also realizing that what had once seemed so necessary was, within a few short years, no longer needed. The Northwestern Ontario Art Association was founded in November 1960 'to upgrade the quality of and appreciation for art' in the region, and brought together member clubs from Nipigon, Schreiber, Dryden, Red Rock, Kenora-Keewatin, Fort Frances, Beardmore, Terrace Bay, Port Arthur, Marathon, and Fort William. For six years, it organized lecture tours, travelling exhibitions, competitions, and twice yearly art courses at the Quietico Conference and Training Centre, but in April 1966 told its clubs that it was suspending operations, for one simple reason: 'you have outgrown your need for us.'[388] The only reason it changed its mind was because funding from the provincial Community Programs Department was contingent on the existence of the umbrella group.

The other encouraging sign in the art world was the growth in the number of small and mid-sized private galleries that could establish relationships with artists, acquaint the buying public with new faces, and help artists sell their work so they could actually make a living with it. In this regard, the relationship between BC artist E.J. Hughes and Max Stern, of the Galerie Dominion in Montreal, is representative of what was going on around the country.

Stern, a refugee from Nazi Germany, arrived in Montreal in 1941 and, thanks to a doctorate in art history and experience in his father's art gallery, was invited to become a partner in Rose Millman's

Dominion Gallery of Fine Arts. Stern and Millman began mounting exhibitions by some of the foremost young modernists in Canada, including Goodridge Roberts, John Lyman, Jean-Paul Riopelle, and Louis Muhlstock, and developed a reputation for being one of the few galleries interested in supporting *art vivant*. In 1951, Stern (who had bought the gallery from Rose Millman in 1947) signed a contract to represent Edward Hughes, a Vancouver-born artist who had been employed in the war art program during the Second World War. Then living at Shawnigan Lake on Vancouver Island (he and his wife had left Victoria because he found the noise irritating), Hughes had little in common stylistically with the other artists Stern represented. As he wrote in 1952, his heart was in realist landscape painting: 'I think I will be predominantly a landscape painter, however, as long as I'm living in Canada, because to me the landscape is so vast and overpowering here and people so "few and far between."'[389]

The correspondence between the two men sheds a fascinating light on the lives of a working artist and his agent. Hughes, unfailingly polite and eager to please, was always happy to take Stern's advice on what might make his work sell better. Stern, for his part, was well aware that art was rarely the path to riches, and did everything he could to secure fair prices for Hughes' work and to ensure that he was paid promptly. Stern put Hughes on a schedule—four paintings every two months—and if the artist sometimes despaired of falling behind, it was because of his perfectionism. 'I wish I could get them all right with the first coat like many of the old masters could,' he wrote to Stern, 'but seem destined to have to rework to make them even passable.' Hughes recognized that he was out of step with the art establishment in Canada; when he was rejected by the Canadian Group of Painters for their 1952–53 show, he told Stern it was because 'the prevailing taste is for abstract and non-objective painting, and my work is headed in the opposite direction,' and worried if his sales would suffer as a result. Later, he revealed his desire to paint things like Mounties, birds, and animals, but realized that it might damage his reputation: 'can you imagine the reception that the National gallery, art critics, and Cdn. Art Magazine would give to such subjects. Done in my realistic manner they would be mostly dismissed as illustrations.'

Edward Hughes eventually prospered as an artist (in 2004, when Hughes was ninety-one, two of his canvases sold in separate auctions for a total of nearly $540,000), but through the 1950s and 1960s it was an uphill struggle—$400 here for a landscape sold to a New York woman to hang in her husband's office, $1,930 there from Standard Oil of New Jersey for the reproduction rights to five paintings of oil tankers. He and Stern developed a mutually beneficial relationship, and it seems likely that Stern's guidance and shrewd management allowed Hughes to continue painting on a full-time basis. More than once, he told Stern that, were it not for their contract, he would have to find other work to pay the bills.

If things were looking up for artists, they were also improving for actors and playwrights. The lack of a professional theatrical tradition had long been a bone of contention for cultural nationalists, but amateur theatre was being energized by the Little Theatre movement, which aimed to foster amateur community theatre and to provide a more cultured alternative to the vaudevilles and nickelodeons that were drawing mass audiences. Some very fine companies emerged—the Vancouver Little Theatre (1921), le Cercle Molière (1925) in St. Boniface, Manitoba, Halifax's Theatre Arts Guild (1931)—but the Earl of Bessborough, the British aristocrat and margarine tycoon who arrived in Canada as Governor General in 1931, had been led to believe that drama in Canada was dead. This was a tremendous disappointment to the man whose country estate boasted the best private playhouse in the British Isles, and in 1933 he established the Dominion Drama Festival [DDF] to bring amateur theatre groups together into an annual national competition. At first it focused on short plays, but after a hiatus during the Second World War, the festival turned to full-length works, although it never quite recaptured the glory days of the 1930s (critics argued that the DDF became too mainstream, with companies sticking to tried-and-true favourites rather than attempting anything innovative). Financial woes forced it to seek support from the private sector, most controversially from Calvert Distillers (an early director had said that, if the DDF were to succeed, 'it will have to be founded on love and whisky'[390]) and the Canadian Association of Broadcasters, and, after going through a number of reorganizations (including changing its name to Theatre Canada in 1970), it eventually collapsed in 1978.

Robertson Davies' curmudgeonly verdict (a staunch supporter of the festival, he also had very high standards and recalled one production that was 'uttered in accents reminiscent of a circular saw striking a knot...With all its virtues the DDF had no place and no understanding for anything new') was probably less representative than Sir Robert Borden's, who credited the festival with starting a movement that 'had spread all over Canada...it was really only beginning and would go on for ever to even greater things.'[391] In fact, when Theatre Canada finally closed its doors, the amateur groups that had constituted it did not disappear, but simply continued under different names. English-Canadian amateur groups in Quebec became the Quebec Drama Festival (1972), later the Quebec Drama Federation (1989), while their French-Canadian counterparts became l'Association Canadienne du Théâtre d'Amateurs, later l'Association Québécoise du Jeune Théâtre (1972–86). On the east coast, the Newfoundland and Labrador Drama Festival (and eventually the Newfoundland High School Drama Festival and the Labrador School Festival) succeeded the DDF.

All of these amateur, semi-professional, and professional theatre groups were finding that attracting and retaining an audience was no longer as difficult as it used to be. Theatre in Newfoundland was energized by a six-year visit from the professional London Theatre Company [LTC], which had a major impact on developing interest among audiences and employing actors and technicians in and around St. John's. When the company disbanded in 1956, some of the members remained in the province and continued as·the Arts Club, building on the successes that the LTC had enjoyed. In Winnipeg, an anonymous benefactor made the Dominion Theatre available to the Winnipeg Little Theatre in 1957, allowing it to expand from eight shows to twenty; at the same time, a semi-professional group called Theatre 77 was planning forty-two performances of five plays. In the 1957–58 season, attendance jumped to 36,000 from the previous year's 6,000, convincing the two groups to merge into the Manitoba Theatre Centre [MTC]. In its first season, attendance climbed again, to 45,000, and the group won a $12,000 grant from the Canada Council for its 1959–60 season. John Hirsch, who became the MTC's first creative director, had a theory about its success: 'There's something about that wide wash of pale blue sky that encourages dreaming, and the pioneering days are still alive in our memories. The ruts that our thinking runs in have not yet had time to deepen into graves for ideas.' But John Hirsch was not the only person who claimed primacy on geographical grounds. As the proposal for a repertory theatre in Calgary put it, that city is a natural place for theatre because of its vitality: 'the foothills of the Rockies, in themselves, contain a Drama…theatre is life. Its home must be a living place.'[392]

In other places, it wasn't the blue sky or the mountains that made the difference, but the active support of municipal and provincial governments. In Vancouver, the city became a major patron of drama when the Board of Park Commissioners agreed to fund Theatre under the Stars, first held in Stanley Park in 1940. Originally conceived 'with the double purpose of enabling local talent a broader means of expression and offering to the public popular musical entertainment in an attractive outdoor setting,' the organization soon became all but professionalized, with full-time employees in its administrative, artistic, and technical departments. By 1948, it had established a permanent scenic studio in a former naval station, where artisans made sets for theatre groups across western Canada and, in the process, generated revenue for the company. The technical directors travelled to New York once or twice a year to keep abreast of the latest theatre innovations, but ticket prices remained lower than the city average because the group had become so adept at fundraising. Indeed, by 1948, the Board of Parks Commissioners was a patron only in that it provided the venue; publicity materials hastened to point out that the company 'represents no public investment from tax monies.'[393]

By 1949, Theatre Under the Stars had become so large that city council decided to reconstitute it as the Vancouver Civic Theatre Society. Its attendance continued to climb, topping 167,000 in 1951, audiences drawn by its mixture of light comedies, musicals, Shakespeare, and the occasional home-grown production. One of the first was 1952's *Timber!*, billed as a 'sensational Canadian musical comedy about B.C.'s loggers…a gay romantic story about Dan Dawson and his logging pals who arrive in Vancouver on a spending spree. Margery Manson, a timber tycoon's daughter, makes her father angry by falling in love with Dan.'[394]

Perhaps the most well-known example of municipal governments taking the initiative occurred in Stratford, Ontario. For nearly a century, Stratford had prospered as a railway town but by the early 1950s, railways were becoming a thing of the past and the city was facing the loss of its single biggest employer. City council was willing to consider just about anything that might fill the void, and when journalist Tom Patterson suggested a Shakespearean festival, it didn't seem like a bad idea. After all, Stratford had already warmly embraced the connection with its English namesake—this was a city whose municipal parks contained every flower mentioned in Shakespeare's plays. So, Patterson was sent forth to the Old Country to try to sell the giants of the English stage on the idea. His first choice, Sir Laurence Olivier, was only mildly interested, but Tyrone Guthrie, from the Old Vic—one of the world's great theatres—agreed to serve as the festival's artistic director. With Guthrie on side, the other pieces fell into place. Alec Guinness, one of the finest actors of his generation, agreed to be the headliner, and Tanya Moiseiwitsch, perhaps the foremost theatre designer of the twen-tieth century, committed to designing the stage and sets. The Stratford Shakespearean Festival was incorporated on 31 October 1952, and on 13 July 1953 the curtain went up on its first production, *Richard III*. It succeeded beyond anyone's wildest expectations. Nearly 200,000 people came from across North America to see *Richard III* and *All's Well That Ends Well*, so many that the festival had to be extended by a week because the tent-theatre was unable to accommodate everyone who wanted tickets.[395] Stratford now hosts one of the largest and most successful theatre festivals in the world, with technical facilities that are second to none, although people who recall the first few seasons spent in the tent beside the Avon River hold it in fond memory.

Because education was a provincial responsibility under the British North America Act, little theatre groups tended to look to their provin-cial governments rather than to Ottawa for support. The Community Programmes Branch of Ontario's Department of Education had a division devoted solely to assisting local amateur theatre groups by providing advice on technical matters, loaning scripts, and helping with the adjudication of drama competitions. The province's Drama Advisor even laid down some principles to ensure the success of a little theatre group: in selecting the plays to perform, the group had to be sensitive to locals interest and tastes; 'stardom and the long hair attitude' should be avoided at all costs; members of the club should be kept as busy as possible, so that they always felt they were contributing to the project; an aggressive and energetic ticket-sales force was essential; and the group had to build a large subscription base, preferably with a waiting list. If these guidelines were followed, any community could have a little theatre that was as successful as the province's best amateur companies, in London, St. Mary's, Woodstock, Simcoe, Hamilton, and Welland.[396]

On the west coast, the British Columbia Drama Association, established in 1932 as the BC Festival Association, quietly folded during the Second World War but was revived in 1954 with support from the Communities Programs Branch of the provincial Department of Education. Its constitution, revised a decade later, declared its aims: 'to promote drama and other allied theatrical forms as a pleasing adjunct to community life in BC; to stimulate and emphasize the value of drama and allied theatrical forms as a recreational activity;...to enlist the support of citizens and government for theatrical activity.' If the sheer amount of theatrical activity in the province is any indication, those aims had already been achieved. In 1950, there were twenty-four drama festivals in the spring season alone, from the Dominion Drama Festival regional competition in January to the Fort St. John Music and Drama Festival in May. In the early 1960s, thirty-one separate festivals between November and June involved groups from every part of the province, including the Quesnel Little Theatre, the North Kamloops PTA Theatre Wing, and the Haney Correctional Institute Players. According to one local thespian, 'we have enthusiasm and zest to do well and... there has existed a true concept of community drama. The basis of that drama is recreation, the gainful and pleasing and enjoyable use of leisure time.'[397] As important as recreation was, however, the growth of little theatre groups was also part of the nation-building project. As the program for the Bastion Studio Theatre put it in 1965, 'the strong wish of Canadians to be on equal artistic terms with Europe and the United States is bringing about the building of community theatres, the formation of professional theatre companies, and the realization that exchanges of talent and ideas are essential to artistic growth.'[398]

The patriotic undertone of the Bastion's bold statement was hardly accidental. By the mid-1960s, the link between culture and nationalism was widely accepted and the fact that nation-building had to include the arts, so long a mantra of the cultural lobby, had become the conventional wisdom. There was also the lucky coincidence of timing. The one hundredth anniversary of Confederation was just two years away, and there's nothing like a major anniversary to convince a government to reach for its wallet. Premier Ernest Manning had decided to mark Alberta's fiftieth birthday in 1955 by erecting the Jubilee Auditoria in Edmonton and Calgary—the first modern, purpose-built performing arts centres in the province. In 1970, Manitoba gave responsibility for celebrating its centennial to the Ministry of Culture, with the result that many of the commemorative projects were related to the arts, including museums, libraries, concert halls, and art galleries. But Canada's birthday took things to an entirely new level. In a very real sense, the Centennial year would celebrate the arts in Canada as much as it would the country's birthday.

The federal government started to think about the celebrations as early as May 1959, and in 1961, the House of Commons passed legislation to create the Centennial Commission, under John Fisher, a household name in Canada thanks to his very popular CBC radio program *John Fisher Reports*. The deputy commissioner was to be Robert Choquette, known in Quebec as the Prince of Poets. His accomplishments were many—three Prix Davids (the first won when he was only twenty-one), a movie, *Le Curé de Village*, and a television series, *La Pension Velder*, the Prix International des Amitiés Françaises for his 1954 epic poem 'Suite Marine'—but his talents did not include administration. Choquette lasted less than a year in the job before the responsibility for representing French Canada on the commission was turned over to a bureaucrat.

It soon became clear that the arts would loom large in the festivities in two respects: Ottawa was willing to fund, on a cooperative basis, infrastructure projects put forward by individual communities, with the emphasis on cultural facilities; and it would also plan and pay for a full slate of cultural events, from small-town concerts and art shows to the Montreal Universal and International Exhibition, better known as Expo '67, that was being held 'in connection with the Celebration of the Centennial of Confederation in Canada.' That celebration would represent, in many respects, the high-water mark of government support for culture.

The first committees to mull over the anniversary plans tackled head on one of the observations of the Massey Report: that Canada was sadly deficient in performing arts centres. Municipalities had started to act in the 1950s when Vancouver's Queen Elizabeth Theatre, the Stratford Festival Theatre, Windsor's Cleary Auditorium, the O'Keefe Centre in Toronto, Fredericton's Beaverbrook Theatre, and Montreal's Place des Arts were opened. But despite the postwar economic boom, as Centennial commissioner John Fisher told an Ottawa audience in 1964, 'opportunities were few and places to perform in were almost non-existent, at least in relation to the development of the modern stage.'[399] So a parliamentary committee under Ellen Fairclough, the first woman to hold a federal cabinet position in Canada, recommended the construction of a national theatre and concert hall in Ottawa, and a string of smaller facilities across the country. The idea picked up steam, thanks in part to the efforts of Frank MacKinnon (the principal of Prince of Wales College in Charlottetown), who had spent years lobbying for a commemorative theatre-art gallery-concert hall-library in the Prince Edward Island capital, where the Fathers of Confederation had met in 1864 to begin the talks that would eventually lead to union. Exactly a century later, five provinces were on side; by October 1964, Newfoundland, PEI, Quebec, Manitoba, and Saskatchewan had all signed cooperative funding agreements to erect performing arts centres as Centennial projects. They would, said John Fisher, 'serve the professional who wants to improve his craft; the student who wants to broaden his knowledge, the layman who wants to be inspired. Let them reach far beyond the field of sheer entertainment, for here will our cultural resources and spiritual forces flourish and live.' The capstone of the chain would be the National Arts Centre, an $18-million project for downtown Ottawa. It would not only 'bring Canada's capital into line with most of the capital cities of the world,' but would also stand as 'a further recognition by the governments concerned of the civic, cultural and artistic achievements of the Canadian people.'[400]

Ironically, just two of the centres, the Fathers of Confederation Memorial Building in Charlottetown and the Arts and Culture Centre in St. John's, actually opened before the Centennial year ended. MacKinnon's plan was helped along because a potato warehouse next to Province House, where the Fathers of Confederation had met, obligingly burned to the ground, leaving the perfect location for the arts centre; at the other end of the spectrum, political and financial considerations pushed back the completion of le Grand Théâtre du Québec to 1971. At the same time, funding was flowing to dozens of other more modest arts centre projects across Canada, along with liberal quantities of advice. The federal government circulated technical reports to help local committees with practical matters such as lighting, sound systems, seating arrangements, and management structures, as well as stacks of pamphlets full of encouraging words and gentle warnings. The most important thing was to get the ball rolling early: 'Carnivals, parades and pageants can be organized on relatively short notice. Enduring, "working" monuments to Confederation require years of preparation.'[401] The Canadian Centenary Council in Ottawa was ready with all manner of help, from guest speakers to tips on fund-raising, and the Canadian Film Institute would loan copies of a half-hour documentary entitled *Quality of a Nation*, a how-to guide for centennial project planners. Then it was simply a matter of bringing together interested people and deciding how the community could best create a lasting memorial to the anniversary of Confederation. The final report of the commission reveals that, in addition to the six large performing arts centres, over 200 other cultural facilities were built with centennial funding, including museums, art galleries, libraries, and conservatories (this is in addition to the 428 community centres erected, many of which were designed with space for local arts groups).

But the commission realized that a cultural infrastructure consisted of more than just bricks and mortar; a library was splendid, but it needed something to loan out. So, Ottawa set aside $130,000 to purchase books for Canadian libraries; each institution was free to choose from the commission's list of available titles, the only provisos being that half of the choices had to be Canadian in subject matter and 20 percent had to be in French. When the final accounting was done, 23,000 books had been distributed free of charge to 451 libraries. The commission also made grants to finance the publication of Canadian books, everything from local histories to broader studies such as *Canadian Heraldry* and *Blackfoot Indian Tribal Legendary*. Taking into account the commission's major publishing venture, the *Dictionary of Canadian Biography*, over $900,000 was funnelled to writers and publishers.

In Centennial-speak, all of these were considered to be 'projects of enduring value'—they would continue to enrich the lives of their

Don Messer's Jubilee, 1960.

communities long after 1967 had passed. But the year also needed events to showcase the best of Canadian culture on the one hand, and to foster the next generation of talent on the other. Indeed, the importance of the performing arts was confirmed by the fact that it was the second largest item in the Centennial Commission's budget. The coordinating body was Festival Canada, best known for organizing a national tour of 248 performances in ninety-eight cities over the course of the year. Two of the touring companies were from outside the country—the National Theatre of Great Britain, under Sir Laurence Olivier, and the New York Philharmonic Orchestra, under Leonard Bernstein—but the rest were uniquely Canadian: the Charlottetown Festival's musical *Anne of Green Gables*; Don Messer and the Islanders; Vancouver's Holiday Theatre, Canada's best known children's theatre troupe; Les Feux Follets, the Montreal-based national folk dance company; le Théâtre du Nouveau Monde, the country's oldest permanent theatre company, which toured its production of Jean-Paul Pinsonneault's *Terre d'Aubé*; the National Ballet of Canada, doing *Swan Lake* and *La Sylphide*; Halifax's Neptune Theatre, with Maritime playwright Arthur L. Murphy's *The Sleeping Bag* and the Irish classic, Sean O'Casey's *Juno and the Paycock*; and the

Stratford Festival Company, which took Shakespeare's *Twelfth Night* and Gogol's *The Government Inspector* across Canada.

There was much more on the menu, however. Festival Canada also commissioned twenty-one new plays and musicals, three new ballets (including Brian Macdonald and Harry Freedman's *Rose Latulippe*, a re-telling of the French-Canadian legend about a devout young girl possessed by the devil, written for the Royal Winnipeg Ballet), and three new operas (including the Canadian Opera Company's *Riel* by Harry Somers and Mavor Moore, a cooperative venture funded jointly by the Centennial Commission, the Canada Council, and the Floyd Chalmers Foundation), and arranged 125 national premiere performances and some 400 other touring shows by the likes of Gordon Lightfoot, the Montreal Symphony Orchestra, and Ian and Sylvia Tyson. The Canadian Music Centre, a non-profit resource centre funded by the Canada Council and music industry organizations, doled out $60,000 to commission new works from more than forty Canadian composers, the only stipulation in their contracts being that the works had to premiere in 1967. In most cases, the money was used to great effect. The Edmonton Symphony used its grant to leverage donations from the private sector, enabling it to offer a much richer commission, while the Czech-born composer Oskar Morawetz combed through volumes of Canadian poetry until he found four poems by Bliss Carman that he turned into a song cycle for baritone Donald Bell.[402] But the most famous song to come out of the Centennial year was Bobby Gimby's infectious *CA-NA-DA*, a shamelessly simple ditty that anyone who was over the age of six in 1967 can probably still sing. And for people who wanted a lasting souvenir, there was the seventeen-album *Music and Musicians of Canada* and the nine-album *Canadian Folk Songs: A Centennial Collection*, both joint efforts of the CBC and the RCA Victor Corporation.

For a country that had often been characterized as a cultural wasteland, the opportunities were dizzying. There was Festival Canada at Home, an advisory body created to help local communities stage their own Centennial shows. The Canadian Folk Arts Council mounted over fifty festivals of folk music, art, and dance across the country. Perspective '67 was a nation-wide competition for young artists, sculptors, printmakers, and artisans that organizers hoped would show 'Canadians everywhere…the promise of a heightened sense of artistic endeavour

Bobby Gimby performs Canada's centennial song, 1967.

and purpose.'[403] A visual arts program helped local galleries mount
Centennial exhibitions; none of them had the scope of the National
Gallery's ambitious retrospective of 300 years of Canadian art, but they
were just as important to their own communities. The Art Gallery of
Greater Victoria put on 'Ten Canadians—Ten Decades,' a retrospective
featuring works from Cornelius Krieghoff to Harold Town. The Western
Canada Art Circuit assembled four special Canadian collections—paintings, prints & drawings, sculpture, pottery & handcrafts—that travelled
through the west in 1967. The Confederation Art Gallery and Museum in
Charlottetown held an exhibition of the works of Robert Harris, which
was entirely appropriate given the ubiquity of reproductions of Harris'
lost painting of the Fathers of Confederation. The Dominion Drama
Festival celebrated 1967 with an all-Canadian program featuring sixty-
two plays, twenty-nine of them premieres. Six new films were specially
commissioned for the Centennial, none more popular than the National
Film Board's Oscar-nominated *Helicopter Canada*, an aerial tour of the
country, or the nine television extravaganzas sponsored by Air Canada.
And then there was the military tattoo that gave 150 performances in
forty-five cities. It was more than simply brass bands and bagpipes, but

a pageant in the tradition of the 1908 Quebec Tercentenary celebrations, a multi-media journey through three centuries of Canada's military history, complete with music, re-enactments, and pyrotechnics, all staged by a cast of 1,700 men and women from Canada's armed forces.

Toronto's Folk Art Festival, part of the centennial celebrations, 1967.

The programs were not always successful. Critics noted that there was a conspicuous abundance of highbrow culture, but precious little that could be considered popular entertainment. Even some of the high culture did not work out as planned. *The Centennial Play* was specially commissioned to be performed by little theatre groups across Canada, but the *Globe* thought it was a classic case of 'the more playwrights you hire the less dramatic entity you are likely to achieve.' A collaborative effort by five of Canada's best known writers, it was test-driven in Lindsay, Ontario, in the fall of 1966 but underwent a major overhaul before its Ottawa premiere on 11 January 1967. The Centennial Commission's chosen director had transformed an old-fashioned dramatic re-telling of Canadian history into a light and frothy revue, and critics felt that it fell awkwardly between the two chairs. Yves Thériault's picture of Quebec as Canada's most swinging province and Robertson Davies' scene set in a 1912 Ontario school room won high praise, but W.O. Mitchell's prairie scenes looked more like Oklahoma than Saskatchewan, Arthur L. Murphy's Confederation

debate between Joseph Howe and Charles Tupper left more than a few
eyelids drooping in the audience, and Eric Nicol drew only sporadic
laughs with his satirical version of Judge Matthew Begbie laying down
the law in a Yukon bar.[404] One drama critic called it 'a two-hour pageant
of scampering naiveté, banality and ineptitude,' while Nicol doubted
that any of the local theatrical troupes that had ordered copies of the
script ever bothered to stage it.[405]

Still, perfection could not be hoped for nor expected; what mattered
was the effort and support. In this respect, the numbers tell the real
story. Between 1963 and 1968, the Centennial Commission spent over
$158 million on projects of national significance, over a third of it
going to cultural works. When the money devoted to local initiatives is
included, the three levels of government spent over $70 million on the
arts—more in five years than successive governments had spent in the
previous three hundred.

And then there was Expo. According to the exhibition's press
releases, 'The "Man and His World" Theme owed it to itself to put the
artist's creative genius in the place to which it is entitled, that is to say,
the first place.'[406] Exposition organizers had taken over the Place des
Arts in downtown Montreal for the entire summer, but also built the
2,000-seat Expo Theatre, the Place des Nations, which could accommodate audiences of over 10,000, and a handful of smaller stages and
bandshells on Île Ste.-Hélène, the artificial island in the St. Lawrence
River made from fill excavated from Montreal's new Métro system.
There was an impressive roster of some of the world's most popular
entertainers: comedian Jack Benny; the legendary actress and singer
Marlene Dietrich; the world-renowned Ballet of Prague; two of Broadway's biggest current hits, *Hello, Dolly* and *The Odd Couple*; *Pop Goes
Australia*, featuring the biggest stars from down under; jazz greats
Duke Ellington, Sarah Vaughan, and Pearl Bailey; the Supremes, then
at the height of their popularity; and countless others. But there was
also excellent representation from the host nation. La Semaine de la
Chanson featured some of Quebec's leading singers, including Pauline
Julien and Gilles Vigneault, who would become passionate advocates
of French-Canadian nationalism. Don Messer's Jubilee introduced fair-
goers to Canada's most popular country and western music. Monique
Leyrac, known as Quebec's ambassador of song, came to Expo after

Anne of Green Gables, one of the most popular productions of Festival Canada, 1967.

a triumphant tour of London, Paris, and Moscow. And it all ended with Charlottetown's Confederation Centre Company performing the musical version of *Anne of Green Gables*.

Perhaps the greatest success of Expo, however, was to provide a buffet of every conceivable form of culture, from the most traditional to the extreme avant-garde. Most Canadians were quite familiar with the former, but Expo exposed them to the most radical and experimental forms of art. Film, for example, went to a whole new level, both in terms of the technology used to create it and the aesthetic behind it. There was *Kaleidoscope*, sponsored, appropriately enough, by Canadian chemical companies, 'an optical mirror show designed to initiate the viewer into the mysteries of color. There,' wrote film critic Judith Shatnoff,

> as you moved from chamber to chamber, sound and light effects became more extreme, images and electronic tracks became more and more abstract, sometimes colliding, more often going their separate ways, until in the last chamber, mirrored walls, floor and ceiling, flashing, whirring incandescent lights, balls of fire and psychedelic explosions were prodded by increased decibels of sound into kaleidoscope symmetry.

Canada '67, funded by the nation's telephone companies, put nine projectors and 12 sound channels in a circular auditorium that held 1,500 people. 'Almost the only truly nationalistic film at Expo,' wrote Robert Fulford, it was 'a cinematic hymn to the glories of Canada, so blatant in its chauvinism that one could hardly imagine Canadians producing it' (in fact they didn't—it was the work of the Walt Disney Studios).[407] Another favourite was *Ontario: A Place to Stand*. As Shatnoff wrote, 'director Christopher Chapman turned a banal 16-minute travelogue into a tour de force of rapidly changing screen size and shape, multiple scenes of the province, life and events—everything going on at once, as it actually does.' But the most talked-about production was the forty-five-minute *Labyrinth*, by Roman Kroiter and the National Film Board, an allegory of the human journey using the ancient myth of Theseus and the Minotaur as a conceptual framework. To call it a mere film is to do it an injustice. Three years and $4.5 million in the making, it took place in a five-storey concrete bunker whose architecture was integral to the viewers' experience as they moved 'through dim, intimate corridors which prepare [them], first to find the hero, then to find the beast which lives inside, then to return, triumphant, to the world.'[408] With images projected on wall and floor screens and sound emanating from hundreds of speakers throughout the building, it was like nothing film-goers had ever experienced. People waited in line for hours to enter *Labyrinth*, and many emerged to go straight back into line again.

Architecturally, the Expo site was as innovative as *Labyrinth*. As far as the Canadian contribution was concerned, the most talked-about work had to be Habitat, by Israeli-born Moshe Safdie, who had immigrated

Habitat, at Expo '67.

to Montreal in 1954. Habitat was essentially a three-dimensional city (although Safdie disliked that term), with the density of an apartment complex and the privacy of detached housing. To achieve this, Safdie used prefabricated concrete units that could be joined together in various ways to make different sized living spaces. It was smaller than Safdie had originally planned (he envisioned a city of a thousands units, complete with shops and a school, but only 158 were actually built) and the apparent randomness of the structure disguised a graceful symmetry. Love it or hate it—a British architecture critic called it a student's fifth-year thesis that somehow managed to get built, while an American praised it as the first real victory of the modern industrial revolution—it was as bold in architectural terms as any structure that graced the island.

That was the artistic triumph of Expo—its sheer scope and variety. Nowhere else could someone listen to Quebec folk singers in the

Futuristic architecture abounded at Expo.

morning, spend the afternoon watching Graeme Ferguson's *Polar Life*, projected in four slowly revolving cinemas with twelve projectors going simultaneously, and stroll through a rose garden filled with abstract sculptures after dinner. Fifty million people had come to Île Ste.-Hélène and few would ever forget what they had experienced.

* * *

In December 1963, cabinet minister Maurice Lamontagne, who emerged as one of Parliament's strongest supporters of the Centennial celebrations, told the House of Commons that 'Since 1867, our country has expanded physically and materially at an increasing rate. It now seems to be calling for a greater soul. It will achieve this only if it intensifies its cultural life, feeding its two main cultural streams and getting them to meet more often.'[409] Expo '67 had done what it could to bring French and English Canada together. Of the fifty million people who passed through the gates, over 30 percent were from Quebec and 20 percent were from the rest of Canada; for many of the out-of-province visitors, this might have been their first opportunity to experience French-

Canadian culture. And there's no question that every possible effort was made to introduce the two streams of culture to one another, as Lamontagne had hoped—so much so that it is difficult to think of anything else the Centennial Commission could have done to promote cultural interchange. But did it work?

As far as English Canada was concerned, it was an uphill struggle. Those who had never travelled to Canada's swingingest province to visit Expo probably held deep-seated preconceptions of a French-Canadian culture that affirmed the province's character as a kind of pre-modern rural theme park. For them, the essence of French Canada could be found in the habitant paintings of Cornelius Krieghoff or in the dialect poetry of W.H. Drummond. Louis Hémon's *Maria Chapdelaine* had sold well in English translation, reinforcing the notion of Quebec as a bastion of rural traditionalism. The ideal of French-Canadian architecture was more likely to be an ancien régime farmhouse than Ernest Cormier's modernist Université de Montréal. The rest of Canada had long regarded Quebec as economically backward and socially unprogressive—why should its culture be any different?

In fact, the province had changed dramatically in the decade after the foundation of the Canada Council, although people outside of Quebec probably did not appreciate the magnitude of those changes. Maurice Duplessis, *le chef* who had run the government as a kind of state/church alliance for nearly twenty years, died in 1959, leaving no successor of his ability or stature. When the provincial Liberals came to power in 1960, they set out to reform government institutions, modernize the educational system by wresting it from the hands of the church, give Québécois and Québécoises a bigger role in running the province's economy, and generally make them *maîtres chez nous*. The transformation, which came to be known as the Quiet Revolution, was probably of more immediate significance to Quebeckers than the Centennial of Confederation, and it was no less important in cultural terms. French-Canadian artists had been among the first to criticize the oppressive nature of the Duplessis years, which some referred to as *la grande noirceur*, an intellectual dark age, and they were among the first to experiment with the new freedom of the 1960s. After the First World War, Duncan Campbell Scott had called for more rage from Canada's artists; in the wake of the Second World War, Quebec would become a hotbed of cultural rage.

The first flash fire came in 1948. Paul-Émile Borduas had been apprenticed as a church decorator when he was sixteen, but six years later made the jump to teaching art, a vocation he would fall back on, often reluctantly, for the rest of his life. Through the early 1940s, Borduas grew more interested in surrealism, which held that the creative impulse flowed from the unconscious; the act of painting should be an automatic process in which the soul of the artist was transferred, spontaneously and without mediation, to the canvas. It's not clear how many people fully appreciated the complexities of surrealist philosophy, but they certainly appreciated Borduas' work; at his first one-man show in 1942, thirty-seven of the forty-five paintings were sold, something that the Group of Seven could only have dreamed of two decades earlier. By the end of the war, he had drawn together a small group of students and disciples who called themselves *Automatistes*, but Borduas was already beginning to feel trapped by his own success. Facing increasing pressure to join the growing international surrealist movement, Borduas opted instead for complete independence. In 1948, he was the driving force behind *Refus global*, which art historian Dennis Reid has called 'perhaps the single most important social document in Quebec history and the most important aesthetic statement a Canadian has ever made.'[410]

Signed by fifteen artists and writers, in addition to Borduas, it was an angry, imaginative, and sometimes incoherent call to arms, a diatribe against the past and a prescription for the future. The villain was Christianity, a repressive creed that had been 'maintained so efficiently for so many centuries at the cost of life's most precious qualities,' and its victims were the 'submissive slaves who, the more wretched they were, the harder they fought to defend it.' But the end was in sight; Christianity was collapsing under the weight of its own excess, and it was up to artists to deliver the *coup de grâce*: 'We must refuse to turn a blind eye to vice, to scams masquerading as knowledge, as services rendered, as payment due.' They would work 'with feverish enthusiasm…because we feel a pressing need for unity.' The result would be a new age of cultural liberation, with people 'freed from their useless chains and turning, in the unexpected manner that is necessary for spontaneity, to glorious anarchy to make the most of their individual gifts.'

Like many such courageous public statements, *Refus global* was devastating to the career of its author. Dismissed from his teaching position at l'École de Meuble, vilified by the church and liberal Catholic intellectuals, and deserted by many of his students, Borduas struggled to make a living in Quebec before finally giving up and moving to New York in 1953. Two years later he moved to Paris, still painting feverishly and producing some of the best work of his career. But the frenetic pace and the intensity of his personality took a toll on his health, and in 1960 Borduas died of a heart attack.

The ripple effect of *Refus global* over the next decade was dramatic. It thrust Quebec modernists into the spotlight, and painters such as Borduas, Jean-Paul Riopelle, and Fernand Leduc developed reputations that placed them among the world's foremost abstract expressionists. The near sell-out of Borduas first one-man show had not been a fluke, and within a decade of his death the work of the *Refus global* signatories—with their thick globs of paint, jarring colour combinations, and bold lines—would carry hefty price tags. It would also help the cause of abstract artists elsewhere in Canada, for, as one critic wrote in *Canadian Art*, 'the thrall of the Group of Seven is still on them, and they lack a clearly defined original purpose of their own.'[411] The success of the Montreal modernists emboldened abstractionists and acted as motivation for the formation of groups such as the Painters Eleven and the Regina Five. They carried to the rest of Canada the spirit of revolution that was behind *Refus global*.

The Painters Eleven. c. 1957.

If there was no earthquake in French-Canadian literature to compare to *Refus global*, there was a succession of novels that jolted society with a progressively more vigorous critique of traditional French-Canadian values. One can find signs of this literary uprising in the late nineteenth century, with the work of the province's first female novelist, Félicité Angers, who wrote under the pseudonym Laure Conan. Conventional and even unremarkable on first reading, her novels repay closer attention, for there is an undercurrent of criticism of the smothering patriarchy, on both an individual and a broader social level, of Quebec society. The early twentieth century saw writers become more daring in their criticism. *Marie Calumet* (1904) by Rodolphe Girard, later the official translator for the House of Commons, poked fun at the church through satiric episodes from the parish St.-Ildefonse, many of them revolving around bodily fluids, laxatives, underwear, and scatological literature, and most involving the pious but earthy Marie (she was a little too earthy for the church, which condemned the book as 'gross, immoral and impious'). Albert Laberge, a sports columnist for *La Presse*, took a harsher view in *La Scouine* (1918), set in the Beauharnois region in the early 1800s. It paints a bleak picture of the world that Krieghoff had idealized: the cheerful, tightly knit family is replaced by suspicious and often malevolent kinfolk; religion is not a comforting certainty but an irrelevancy that survives only as a reflex; and the land, rather than being the source of health and prosperity, is characterized as leprous and cancerous. The novel was so controversial that its first print run was just fifty copies; it was not republished in its entirety until 1972. Anti-clericalism also runs through Jean-Charles Harvey's *Les demi-civilisés* (1934), which added a critique of moral and intellectual repression and a condemnation of English-Canadian domination of Quebec's economy. For attacking the three pillars of the Duplessis state, Harvey was condemned by the church and fired as director of the province's office of statistics. Ringuet's *Trente arpents* (1938) turned the rural idyll on its head, the farmer's absolute devotion to his land ultimately driving him from it, while Gabrielle Roy's *Bonheur d'occasion* (1945) laid bare the miseries of life in working-class Montreal in an early example of the urban realist novel. André Langevin brought existentialism to French-Canadian literature with novels such as *Poussière sur la ville* (1953), which explored the suffering of people trapped in a pointless existence. Claude-Henri Grignon's *Un homme et son péché* had an even longer shelf life. First published as a novel in 1933, it inspired an enormously popular radio serial that ran for twenty-six years and sometimes garnered an 80 percent share of the listening audience, and two film versions, in 1948 and 1950. Grimmer than *Trente arpents*, it revealed the seamier side of Quebec rural life, particularly in its fearless depiction of a greedy peasant's abusive relationship with his wife.

A young Gratien Gélinas performs in *Les Deux Canards*, 1933.

For many young intellectuals, the status of the theatre in French Canada symbolized all that was wrong with culture in the old Quebec. The repression of the nineteenth century, when Bishop Bourget had warned theatre-goers that 'they play with the devil...[and] as a consequence, renounce the happiness promised by Jesus Christ,' continued into the twentieth. The church could no longer order the closure of theatres, but it retained the right to preview plays and edit scripts; if a work was found wanting, as was the case with a play by the French writer Henri Bernstein in 1907, clerics felt a responsibility to forbid Roman Catholics from attending. By the interwar era, serious theatre had almost ceased to exist—audiences preferred either movies or frothy revues that presented sketch comedy to a largely male audience (the theatre remained a sphere that the respectable woman should not frequent). But in these sketches, we see the roots of the same critique of

French-Canadian society that characterized art and literature. Gratien Gélinas' *Les fridolinades* (1937–46), for example, tossed witty barbs at religious, political, and economic elites, a formula that would reappear in *Tit-Coq*, arguably Gélinas' most well-known work. Its premiere came in the same year as *Refus global* and if its criticism of contemporary Quebec was more muted, it was no less pointed; Gélinas' outcast orphan was trapped in a social order that stifled his dreams, his every attempt to break free simply putting him into a deeper hole. Even more controversial was Claude Gauvreau's *Les oranges sont vertes*. Gauvreau had been one of the signatories of the *Refus global*, and he brought the same ideology to his play, a surrealist experience in which the artist and his friends are ultimately destroyed by society because they threaten the social order.

When the Quiet Revolution brought rapid changes to that social order, writers who had been pushing the boundaries in the 1950s became even more innovative and adventurous, just as Borduas and his followers had done. Novelists such as Hubert Aquin and Réjean Ducharme introduced characters who were avowedly revolutionary, and who sought nothing less than the rejection of every social and cultural value of previous generations. At the other end of the spectrum, Roch Carrier and Jacques Ferron used parody and ridicule masterfully to achieve the same subversion of the old order. But if there was one work that symbolized the cultural shift in Quebec, it was Michel Tremblay's *Les Belles-Sœurs* (1968). Tremblay came from a working-class background in Montreal, and turned down a scholarship that would have opened doors to a university education and a professional career. By his own admission, that path would have prevented him from writing the kind of plays that solidified his reputation as one of the province's greatest playwrights. It certainly would have kept him from writing *Les Belles-Sœurs*, the first play performed entirely in *joual*, the street slang of urban French Canada. *Joual* had already found its way into novels published earlier in the 1960s, but to hear it on stage in a major theatre was entirely different. Many critics hated it—they accused the profanity-laced dialogue of debasing French-Canadian culture—but its attack on the Catholic ideal of the family, in which the home became not a haven but a place of abuse, excess, and misery, ensured it would have lasting impact on literature in Quebec. It affirmed, if any such affirmation was needed, that culture in Quebec was finally free of the burden of traditionalism. For French-Canadian artists, that was as much of a reason to celebrate as the country's one hundredth birthday.

———•◦•———

In April 1968, Hilda Neatby, one of the Massey commissioners, spoke at a dinner of the Saskatchewan Registered Music Teachers Association honouring May Woodley Benson and Dorothy Bee, two of the province's pioneers in music education. Neatby, probably still basking in the cultural flowering of the Centennial year, used the occasion to reflect on the place that the arts had come to occupy in the life of the nation. 'They may be uneconomic subjects,' she said about things cultural, 'but they do lie at the centre of life and its central purpose to know truth and enjoy beauty.'[412]

Truth and beauty, of course, are subjective, and do not necessarily go hand in hand. While Neatby might have accepted the truth of *Les Belles-Sœurs*, would she have described it as beautiful? But one of the most important steps in the maturation of Canadian culture was accepting that beauty could be found in the realist landscapes of Edward Hughes as much as in the abstract expressionism of Jean-Paul Riopelle. For decades, modernists in the cultural lobby had complained about gatekeepers—private and corporate patrons, government departments, the old guard that had long dominated organizations like the Royal Canadian Academy and the Canadian Authors' Association—who had constricted the freedom of artists on every conceivable ground. Now, to use a well-worn metaphor, the tent was getting larger; opportunities were becoming available for artists whose muses took them away from the old mainstream.

Neatby also reminded her audience of a word that had bedevilled the cultural lobby for centuries: uneconomic. The inability to make a living in the arts had long been an obstacle to Canadians, but new forms of government support and a more affluent and culturally aware public were changing that. As people began to think of culture as an industry, and a potentially profitable one at that, they began to see an even greater role for governments. Funding culture was no longer enough; government intervention was necessary so that the regulatory and protectionist power of the state could be put to work for the arts, just as it had long done for any other product harvested or manufactured by Canadians.

Chapter 16

The Regulatory State

'Canada has one decade remaining in which its members have to make up their minds whether they want to remain a distinct political, cultural and geographical national entity.' Those apocalyptic words, spoken by a communications professor from Loyola University, surely got the attention of the Special Senate Committee on the Mass Media in 1970.[413] It was just three years after the Centennial, and the extinction of Canadian cultural distinctiveness was already being foretold. And yet the comment conveyed the sense of urgency that many in the arts lobby felt: that there might never be another chance to capitalize on governments' interest in culture by creating a permanent support infrastructure. But could they have envisioned what would eventually evolve? The Montreal Regional Arts Council, the Canadian Music Centre, the Standing Committee on Broadcasting, Films and Assistance to the Arts, the Advisory Arts Panel of the Canada Council, the Federal-Provincial Committee on the Future of French-Language Television, the Playwrights' Circle, the Newfoundland and Labrador Film Development Agency, the Girard-Peters Task Force Report on the Economic Status of Television—when the arts lobby called for government intervention in culture, it probably did not foresee the bewildering web of agencies and reports aimed at promoting and protecting Canadian culture.

Much of this bureaucratic infrastructure emerged from the realization that, whatever value culture had as an expression of national spirit, it was becoming an increasingly important economic sector, employing thousands of Canadians and generating billions of dollars in economic activity. So, the debate over how to fund Canadian culture became inextricably intertwined with the debate over how to protect it, particularly from the incursion of culture from the United States. This was not a new conundrum—writers and publishers had been worrying about it since the nineteenth century—but it became acute in the twentieth. The radio debate had highlighted the problems of dealing with a cultural product that could not be stopped at the border; its successor, television, simply made things more difficult, in part because it involved much higher costs.

The federal government, having gotten its feet wet in the waters of regulation with radio and television, was eventually forced to take protectionist measures in other cultural sectors, particularly in magazine publishing and music broadcasting. At the same time, Ottawa finally took action for the benefit of artists in the matter of copyright law. But the underlying story of the period was the evolution of a cultural infrastructure that resembled other parts of the government: it was over-bureaucratized, filled with agencies whose mandates overlapped or conflicted, consumed excessive amounts of money in administration, dogged by inefficiency, and moved ponderously slowly. Still, artists made the best of it.

———•◦•———

Things had come a long way since the early years of the twentieth century, when the number of government agencies devoted to the promotion of culture could be counted on one hand. And it was not all a result of the cultural flowering of the Centennial era. In 1948, Saskatchewan established the first provincial, arm's-length arts council, the Saskatchewan Arts Board, and in 1959 Alberta became the first province to create a government branch responsible for cultural matters. After that, the floodgates opened—the Quebec Department of Cultural Affairs in 1961 (now the Ministry of Culture and Communications, with responsibility not only for culture, but language and immigration as well), the Ontario Arts Council in 1963, the Manitoba Arts Council in 1965, the Manitoba Department of Culture in 1970, the Saskatchean Department of Culture in 1972, the Nova Scotia and Newfoundland Departments of Culture in 1973, the British Columbia and Prince Edward Island arts agencies in 1974, the Ontario and New Brunswick Departments of Culture in 1975. And this does not even account for all of the other government and non-governmental agencies—such as Ontario's public broadcaster TVO (1970), SaskFilm (1989), the Nova Scotia Film Development Corporation (1990)—that were created to fill holes in the cultural quilt. Federally, cultural matters were handled by the Secretary of State until they were taken over by the new Department of Communications in 1980. In 1993, this was reorganized into the Department of Canadian Heritage.

Aside from the bureaucracy, there were government-sponsored studies and task forces—literally dozens of them in the decades after the Centennial—intended to examine the state of culture generally or specific media in detail. Some of them were high-profile and comprehensive, such as the blue-ribbon Federal Cultural Policy Review Committee (1982), under chair Louis Applebaum and co-chair Jacques Hébert. After hearings in eighteen cities and nearly 1,400 submissions, it produced a sweeping list of recommendations: that key cultural bodies like the Canada Council and the CBC be immune from political direction; that the CBC stop selling commercial airtime and exist as an alternative to private broadcasters; that new agencies be established to assist the cultural sector; that funding levels for art galleries, the publishing industry, and film production be boosted; and that authors receive compensation for their books that circulated through public libraries (this came into effect with the establishment of the Public Lending Right program in 1986).

But it's hard to resist the conclusion that most of these studies were simply reinventing the wheel. Clearly, the government's way of dealing with the cultural lobby (and with any other lobby, for that matter) was to strike a task force or commission a report, to put off dealing with the substantive issues at hand. The fact that most of the advice was the same—it identified the same problems, came to the same conclusions, and put forward the same recommendations—did not seem to matter. There was always the obligatory statement that culture played an 'essential role in the maintenance of Canada's identity and sovereignty' and that Canadian artists had to continue 'the unending search for the highest possible quality.'[414] And then came the suggested remedies, which varied from sector to sector but always involved a higher level of government support: a Feature Film Fund (1986) for the 'production and distribution of high quality films with a high level of Canadian content'; a Cultural Industries Development Fund (1990), to assist 'entrepreneurs working in book and magazine publishing, sound recording, film and video production and multimedia'; a 5 percent increase in government arts funding, more support for the Canada Council, amendments to the copyright act to give better compensation to artists, and stable CBC funding, all recommendations contained in the Federal Standing Committee on Communications and Culture's report *Ties That Bind* (1992). Time after time, committees and task forces came to the same conclusion: culture was essential in maintaining Canadian identity, and it should be more generously funded by all levels of government.

The sub-text of many reports was the notion that culture was growing in economic importance, and should be treated like other sectors of the economy. Despite the fact that Ontario's Royal Commission on Book Publishing (1972) recognized that 'the cultural implications of book publishing far outweigh the economic implications to society,' the language of the economist and the marketer became ever more prevalent in government and industry reports. The Book Publishing Industry Development Program, announced in 1986, was intended to 'promote Canadian publishers in Canada and around the world' through 'strategic support' and assistance with export marketing. The Canadian Conference of the Arts, an outgrowth of the 1941 Kingston Conference of Canadian Artists, began producing reports with titles such as *Tax Reform and the Arts* (1970), *Culture as a Growth Sector in Canadian Development* (1982), *The Roles of the Arts and Cultural Industries in the Canadian Economy* (1985), and *A Strategy for Funding of the Arts* (1990). The Status of the Artist Act (1992), although it affirmed 'the importance of the contribution of artists to…developing and enhancing Canada's artistic and cultural life, and in sustaining Canada's quality of life,' was essentially a blueprint for labour relations between workers and management.[415] A brief presented by the Canadian Film and Television Production Association in 2005 hit all the right notes about feature films making 'an important contribution to the cultural lives of Canadians…[by] captur[ing] unique perspectives on domestic or international issues…[and] present[ing] complex and sometimes difficult subjects from a distinctively Canadian point of view,' but the arguments it put forth were largely economic. It placed particular emphasis on films like *Resident Evil: Apocalypse* and *White Noise*, films that were not distinctively Canadian but that 'export better overall…[and] have traditionally attracted higher levels of foreign financing.'[416] It could be argued that, in remarks like this, the line between film as art and film as commodity had been crossed.

The conjunction of the bureaucratization and the commodification of culture can be seen clearly in Newfoundland. In 1971, arts policy in the province was turned over to the new Division of Cultural Affairs, which assumed responsibility for the Newfoundland Public Libraries Board and the Arts and Letters Competition the following year. In 1980 came the Newfoundland and Labrador Arts Council, created by the government of Brian Peckford, followed by the short-lived Publishers' Assistance Program to aid the province's book industry, the Sustaining Grants Programme for performing arts companies, the literary and visual arts, and provincial arts organizations, and the Art Procurement Programme to purchase art for public buildings. With the necessary bureaucracy in place, the Provincial Arts Policy Committee of 1990, chaired by Patrick O'Flaherty, articulated a vision of culture that was increasingly becoming the norm across Canada: 'The arts are not a frill, but an industry which is worth investing in. Public money put into the arts is no more a "subsidy" than taxpayers' dollars put into the fishery, agriculture, mining, forestry, post-secondary education, and offshore oil. Artists are just as deserving of government support in their efforts to make a decent living as other occupations and professions.'[417] The impact of the report could be seen in the Canada/ Newfoundland Cooperation Agreement on Cultural Industries, a four-year deal signed in 1992 that set aside $5 million to help artists with research and development, marketing, and distribution; when the deal expired, it was replaced by the Canada/Newfoundland Agreement on Economic Renewal, which earmarked $3.75 million for culture. The connection between culture and the economy was further strengthened by premier Clyde Wells' 1992 Strategic Economic Plan, which included nearly two dozen proposals to assist arts groups. As historian Ronald Rompkey observed, the plan may have overstated the case in claiming that Newfoundland had a disproportionate number of artists relative to its population (it was 'as if Newfoundlanders and Labradorians had received an evolutionary benefit not visited upon any other province of Canada or any other culture of the world,' he wrote[418]), but it had a major impact on the way government viewed culture. It led to the creation of the Department of Tourism and Culture, whose policy statement *A Vision for Tourism* (1994) argued that the province could reap significant economic benefits from its artists, who were becoming increasingly popular with consumers 'for their unique styles and point of view.'[419]

The Newfoundland example is instructive in two respects. First, bureaucracies cost money, and every dollar that goes into the creation or administration of a new program is a dollar that does not reach the artists themselves. Between 2001–2 and 2002–3, the operating expenses for the Department of Canadian Heritage grew by a whopping 67 percent, from $52 million to over $87 million; it is unlikely that many of the department's programs enjoyed a 67 percent funding increase over a single year. On a smaller scale is the Cultural Capitals of Canada awards program, intended to support 'municipalities for special activities that harness the many benefits of arts and culture in community life.' Its two-year budget was $5 million, but fully 20 percent of that apparently went to administrative expenses rather than to the artists and cultural groups being rewarded. Sometimes, the bureaucratic decisions were more than a little perplexing. When the federal government approved the $23 million Music Entrepreneur Program [MEP] in 2001 as a mechanism for financing improvements in the recording infrastructure, especially for small labels, it made Telefilm Canada responsible for it. Because Telefilm Canada has never been in the recording business, it had to create a new administrative infrastructure to administer the MEP, eating up money that could have been used to benefit record producers.

Equally noteworthy is the assumption of the Newfoundland government (one shared by every other level across Canada) that the arts was an industry. A book or a painting was like cod or potash: it provided employment and generated economic activity, and so was deserving of government support. In a very real sense, culture became a commodity and like any other commodity it spawned government departments and agencies to monitor it, grant programs to assist it, and a regulatory regime to protect it. The rhetoric of culture as an element of nation-building was never far from the surface, but increasingly it was subsumed in the ideology of culture as a product.

This was certainly what motivated the Canadian Film Development Corporation [CFDC], established in 1968 with $10 million in federal money. As its chair, Georges-Émile Lapalme, told a parliamentary committee in 1969,

> any film that has a chance of developing the Canadian film industry, even if that film is not particularly interpretive of Canada to Canadians, would still be considered and possibly invested in by us. [We are] a specialized bank established to provide financial assistance on the basis of which a Canadian feature film industry can be launched. We are not filmmakers, we are just investing money and making loans…If we were to judge our scripts from an intellectual and cultural point of view we would not be a bank anymore.[420]

Regrettably, the CFDC was not especially effective as either a bank or a cultural arbiter. By 1971, it had funded sixty-four films; only three of them had generated a profit, and not many more had won critical acclaim. One of the few that did was Don Shebib's *Goin' Down the Road* (1970), a gritty and realistic account of two Maritimers seeking their fortunes in Toronto. The CFDC's successor, Telefilm Canada (1984), had to be more discriminating in its approach to financing, as did the agencies that were charged with regulating what was arguably the most important cultural medium of the twentieth century, television.

———•••———

'Great faith is put in broadcasting,' observed a government committee in 1970. Television

> must lighten our drab little lives, sell the soaps or instant puddings we manufacture, bring war into our living rooms, present politicians before us with unretouched warts, amuse the baby, enlighten the mother, show us the increasingly insane and violent world around us, and then reassure us that nothing like that could ever happen to us in our wonderful world of frozen dinner, aphrodisiac shampoos, and deodorant soaps.

It was the only medium that Canada's Parliament had specifically delegated as the protector and nourisher of the nation's cultural, political, social, and economic fabric, yet 'we rely for this on the same medium that is the principal advertising mainstay of the soap industry.'[421]

Tuning in, Calgary, 1953.

The proud birth of Canadian television has become the stuff of legend. On the evening of 8 September 1952, hundreds of thousands of people gathered in living rooms across the country to watch as CBLT in Toronto began broadcasting. The viewing audience was eager and expectant on that Monday evening, and at precisely 7:15 PM, the first image of Canadian television, the station's logo, appeared on their screens—upside down. Next came Percy Saltzman and the weather report, a puppet show starring Uncle Chichimus, Pompey, and Holly Hock, and the evening news. At 8 PM the official opening ceremonies were aired, with various dignitaries from government and the network and a message from Prime Minister St. Laurent. The new medium, it read,

should stimulate a real appreciation of the creative resources of our own people. It should be a new means of self-expression for Canada. Our television should foster new interest in many aspects of Canadian life, and so help build mutual understanding within the nation…It should contribute to the full development of an enriched family and national life in Canada…This new service will undoubtedly bring much to entertain and interest you in your leisure hours. But it will also be offering wide new opportunities for Canadian talent and abilities.[422]

Those talents were then put on display with a variety show, a recital by the Leslie Bell Singers, and a selection of performances from the CBC station in Montreal that followed. To end the broadcast, the network aired Canada's first ever re-run, when the 7:30 news magazine was repeated.[423]

The legend, however, leaves out a few important details. The CBC station in Montreal, CBFT, had actually gone to air two days earlier, with a production of *Aladdin and His Lamp*, but most accounts ignore this. Even then, CBLT was on the air hours before the official sign-on at 7:15, thanks to the lucky coincidence of the notorious Boyd Gang escaping from Toronto's Don Jail. As A.D. Dunton, the chair of the network's board of governors, was addressing a news conference that afternoon in the CBC's Jarvis Street studio, the television monitors in the press room began showing images and descriptions of the convicts. Without missing a beat, Dunton pointed to one of the mug shots and observed drily, 'Canadian talent.'[424]

An early CBC television weather broadcast, 1954.

Nor were the Montreal and Toronto broadcasts the first in Canada. On 21 August 1931, an experimental station owned by the James A. Ogilvy department store in Montreal sent the nation's first television signal all of 102 metres. The following month, the federal government authorized experimental stations in Toronto, Montreal, Mont-Joli, Saskatoon, and Vancouver, but it was not until 19 July 1932 that the Montreal station, VE9EC, jointly owned by radio station CKAC and the newspaper *La Presse*, transmitted the first television broadcast that could be picked up by commercial sets. Unfortunately, the pictures, intended to be black and white, were bright red. Better signals were available from stations in the United States, but even then the offerings were not especially generous. At the time of VE9EC's broadcast, the television listings in central Canada provided just one option, station W2XCD in Passaic, New Jersey, which offered five unidentified programs between 9 and 10:30 PM.[425]

Even so, Canadians soon became enamoured of television, so much so that the CBC began formulating a policy in 1949, using the expertise of its television guru, Alphonse Ouimet, who had been involved in the first experiments in the early 1930s. The plan called for production and studio facilities in Montreal and Toronto, and by the time those stations went on the air, as many as 100,000 Canadians had sets and those within signal range of the US border were avid watchers of American programming. Not that watching was cheap. The same newspaper that carried an advertisement for CBLT's first broadcast carried one for the grand opening of Binnington's TV showroom. The day's special was a seventeen-inch black and white RCA Victor television in a walnut case for $329.50, or over $2,600 in current values.[426]

Price appeared to be no object, however, because television's popularity grew enormously in the early years. Within a year, the CBC was broadcasting thirty hours of programming a week and its first private affiliate, CKSO in Sudbury, Ontario, began operations. More new stations, both network and private affiliates, took to the airwaves every year—seventeen in 1954, ten in 1955, four in 1956, eight in 1957, five in 1958—and in 1958 the Cross-Canada Microwave Network was completed, linking eight CBC stations and thirty-four private affiliates from Victoria to Sydney; the occasion was marked with the broadcast of a commemorative program, *Memo to Champlain*. By that time, the

French and English stations together reached 85 percent of the nation's population.

Once it became clear that television was here to stay, the old debate about cultural nationalism reared its head. That cloud had always hung over radio—'the State or the United States'—and the government of the day had agreed. In announcing the creation of the Canadian Radio Broadcasting Commission in 1932, Prime Minister R.B. Bennett had said that its role was to exert 'complete control of broadcasting from Canadian sources...[for the] communication of matters of national concern...[and the] diffusion of national thought and ideals...[to foster] national consciousness...[and to strengthen] national unity.'[427] The same sentiment was echoed in the report of the Royal Commission on Broadcasting (1955), created under chair Robert Fowler to consider the financial aspects of broadcasting in Canada. The Fowler report dismissed the arguments put forth by private broadcasters that the CBC was perfectly capable of achieving the cultural goals set out for broadcasting in Canada, and suggested that private radio and television stations should be subject to the same minimum domestic content standards as the CBC, with those standards being enforced by an independent regulatory body (the Board of Broadcast Governors). Furthermore, those stations should be domestically owned. 'In broadcasting,' the report stated, 'dealing as it does with media of public information and wielding so great an influence on opinion, we feel that facilities should be kept substantially in Canadian hands.'[428] The spirit of the report, if not the exact language, found its way into the Broadcasting Act of 1958, which laid down that 'Canada was to have a national broadcasting system...that is basically Canadian in content and character.' To meet that goal, the legislation mandated that 45 percent of programming had to be 'Canadian in nature.'

But there was a key difference between radio and television. Radio had cultivated an enthusiastic following during the Second World War, when the majority of listeners chose the CBC over stations from the United States because they wanted to hear about the Canadian war effort, not the American. With television, however, Canadians had two decades to become attached to programming from the United States before any domestically produced alternatives were available. The habit of watching American television would be a hard one to kick.

Indeed, viewers were already beginning to chafe at the CBC's monopoly. About a quarter of Canadians were close enough to transmitters in the United States to pick up their signals, but everyone else had to choose between watching the CBC or nothing. Two forces began to exert themselves: a realization that, because of high consumer demand for American programs such as *Kukla, Fran and Ollie*, and *The Jack Benny Show*, advertising revenues for those programs were correspondingly higher; and growing calls that the government open up television to competition, rather than hiding behind the fig-leaf of private affiliates. In both cases, consumer demand won out. In 1958, Prime Minister John Diefenbaker announced that broadcast licenses would soon be available to private stations. A number of individual stations were approved over the next few years, and in 1961 some of them came together to form CTV, the nation's first private network. The first private French-language broadcaster, Télémetropole, was licensed in 1961; a decade later, Télé-Diffuseurs Associés became Canada's first private French-language network.

The other important development was that the public broadcaster began purchasing more and more American programming, using the higher advertising revenues to develop Canadian content. With its mandate to promote Canadian identity and culture, the CBC had to be careful about the amount of foreign content it broadcast, but private stations were under no such constraints. Most loaded their schedules with American content, the sole exception being in Quebec, where language helped to insulate viewers from US programming. Montreal became the world's most important centre of French-language television production, and Quebec's broadcasters aired more home-grown programs than any other province. Grignon's *Un homme et son péché* and Lemelin's *Les Plouffe* drew critical acclaim and immense audiences, and just as Aberhart and Smallwood had with radio, ambitious Québécois recognized the influence of television; René Lévesque is just the best known telejournalist who parlayed his popularity on the small screen into a political career. The CBC, rather than risk losing out on the prime advertising revenues, followed the trend towards American programming. The Board of Broadcast Governors responded in 1960 by decreeing that all stations had to air at least 50 percent Canadian content, but many private stations produced cheap game shows and talk shows for the daytime hours, which kept the evening hours free for the more lucrative imports.

Ironically, while cultural nationalists in Canada were lamenting the fact that television seemed to be going down the same slippery slope that radio had in the 1920s and 1930s, critics outside the country had high praise for Canadian television. In *The New York Times* entertainment writer Paul Gardner referred to the 'Theatrical Riches on Canadian TV' and complimented the public broadcaster for its determination 'to offer an abundance of modern and classical theatre that can only make us feel foolishly left out.' While admitting that the CBC aired its fair share of low-brow American programming, Gardner was impressed that there were always at least three hours a week of serious, challenging drama. Actors from the United States were drawn to Canadian television because it offered the opportunity to do something innovative and exciting, instead of dull gunfighters and doctors sleep-walking through American programs. Furthermore, CBC producers such as Daryl Duke, who created the half-hour series *Quest*, were always on the lookout for new and experimental plays to transform into teledramas. Gardner was particularly impressed by Duke's willingness to tackle *The Brig*, which he described as 'a shattering non-play' that had recently opened off Broadway. 'It suits the nature of our series,' said Duke, 'which is to confront our television audiences with a tough notion of themselves.' In Gardner's view, the CBC offered something that television in the United States did not: programming that challenged the viewer and attempted to advance the art form.[429]

But to continue on that tack proved to be a challenge. In 1964, the Fowler Broadcasting Committee was struck to examine the effectiveness of the Canadian content element of the 1958 Broadcasting Act. In 1965, the CBC's evening schedule included 57 percent Canadian content, but the average private station had just 34 percent Canadian programming during the evening hours. The government remained committed to using television as an agent of national unity, the 1966 White Paper on Broadcasting stating that 'a national system of radio and television broadcasting in Canada is an essential part of the continuing resolve for Canadian identity and Canadian unity.'[430] To achieve that, the new Broadcasting Act of 1968 replaced the Board of Broadcast Governors with the Canadian Radio-Television Commission [CRTC] (later the

Canadian Radio-Television and Telecommunications Commission) and upped the Canadian content quota to 60 percent. At the same time, the CBC slowly boosted its proportion of Canadian programming, from 52 percent in the 1967–68 season to 74 percent in 1983–84 (when, interestingly, the Canadian content on the French-language CBC was only 69 percent). The White Paper also reminded the CBC of the importance of its holding a 25 percent share of television advertising revenue and 4 percent of radio advertising revenue; this money would then be funnelled back into the production of Canadian programming. But by 1968, television ad revenues had slipped to 23.9 percent and radio revenues to 1.8 percent, so low that CBC president George F. Davidson considered making CBC radio entirely non-commercial (this was done in 1975, the same year that CBC-FM was inaugurated).

Sensing that they were gaining the upper hand, private broadcasters continued their battle against their government-subsidized competitor. The Canadian Association of Broadcasters [CAB] would have preferred to see the CBC get out of broadcasting altogether, and confine itself to producing programs that would then be distributed (free of charge, of course) to private stations. The CAB's fallback position was that CBC television should be non-commercial, so it was not competing with private networks for scarce advertising dollars. Neither of these arguments found much sympathy with the Special Senate Committee on Mass Media, which held hearings through 1970. With a sense of humour that is rare in such documents, the report concluded that 'private broadcasters, no matter how sophisticated their individual thought, seem by group interaction to achieve a level perhaps best described as neanderthal.' Pointing out that private networks had done well financially under the status quo, the committee was unable to understand why the CAB should resist having to divert some of its healthy profits into funding Canadian programming. Nor did it agree that the revenues of private broadcasters should be boosted even more by cutting out the CBC and letting the private sector scoop up all of the advertising revenues. It was flummoxed by the CAB's argument that viewers actually preferred more commercials in their television programs, and rejected the notion that private stations had done more than the CBC to foster Canadian talent, unless one subscribed to the CAB's belief that 'commercials...represent the finest flowering of the television art.' No one could argue that the

CBC was a paradigm of economic efficiency—it spent $1 in production costs to generate 54¢ in advertising revenues—but the committee was certain that it should remain the cornerstone of Canada's cultural policy where television was concerned.[431]

Through these years, the federal government struggled to balance its cultural and national objectives with the financial bottom line. In 1983, the Department of Communications' paper *Towards a New Broadcasting Policy* recommended maintaining the broadcasting status quo and increasing Canadian content even more through incentives to private production companies. The mechanism, as laid out in the new National Film and Video Policy (1984), was the Broadcast Program Development Fund, to be administered by the Canadian Film Development Corporation (later Telefilm Canada). Two years later, the Department of Communications Task Force on Broadcasting Policy issued the Caplan-Sauvageau Report, which endorsed public broadcasting, especially the CBC, as a pillar of Canadian culture and proposed a series of tax and funding incentives to improve Canadian content production. But then budget cuts forced the CBC to close eleven of its regional bureaus, a move that provoked a storm of outrage from the listening public.

The Broadcasting Act of 1991 continued in the mode of its predecessors, with an explicit nation-building agenda. The broadcasting system was intended to 'safeguard, enrich and strengthen the cultural, political, social and economic fabric of Canada…[and] encourage the development of Canadian expression by providing a wide range of programming that reflects Canadian attitudes, opinions, ideas, values and artistic creativity, by displaying Canadian talent in entertaining programming.' To that end, the programming should be 'predominantly and distinctively Canadian' and should 'contribute to shared national consciousness and identity.'[432] But again the policy rhetoric was not matched by financial support. In 1995, the CBC was hit with more budget cuts, its allocation dropping from $1.2 billion in 1990 to $820 million in 1999; at the same time, the budget of Canadian Heritage was to be reduced by $675 million. Despite the fact that the Liberals had promised long-term stable funding for the CBC and Heritage Minister Sheila Copps engaged in intense lobbying efforts on behalf of the broadcaster, the government demonstrated that contributing to a shared national consciousness and identity was a laudable goal, but only if the price was right.

For the rest of the decade, Canadian Heritage and its supporters waged an ongoing battle to pressure Ottawa to back up its rhetoric with firm financial commitments. In 1996, Canadian Heritage commissioned the Mandate Review Committee, headed by former CRTC chief Pierre Juneau, to examine the CBC, Telefilm Canada, and the National Film Board. The conclusions were predictable: much of Canadian cultural production wouldn't be possible without government assistance; US cultural influence on Canada was growing; and the CBC, because of its importance as a distinctly Canadian cultural voice, should be funded through a permanent tax. The same year, the federal government stepped up with the Canada Television and Cable Production Fund, which provided $200 million to help finance Canadian television programming; it was funded jointly by the federal government, Telefilm Canada, and cable companies, which were required to contribute to the fund as a condition of receiving their licenses. The effectiveness of the program was called into question in 1999, however, when the CRTC released its review *Building on Success: A Policy Framework for Canadian Television*, which once again pointed out the need to improve the financial success of Canadian programs in areas other than news and sports, and to increase the amount of Canadian programming during peak viewing hours. The central problem to all of this recommending and regulating was economic. The reality of the television business was that it cost about $1 million to produce an hour of television programming, but only $100,000 to buy an hour of programming from another country. If the government was going to keep cutting the CBC's budget, the broadcaster simply could no longer afford to produce Canadian content. The tension between cost and content, it seemed, was irreconcilable.

Television was not the only medium in which the federal government had to find creative ways to protect Canadian culture. Controlling printed material had been easy in the early days—publications that were deemed to be objectionable either in terms of content or their possible impact on Canadian competitors could be stopped or taxed at the border—but the tremendous growth of the periodical industry after the Second World War, particularly in the United States, and the gradual takeover of Canadian newsstands by foreign publication forced Ottawa into action. As a government committee noted in 1970, periodicals were every bit as important to national identity as broadcasting: 'magazines constitute the only national press we possess in Canada…Magazines, in a different way from any other medium, can help foster in Canadians a sense of themselves.'[433]

The stakes were high enough for the government to strike the Royal Commission on Publications in September 1960 to examine the impact of foreign periodicals on Canada, particularly with respect to the relationship between competition and national identity. The commission was headed by Grattan O'Leary, a respected writer and journalist who had long been a proponent of cultural nationalism—O'Leary wrote that communications, and especially the magazine industry, constituted 'the thread which binds together the fibres of our nation'—but in the end the report was as much about economics as identity. It found that there were 661 periodicals on sale in Canada, but that Canadian publications held just a quarter of the market.[434] The main offenders, in the eyes of Canadian publishers, were *TIME* and *Readers Digest*, which had pioneered the split-run edition: a magazine with editorial content produced almost exclusively in the United States, but with advertising targeted at Canadian readers. Because the cost of the content was covered by advertising revenue generated in the much larger US market, split-run editions charged ridiculously low advertising rates to Canadian companies, rates that Canadian periodicals could not hope to match. In response, the commission recommended that the income tax deduction on advertising aimed at Canadians but appearing in foreign publications be scrapped. Some companies urged that the legislation be grandfathered, so that it would not apply to *TIME* and *Readers Digest* but only to future split-run magazines, but publisher and philanthropist Floyd Chalmers had little time for his US competitors: 'the parasitical character of these publications suggests that they are not particularly entitled to sympathetic or generous treatment,' he growled.[435]

Gradually, the government introduced measures to curb the impact of split-runs on the Canadian magazine industry. In 1965, the Income Tax Act was amended to prohibit Canadian companies from claiming the expenses for advertising in periodicals that were anything less than 75 percent Canadian-owned; a later amendment added the qualification that, to gain a tax credit, the publication had to have at least 80 percent Canadian content. The same year, the now infamous Tariff Code 9958 was put in place: any split-run edition with more than 5 percent of its advertising directed at the Canadian market would be stopped at the border.

But technology complicated the situation even further in 1993, when Sports Illustrated began transmitting its content electronically across the border and printing its split-run edition in Canada. It was filled with advertisements directed at Canadian consumers that went for fire-sale prices—a full-page colour advertisement in Sports Illustrated Canada costs $6,250, while the very same advertisement in SI's New England edition cost $18,688, and $25,400 in Maclean's. Although the practice violated the spirit of Canadian legislation, it was all perfectly legal. It also had the potential to devastate the Canadian magazine industry, which claimed that split-run editions gave their publishers a profit margin of 80 percent, while the average Canadian magazine enjoyed a mere 4 percent profit margin.[436] Ottawa was quick to strike a task force to study the situation, and its 1994 report painted a bleak picture of the industry. Compared to 1960, the 1,440 Canadian titles in circulation enjoyed a 67.6 percent share of annual sales but accounted for only 25.5 percent of the circulation revenue, and over half of them showed no operating profit; the average profit margin was even lower than the industry itself admitted, at 2.36 percent. Of the fifty highest circulation English-language magazines in Canada, twenty-one were imported from the United States; on the average newsstand in English Canada, fewer than one in five magazines was Canadian (in French Canada, 95 percent of periodicals were Canadian). If other US publishers followed the example of SI Canada, the Canadian magazine industry would be gutted; the task force estimated that 40 percent of advertising revenues would be diverted to American publishers, and 94 percent of the country's profitable magazines would be driven into the red. This was not just an economic threat, but a threat to a cultural institution. 'We must continue to find ways to maintain a place for the rich tapestry of ideas and information we now have in Canadian periodicals,' declared the report. Magazines were an 'essential part of Canadian cultural development…one of the "vital links" that permit Canadians to exchange ideas and information with one another…Like the image in a mirror held in our own hands, they give us an unclouded vision of ourselves…They blend knowledge, entertainment and ideas, and are both timely and enduring.'[437]

Ottawa was quick to act on the task force's key recommendations. Tariff Code 9958 was retained, and in 1995 the federal government put an 80 percent excise tax on split-run editions whose editorial content was not substantially Canadian but whose advertising was. US trade officials responded just as quickly by lodging four complaints with the World Trade Organization. In March 1997, the world body ruled against Canada on all but one complaint. Tariff Code 9958, the 80 percent excise tax, and the commercial publications mail rates (which set differential postage rates for domestic and foreign publications) were all judged to be out of order; only the government's postal subsidy program, allowing certain periodicals to enjoy lower postage rates within Canada, was ruled acceptable.

The decision was based on the understanding that a cultural product, in this case a magazine, was the same as a washing machine, but the Canadian government took a very different position. The Minister for International Trade, Art Eggleton, announced that Ottawa would appeal the ruling, while Minister of Canadian Heritage Sheila Copps tried to refocus attention on the cultural implications of the ruling. 'The final report states very clearly that this decision does not take issue with the ability of any WTO member to take measures to protect its cultural identity,' she stated. 'Canada will continue to promote its cultural objectives and ensure that Canadians have access to magazines that speak to us about our own country.'[438]

The immediate legislative response was Bill C-55, which directed that 'No foreign publisher shall supply advertising services directed at the Canadian market to a Canadian advertiser or to a person acting on their behalf.' Not surprisingly, US trade representatives reacted badly, accusing Canada of perpetuating 'longstanding anti-competitive policies' and being 'protectionist and discriminatory.' Rhetoric was one thing, but in January 1999 Canadian newspapers reported the United States was considering slapping retaliatory tariffs on steel, textiles and clothing, wood, and plastics exports, measures that could have cost as much as $4 billion.[439] Eggleton was not keen on doing battle where big-ticket exports were concerned, but Copps refused to be cowed. She responded by meeting with French government representatives and opening lines of communication with Ireland and Italy about forging ties with, as she put it, 'allies that fear the Americanization of culture around the world…If the Americans insist on pursuing their domination of the world cultural community by using all the instruments at their disposal, they will expect the same in return. We are prepared to use all the tools in our arsenal to fight the decisions that restrict our capacity to build our own culture.'[440]

But Copps was a lone voice in cabinet, and in May 1999 Bill C-55 was softened by a number of compromises that gave foreign publishers limited access to the Canadian market as long as their publications contained a majority of Canadian content and they were willing to start new periodicals in Canada. Split-run editions with less than half Canadian content could contain only 12 percent of advertising directed at Canadian consumers, a figure that would rise to 18 percent in the third year of the agreement. To soften the blow even more, the federal government came up with the Canadian Magazine Fund in 1999, a $150-million, three-year subsidy program available to magazines that had majority Canadian control and ownership and at least 80 percent Canadian editorial content. Only time will tell if these measures would be enough to preserve 'the rich tapestry of ideas' that constituted Canadian magazines.

—•—

If the economic dimension is removed, the battle over the magazine industry was a battle over one thing: Canadian content. Legislating a certain level of domestic content in cultural media was not a Canadian invention, and indeed Canadian regulations in this regard are weaker than those in other countries. Theatres in Spain must show one day of European Union [EU] films for every three days of non-EU films they show. In 1993, the government of Mexico decreed that 30 percent of screen time in the country's cinemas had to be devoted to Mexican films. The Italian government rebates the box office taxes to cinemas showing Italian-made films. In Australia, 55 percent of television programs must be produced domestically. French radio and television stations are required to broadcast 60 percent EU programming, 40 percent of which had to be French.[441]

But of all these countries, only Mexico is as close to the world's largest exporter of culture as Canada, and even then the common language gives a greater sense of urgency to the campaign to foster domestic content. The battle has been fought in many arenas. In 1972, the playwrights committee of ACTRA and the Playwrights' Circle surveyed the offerings of the nation's theatres over the previous few seasons and determined that only 19 of 108 plays had been Canadian; their recommendation to the Advisory Arts Panel of the Canada Council was that any theatre receiving government subsidies should perform 50 percent Canadian works.[442] In 1977, the Quebec Minister of Culture actually took a step in that direction, ordering that every theatre receiving government money had to produce at least one new Quebec work each season. In classical music, the Canadian Music Council suggested a quota system: orchestras that received government grants should be required to employ a certain number of Canadian soloists, while the major opera companies should be required to perform a certain number of Canadian operas, perhaps one every two or three years, for which the government should provide funding for composers and librettists.[443]

But the term CanCon has always been associated most closely with the music industry, and it was the state of commercial radio that started the drive to Canadian content legislation. There were plenty of Canadian bands in the pre-Beatles era—Edmonton's Wes Dakus and the Rebels, The Gemtones from Moncton, Les Diables Noirs, The Stripes of Vancouver (featuring Ian Tyson)—but few got the radio airplay that their counterparts from the United States enjoyed. 'Canada has a booming record Industry,' wrote Jerry Ross in the *Toronto Telegram* in 1964, '(but only because it's 95 percent American)…We have so many good records available to us from the States that there's really not much point in doing a great deal of recording up here.' This state of affairs did not sit well with the magazine *RPM*, founded in 1964 and sometimes referred to as the conscience of Canada's music industry. At first, it was less than enthusiastic about CanCon regulations, believing that 'a soft policing by the broadcast industry alone would bring about the necessary musical nationalism.'[444] Its solution was the Maple Leaf System, under which twelve stations across Canada would review Canadian singles every week and select those to be given regular airplay and promotion. Regrettably, the soft policing was unsuccessful because, as the journal's editor later

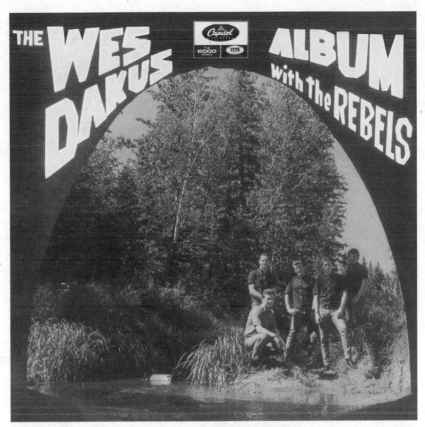

Canadian Rock and Roll in the late 1950s: Wes Dakus and the Rebels.

put it, the Maple Leaf System 'would have required courage on the part of the members and stations involved and unfortunately Canadian radio has been capable of very little creativity and courage.'[445]

In 1968, publisher Stan Klees used the pages of *RPM* to sketch out a new system, under which 25 percent of all programming on Canadian radio had to be 100 percent Canadian in its production, creation, performance, and control. A year later, after extensive hearings by the CRTC, the MAPL system was put in place. Each song would be assessed in four categories—music, artist, production (either recorded or performed wholly in Canada and broadcast live in Canada), and lyrics—and if it was Canadian in two of the four, it qualified as Canadian content. Under the current regime, commercial radio stations must ensure that 35 percent of their popular music selections broadcast on weekdays between 6 AM and 6 PM are Canadian; ethnic stations have to meet a threshold of 7 percent Canadian content, while French-language stations

Canadian content regulations were the butt of many editorial cartoons, 1979.

are bound to air 65 percent of their popular music selections in French (55 percent on weekdays between 6 AM and 6 PM). According to the government, the MAPL system's 'primary objective—a cultural one—is to encourage increased exposure of Canadian musical performers, lyricists and composers to Canadian audiences. The secondary objective—an industrial one—is to strengthen the Canadian music industry, including both the creative and production components.'

Not surprisingly, CanCon regulations have provoked bitter debate since they came into force. The Canadian Music Publishers Association, calling the lack of domestic talent heard on Canada's airwaves in the 1960s 'a national cultural disgrace,' has had nothing but praise: 'The best thing about CanCon is that it costs taxpayers nothing and adds so much to our cultural life and to the lives of those who create and promote sound recordings in Canada.'[446] The Canadian Recording Industry Association wants the quota to remain at 35 percent, while the Canadian Independent Record Production Association would like to see the bar set at 45 percent; and the Society of Composers, Authors and Music Publishers of Canada is lobbying for 51 percent CanCon. The Canadian Association of Broadcasters, on the other hand, wants a reduction to 25 percent, and French-language commercial radio stations want to see their quota drop from 65 percent to 45 percent French-language content, on the grounds that young listeners are turning away from French-language stations because they prefer English music. The conservative think-tank the Fraser Institute goes even farther, declaring that 'the present CanCon regulations have almost no redeeming social value. They are based largely on citizenship, not on the substantive Canadian content of TV programs or musical recordings. After several decades, there is no evidence of any link between CanCon regulations, national identity, and cultural sovereignty—the key stated objectives of the Broadcasting Act.' The major beneficiaries of the legislation have been companies that produce dubious 'Canadian' content. It is not about national identity or cultural sovereignty; protecting jobs is now the primary rationale. For that reason, all regulations on broadcasting content should be abolished to eliminate the possibility of US trade retaliation in sectors that could be more economically damaging.[447]

But in all likelihood, CanCon regulations are here to stay, and indeed they have spread to other cultural sectors. The MAPL equivalent for television and film is administered by the Canadian Audio-Visual Certification Office, which uses a complicated formula to determine if a film or television program is eligible under one of the many federal funding programs. Each element of a production—director, scriptwriter, lead actor, art director—is worth one point, and different genres and funding programs require a different number of points to qualify as Canadian. The key common requirement is that the production 'must speak to Canadians about, and reflect, Canadian themes and subject matters.'

———•—

In the three decades after the creation of the Canada Council, the three levels of government had assembled an impressive array of funding mechanisms, agencies, and support programs to meet the goal of fostering a culture that would 'speak to Canadians.' Ironically, the area that had the greatest potential to be of direct benefit to artists— copyright legislation—was the very field in which governments seemed most reluctant to act.

With the exception of a few superstars, artists had generally existed at the low end of the income scale—the starving artists of the nineteenth century were alive and well in the twentieth, partly because of their own temperament. In the words of a lawyer for the Canadian Arts Council in 1949,

> the creative artist is, generally speaking, prone to neglect his own material interests and to be, at times, more than careless of his legal rights. This attitude may operate to the benefit of the world at large in that it tends toward the increased production of artistic masterpieces, but it does not help to keep the creative artist alive and, while it may be good for his soul it does not benefit his digestion.[448]

For orchestral musicians, salaries were miserly, particularly when compared to what musicians in the United States earned. In the early 1970s, a typical symphony player in Vancouver was guaranteed only thirty weeks' work for a total wage of $4,050; the same player in Boston, Chicago, or New York worked for fifty-two weeks of the year, earning over $15,000 in the process.[449] Statistics from 1993 reveal that the average annual income from cultural sources was $20,300, with great variation between painters and sculptors ($7,800) and directors, producers, and choreographers ($35,800)—significantly, given the bureaucratization of culture, artists earned considerably less than others employed in the cultural sector, like arts administrators, curators, and fund-raisers ($31,300).[450] Furthermore, the tax structure was positively punitive. Gwethalyn Graham's novel *Earth and High Heaven* (1944) topped the US best-seller list for over a year, selling more than a million copies. A major Hollywood studio bought the screen rights for $100,000, and Graham's agent also sold the novel as a serial to the big US magazine *Colliers* for $40,000. But Canadian tax law of the time considered royalties to be unearned income, so the federal government took almost everything Graham earned; she never wrote another book, and when she died prematurely at age fifty she was making ends meet by marking assignments for a Montreal high school.

Arts groups lobbied long and hard for legislation that would allow creators to realize the full financial benefits of their success, but it was an uphill struggle. The legislation that came into effect on 1 January 1924 was a qualified victory—copyright was extended to fifty years after the creator's death, works published outside of Canada (or not published at all) were protected, and the range of media that was protected broadened considerably—but having been enacted, the law sat. There were minor amendments in 1936 and in the 1960s and 1970s but for all intents and purposes, the cultural property rights of an artist in 1975 were protected by a fifty-year-old law that had been drawn up before the advent of sound film, videotape, television, photocopying, digital storage and retrieval, and computers. Moreover, when the government began serious consideration of revising copyright legislation in the late 1970s, it did so under the assumption that culture was a commodity, and that copyright should protect a much wider range of activities than the Canadian Authors Association could have imagined in the 1920s. Typical in this regard was a 1977 proposal written for Consumer and Corporate Affairs Canada. It contained the implicit assumption that artists were valued members of society and that copyright allowed them to get the maximum remuneration for their creativity. But explicit was the notion that copyright was fundamentally an economic mechanism. The sector that was considered to be 'copyright industries' had expanded to include commercial printing, toy and game manufacturing, signs and displays, advertising, certain retail establishments like florists and opticians, and services to business management like public opinion polling and greeting card design. At the same time, the conclusions of the report were peppered with econospeak, with phrases like 'growing imbalance of international payments,' 'interests of entrepreneurs,' and 'matters that do not reflect their economic positions.'[451]

However, it took another twenty years for the law to change, with the new Copyright Act receiving royal assent in April 1997 (although some of its provisions did not come into effect until October 1999). By that time, copyright had become a technological matter as well as a cultural and economic one. Digitization and the internet meant that cultural materials could be transmitted around the globe in an instant, with no compensation returning to the creator. Many kinds of media were vulnerable, but music became the flashpoint, thanks to the popularity of websites such as Napster, which allowed the illegal copying (or pirating) of music. So, two of the key elements to the new legislation were a levy on blank recordable media (with the proceeds going to compensate performers for the pirating of their work) and a stipulation that the act undergo a comprehensive review after five years, as part of an ongoing process of copyright reform.[452] The debate over Canada's copyright regime remains bitter, but in some ways it goes at cross-purposes. The president of the Canadian Recording Industry Association refers to the government's failure to act as having cost the industry nearly $600 million in revenues and 20 percent of its workforce, while Steven Page of the rock group the Barenaked Ladies and a leading voice of the Canadian Music Creators Coalition argued that industry lobbying is not done for the benefit of artists, but for 'propping up business models in the recording industry that are quickly becoming obsolete and unsustainable...[and] preserving foreign-based power structures and further entrenching the labels' role as industry gatekeepers.'[453] With technology moving faster than the legislative process, the issue seems intractable. The most that can be said is that future artists will not have to work under a copyright regime that was designed during their grandparents' generation.

The evolution of a cultural bureaucracy has drawn mixed reviews from artists: few of them are completely satisfied with the way things have evolved, but none of them would be willing to return to the pre-Canada Council days. However, there is a striking contrast between the rhetoric emanating from government, and what artists have to say about the brave new world in which they work. Not surprisingly, the government's language is fulsome and laden with high principles. As a 1999 policy paper put it,

> Cultural policy is the expression of a government's willingness to adopt and implement a set of coherent principles, objectives and means to protect and foster its country's cultural expression. In

an age when countries are becoming increasingly interdependent economically and politically, promoting cultural expression by means of a coherent cultural policy for the arts is a valuable way to emphasize and define what distinguishes one country from another.

Canadian magazines as agents of nation building. c. 1949–50.

The same paper was no less idealistic about the place of the artist in the community: 'The role of artists is not only to mirror the values of the society in which they lives, but also to reflect on the issues that society must address if it is to know itself better. The role of the State in this regard is to support artistic activity, to provide creators with conditions favourable to the practice of their art, and to ensure access to their work by the general public.'[454]

The Sarnia, Ontario–born conductor and composer R. Murray Schafer gave a rather different perspective in a newspaper editorial. 'There is no such thing as instant culture,' he wrote; in trying to create culture rather than leaving its development up to time, we may create 'planned culture, complete with cultural commissars to administer large government grants.' He was concerned that every Canadian community would eventually seek to acquire culture in same way, through government grants, which would inevitably bring interference. At first, the interference would be indirect, but in time, 'government inspectors will hound every artist in the nation and corral him into one of their projects…come the day, art will no longer be allowed to be individualistic and haphazard; rather it will be pre-planned by the arts administrators like a big market garden.'[455]

The few isolated voices who raised such concerns shortly after the publication of the Massey Report had been drowned out by the sighs of relief as the government finally indicated an interest in funding culture. But is Canada headed towards the kind of cultural politburo that Murray Schafer foresaw? At the moment, the question in unanswerable, except to say that it very much depends on where one sits in the cultural hierarchy.

Chapter 17

Towards the Future

'A country can be said to be culturally sovereign if it has the freedom to make the necessary decisions on its cultural future; that is, if it enjoys the necessary freedom to promote the creation, distribution, preservation and accessibility of its cultural production across its territory... The omnipresence of American cultural products threatens Canada's cultural identity.'[456] So wrote the authors of a report on Canada's arts policy in 1999, at a time when the battles over the government's regulation of culture on the home front and its attempts to protect Canadian culture on the international stage were intense.

There is much in this short comment that relates to the fortunes of Canadian culture in the early twenty-first century. Cultural sovereignty is one thing, but how does it relate to cultural nationalism—has one superseded the other? The reference to what has been called the US military-entertainment complex (only partly in jest) is also revealing, in that artists and governments continue to struggle with the challenges of being next door to the world's largest exporter of culture, a struggle complicated by the fact that we share a common language. Technology has made the spread of culture easy, instantaneous, and very difficult to control, so cultural sovereignty and cultural nationalism are becoming global issues; Canada is not alone in recognizing that protecting a national culture can no longer be the subject of bilateral negotiations, but must form part of a larger international agenda.

Despite these challenges, Canadian culture has made remarkable strides in recent decades, and signs for the future are promising. Some of this progress has been the result of government regulation and protection, but much has stemmed from the ongoing maturation of the arts and the artist in Canada. Something of our inferiority complex has worn off, and we have become more willing to celebrate the success of our artists, domestically and internationally. But at the same time as the arts are looking forward, they are also looking backwards, with a new interest in and respect for those who laid the groundwork for Canadian culture in past centuries.

---·•·---

As the debates over split-run editions in the magazine industry and Canadian content regulations on commercial radio were playing out, it was already starting to dawn on some people that culture would soon have to be dealt with on a much broader level, rather than in negotiations over certain sectors. The General Agreement on Tarriffs and Trade, which Canada joined in 1947, had a cultural dimension, extending 'most favoured nation' trading status to trading partners covered under the agreement; one article, for example, exempted those partners from quotas that had been created to regulate film production. But few people knew or cared about GATT and its impact on Canadian culture in the late 1940s; it would be another three decades before international trade agreements would mobilize the cultural lobby in Canada.

The impetus came in the 1980s, with the realization that free trade with the United States, and eventually through all of North America, had the potential to affect Canadian culture. If trade was to be truly free, could the Canadian government continue to offer grant programs to the magazine and book publishing industries? Could it enforce Canadian content regulations on radio and television? Could it offer tax credits and other financial incentives to the feature-film industry? Or, would those measures be declared unfair trade practices or illegal subsidies? Many in the arts lobby feared the worst: that government support programs, long so important in building culture, would be sacrificed on the altar of free trade in manufactured goods.

The Free Trade Agreement [FTA] with the United States was signed on 2 January 1988 by Prime Minister Brian Mulroney and President Ronald Reagan. The negotiations had lasted nearly two years, teetered on the verge of collapse more than once, and saw Canadian public opinion on the issue shift from overwhelming support to virtual deadlock. It took a federal election to secure the passage of the deal through the House of Commons, but the bitterness of the debate never really subsided. Indeed, it was brought to the surface again in 1993 when, in one of his last acts as prime minister, Mulroney watched over the passage of the North American Free Trade Agreement [NAFTA].

Since then, neither the pro-free trade lobby, which predicted an era of unparalleled prosperity after the deals, nor the anti-free trade lobby, which foresaw Canada being driven back to the nineteenth century as jobs and investment flowed south, to the lands of low wages, have been proven right. Indeed, it will be at least another generation before the impact of the FTA and NAFTA can be determined with any degree of assurance. This is also true for its impact on Canadian culture. The federal government declared the agreements to be 'qualified victories' for artists; paragraph 1 of Article 2005 of NAFTA states that cultural industries are exempt from provisions affecting other industries, but there is also a notwithstanding clause that could allow the United States to 'take measures of equivalent commercial effect' in response to new Canadian initiatives in support of the cultural sector.

Because of this contradiction, the federal government remained vigilant and in 1995 formally identified culture as the third pillar of Canadian foreign policy, along with security and economic prosperity. That same year, when Canada and other countries from the Organisation for Economic Co-operation and Development [OECD] council agreed to negotiations aimed at achieving a Multilateral Agreement on Investment [MAI], a kind of free trade in international finance, the government made it clear that culture would be exempt. As Minister of International Trade Sergio Marchi put it, 'We will retain the right to enact laws in all areas…we will still be able to impose restrictions on foreign investment in sectors—like culture.'[457]

The matter became moot in October 1998 when OECD officials decided to end the MAI negotiation process; but as a pre-emptive strike, Ottawa took the initiative in organizing the International Network on Cultural Policy, a group of ministers of culture from more than forty countries around the world. Its rhetoric is all about promoting cultural diversity, but implicit is a recognition that countries have to be able to take measures to protect their own indigenous cultures against imports, regardless of international trade agreements. In short, the network accepted the fundamental argument that culture is not a commodity like wheat or cars, and must be governed by a different set of international agreements.

To explore the possibilities in this area, the federal government has supported the International Network on Cultural Diversity [INCD], a non-governmental organization aimed at finding common ground between countries interested in protecting their indigenous cultures as a means to secure cultural diversity. In 1999, the Canadian arm of the INCD put forward a position paper outlining the options. In its view, Canada (and most other countries, for that matter) had reached a crossroads:

> Over the past few years, cultural policies designed for our own cultural industries have come under close international scrutiny. As a nation, we believe in the benefits of open markets, but we are concerned about the effect that global trade, combined with rapid technology change, may have on our ability to promote Canadian culture...As is clear from events over the past few years, the cultural exemption has its limits. It is time for Canada to make some crucial decisions. Do we define ourselves simply as the producers and consumers of tradeable goods and services? Or are we prepared to step forward and reaffirm the importance of cultural diversity and the ability of each country to ensure that its own stories and experiences are available both to its own citizens and to the rest of the world?

Not surprisingly, the report favoured positive action, and affirmed the importance of culture to the fabric of the nation:

> Our culture—our ideas, songs and stories—gives meaning to who we are as Canadians. Through cultural products, such as sound recordings, books and films, we express ideas and perspectives, and we share stories and images that are uniquely Canadian—among ourselves and with the rest of the world. Cultural products are 'brain and soul foods' that help us communicate with others and share differing views. They entertain, and they inform. They help shape our sense of identity. They add richness to our lives. In Canadian books, magazines, songs, films and radio and television programs, we are able to see and understand ourselves. We develop a more cohesive society and a sense of pride in who we are as a people and a

nation…Culture is also a critical tool in the task of nation building. Canadian culture represents the values that make us unique from other nations.

As a result, waving the white flag and allowing culture to be subject to market forces was not an option:

> The Canadian government invests in promoting culture, just as it invests in other activities that benefit its citizens, such as protecting the public health, protecting the environment and maintaining a defence force. In this way, the government acknowledges that cultural products are not simply commodities that can be packaged and sold. Cultural goods and services are different from the goods and services of other industries, and should be treated differently.

The alternatives, then, were four: to negotiate a broader cultural exemption, to ask for no commitments on culture, to deal with cultural issues sector by sector, or to create new international agreements on cultural diversity. The report came out strongly in favour of the last option, which would

> recognize the importance of cultural diversity; acknowledge that cultural goods and services are significantly different from other products; acknowledge that domestic measures and policies intended to ensure access to a variety of indigenous cultural products are significantly different from other policies and measures; set out rules on the kind of domestic regulatory and other measures that countries can and cannot use to enhance cultural and linguistic diversity; and establish how trade disciplines would apply or not apply to cultural measures that meet the agreed upon rules.[458]

One would have expected artists to be four-square behind such a recommendation, but there has long been some suspicion of the kind of cultural nationalism implicit in the proposal. Such concerns were raised in the 1920s, when some members of the arts lobby believed that cultural nationalism should be a thing of the past, and that the arts should be international rather than merely national (and by national, they typically meant parochial). This view came out clearly in architecture, where the International Style was an implicit rebuke to the notion of national forms of architecture, but it underpinned much of modernist culture generally. The members of the Painters Eleven were typical in this regard. They never pretended or aspired to be a national school of art and, rather than portraying themselves as apostles of a Canadianness in painting, they actively sought out inspiration and ideas from painters around the world. As one of their boosters wrote in 1958, its members were 'of the generation which has reacted to an unthinking nationalism in culture. Our painters…have begun to doubt that we can build undisturbed any obvious or fixed Canadian pattern in this world of flux.' Jack Bush, one of the members of the group, was even blunter: 'Being a Canadian is secondary for me. After all, what's the point in being a painter if you don't try to be the best painter in the world?'[459]

The great irony is that this is precisely the kind of ambition that sent talented Canadians to foreign cities in the late nineteenth and early twentieth centuries, much to the dismay of cultural nationalists of the day. Samuel Marchbanks, the alter ego of novelist Robertson Davies, may have lamented the fact that 'Canada exports brains and talent with the utmost recklessness,' leaving the nation with 'one of the lowest artistic and aesthetic standards in the world,' but he did not recognize that many of these expatriates probably had the same ambition as Jack Bush.[460] Marchbanks and many others believed that when Canada exported its artists, it was a sign of weakness, inadequacy, and colonialism, but maybe it was also a sign of their drive, determination, and desire to prove themselves against the world's best. Our national character has often predisposed us to see the glass as being half-empty, but perhaps it has always been half-full, and then some. At last, we may be starting to recognize that.

Unlike a century ago, when artists like Margaret Anglin and Emma Albani were forgotten as Canadians once they achieved success and took up residence elsewhere, we now tend to embrace anyone who was born here, whether or not their successes were achieved in Canada. Anglin and Albani were followed by others. Fay Wray (Cardston, Alberta)

Guy Lombardo on CBC Radio, 1950.

and Mary Pickford (Toronto) became two of the most popular and highly paid stars of the silent-film era. Guy Lombardo and his Royal Canadians, a band that first performed in Grand Bend, Ontario, in 1919, relocated to the US five years later and went on to sell over 300 million recordings, making it the most successful dance band of the day (and for decades, a staple of New Year's Eve celebrations in New York, where their midnight rendition of *Auld Lang Syne* was as famous in its day as the ball drop in Times Square is today). And how often are we reminded that actors Pamela Anderson (Ladysmith, British Columbia), Jim Carrey (Newmarket, Ontario), Michael J. Fox (Edmonton), director James Cameron (Kapuskasing, Ontario), producers Lorne Michaels (Toronto) and Daniel Goldberg (Hamilton, Ontario), singers Paul Anka (Ottawa) and Hank Snow (Brooklyn, Nova Scotia), and a host of others were born in Canada? Indeed, the number of Canadians finding fame in fortune south of the border was sufficient to inspire the biting 1985 mockumentary *The Canadian Conspiracy*, about the federal government using moles in the US entertainment industry to subvert the country. Some of these performers maintain closer ties to their native land than others—Shania Twain (Timmins, Ontario), whose success in the country crossover market enabled her to live in comfort and seclusion in Switzerland, returns to Canada occasionally (once to host the Canadian music awards, decked out in gowns modelled on the jerseys of Canada's National Hockey League teams), while director Norman Jewison (Toronto) founded the Canadian Film Centre in 1988 to help young filmmakers get the training they need to break into the industry. Mike Myers (Scarborough, Ontario), of Austin Powers fame, flies the maple leaf by being seen regularly at hockey games in California.

We have also laid claim to people such as the legendary architect Frank Gehry, who was born in Toronto but moved to the United States when he was a teenager. Gehry is recognized as one of the world's most daring and innovative architects for projects such as the American Centre in Paris, the Guggenheim Museum in Bilbao, Spain (which was named the building of the century), the Experience Music Project in Seattle, and the Nationale-Nederlanden Building in Prague, all of which are characterized by his signature style—shiny metal cladding, asymmetrical shapes, and rippling surfaces that seem unrelated to any architectural tradition, or indeed to gravity itself. Gehry is frequently referred to as a Canadian architect, despite the fact that he has not lived in Canada since he was seventeen and did not undertake a major project in Canada until 2002, when his design for the Le Clos Jordan vineyard in the Niagara peninsula was announced.

Carrey, Twain, and Gehry are a little like the émigré artists of the nineteenth and early twentieth centuries—from Paul Peel and Calixa Lavallée to May Agnes Fleming and Basil King—in that there is little in their work to identify them as Canadian. But even more encouraging is the success of distinctly Canadian artists who have found that they can work around the world without being characterized as *vendus*, like their predecessors of the post-Confederation era were.

Television has become an object lesson of how regulation and a burgeoning domestic talent pool can go hand in hand to build a body of high-quality programming that attracts attention both at home and abroad. The CRTC has continued its efforts to boost Canadian content, not only on the CBC and private networks, but also on new cable channels (the first of which, MuchMusic and The Sports Network, were licensed in 1984) and direct-to-home [DTH] satellite services. When the Global Ontario network's license was renewed in 1986, it had to commit to running 200 hours of original Canadian programming (not including news and sports) each year from 1988 to 1990, increasing to 250 hours in 1991; CTV was also bound to increase Canadian content when its license was renewed in 1987. The same year, CBC was given a long-term goal of 90 percent Canadian content overall, with fully 50 percent of its French and English programming being purchased from the Canadian independent production sector; in the short term, the network's 1994 license renewal set benchmarks of 65 percent Canadian content for the English network and 75 percent for the French network. As the number of cable channels grew to include stations such as Bravo!, Showcase, Le Réseau de l'Information, and Canal D, they were expected to invest a percentage of each year's profits in Canadian productions, and when DTH satellite services were approved in 1995, license holders were required to devote 5 percent of their gross broadcast revenues to an independent production fund.

The impact of these measures has been to boost both the number and the quality of domestically produced programs. Some became fixtures on Canadians' television screens without ever breaking into foreign markets. *La famille Plouffe*, based on the novel by Roger Lemelin, moved from radio in 1953 to become one of the most popular and critically acclaimed programs on Quebec television. Long-running favourites such as *The Friendly Giant* and *Mr. Dressup* delighted children, their children, and then their grandchildren. Sketch comedies *The Royal Canadian Air Farce* and *This Hour Has 22 Minutes* (the latter a take-off on the controversial 1960s public affairs program *This Hour Has Seven Days*) have brought us such memorable characters as the lovable Scots lunatic Jock McBile, cultural pundit Gilbert Smythe Bite-Me, Jerry Boyle of the Newfoundland Separation Federation, the perpetually perspiring Indo-Canadian Raj Binder, and the formidable Marg Delahunty, better known as the Princess Warrior.

Other programs became successful export commodities. After leaving the Canadian Army Show, Johnny Wayne and Frank Shuster began four decades of enormously popular specials on the CBC, the BBC, and NBC (at first, they were bigger in the United States than in Canada, and made a record number of appearances on *The Ed Sullivan Show*). When the CBC sold a package of eighty half-hour Wayne and Shuster specials to television networks around the world in 1980, it was the corporation's biggest syndication sale to date. The Degrassi franchise, which began in 1979 as *The Kids of Degrassi Street*, has become an international television powerhouse, its four incarnations eventually being watched from the United States and Britain to Yemen and China. *Due South*, which began as a made-for-television movie in 1994, became the first Canadian-made series to make the prime-time schedule of a major US network. Created by Oscar-winner Paul Haggis, a native of London, Ontario, it featured Paul Gross as a Mountie in Chicago, and a host of Canadian references, including the canine sidekick Diefenbaker and characters named Esther Pearson, Mackenzie King, Louise St. Laurent, and Buck Frobisher. *Due South* was eventually broadcast in over 100 countries, including Japan, Finland, Iran, and Germany. *Da Vinci's Inquest*, a gritty crime drama about a coroner in Vancouver, enjoyed huge critical and popular acclaim in over forty-five countries during its eight-year run. Red Green, the creation of comedian and producer Steve Smith, has generated a cult following around the world, a handful of books, a successful Hollywood feature film, invaluable publicity for duct tape, and new currency for quintessentially Canadian phrases like 'Keep your stick on the ice.' *Second City TV* began on Global in 1976 and bounced from network to network (winning two Emmy awards in the process) until its final season in 1983–84. Inspired by the Second City stage show, *SCTV* was a fictional television station run by the oily Guy Caballero (Joe Flaherty) in the town of Melonville, the bailiwick of the melon-headed mayor Tommy Shanks (John Candy). Not only did it launch the careers of such stars as Candy, Eugene Levy, Martin Short, and Catherine O'Hara, but it created unforgettable characters: Sammy Maudlin and Bobby Bittman, vacuous Hollywood lounge performers; Mel Slirrup, an insecure geek whose rock and roll show featured music that no one liked; the surrealistic Ed Grimley, his pants firmly buckled around his chest; Yosh and Stan Schmenge and their polka band the Happy Wanderers; and perhaps most notably (because it was added to satisfy demands for Canadian content) the two hosers Bob and Doug McKenzie, who cracked open cans of beer, argued about the week's topic, and ended every sentence with 'eh?'

At the same time, we have become more enthusiastic about celebrating our own successes. The music industry has the Junos, founded by *RPM* magazine in 1970 and named in honour of Pierre Juneau, who was chair of the CRTC when Canadian content regulations were legislated, the Canadian Country Music Awards, also founded by RPM and taken over by the Canadian Country Music Association in 1982, and the East Coast Music Awards. Quebec's Prix David is now part of Les Prix du Québec, which hands out $30,000 to distinguished recipients in eleven categories, including literature, visual arts, theatrical arts, cinema, and the advancement of the French language. There are dozens of awards given by the three levels of government, universities, private foundations, and corporations; among the richest are the Molson Prize of $50,000, for distinguished achievement in any area of culture, and the Giller Prize, established in 1994, which awards $50,000 to the year's best Canadian novel or short story collection.

But Canadians have also become fixtures on the international awards scene, in virtually every cultural medium. The National Film Board has been a frequent winner at the Academy Awards, taking eleven Oscars (including an honorary award in 1989) for documentary and short films since the Board's creation in 1939, and Canadian pictures are breaking into other categories as well. In 1986, Quebec filmmaker Denys Arcand's *Le Déclin de l'empire américain* became the first Canadian feature film to receive an Oscar nomination as Best Foreign Language Film, an award he won in 2003 with *Les invasions barbares*. Both films, as well as Arcand's critically acclaimed *Jésus de Montréal* (1989), were also honoured with awards at the Cannes International Film Festival. Anne Murray, Celine Dion, and Shania Twain have all won multiple Grammy Awards, but few Canadians have been honoured by the Academy for Recording Arts and Sciences as frequently as St. Catharines, Ontario accordionist Walter Ostanek, known as Canada's Polka King, who has garnered more than a dozen nominations and three Grammys over his long career.

The Man Booker Prize, established in 1968 as the Booker-McConnell Prize to honour each year's best novel by a Commonwealth writer and now one of the richest literary prizes in the world, has been a showcase for Canadian fiction. Margaret Atwood is one of the few five-time nominees; other multiple nominees are Mordecai Richler, Brian Moore, and Rohinton Mistry, while the most recent Canadian winners are Atwood for *The Blind Assassin* (2000) and Yann Martel for *Life of Pi* (2002). Even more lucrative is the IMPAC Dublin Literary Award, now worth 100,000 euros to the best novel drawn from a list generated by 180 public library systems in forty-three countries. The first Canadian winner was Alistair

MacLeod's *No Great Mischief* (2001) and the most recent is Rawi Hage's *DeNiro's Game* (2008), but Canadian nominees have been many—Jane Urquhart's *Away* (1996), Rohinton Mistry's *A Fine Balance* (1997), Guy Vanderhaeghe's *The Englishman's Boy* (1998), Atwood's *The Blind Assassin* (2002), Douglas Glover's *Elle* (2005), Frances Itani's *Deafening* (2005), and Thomas Wharton's *The Logogryph* (2006). Even more interesting is which libraries have nominated Canadian novels. Atwood's *Alias Grace* (1998), for example, drew nominations from Chicago; Kansas City; Miami; Washington, DC; Toronto; Richmond, Virginia; Portland, Oregon; Durban, South Africa; London; Mainz, Germany; Oslo, Norway; Wellington, New Zealand; and Adelaide and Hobart in Australia, while Mistry's *Family Matters* (2004) was nominated by institutions in Adelaide, Halifax, Ottawa, Mariehamn (Finland), Bergen (Norway), Johannesburg, Springfield (Illinois), Cincinnati, Kansas City, and San Jose (California). One can only be encouraged by the international appeal of Canadian literature; as Robertson Davies wrote, 'national literature is a mirror in which the nation sees its face…Canadian writers have been busily silvering and polishing the mirror for home use, and at the same time painting a portrait which others lands have inspected with interest and friendly approval.'[461] Yet this was hardly a new development for, as we have seen, in the decades before Robertson was born, many Canadian writers gained international fame, and sometimes fortune, by telling Canadian stories to the world. Seeing Margaret Atwood as a latter-day L.M. Montgomery or Alistair MacLeod as an heir to Ralph Connor may offend the *literati* of today, but the parallels cannot be ignored.

That's not to say that culture in Canada has reached a kind of golden age; there are some worrying trends that give pause to artists and arts administrators, even though statistics reveal that culture has become a profitable commodity. Although government support has dropped slightly in real terms (when inflation is factored in, the three levels of government spent 0.3 percent less on the arts in 2003 than they had in 1993[462]), Canadians have more than picked up the slack as enthusiastic consumers. In 2003, we spent $22.8 billion on cultural goods and services (compared to $7.4 billion that governments put in), or

3.2 percent of total consumer spending; that translated to $758 per person, from a high of $838 in Alberta to a low of $607 in Newfoundland. Taking account of inflation, cultural spending grew 19 percent between 1997 and 2003. The biggest categories were home entertainment (including such things as cable and satellite fees, DVD rentals, audio and video components, and blank audio and video tapes), which accounted for 52 percent of spending, or $13 billion, and reading material, which constituted another 19 percent of spending, or $4.8 billion.[463]

But the habit (some would say the necessity) of reducing culture to a balance sheet of debits and credits has led to considerable tension between the business model and the traditional arts model. The two ends of the spectrum are represented by Duncan Low, the former executive director of the Vancouver East Cultural Centre ('The only real difference between us and other businesses is that we're selling the performing arts. We get subsidies, sure, but so do cattle farmers and Bombardier') and Angus Ferguson, artistic director of Dancing Sky Theatre in Meacham, Saskatchewan ('We're not producing a product, we're talking to people…If people aren't coming into the theatre, then there's a problem, but that's not measuring our success in monetary terms. We do our work for different reasons'). The gulf between the two opposing viewpoints can be accounted for partly by the difference in scale—the VECC is a million-dollar-a-year enterprise, while the theatre in Meacham (population 85) seats just 100 people—but it also reflects a fundamental disagreement over the nature of culture itself. Clearly, there is enormous pressure for arts groups to be financially viable and more aggressive in demonstrating their contribution to the nation's economy, but artists like Ferguson are obviously uncomfortable with current trends. When the Canadian Conference of the Arts uses terms like 'community economic development' and 'asset-mapping,' in which a community's tangible and intangible assets (including the arts) can be used to sell it as a desirable place to live and do business; when its discussion of the Stratford Festival opens not with praise for its artistic achievement or its success as a training ground for Canadian talent, but with an anecdote about how the Festival helped to create a thriving florist shop in downtown Stratford; when it refers to 'The cultural industries and their near-cousins, the information industries' as being central to 'the "creative economy"—those activities which generate economic value through the creation of intellectual property rather than physical products'—such things make some artists squirm uncomfortably. Silver Donald Cameron wrote in the same CCA publication that 'Though artists do not always like the fact, or even recognize it, they are operating businesses. If they were as good at business as they are at their art, they would be very prosperous people.' Cameron's comment calls to mind Sir Robert Borden's assessment of John MacGillivray, the fine Haligonian portrait painter for whom he was sitting in 1934: '[he is] of high nervous temperament...lives for the most part in dreamland; but he seems thoroughly unconscious of this characteristic...his physique is not very strong; and he does not know how to care for himself. I bestowed upon him much good advice which probably had as much effect as if delivered to empty air on the banks of the Rideau river.'[464] Should artists like MacGillivray be good at business, Angus Ferguson might ask? Isn't it enough to be good at art?

There is an even greater contradiction at work here. In international trade negotiations, the federal government (with the backing of arts organizations) has taken the position that culture, even with the economic benefits it yields, is not a commodity like shovels or softwood lumber. It should not, therefore, be governed by rules covering trade in other sectors. But on the home front, a very different message prevails. As Duncan Low put it, culture is not so very different from beef or railway carriages—it is a business that creates products to be sold, and arts organizations that want to succeed would do well to keep that in mind. One wonders how Canadian trade negotiators would reconcile this mixed message if they ever had to confront it at the bargaining table.

But the CCA and those who embrace its business model for the arts would argue that their way is crucial because Canada remains a net importer of cultural products and services. According to 2004 figures from Statistics Canada, the country imported nearly twice as much cultural material (in dollar value) as it exported; the only area in which Canada was a net exporter was photography.[465] To cite just one sector, Canada is at the bottom of the list in the amount of domestic content appearing in its cinemas. In 1999, it was at 2.1 percent, so a government policy paper called for concerted efforts to increase that to 5 percent within five years. However, the situation actually deteriorated: in 2003, English-language Canadian films accounted for just 0.7 percent of total box office receipts (French-language films performed much better, making up 17.1 percent of total box office receipts in 2003).[466] Even had the government's target been met, it's a very small step from importing 95 percent of cinematic content to importing 100 percent. If the alternative is the extinction of the Canadian film industry, in this case perhaps pursuing an aggressive business model is the lesser of evils.

There remains the continuing problem of regional disparity in government funding for the arts. In 2007–8, $106 million, or over one-third of the Canada Council's total grants, went to Ontario and Quebec; Prince Edward Island received just $500,000, the same as Yukon and Nunavut, despite having over four times the population of either. Federal funding generally favours the eastern provinces, where it is greater than provincial funding; from Manitoba west, on the other hand, provincial governments contribute more to culture than Ottawa. And there is a considerable gap between Quebec, which receives the highest level of government funding per capita at $297, and Alberta, which receives just $160 per capita.[467] Indeed, the very notion of government funding for culture is still contentious. In March 2006, Ontario finance minister Dwight Duncan drew fire for presenting a budget that favoured the 'urban arts crowd' over other sectors, especially agriculture. He promised to extend tax credits for film production, boost the Ontario Interactive Digital Media Tax Credit, create a $7.5 million fund for artistic development, and provide an additional $49 million in capital funding to the Art Gallery of Ontario, the National Ballet School, the Gardiner Museum of Ceramic Art, the Canadian Opera Company, and a variety of other arts institutions. Farmers had to make do with $2.5 million over five years for 'outstanding farm innovators' and a new $25 million facility at the Ontario Veterinary College. Newspaper headlines like 'Despite needs, farmers given short shrift in favour of arts' did little to endear other sectors to the arts community, especially when Toronto's six major cultural institutions were back at Duncan's door two months later asking for another $49 million.

———————

Debates over funding inequalities are nothing new—in the 1950s Norman Mackenzie had warned about the political consequences should

the Canada Council be seen to favour central Canadian institutions—
but they are not the only continuities worth noting. One of the most
interesting is a revived interest in aboriginal art that echoes the fascination expressed by the first Europeans to encounter Canada's natives
centuries earlier. Some native artists have embraced new forms, such as
image painting, a catch-all term that encompasses a variety of figurative
and representational approaches, often involving mixed-media work.
Image painting has been particularly effective in documenting and
protesting injustice and inequality, and has found able practitioners in
artists such as George Littlechild, a Plains Cree from Hobbema, Alberta,
Shelley Niro, a Mohawk trained at the Ontario College of Art, and Jane
Ash Poitras, a Chipewyan who was raised by a German-Canadian widow
and did not reclaim her native ancestry until she was a young adult. In
their work, traditional native cultural symbols and images combine with
modern techniques and practices to create striking expressions of native
grievance and empowerment. Playwright Tomson Highway brought the
same sensibility to the stage, particularly with *The Rez Sisters* (1987), a
brash and playful tale of seven women on a pilgrimage to the world's
biggest bingo palace, and *Dry Lips Oughta Move to Kapuskasing* (1990),
a powerful and much more sombre examination of the peculiarities of
seven men on a reserve. Highway's work has been produced in Canada
in French and English, and has also been performed in other countries,
bringing to a wide audience the realities of natives' relationship to a
non-native society that has marginalized them.

By the same token, aboriginal filmmakers and producers have
embraced the new media of television and cinema to tell their stories.
One of the most striking successes was *Atanarjuat* (*The Fast Runner*)
in 2001, which brought to the big screen an ancient Inuit legend from
the north Baffin region. The first feature film to be written, produced,
directed, and acted by Inuit, it captured over a dozen major awards
at film festivals around the world. On the small screen, Television
Northern Canada, which had been broadcasting native programming
since 1991, was transformed into the Aboriginal People's Television
Network. Launched in 1999, APTN offers over 70 percent Canadian
content aimed at both aboriginal and non-aboriginal audiences. With
three-quarters of the network's staff being members of First Nations and
nearly a third of its programming airing in a range of native languages,

APTN has provided an important outlet for aboriginal artists, producers, and technicians.

Just as significant has been the effort to recapture the traditional skills of native craftspeople, in part because of the importance of preserving cultural practices, but also because native art has become increasingly popular with collectors around the world. As anthropologist Ruth Phillips describes, aboriginal arts and crafts had been popular trade goods with the earliest explorers and settlers, and in the nineteenth century with tourists who came into contact with native craftspeople thanks to the growing railway network. But both the supply of and demand for native arts and crafts was in decline by the early twentieth century. In native communities, almost everyone was an artisan of one kind or another, but when men started to be drawn away to better paying jobs (Phillips notes that, for Iroquois men, steel working brought in considerably more money than carving), it was left to women to try and fill the void, often by moving into arts that had traditionally been male-dominated. With fewer working artists, productivity obviously fell. But there was also less of a void to be filled. In the early twentieth century, decorative tastes moved towards simpler objects and away from the ornate beadwork and weaving produced by natives. At the same time, cheap, mass-produced goods started to appeal more to consumers who had bought native work for utilitarian purposes. But most importantly, the intrinsic value of native art was compromised by cheap reproductions that started to flood the market, calling into question native identity as a whole. Was that woven basket made by a Canadian aboriginal artist, or in an Asian sweat-shop? And what about the person selling it—was she really a native? Aboriginal art became devalued to such a point that when Seneca artist Tom Hill told his father he wanted to study art, the brusque response was, 'What are you going to do, wrap yourself up in a damn blanket and sell Indian art to the tourists for the rest of your life?'[468]

It was partly to reverse this trend that white artists, gallery owners, and art dealers began to seek out native sculptors, painters, and artisans to show and sell their work. Their motives were not always disinterested—some recognized a growing demand for aboriginal art, and the opportunity to cash in on it—but many were genuinely keen on promoting native artists and encouraging their work. One of

Inuit artist Kenojuak at Cape Dorset, with examples of her work, 1961.

the most effective programs has involved Inuit art. In October 1965, Canadian Arctic Producers of Ottawa was created at the behest of the federal government as an agent for Inuit artists; a non-profit marketing organization (now an arm of Arctic Co-operatives Limited), it sells to galleries rather than to individuals and guarantees the authenticity of its products through the igloo trademark, whose use is restricted by Ottawa to bona fide Inuit artists. Over the years, many local groups took advantage of such marketing networks, including the West-Baffin Eskimo Co-operative of Cape Dorset. It employed a group of native artists who worked on carving, print-making, textiles, and other crafts over the winter months; each spring, the co-operative's art director bought everything and shipped it to galleries around the world, demand having been heightened by exhibitions of Inuit art in Canada, the United States, and Europe. As Dorothy Eber wrote, the pieces have 'immense historic and economic value—they record the old Eskimo life and they also sustain the new...increasing numbers all over the world are finding delight in contemplation of an art that is tied to life—a hard life that an ingenious people found so well worth living.'[469]

In Nunavut, the government has taken the initiative through the Department of Culture, Language, Elders and Youth, with a mandate 'To preserve and enhance Nunavut's culture, heritage and languages.' Its grant program provides funding to individual artists and cultural organizations, and relies for advice on the five-member Nunavut Arts Council, created 'to recruit more young people into the arts, and to see that the performing arts thrive and flourish.' The government also supports the Nunavut Arts and Crafts Association, a non-profit group incorporated in October 1998 that uses conferences, workshops, the yearly Nunavut Arts Festival, and other events to promote and market the work of local carvers, print-makers, potters, painters, photographers, jewellers, and seamstresses.

Natar Ungalaaq, the lead in *Atanarjuat* (*The Fast Runner*).

Across Canada, similar efforts are underway to revive and preserve age-old cultural practices in aboriginal communities. There is Theytus Books (the name is taken from the Salish word meaning 'preserving for the sake of handing down'), established in 1980 as Canada's first aboriginal publisher as a vehicle to disseminate native culture. The Simon Charlie Society near Duncan, British Columbia, was established as the only carving school in the Coast Salish region and later expanded to teach weaving, painting, basket-making, and other crafts (it has received financial support from a variety of sources, including the funds established by the Anglican and United Churches as part of their attempts to make restitution for the wrongs committed in native residential schools). Significantly, the society was as much about preserving these crafts as providing economic opportunities for native communities: 'Carving and other crafts are actually sacred arts, but to survive they have also become articles of commerce. You can learn to carve here—but you can also take training for self-employment,' observed a former executive director of the Society. 'The idea is to create several micro-businesses with revenue streams which will eventually support the society.'[470] That old arts could be made profitable again was clear by the career of Bill Reid, born in Vancouver of a Haida mother and a Scots-American father. Not until he became an adult did Reid truly embrace his native heritage, and in time be became one of the most famous aboriginal sculptors in Canada, with such major works as *Haida Village* at the University of British Columbia, *The Chief of the Undersea World* for the Vancouver Aquarium, and *The Spirit of Haida Gwaii* for the Canadian Embassy in Washington.

Reid was largely responsible for the revival of northwest native art, but not all of his fellow artists have been as fortunate. It takes time to bring real change to the lives of aboriginal artists, and many remain at the low end of the economic scale as compared to other artists. The 2001 census reported that there were 3,100 aboriginals among the 130,700 artists in Canada; their average earnings were $16,900 a year, nearly 30 percent less than the annual earnings of non-native artists.[471] Even the National Gallery of Canada has come on board. For much of its first century it showed only sporadic interest in native art (for years, the only aboriginal work in its published catalogue was a miniature argillite totem pole from Skidegate, in the Queen Charlotte Islands[472]) and it was not until 2006 that the gallery held its first solo exhibition by an aboriginal artist when it mounted 'Norval Morrisseau: Shaman Artist,' featuring the Anishnaabe painter known as Copper Thunderbird or the Picasso of the North. But the gallery's exhibition policies brought into focus a larger debate—the ownership of aboriginal art. The acquisition of native art in the nineteenth and early twentieth centuries, by Canadian and foreign collectors, took a number of forms: many pieces were bought or commissioned from native artists eager to earn money from their skills, but others were acquired in dubious trades, or simply stolen. The notion that these pieces could have deep religious, social, and cultural significance to their communities was barely considered. But recent decades have seen a growing awareness that the 'collecting' of native art was, in many cases, little more than theft; as a result, thousands of pieces have been returned to the descendants of the craftspeople who created them,

OLD · TIME

SONGS

OF

NEWFOUNDLAND

THIRD EDITION 1955

PUBLISHED FOR FREE DISTRIBUTION BY

GERALD S. DOYLE

LIMITED

ST. JOHN'S NEWFOUNDLAND

Gerald Doyle's collection of Newfoundland folk music, first published in 1927.

so they can once again play the role in native culture that they had before European notions of art as a commodity reached North America.

The new popularity of aboriginal art is not the only case of the old becoming new again. In honour of the International Year of the Child in 1979, the Ontario Arts Council commissioned composer Howard Cable to write *Sing Sea to Sea*, an orchestral/choral work based on folk songs that exposed a new generation of Canadians to classics such as *Bonavista Harbour*, *Un Canadien errant*, *The Black Fly Song*, *The Red River Valley*, *Alberta Homestead*, and *Up the Yucletaw, Great Grandma*.[473] Over two decades later, the Newfoundland quartet Great Big Sea had built an ardent fan base for their mix of infectious pop tunes and traditional Maritime folk music. They took the passion for the music of their ancestors a step further in 2005, with the release of *The Hard and the Easy*, a collection of Newfoundland folk songs, many of them taken from booklets published by a St. John's merchant who reprinted the songs to attract customers to his products. Great Big Sea's fans have embraced the centuries-old music with enormous fervour, as much for their musical quality as for their local colour. As the band members are fond of pointing out, what other CD includes not one but two songs about horses falling through the ice on ponds?

Great Big Sea in concert. Undated.

The National Gallery of Canada has been plagued by the same kind of controversies over its acquisitions policy that had dogged it in the early twentieth century. Its new Moshe Safdie/Parkin Partnership–designed building opened in 1988 to great fanfare, but the gallery drew fire for its 1989 purchase of US colour-field painter Barnett Newman's *Voice of Fire* (1967)—as much for its style (a Manitoba MP said that it could be done with 'two cans of paint and two rollers and about ten minutes') as for the belief that the $1.8 million purchase price should have gone to the work of Canadian artists. The gallery's 1993 purchase of another modernist work, Mark Rothko's *No. 16* (1957), for $1.8 million also caused controversy, but there was no similar uproar when it paid $3.45 million for Guido Reni's *Jupiter and Europa* (1636) or $4.2 million for the sixteenth-century Italian artist Francesco Salviati's *Virgin and Child with an Angel*, which now holds the record as gallery's single most expensive purchase. The echoes of a century-old debate over what the gallery should purchase are unmistakable.

The canonization of Canadian literature also calls forth echoes from the late nineteenth and early twentieth centuries, when critics expressed concern at how the so-called classics of Canadian literature would stand up against the world's best and questioned the indiscriminate praise showered on certain writers simply because they were Canadian. The most recent effort at canonization began in 1958, when McClelland and Stewart launched the New Canadian Library, under general editor Malcolm Ross; when he retired in 1978, the library had grown to 168 titles. In the intervening twenty-one years, the word 'classic' had crept into the rhetoric, perhaps suggesting to the average book-buyer that the collection represented the collected wisdom of critics and editors in selecting the best literature that Canada had to offer. In fact, as Robert Lecker has shown, inclusion in the series was based largely on economic factors, at least in the early years. What mattered was less the aesthetic quality of a work than it was the potential sales it might generate in the university market, as well as the cost of acquiring publication rights. So, of the first four titles selected, Frederick Philip Grove's *Over Prairie Trails* was already owned by McClelland and Stewart, Morley Callaghan's *Such Is My Beloved* and Sinclair Ross' *As For Me and My House* could be purchased cheaply, and Stephen Leacock's *Literary Lapses* was worth the price because it would sell well enough to carry other, less popular titles. This focus on economics over aesthetics continued; of the 200 early documents on the New Canadian Library that Lecker consulted in the McClelland and Stewart archives, only five dealt with the literary merits of any potential addition to the series; in most cases, decisions were made based on estimated sales, the cost of rights, and book length.

The New Canadian Library continues, with considerably more intellectual rigour applied to the selection process, but questions remain about the canonization of CanLit. In 1997, *Toronto Star* critic Philip Marchand raised some hackles by calling into question the reverence paid to certain Canadian superstars: 'No one who has read them [the classics of world literature] at all widely can read, say, Laurence or Atwood or Davies, and not recognize that they are, when all is said, minor writers… no amount of boosterism can turn them into major works.' He had some sharp barbs about all of the great modern Canadian writers. Of Michael Ondaatje's writing, he noted that it was 'the kind of verbal embroidery that is called "beautiful prose" by people who like gobs of marmalade on their toast,' while Timothy Findley, it seemed to Marchand, 'did not spend hours…in an agonizing search for the mot juste,' instead falling back on 'something of a stylistic tic, which is the creation of sentences consisting of a single word or phrase, employed the way radio soap operas used to call upon ominous chords from the organ.' He was even harsher about the work of Margaret Laurence, called by one scholar 'the Canadian literary matriarch and our most revered cultural figure.' Marchand would have none of it: 'If it is an advantage for a novelist to have an interesting mind, Margaret Laurence was always writing under a handicap.'[474] Marchand's essay was written before Canadian authors became perennial contenders for international literary awards and one senses something of the distinctly Canadian inferiority complex in his remarks, but in 2005 columnist Anne Kingston wondered if Canadian literature was plagued by the tendency of critics to tread lightly when reviewing the works of canonical writers. 'Are Canada's literary lions protected from unvarnished criticism?,' she wondered, because 'timorous critics' lacked the nerve or the detachment to deal objectively and honestly with CanLit superstars? There is in such comments more than a faint echo of earlier critics such as one in the *Globe* in 1889, who warned that 'nothing but evil can ensue from indiscriminate and rapturous applause of verses, stories, or essays on the mere ground of their production by inhabitants of this country.'[475]

On a broader level, revivals of all sorts are becoming more and more popular. In 1976, Cameron Smith of the *Globe and Mail* wrote to novelist Gabrielle Roy that he was planning to bring back the column 'The Mermaid Inn,' which had been a fixture of the Canadian literary scene in the 1890s. He wanted to retain 'the homey feel of the writing and the breadth of the subject matter' of the original, and asked for Roy's contribution.[476] Former street performers Guy Laliberté and Daniel Gauthier founded Cirque du Soleil in Paris in 1984, later moving it to Montreal. Now with permanent shows in Las Vegas and Walt Disney World, in addition to its touring companies, it represents the pinnacle of the modern circus as an art form, with its cast of aerialists, trampolinists, acrobats, dancers, and a host of other performers. Even so, it should claim as its ancestors the great travelling circuses of the late eighteenth and nineteenth centuries, which brought death-defying stunts to mass audiences across Canada. In 2004, McClelland and Stewart announced a repackaging of the New Canadian Library, with the slogan 'A bold new look for the same great books'; nothing published before the First World War made it on to the catalogue's cover, but the publisher did affirm its determination to keep in print more than two centuries of Canadian writing. John Richardson's *Wacousta*, which had never made any money for the unfortunate major, was republished in 2005 by Barrie, Ontario author Heather Kirk, who shortened and updated the original text so it would appeal to modern readers. Reaching even farther back into European culture in North America, a Halifax director announced plans to mount a production of Marc Lescarbot's *Le Théâtre de Neptune*, four centuries after it became the first play to be performed in North America. With the revival of aboriginal art and the staging of Lescarbot's play, Canadian culture has come, in some ways, full circle.

Conclusion

In 1963, Herman Geiger-Torel, the long-time director of the Canadian Opera Company, told the *Globe* that 'The hockey player in Canada is much more worshipped than the opera star, it's true. I have nothing against that but I'm sure that the opera star, as the theatre star, will be able, in about 50 years, to compete with a hockey or baseball star.'[477] If we take Geiger-Torel's comment in a more general sense, as a reflection on the standing of the artist in society, it provides a useful vantage point for some concluding thoughts on the place that Canadian culture occupies in the early twenty-first century.

Although the hockey playoffs bump virtually every other program from the CBC television schedule each spring and *Hockey Night in Canada* remains one of the strongest performers in terms of ratings, there are indications that Geiger-Torel was more prescient than we might imagine. According to statistics from 2003, Canadians' spending on the arts is nearly double what they spend on live sporting events, and nearly twice as many households spend some money on live performing arts as on live sports.[478] And when the CBC launched its search for The Greatest Canadian, the one hundred finalists included thirty-six people from the arts, including singers Stompin' Tom Connors (#13) and Gordon Lightfoot (#33), pianist Glenn Gould (#55), novelist L.M. Montgomery (#57), children's author Robert Munsch (#78), painter Emily Carr (#85), and novelist Mordecai Richler (#98). Only seventeen of the top one hundred were sports figures.

But what's in a list? Three times since 1984, the Toronto International Film Festival has pronounced on the top ten Canadian films ever made; what are we to make of the fact that *Mon oncle Antoine* topped the first two lists but disappeared entirely from the 2004 version, to be replaced at the top by *C.R.A.Z.Y.*? Clearly, lists reflect many things—the predilections of the compilers, the method of calculation, the nature of current trends, and any number of other imponderables. In the spring of 1999, the University of Toronto Bookstore *Review* published its list of the best one hundred Canadian books, as compiled by a jury of five who gathered in a downtown pub and thrashed out the subject over a few pints. 'Another afternoon, another pub, or even a different table might have produced a different list,' observed *Review* editor Nicholas Pashley.[479]

But lists can also be very revealing. In 1999, the Modern Library, an imprint of the US publisher Random House, assembled a distinguished panel to come up with the top one hundred English-language novels published in the twentieth century; the lack of Canadian content on the list (unless one counts *Under the Volcano* by Malcolm Lowry, who is often considered Canadian because of the fifteen years he and his wife spent living in a shack on the beach near Dollarton, British Columbia) may well bear out Philip Marchand's comment that the stars of CanLit are, at best, minor writers. The publisher's subsequent list, of the top 200 novels published since 1950, was kinder to Canada and included works by Margaret Atwood, Robertson Davies, Mavis Gallant, Alice Munro, Margaret Laurence, Alistair MacLeod, Rohinton Mistry, Brian Moore, Michael Ondaatje, and Mordecai Richler; that list, in contrast, may suggest that Canadian writing did not come of age until after the Second World War. But more interesting than either of these lists was the Top 100 list compiled from the over 200,000 ballots cast on the Modern Library's website. Davies made the grade with *Fifth Business* (#40) and *The Cunning Man* (#99), as did Lowry's *Under the Volcano* (#39) and Atwood's *The Handmaid's Tale* (#53), but the big winner was Ottawa fantasy novelist Charles de Lint, who scored the top Canadian entry at #35 and had eight books on the list altogether. In few other contexts is the gulf between what receives the stamp of approval from the *literati* (high culture) and what is most widely read (popular culture) more evident.

These albeit-imperfect lists also provide a window into the tension between the traditional and the modern. In 1999, *Quill & Quire* asked thirty-seven academics, writers, booksellers, and librarians to nominate the 'most interesting, important and influential' books of twentieth-century Canadian fiction. The 270 titles submitted were eventually winnowed down to forty, with Margaret Laurence's *The Stone Angel* (1964) at the top. Significantly, the earliest novel on the list was *Anne of*

Green Gables (1908) at #10, and only four of the forty were published before the Second World War.[480] Is new Canadian fiction really better than old, or did the results simply reflect the preferences of the panelists? One might ask the same question of Donna Bennett and Russell Brown's *A New Anthology of Canadian Literature* (2003), an abridged version of an earlier two-volume anthology. Over eighty authors were represented, but only twenty-five of them were born before 1900. Are twentieth-century writers superior to those who came before them, or do anthologizers simply prefer what they are familiar with? In compiling *Canadian Poets*, J.W. Garvin chose for the first edition (1916) the poets he grew up with, and had trouble discarding any of them to make way for the modernists when it came time to do a second edition (1926). Perhaps Bennett and Brown selected the writers they were most comfortable with (and had trouble discarding any of them to make way for the traditionalists).

Anthologizing, of course, is a thankless task. Garvin was pilloried by later generations of scholars, critics, and authors for his choices; Bennett and Brown may well face similar barbs in the coming decades. Culture is full of writers, artists, sculptors, and composers who were lionized as geniuses of transcendent talent in their own day, only to fall prey to the vagaries of public or academic taste and, in later decades, have their work ridiculed as puerile and amateurish. Most modern critics would regard anthologies such as W.D. Lighthall's *Canadian Poems and Lays: Selections of Native Verse Reflecting the Seasons, Legends and Life of the Dominion* (1894) and Theodore H. Rand's *A Treasury of Canadian Verse: With Brief Biographical Notes* (1900) as virtually unreadable today. How many of the names in current anthologies and Top 100 lists will suffer the same fate in the next century?

The historian's job is not one of making predictions, but the continuities in a history of Canadian culture offer some intriguing lessons. The journey towards distinct Canadian forms of expression has been slow and halting, but we must keep in mind that other countries did not pluck their cultures fully formed from the ether. As Sara Jeannette Duncan wrote in 1886, Canadians should resist the temptation 'to nip north-putting buds by contemptuous comparison with the full blown production of other lands' because such a tendency was 'a distinctly colonial trait.'[481] Her remark points to the typically Canadian tendency towards self-deprecation, especially where culture is concerned. In the early nineteenth century, for example, the cultural life of Canada was probably no better or worse than what could be found in any provincial town in Britain or the United States. The critic who reviewed an 1830 art exhibition at Dalhousie College for the *Halifax Monthly* was probably right in arguing that the artistic production of 13,000 Haligonians would compare favourably to that of a similar number of people anywhere else in the British Empire. Or, as the *Christian Guardian* put it in defending Upper Canada against Anna Jameson's characterization of it as a community of philistines, 'We would venture to assert that in Upper Canada there is twice the number of newspapers read, in proportion to the population that there is in any county, city, town or village, in England.'[482]

A key part of the journey towards cultural distinctiveness has been the transition from traditional to more modern cultural forms, but this is also more complicated than it seems. Modernism as a genre is typically regarded as a child of the early twentieth century, but new art forms are constantly evolving. With surprising rapidity, the avant-garde becomes the mainstream and then the traditional. As the members of the Group of Seven fully realized, it took little more than a generation for their work to move from drawing praise as the vanguard of Canadian art to drawing criticism for being repetitious, formulaic, and, yes, old-fashioned. The fact that every generation of artists does something new means that the previous generation inevitably starts to look passé. The wonder is how few people involved in the arts have recognized this. When Eric Brown of the National Gallery of Canada said in 1915 that 'A younger generation is coming to the fore, trained partly in Canada, believing in and understanding Canada…These artists are painting their own country and realizing its own splendours and its character…Many are convinced that they are looking into the dawn of a new era in Canada which will glorify their country and help its people towards a better understanding of one of the greatest refining influences in Canadian life,'[483] he genuinely believed that Canada was on the verge of a new era of cultural expression. But we can find similar comments from the eighteenth century right up to last week—the fact is that Canada has always been in the verge of a new era of cultural expression. A reality of that process is that today's avant garde soon become tomorrow's conservatives.

Modernists, too, generally regard themselves as opposed to cultural nationalism, but few would deny that there is still such a thing as a national culture, despite the international orientation of modernism and the effects of globalization. And few would deny that it should be fostered, by the regulatory and protectionist arms of the state if necessary. Even if cultural nationalism has been a destabilizing force in the world (many people would argue that any form of nationalism is destabilizing), the notion of one world culture is a pipe-dream, for history tells us that it will almost inevitably come at the expense of cultural diversity. In the arts, the strong usually prevail. One need only to look at the fortunes of aboriginal culture in the decades after contact to see this process at work. The loss of centuries-old craft skills, the extinction of native languages, the outlawing of cultural practices— these are the consequences when states embark on what amounts to cultural imperialism. All too often, an unprotected culture falls prey to homogenization and assimilation.

But there is more at stake than what artists produce; it's not just about paintings, buildings, books, and songs, for culture is more than just the sum of the individual works created. Again, the history of aboriginal culture offers an object lesson, for as it began to crumble under the European assault (sometime well meaning, sometimes not), it took aboriginal identity with it. And so it would be in any society, for the fundamental relationship is not between culture and nationalism, but culture and identity. If there is one underlying notion that generations of artists and their supporters have agreed on, it's that a collective identity cannot exist without a distinct culture to express it. 'Art is what makes a nation articulate, not painting alone but literature, drama, music, sculpture and architecture, and every great nation must create these things for itself,' said the painter A.Y. Jackson in 1925. 'Art is the voice of the nation speaking through time.'[484] It has taken a long time for Canadians to learn to speak for themselves; we owe it to ourselves to keep doing so.

Endnotes

1. Frances Brooke, *The History of Emily Montague* (London: J. Dodsley, 1769), 216–17.
2. Quoted in Thomas E. Tausky, *Sara Jeannette Duncan: Novelist of Empire* (Port Hope, ON: P.D. Meany Publishers, 1980), 117–18.
3. Quoted in Claude Bissell, 'Literary Taste in Central Canada during the Late Nineteenth Century,' *Canadian Historical Review* 31/3 (September 1950), 248.
4. Library and Archives Canada: RG69, vol. 423, f. National Arts Centre, G. Hamilton Southam, 'The Meaning of the Arts Centre: Address before the Ottawa Women's Canadian Club,' 27 April 1965.
5. University of Regina Archives: 87-6 Howard Layton Brown Papers, box 1, file 'Canada Council,' quoted in 'Notes for Remarks by director André Fortier at International Conference of Symphony and Opera Musicians, Montreal, 28 August 1972.'
6. University of British Columbia Archives and Special Collections: Players Club Papers, box 2, scrapbook, letter to editor, *Ubyssey*, 16 March 1934.
7. City of Vancouver Archives: AM 807, 588-A-7 Sheila Neville Papers, f. 8, Mrs J. Richardson, 'Progress and Problems of Larger City Drama Groups,' 1948.
8. Banff Centre Archives: 1990-58 Irene Prothroe Papers, box 3, Jamie Portman, 'Program,' n.d.
9. Hugh MacLennan, 'Fiction in Canada—1930 to 1980,' in W.J. Keith and B.-Z. Shek, *The Arts in Canada: The Last Fifty Years* (Toronto: University of Toronto Press, 1980), 34–35.
10. Southam, 'The Meaning of the Arts Centre.'
11. Olive P. Dickason, *Canada's First Nations: A History of Founding Peoples from Earliest Times* (Don Mills, ON: Oxford University Press, 2002), 10; Mary E. Southcott, *The Sound of the Drum: The Sacred Art of the Anishnabec* (Erin Mills: Boston Mills Press, 1984), 10; Robin K. Wright, *Northern Haida Master Carvers* (Vancouver: Douglas and McIntyre, 2001), 5–6.
12. Samuel Hearne, *A Journey from Prince of Wales's Fort, in Hudson's Bay, to the Northern Ocean: Undertaken by Order of the Hudson's Bay Company for the Discovery of Copper Mines, a North West Passage, &c. in the Years 1769, 1770, 1771 & 1772* (London: A. Strahan and T. Cadell, 1795), 263.
13. Edmund Carpenter, 'Image Making in Arctic Art,' in Gyorgy Kepes, ed., *Sign Image Symbol* (New York: George Braziller, 1966), 212.
14. Franz Boas, *Primitive Art* (New York: Dover Publications, 1955 [1927]).
15. George Heriot, *Travels through the Canadas, Containing a Description of the Picturesque Scenery on some of the Lakes and Rivers; with an Account of the Productions, Commerce, and Inhabitants of those Provinces* (London: Richard Phillips, 1807), 82.

16. C. Stuart Houston, ed., *Arctic Artist: The Journal and Paintings of George Back, Midshipman with Franklin, 1819–1822* (Montreal: McGill-Queen's University Press, 1994), 101.

17. Reuben Gold Thwaites, ed., *The Jesuit Relations and Allied Documents: Travels and Explorations of the Jesuit Missionaries in New France, 1610–1791*, vol. 6 (Cleveland: Burrows, 1897), 18.

18. Diamond Jenness, *The Sarcee Indians of Alberta* (Ottawa: Department of Mines and Resources/National Museum of Canada, n.d.), ch. 6.

19. Eldon Yellowhorn, 'Before the Alberta Century,' in Jack W. Brink and John F. Dorman, eds., *Archaeology in Alberta: A View from the New Millennium* (Medicine Hat: Archaeological Society of Alberta, 2003), 329.

20. Robert McGhee, *Ancient People of the Arctic* (Vancouver: UBC Press, 1996), 159, 162.

21. Otis T. Mason, 'Basket-Work of the North American Aborigines,' *Report of the National Museum, 1884* (Washington, DC: United States National Museum, 1885), 293.

22. Roy Carlson, ed., *Indian Art Traditions of the Northwest Coast* (Burnaby, BC: Archaeology Press/Simon Fraser University, 1976), 101.

23. Bill McLennan and Karen Duffek, *The Transforming Image: Painted Arts of the Northwest Coast First Nations* (Vancouver: UBC Press, 2000), 55.

24. Quoted in Dickason, *Canada's First Nations*, 18; quoted in Leslie Drew and Douglas Wilson, *Argillite: Art of the Haida* (North Vancouver: Hancock House, 1980), 28; quoted in Dickason, *Canada's First Nations*, 15.

25. Thwaites, ed., *The Jesuit Relations and Allied Documents*, vol. 66 (Cleveland: Burrows, 1900), 147.

26. François-Marc Gagnon, 'Conversion Through the Printed Image,' in Patricia Lockhart Fleming, Gilles Gallichan, and Yvan Lamonde, eds., *History of the Book in Canada*, vol. 1, *Beginnings to 1840* (Toronto: University of Toronto Press, 2004), 19.

27. Alfred Goldsworthy Bailey, *The Conflict of European and Eastern Algonkian Cultures, 1504–1700: A Study in Canadian Civilization*, second edition (Toronto: University of Toronto Press, 1969 [1937]), 148–51.

28. Ibid., 47.

29. William Kirby, *The U.E.: A Tale of Upper Canada* (Niagara, ON: n.p., 1859).

30. Rev. J.P. Hicks, ed., *From Potlatch to Pulpit: Being the Autobiography of the Rev. William Henry Pierce, Native Missionary to the Indian Tribes of the Northwest Coast of British Columbia* (Vancouver: Vancouver Bindery, 1933), 126–27.

31. Edward Parry, *Memoirs of Rear-Admiral Sir W. Edward Parry, Kt* (London: Longman, Brown, Green, Longmans, & Roberts, 1857), 116.

32. J. Russell Harper, *Painting in Canada: A History* (Toronto: University of Toronto Press, 1977), 19.

33. Louis Armand de Lom d'Arce, Baron de Lahontan, *New voyages to North America: containing an account of the several nations of that continent, their customs, commerce, and way of navigation upon the lakes and rivers, the several attempts of the English and French to dispossess one another* (London: Printed for H. Bonwicke, 1703).

34. Quoted in Leonard E. Doucette, *Theatre in French Canada: Laying the Foundations, 1606–1867* (Toronto: University of Toronto Press, 1984), 10.

35. Ibid., 23.

36. Margaret M. Cameron, 'Play-Acting in Canada during the French Regime,' *Canadian Historical Review* 11/1 (March 1930), 17.

37. Harold D. Kalman, *A History of Canadian Architecture*, vol. 1 (Don Mills, ON: Oxford University Press), 59.

38. Harper, *Painting in Canada*, 25.

39. Gérard Tougas, *History of French-Canadian Literature*, trans. Alta Lind Cook (Toronto: Ryerson Press 1966), 5.

40. Doucette, *Theatre in French Canada*, 69, 72.

41. Thomas Cary, *Abram's Plain: A Poem* (Quebec: T. Cary, 1789), 10.

42. Gwendolyn Davies, 'Consolation to Distress: Loyalist Literary Activity in the Maritimes,' *Acadiensis* 16/2 (spring 1987), 56.

43. Quoted in Yashdip Singh Bains, 'The New Grand Theatre: Halifax 1789–1814,' *Nova Scotia Historical Quarterly* 10/1 (1980), 5; quoted in Franklin Graham, *Histrionic Montreal: Annals of the Montreal Stage* (New York: B. Blom, 1969), 19.

44. Quoted in Mary Elizabeth Smith, *Too Soon the Curtain Fell: A History of Theatre in Saint John, 1789–1900* (Fredericton: Brunswick Press, 1981), 33–35.

45. 'On Opening a Little Theatre in the City, on Monday the 5th January Inst.,' *The Royal Gazette and the New-Brunswick Advertiser*, 20 January 1795.

46. Davies, 'Consolation to Distress,' 58–59.

47. Quoted in D.C. Harvey, 'The Intellectual Awakening of Nova Scotia' in G.A. Rawlyk, ed., *Historical Essays on the Atlantic Provinces* (Toronto: McClelland and Stewart, 1967), 110.

48. Quoted in George L. Parker, 'Courting Local and International Markets,' in Fleming, Gallichan, and Lamonde, eds., *History of the Book in Canada*, vol. 1, 345; quoted in George L. Parker, *The Beginnings of the Book Trade in Canada* (Toronto: University of Toronto Press, 1985), 21.

49. Tougas, *History of French-Canadian Literature*, 5.

50. Quoted in Bains, 'The New Grand Theatre,' 14,

51. Quoted in Gwendolyn Davies, '"Good Sense and Sound Taste": *The Nova-Scotia Magazine* (1789–92),' in Terry Whalen, ed., *The Atlantic Anthology*, vol. 3, *Critical Essays* (Charlottetown: Ragweed Press, 1985), 10.

52. Michel Verrette, 'The Spread of Literacy,' in Fleming, Gallichan, and Lamonde, eds., *History of the Book in Canada*, 168, 171; Leonard E. Doucette, *Theatre in French Canada*, 81.

53. *La Minerve*, 18 May 1851, 2.

54. Alan S. Downer, ed., *The Memoir of John Durang, American Actor, 1785–1816* (Pittsburgh: Historical Society of York County, 1966).

55. Captain Horton Rhys, *A Theatrical Trip For a Wager!: Through Canada and the United States* (London: Charles Dudley, 1861).

56. Susanna Moodie, *Life in the Clearings Versus the Bush* (London: R. Bentley, 1853), 95–97.

57. Smith, *Too Soon the Curtain Fell*, 38.

58. Quoted in Edwin C. Guillet, *Pioneer Inns and Taverns*, vol. 4 (Toronto: Ontario Publishing, 1958), 140.

59. Chad Evans, *Frontier Theatre: A History of Nineteenth Century Theatrical Entertainment in the Canadian Far West and Alaska* (Victoria: Sono Nis Press, 1983), 83.

60. Ibid., 32, 81.

61. Quoted in Phyllis Blakeley, 'Music in Nova Scotia, 1605–1867,' part 1, *Dalhousie Review* 31/2 (summer 1951): 99.

62. Jesse Edgar Middleton, 'The Theatre in Canada,' in Adam Shortt and Arthur G. Doughty, eds., *Canada and Its Provinces: A History of the Canadian People and Their Institutions by One Hundred Associates*, vol. 12 (Toronto: Glasgow, Brook and Company, 1914), 657.

63. Provincial Statutes of Canada, 9 Victoria (1846), 966; Journal of the House of Assembly of New Brunswick from February to April 1850 (Fredericton: C. Sower, 1850), clxxv.

64. Emigrant Lady, *Letters from Muskoka* (London: R. Bentley, 1878), 263–64

65. Canniff Haight, *Country Life in Canada Fifty Years Ago: Personal Recollections and Reminiscences of a Sexagenarian* (Toronto: Hunter-Rose, 1885), 3, 89, 181.

66. Frances Stewart, *Our Forest Home: Being Extracts from the Correspondence of the late Frances Stewart* (Toronto: Presbyterian Printing and Publishing, 1889), 92–93; Robert Mudie, *The Emigrant's Pocket Companion: containing what emigration is, who should be emigrants, where emigrants should go: a description of British North America, especially the Canadas, and full instructions to intending emigrants* (London: J. Cochrane, 1832).

67. Frances Beaven, *Sketches and Tales Illustrative of Life in the Backwoods of New Brunswick, North America: Gleaned from Actual Observation and Experience During a Residence of Seven Years in that Interesting Colony* (London: G. Routledge, 1845), 31; Anna Jameson, *Winter Studies and Summer Rambles in Canada* (London: Saunders and Otley, 1838), 443.

68. Stewart, *Our Forest Home*, 38.

69. Quoted in Bertrum H. MacDonald, 'Print in the Backwoods,' in Fleming, Gallichan, and Lamonde, eds., *History of the Book in Canada*, 184; Emigrant Lady, *Letters from Muskoka*, 161.

70. Audrey Saunders Miller, ed., *The Journals of Mary O'Brien, 1828–1838* (Toronto: Macmillan, 1968), 35, 139.

71. H.H. Langton, ed., *A Gentlewoman in Upper Canada: The Journals of Ann Langton* (Toronto: Clarke, Irwin and Company, 1950), 7 November 1842, 170; Beaven, *Sketches and Tales Illustrative of Life in the Backwoods of New Brunswick*, 129.

72. Ibid., 40; MacDonald, 'Print in the Backwoods,' 186.

73. Stewart, *Our Forest Home*, 162.

74. J.I. Little, ed., *Love Strong as Death: Lucy Peel's Canadian Journal, 1833–1836* (Waterloo, ON: Wilfrid Laurier University Press, 2001), 199; T.W. McGrath to Rev. Thomas Radcliff, January 1832, in Rev. Thomas Radcliff, ed., *Authentic Letters from Upper Canada* (Toronto: Macmillan, 1953), 67.

75. Oliver Goldsmith, 'The Rising Village,' in *The Rising Village, with other Poems* (Saint John: J. M'Millan, 1834).

76. Letter of February 1833, in Radcliff, ed., *Authentic Letters from Upper Canada*, 184; Little, *Love Strong as Death*, 116.

77. Wilfrid Eggleston, *The Frontier and Canadian Letters* (Toronto: McClelland and Stewart, 1977), 78, 81.

78. Richard M. Saunders, 'The Cultural Development of Newfoundland Before 1760,' in R. Flenley, ed., *Essays in Canadian History Presented to George Mackinnon Wrong for his Eightieth Birthday* (Toronto: Macmillan, 1939), 345.

79. Michael Bird, *Canadian Folk Art: Old Ways in a New Land* (Toronto: Oxford University Press, 1983), 4.

80. J. Russell Harper, *A People's Art: Primitive, Naïve, Provincial, and Folk Painting in Canada* (Toronto: University of Toronto Press, 1974), 16, 18

81. Bird, *Canadian Folk Art*, 4.

82. Marius Barbeau, 'Folk Songs of French Canada,' in *The Empire Club of Canada Speeches, 1929* (Toronto: Empire Club of Canada, 1930), 7 March 1929.

83. George Head, *Forest Scenes and Incidents, in the Wilds of North America; being a diary of a winter's route from Halifax to the Canadas* (London: John Murray, 1829), 342.

84. Alexander M'Lachlan, *The Emigrant, and Other Poems* (Toronto: Rollo & Adam, 1861), 75; Marius Barbeau, 'Folk Songs of French Canada,' in *The Empire Club of Canada Speeches, 1925* (Toronto: Empire Club of Canada, 1926), 9 April 1925.

85. Saskatoon Public Library: Doc 88-16G, 'Music in Saskatoon,' n.d.; Doc 88-16M, 'Historical Sketch of the Battlefords,' n.d.

86. Cornwall Bayley, *Canada: A Descriptive Poem, Written at Quebec, 1805* (Quebec: John Neilson, 1806).

87. Goldsmith, 'The Rising Village.'

88. British Columbia Archives: Edythe Hembroff-Schleicher Papers, MS-2792, box 4, file 9 'The Island Arts and Crafts Club,' in *The Week* (Vancouver), 19 October 1912.

89. Stewart, *Our Forest Home*, 140.

90. *Le Pays*, December 1856, quoted in John R. Porter, 'The Market for Paintings: Basic Needs versus Artistic Taste,' in Mario Béland, ed., *Painting in Quebec, 1820–1850: New Views, New Perspectives* (Quebec: Musée du Québec, 1992), 33.

91. *Novascotian*, 18 May 1837, 154.

92. Quoted in Harper, *Painting in Canada*, 104; *North Pacific Times* [New Westminster, BC], 23 November 1864.

93. Quoted in Jim Blanchard, 'Anatomy of Failure: Ontario Mechanics' Institutes, 1835–1895,' *Canadian Library Journal* 38/6 (December 1981), 393; quoted in Laura J. Murray, 'The Uses of Literacy in the Northwest,' in Fleming, Gallichan, and Lamonde, eds., *History of the Book in Canada*, 190.

94. Quoted in Lorne D. Bruce, 'The Aims of the Public Library Movement in Late Victorian Ontario,' in Peter F. McNally, ed., *Readings in Canadian Library History*, vol. 2 (Ottawa: Canadian Library Association, 1996), 99; quoted in Heather Murray, *Come, Bright Improvement!: The Literary Societies of Nineteenth-Century Ontario* (Toronto: University of Toronto Press, 2002), 25.

95. Quoted in ibid., 3.

96. Paul Axelrod, *The Promise of Schooling: Education in Canada, 1800–1914* (Toronto: University of Toronto Press, 1997), 66; David Alexander, 'Literacy and Economic Development in Nineteenth Century Newfoundland,' *Acadiensis* 10/1 (autumn 1980), 7, 10–11.

97. Michel Verrette and Yvan Lamonde, 'Literacy and Print Culture,' in Yvan Lamonde, Patricia Lockhart Fleming, and Fiona A. Black, eds., *History of the Book in Canada*, vol. 2, *1840–1918* (Toronto: University of Toronto Press, 2005): 452–58; quoted in Bruce, 'The Aims of the Public Library Movement in Late Victorian Ontario,' 96.

98. J.J. Talman Regional Collection, D.B. Weldon Library, The University of Western Ontario: 'Hellmuth Ladies' College, London, Ontario. Incorporated 1869.'

99. Quoted in Bruce Curtis, '"Littery Merit," "Useful Knowledge," and the Organization of Township Libraries in Canada West, 1840–1860,' *Ontario History* 78 (1986), 300.

100. Quoted in Murray, *Come, bright Improvement!*, 34; quoted in Michael Pearson, 'Some Aspects of Early Ontario Libraries,' *Ontario Library Review* 51 (1967): 74; quoted in Bruce, 'The Aims of the Public Library Movement in Late Victorian Ontario,' 100.

101. Quoted in W.D. Caskey, 'Ontario's Oldest Library,' *Ontario Library Review* 23/3 (August 1939), 284.

102. Quoted in Kenneth Donovan, 'May Learning Flourish: The Beginnings of a Cultural Awakening in Cape Breton during the 1840s,' in Kenneth Donovan, ed., *The Island: New Perspectives on Cape Breton History, 1713–1990* (Sydney, NS: Acadiensis Press, 1990), 108.

103. Quoted in Curtis, '"Littery Merit," "Useful Knowledge," and the Organization of Township Libraries in Canada West,' 287.

104. Quoted in ibid., 286.

105. Quoted in Pearson, 'Some Aspects of Early Ontario Libraries,' 75.

106. Quoted in Curtis, '"Littery Merit," "Useful Knowledge," and the Organization of Township Libraries in Canada West,' 304.

107. Quoted in ibid., 293.

108. Quoted in ibid., 299.

109. Quoted in ibid., 303.

110. *Victoria Colonist*, 10 October 1859; *New Westminster Times*, 11 October 1859.

111. Madge Wolfenden, 'Books and Libraries in Fur-Trading and Colonial Days,' *British Columbia Historical Quarterly* 11/3 (July 1947), 160.

112. Quoted in Murray, *Come, Bright Improvement!*, 39.

113. *Napanee Standard*, 26 June 1860 and 6 March 1865, quoted in James A. Eadie, 'The Napanee Mechanics' Institute: The Nineteenth Century Ontario Mechanics' Institute Movement in Microcosm,' *Ontario History* 68/4 (December 1976), 214–15.

114. Quoted in ibid., 212; quoted in Elizabeth Mitchell, 'From Mechanics' Institute to Corby Public Library: The Development of Library Service in Belleville, Ontario, 1851–1908,' in McNally, op. cit., 154.

115. Quoted in Donovan, 'May Learning Flourish,' 104.

116. Quoted in Jennifer R. Johnson, 'The Availability of Reading Material for the Pioneer in Upper Canada: Niagara District, 1792–1842' (MA thesis, The University of Western Ontario, 1982), 81; Mary Lu MacDonald, 'English and French-Language Periodicals and the Development of a Literary Culture in Early Victorian Canada,' *Victorian Periodical Review* 26/4 (winter 1993), 222.

117. Quoted in Mitchell, 'From Mechanics' Institute to Corby Public Library,' 156.

118. Quoted in Murray, *Come, Bright Improvement!*, 36; quoted in Allan C. Dunlop, 'The Pictou Literature and Scientific Society,' *Nova Scotia Historical Quarterly* 3 (June 1973), 99.

119. Public Archives of Manitoba: MG10 C2 Griswold Reading Club Papers.

120. Quoted in Ellen L. Ramsay, 'Art and Industrial Society: The Role of the Toronto Mechanic's Institute in the Promotion of Art, 1831–1883,' *Labour/Le Travail* 43 (Spring 1999), 76.
121. Quoted in Porter, 'The Market for Paintings,' 31.
122. *Montreal Herald*, 28 February 1865, 2; quoted in Porter, 'The Market for Paintings,' 32.
123. Quoted in Bruce, 'The Aims of the Public Library Movement in Late Victorian Ontario,' 108; quoted in Blanchard, 'Anatomy of Failure,' 398.
124. Quoted in Eadie, 'The Napanee Mechanics' Institute,' 212, 218.
125. *The Bee* [Pictou], quoted in Dunlop, 'The Pictou Literature and Scientific Society,' 103.
126. Quoted in Eadie, 'The Napanee Mechanics' Institute,' 218.
127. *New Westminster British Columbian*, 21 December 1864.
128. Quoted in Eadie, 'The Napanee Mechanics' Institute,' 219; quoted in Blanchard, 'Anatomy of Failure,' 396.
129. Quoted in Pearson, 'Some Aspects of Early Ontario Libraries,' 74.
130. Quoted in Mitchell, 'From Mechanics' Institute to Corby Public Library,' 155.
131. Quoted in ibid., 158; quoted in Eadie, 'The Napanee Mechanics' Institute,' 220.
132. Quoted in Michael Peterman, 'Literary Cultures and Popular Reading in Upper Canada,' in Fleming, Gallichan, and Lamonde, eds., *History of the Book in Canada*, vol. 2, 399.
133. Quoted in Curtis, '"Littery Merit," "Useful Knowledge," and the Organization of Township Libraries in Canada West,' 305.
134. Quoted in Johnson, 'The Availability of Reading Material for the Pioneer in Upper Canada,' 95.
135. Quoted in Murray, 'Frozen Pen, Fiery Print, and Fothergill's Folly: Cultural Organization in Toronto, Winter 1836–37,' *Essays on Canadian Writing* 61 (spring 1997), 53.
136. Quoted in Murray, *Come, Bright Improvement!*, 74.
137. Quoted in Bruce, 'The Aims of the Public Library Movement in Late Victorian Ontario,' 102.
138. Edward Hartley Dewart, *Selections from Canadian Poets: With Occasional Critical and Biographical Notes, and an Introductory Essay on Canadian Poetry* (Montreal: John Lovell, 1864), xiv.
139. Quoted in John R. Porter, 'The Market for Paintings: Basic Needs versus Artistic Taste,' in Béland, ed., *Painting in Quebec, 1820–1850*, 27.
140. *British Colonist* [Toronto], 2 January 1849, 2.
141. Daniel Wilson, 'Canadian Poetry,' *Canadian Journal of Science and Literature* 3 (1858): 17–27; G. Mercer Adam, 'Nationalism and the Literary Spirit,' *The Week* 5 (19 January 1888), 118.
142. Dewart, *Selections from Canadian Poets*, introductory essay.
143. Letter of 12 November 1856, in W.A. Langton, ed., *Early Days in Upper Canada: Letters of John Langton from the Backwoods of Upper Canada and the Audit Office of the Province of Canada* (Toronto: Macmillan, 1926), 292–93.
144. 29 July 1834, quoted in Carol D. Lowrey, 'The Society of Artists & Amateurs, 1834: Toronto's First Art Exhibition and Its Antecedents,' *Canadian Art Review* 8/2 (1981), 114.
145. *New Era*, 10 June 1857; D'Arcy McGee, 'Protection for Canadian Literature,' *The New Era*, 24 April 1858, 2.

146. Thomas D'Arcy McGee, *Canadian Ballads and Occasional Verses* (Montreal: J. Lovell, 1858), preface.

147. D'Arcy McGee, 'The Mental Outfit of the New Dominion,' in Carl Ballstadt, ed., *The Search for English-Canadian Literature: An Anthology of Critical Articles from the Nineteenth and Early Twentieth Centuries* (Toronto: University of Toronto Press, 1975), 93.

148. Henry J. Morgan, *Bibliotheca Canadensis, or, a Manual of Canadian Literature* (Ottawa: n.p., 1867), introductory remarks.

149. Pelham Edgar, 'A Fresh View of Canadian Literature,' *University Magazine* 11 (October 1912): 479–86.

150. Quoted in Norman Shrive, *Charles Mair: Literary Nationalist* (Toronto: University of Toronto Press, 1965), 13.

151. William Foster, 'Address to the Canadian National Association' (1875), quoted in Claude Bissell, 'Literary Taste in Central Canada during the Late Nineteenth Century,' *Canadian Historical Review* 31/3 (September 1950), 239.

152. Quoted in Alfred Goldsworthy Bailey, *Culture and Nationality: Essays by A.G. Bailey* (Toronto: McClelland and Stewart, 1972), 71.

153. Quoted in Dennis R. Reid, *'Our Own Country Canada': Being an Account of the National Aspirations of the Principal Landscape Artists in Montreal and Toronto, 1860–1890* (Ottawa: National Gallery of Canada, 1979), 110; *Canadian Monthly* 3 (June 1873), 546.

154. *The Week* 3/44 (30 September 1886), 707; Sara Jeannette Duncan, *The Imperialist* (Toronto: McClelland and Stewart, 1961 [1904]), 48.

155. J.E. Collins, *Life and Times of the Right Honourable Sir John A. Macdonald, K.C.B., D.C.L., &c, Premier of the Dominion of Canada* (Toronto: Rose Publishing, 1883), 442.

156. *The Week* 1/28 (12 June 1884), 439; *Prince Albert Daily Times*, 29 November 1882.

157. Quoted in Read, *"Our Own Country Canada"*, 277–78.

158. Quoted in Moncrieff Williamson, *Robert Harris, 1849–1919: An Unconventional Biography* (Toronto: McClelland and Stewart, 1970), xvii.

159. Sir John Bourinot, 'Literature and Art in Canada,' *Anglo-American Magazine*, February 1900, 104; 'At the Mermaid Inn,' *Globe*, 27 February 1892, 8.

160. Quoted in Harold D. Kalman, *A History of Canadian Architecture*, vol. 2 (Don Mills, ON: Oxford University Press), 565.

161. Quoted in Kelly Crossman, *Architecture in Transition: From Art to Practice, 1885–1906* (Montreal: McGill-Queen's University Press, 1987), 115.

162. Quoted in ibid., 116.

163 Quoted in D.M.R. Bentley, *The Confederation Group of Canadian Poets, 1880–1897* (Toronto: University of Toronto Press, 2004), 43; quoted in Malcolm Ross, ed., *Poets of the Confederation: Duncan Campbell Scott, Archibald Lampman, Bliss Carman, Charles G.D. Roberts* (Toronto: McClelland and Stewart, 1960), vii–viii.

164 Quoted in Bentley, *The Confederation Group of Canadian Poets*, 101, 108.

165 Quoted in Shrive, *Charles Mair*, 50–51.

166 Quoted in ibid., 188; *Orillia Packet*, 2 April 1886.

167 See Bentley, *The Confederation Group of Canadian Poets*, 276–86.

168 *The Week* 3/44 (30 September 1886), 708; *Canada* [Benton, NB], May 1891, quoted in Bentley, *The Confederation Group of Canadian Poets*, 109; quoted

in S.M. Beckow, 'From the Watch-towers of Patriotism: Theories of Literary Growth in English Canada, 1864–1914,' in *Journal of Canadian Studies* 9/3 (1974), 12.

169   *The Nation* 2 (14 May 1875), 226; *Forum* 28 (1899), 752.

170   Dewart, *Selections from Canadian Poets*, introductory essay; quoted in Bissell,. 'Literary Taste in Central Canada,' 248.

171   'The Mermaid Inn,' *Globe*, 19 March 1892, 8–9; quoted in Beckow, 'From the Watch-towers of Patriotism,' 4.

172   *Montreal Star*, 31 January 1888, 2.

173   Collins, *Life and Times of the Right Honourable Sir John A. Macdonald*, 464.

174   Louis Prosper Bender, *Literary Sheaves; or, La Littérature au Canada français. The Drama, History, Romance, Poetry, Lectures, Sketches, &c* (Montreal: Dawson Brothers, 1881), 201.

175   Quoted in Shrive, *Charles Mair*, 214.

176.   Quoted in Charles C. Hill, 'George Wade's Monuments to Sir John A. Macdonald,' *Journal of Canadian Art History* 22/1&2 (2001), 20.

177.   D'Arcy McGee, 'Protection for Canadian Literature,' *The New Era*, 24 April 1858, 2.

178.   Quoted in George Parker, 'The Canadian Copyright Question in the 1890s,' *Journal of Canadian Studies* 11/2 (May 1976), 50.

179.   Quoted in ibid., 52.

180.   Goldwin Smith, 'What is the Matter with Canadian Literature,' *The Week* 11 (31 August 1894), 950–1.

181.   Rosanna Leprohon, *Antoinette De Mirecourt, or, Secret Marriage and Secret Sorrowing: A Canadian Tale* (Montreal: Lovell, 1864), introduction; *The Week* 7/4 (27 December 1889), 60.

182.   J.E. Middleton, in Adam Shortt and Arthur G. Doughty, eds., *Canada and its Provinces: A History of the Canadian People and their Institutions by One Hundred Associates*, vol. 12, *Arts and Letters* (Toronto: Glasgow, Brook and Company, 1914), 661.

183.   Frederic Robson, 'The Drama in Canada,' *Canadian Magazine* 31/1 (May 1908), 58–59, 61.

184.   B.K. Sandwell, 'The Annexation of our Stage,' in *Canadian Magazine* 38/1 (November 1911), 23.

185.   Robson, 'The Drama in Canada,' 58.

186.   George Monro Grant, ed., *Picturesque Canada: The Country As It Was and Is* (Toronto: James Clarke, n.d.), preface.

187.   *The Week* 1/6 (10 January 1884), 91; quoted in Reid, 'Our Own Country Canada', 299.

188.   Quoted in Russell J. Harper, *Painting in Canada: A History* (Toronto: University of Toronto Press, 1977), 215–66; quoted in Muriel Miller, *George Reid: A Biography* (Toronto: Summerhill Press, 1987), 100.

189.   Quoted in Reid, 'Our Own Country Canada', 438.

190.   Quoted in Crossman, *Architecture in Transition*, 15.

191.   Quoted in ibid., 26.

192.   Quoted in ibid., 109.

193.   Quoted in Susan Wagg, *Percy Erskine Nobbs: Architect, Artist, Craftsman* (Montreal: McGill-Queen's University Press, 1982), 1, 16.

194.   Quoted in Crossman, *Architecture in Transition*, 121.

195.   Quoted in George L. Parker, 'Courting Local and International Markets,' in

Fleming, Gallichan, and Lamonde, eds., *History of the Book in Canada*, vol. 1, 345.

196. Quoted in ibid., 349.

197. Quoted in Janet Friskney, 'Beyond the Shadow of William Briggs: Canadian-Authored Titles and the Commitment to Canadian Writing,' part 2, *Papers of the Bibliographical Society of Canada* 35/2 (fall 1997), 170.

198. Quoted in Carole Gerson, 'Canadian Women Writers and American Markets, 1880–1940,' in Camille R. La Bossière, ed., *Context North America: Canadian/ U.S. Literary Relations* (Ottawa: University of Ottawa Press, 1994), 112.

199. Charles W. Gordon, *Postscript to Adventure: The Autobiography of Ralph Connor* (New York: Farrar and Rinehart, 1938), 148, 150.

200. Wilfrid Eggleston, ed., *The Green Gables Letters: From L.M. Montgomery to Ephraim Weber, 1905–1909* (Toronto: Ryerson Press, 1960), 46, 59, 80.

201. Quoted in Friskney, 'Beyond the Shadow of William Briggs,' 189.

202. John Lennox and Michele Lacombe, eds., *Dear Bill: The Correspondence of William Arthur Deacon* (Toronto: University of Toronto Press, 1988), 168; University of Manitoba Archives: MSS 56 Ralph Connor Papers, box 33, file 3, letter 28 January 1907.

203. Quoted in Friskney, 'Beyond the Shadow of William Briggs,' 189.

204. Quoted in *At the Mermaid Inn: Wilfred Campbell, Archibald Lampman, Duncan Campbell Scott in 'The Globe' 1892–93*, introduction by Barrie Davies (Toronto: University of Toronto Press, 1979), xvi.

205. Quoted in Faye Hammill, 'Sara Jeannette Duncan in the "Camp of the Philistines,"' *Journal of Canadian Studies* 32/3 (summer 1997), 165–6.

206. G. Mercer Adam, 'Literature, Nationality and the Tariff,' *The Week* 7/4 (27 December 1889), 59–60.

207. Letter of 22 March 1911, quoted in Nicole Cloutier, *James Wilson Morrice 1865–1924* (Montreal: Musée des Beaux-Arts, 1985), 55.

208. *Toronto Star*, 2 June 1898, 5.

209. *New York Times*, 8 January 1958, 47.

210. Stephen Leacock, *Moonbeams from the Larger Lunacy* (New York: John Lane, 1915), preface.

211. *Canadian Literary Mecca* (1891), quoted in John Coldwell Adams, *Seated With the Mighty: A Biography of Sir Gilbert Parker* (Ottawa: Borealis Press, 1979), 67; 'At the Mermaid Inn,' *Globe*, 7 January 1893, 6.

212. 'At the Mermaid Inn,' *Globe*, 4 March 1893, 6; quoted in Thomas E. Tausky, *Sara Jeannette Duncan: Novelist of Empire* (Port Hope, ON: P.D. Meany Publishers, 1980), 269.

213. Quoted in Williamson, *Robert Harris*, 99.

214. George Stewart, Jr., 'Letters in Canada,' *The Week* 4 (16 June 1887), 461–62; 'At the Mermaid Inn,' *Globe*, 16 April 1892, 6.

215. 'At the Mermaid Inn,' *Globe*, 22 October 1892, 8; *The Week* 7 (27 October 1890), 746.

216. Quoted in Tausky, *Sara Jeannette Duncan*, 270; Misao Dean, *A Different Point of View: Sara Jeannette Duncan* (Montreal: McGill-Queen's University Press, 1991), 10.

217. Quoted in Cheryl MacDonald, *Emma Albani: Victorian Diva* (Toronto: Dundurn Press, 1984), 184; Library and Archives Canada: W.L.M. King Diary, 16 April 1925.

218. Mary Rubio and Elizabeth Waterston, *The Selected Journals of L.M.*

Montgomery, vol. 2, *1910–1921* (Toronto: Oxford University Press, 1987), 150; Francis W.P. Bolger and Elizabeth Epperly, eds., *My Dear Mr. M: Letters to G.B. MacMillan* (Toronto: McGraw-Hill Ryerson, 1980), 70–73.

219. Laurel Boone, ed., *The Collected Letters of Charles G.D. Roberts* (Fredericton: Goose Lane Editions, 1989), 300–1.

220. Quoted in Maria Tippett, *Stormy Weather: F.H. Varley, A Biography* (Toronto: McClelland and Stewart, 1998), 84; quoted in Maria Tippett, *Art at the Service of War: Canada, Art, and the Great War* (Toronto: University of Toronto Press, 1984), 5.

221. Toronto *Star*, 9 September 1914, 6; 7 October 1914, 6.

222. University of Manitoba Archives: MSS11 Men's Musical Club of Winnipeg Papers, box 1.

223. City of Victoria Archives: PR182 29C8 Reginald Hincks Papers.

224. John W. Garvin, *Canadian Poets* (Toronto: McClelland, Goodchild and Stewart, 1916), 5; Carrie Ellen Holman, ed., *In the Day of Battle: Poems of the Great War* (Toronto: William Briggs, 1918), note to 3rd edition.

225. Walter McRaye, *Town Hall Tonight* (Toronto: Ryerson Press, n.d.), 71.

226. *Spectator* [Hamilton], 3 February 1917.

227. Lindsay Crawford, 'The Roll of Honour,' *Canadian Magazine* 48/4 (February 1917), 392.

228. Review of *Living Bayonets*, in *The Rebel* 3/5 (March 1919), 237.

229. Quoted in Tippett, *Art at the Service of War*, 23.

230. Quoted in ibid., 26, 90.

231. Quoted in ibid., 28.

232. Quoted in ibid., 15.

233. Quoted in ibid., 11; Richard Clive Cooper (South Vancouver), House of Commons, Debates, 10 March 1919, 340.

234. Quoted in Tippett, *Art at the Service of War*, 77.

235. *Spectator*, 1 October 1918; *Canadian Bookman* 1/1 (January 1919), 48.

236. J. Lewis Milligan, 'The Poet and the War,' *Canadian Magazine* 45/3 (July 1915), 234; review of Durkin, *Fighting Men of Canada*; Thomas, *Songs of an Airman*, and McGillicuddy, *The Little Marshal*, in *Canadian Magazine* 52/5 (March 1919), 977–78.

237. Fred Jacob, 'The War Poets,' *Saturday Night*, 26 August 1918, 3.

238. University of Saskatchewan Archives: MG87 A.F.L. Kenderdine Papers, vol. 3, f. 10.

239. Quoted in Clarence Karr, *Authors and Audiences: Popular Canadian Fiction in the Early Twentieth Century* (Montreal: McGill-Queen's University Press, 2000), 195; Harcourt Farmer, 'Play-writing in Canada,' *Canadian Bookman* 1/2 (April 1919), 55.

240. British Columbia Archives: MS-2792, Edythe Hembroff-Schleicher Papers, box 4, f. 9, 'Art after War,' Victoria *Times*, 4 May 1917.

241. Estelle M. Kerr, 'The Etcher's Point of View,' *Canadian Magazine* 48/2 (December 1916), 158; review of *The New Poetry*, in *Saturday Night*, 1 September 1917, 8.

242. R.A. Falconer, 'The New Imperial Allegiance,' *University Magazine* 15 (1916), 14; W.D. Lighthall, 'Canadian Poets of the Great War,' *Proceedings and Transactions of the Royal Society of Canada*, 3rd ser., vol. 12 (1918): xli–lxii.

243. Arthur Beverly Baxter, 'The Birth of the National Theatre,' *Maclean's*, February 1916, 27, 29.

244. University of British Columbia Library and Special Collections: Alfred Myrick Pound Papers, box 1, 'Canadian Authors,' given to Vancouver Poetry Society, 18 December 1919; Kenderdine Papers, vol. 3 f. 10, lecture 'Development of Canadian Art,' undated.

245. B.K. Sandwell, 'The Influence of Art and Literature,' in E.A. Victor, ed., *Canada's Future: What She Offers After the War* (Toronto: Macmillan, 1916), 169.

246. *Dalhousie Review* 1/1 (1921), 3–4.

247. *Canadian Forum*, 1/1 (October 1920), 1.

248. 'The New Era,' *Canadian Bookman* 1/1 (January 1919), 8–9.

249. Quoted in Karr, *Authors and Audiences*, 194.

250. Quoted in Maria Tippett, *Making Culture: English-Canadian Institutions and the Arts before the Massey Commission* (Toronto: University of Toronto Press, 1990), 82.

251. Men's Musical Club of Winnipeg Papers, box 1, f. 1, 'A Short History of the Men's Musical Club,' n.d.

252. Duncan Campbell Scott, 'Poetry and Progress,' *Proceedings and Transactions of the Royal Society of Canada*, 3rd ser., vol. 16 (1922): xlvii–lxvii.

253. Letter of 5 April 1917, quoted in D.M.R. Bentley, *The Confederation Group of Canadian Poets,* 292.

254. University of British Columbia Library and Special Collections: Alfred Myrick Pound Papers, box 1, f. 5.

255. University of Saskatchewan Archives: MG87 A.F.L. Kenderdine Papers, vol. 3 f. 10, Prof. G.W. Snelgrove, 'Art in Saskatchewan,' undated; University of Calgary Library and Special Collections: MsC 206 Agnes Aston Hill Papers, box 2, f. 7 uncited article, early 1930s.

256. Vincent Massey, 'The Prospects of a Canadian Drama,' *Queen's Quarterly* (October–December 1922): 194–212; *Le Nigog*, 1/2 (February 1918), 44–48.

257. A.J.M. Smith, 'Wanted: Canadian Criticism,' *Canadian Forum* 8/91 (April 1928), 600; Alfred Myrick Pound Papers, box 1, f. 5, unidentified talk

258. A.J.M. Smith, 'A Rejected Preface,' *Canadian Literature* 24 (spring 1965), 7.

259. Quoted in Kalman, *A History of Canadian Architecture*, vol. 2, 749.

260. *Canadian Bookman* 6/7 (July 1924), 164.

261. Quoted in Charles C. Hill, *The Group of Seven: Art for a Nation* (Toronto: McClelland and Stewart, 1995), 142.

262. Anthony Bertram, 'The Palace of Arts, Wembley,' *Saturday Review*, 7 June 1924, 16; *Art News* [New York], *Press Comments on the Canadian Section of Fine Arts, British Empire Exhibition, 1924–1925*, 16.

263. Lawren Harris, 'The Group of Seven in Canadian History,' in *Canadian Historical Association Historical Papers* (1948), 29.

264. H.W. Gadsby, 'The Hot Mush School, or Peter and I,' *Toronto Daily Star*, 12 December 1913, 6; *Montreal Daily Star*, 23 May 1913, 2.

265. *Saturday Night*, 18 March 1916, 5; 8 November 1924, 1.

266. *Toronto Star*, 20 May 1922, 7; *Ottawa Citizen*, 29 December 1928, 19.

267. *Toronto Star*, 27 January 1925, 6; 4 September 1924, 6.

268. Bertram Brooker, *Yearbook of the Arts in Canada, 1928–1929* (Toronto: Macmillan, 1929), 185.

269. Harris, 'The Group of Seven in Canadian History,' 38; quoted in Hill, *The Group of Seven*, 288.

270. F.B. Housser, *A Canadian Art Movement: The Story of the Group of Seven*

(Toronto: Macmillan, 1926), 17, 24; Harris, 'The Group of Seven in Canadian History,' 31.

271. Quoted in Ann Davis, 'A Study in Modernism: The Group of Seven as an Unexpectedly Typical Case,' *Journal of Canadian Studies* 33/1 (Spring 1988), 114.

272. *Toronto Star*, 4 September 1924, 6.

273. Quoted in Margaret E.R. Davidson, 'A New Approach to the Group of Seven,' *Journal of Canadian Studies* 4/4 (November 1969), 15.

274. Quoted in ibid., 14.

275. Wyly Grier and A.Y. Jackson, 'Two Views of Canadian Art,' in *The Empire Club of Canada Speeches, 1925* (Toronto: Empire Club of Canada, 1926), 113.

276. Archibald MacMechan, *Head-waters of Canadian Literature* (Toronto: McClelland and Stewart, 1924), 215; 'The National Consciousness Idea,' *Canadian Bookman* 11/5 (May 1929), 116; 'A Plea for Tolerance,' *Canadian Bookman* 6/5 (May 1924), 110.

277. J.M. Gibbon, 'Rhymes With and Without Reason,' *Canadian Bookman* 1/1 (January 1919), 4.

278. *Canadian Mercury*, December 1928, 3.

279. Quoted in Leo Kennedy, 'The Future of Canadian Literature,' *Canadian Mercury* 1/5–6 (April–May 1926), 100.

280. Smith, 'A Rejected Preface,' 7; quoted in Patricia Morley, *As Though Life Mattered: Leo Kennedy's Story* (Montreal: McGill-Queen's University Press, 1994), 43.

281. Watson Griffin, *The Gulf of Years* (Toronto: Point Publishers, 1927), 167–70.

282. 'Plea for Purity,' *Canadian Bookman* 6/3 (March 1924), 64.

283. Quoted in Morley, *As Though Life Mattered*, 62.

284. Leo Kennedy, 'The Future of Canadian Literature,' *Canadian Mercury*, December 1928; A.J.M. Smith, 'Wanted: Canadian Criticism,' *Canadian Forum* 8/91 (April 1928), 27.

285. Kennedy, 'The Future of Canadian Literature,' 101.

286. Deacon to Salverson, 28 February 1931, in Lennox and Lacombe, eds., *Dear Bill*, 122.

287. Quoted in Lyn Harrington, *Syllables of Recorded Time: The Story of the Canadian Authors Association, 1921–1981* (Toronto: Simon and Pierre, 1981), 133.

288. Ralph Connor, *Postscript to Adventure: The Autobiography of Ralph Connor* (New York: Farrar and Rinehart, 1938), 150.

289. *La Presse*, 29 June 1896.

290. University of Manitoba Archives: MSS 56 Ralph Connor Papers, box 33, f. 6, letter 25 October 1919.

291. Ibid., box 33, f. 6, Connor to Ernest Shipman, 5 May 1920; Shipman to Connor, 8 May 1920.

292. Helen Creighton, *Songs and Ballads from Nova Scotia* (Toronto: J.M. Dent & Sons, 1933), preface.

293. Georges Bouchard, *The Renaissance of the Rustic Arts* (Ottawa: private, 1932), 3.

294. Ibid., 5.

295. Canadian Handicrafts Guild, *Annual Report 1939* (Montreal: Canadian Handicrafts Guild, 1939), 12.

296. Canadian Handicrafts Guild, *Annual Report 1938* (Montreal: Canadian Handicrafts Guild, 1938), 28.

297. Ibid., 4; Bouchard, *The Renaissance of the Rustic Arts*, 15.
298. Public Archives of Manitoba [PAM]: MG10 C51 Searchlight Book Club Papers.
299. PAM: P882 and P883 Hawthorne Women's Club Papers.
300. Glenbow Museum: M907 Frederick John Niven Papers, box 1, f. 6, Agnes Wells, Britannia Beach, BC, to Niven, 3 October 1944.
301. Whyte Museum: M451 Margaret and Henry Greenham Papers, f. 7, brochure for Mountain School; f. 9, The Literary Dramatic Club.
302. PAM: P5015a Women's Art Club (Portage la Prairie) Papers, f. 4.
303. PAM: MG10 G16 Winnipeg Little Theatre Papers, newsletter *The Bill*, August 1932.
304. Winnipeg Little Theatre Papers, announcement of 5th season, 1925–26.
305. Medicine Hat Museum and Art Gallery [MHMAG]: M72.282 May Laidlaw Papers, program for Medicine Hat Amateur Operatic Society production of *Merrie England*, 14–15 December 1928 .
306. City of Victoria Archives: Audrey Johnson Papers, box 4, 'Langham Court Theatre.'
307. MHMAG: M87.16.1-2 Irva Fleming Papers, souvenir program for school music and dramatic festival of the Medicine Hat inspectorate, 2–3 May 1935.
308. Whyte Museum: M72 Helen Jo and Ernest Kennedy Papers, accession 361, f. 10. Program for Banff School of Fine Arts, undated [1933].
309. Quoted in Hill, *The Group of Seven*, 145; A.J.M. Smith, 'Canadian Poetry: A Minority Report,' *University of Toronto Quarterly* 8/2 (January 1939), 131; Harris, 'The Group of Seven in Canadian History,' 30.
310. Deacon to Morley Callaghan, 14 September 1932, in Lennox and Lacombe, *Dear Bill*, 132.
311. Quoted in Karen Smith, 'Community Libraries,' in Fleming, Gallichan, and Lamonde, eds., *History of the Book in Canada*, vol. 1, 148.
312. Quoted in Hill, *The Group of Seven*, 147.
313. Quoted in ibid., 39.
314. Mary Alexander, 'Little Theatres in the West,' *Maclean's* 36/17 (1 October 1921), 52.
315. Glenbow Museum: M1134 Inglis Sheldon Williams Papers, box 1, f. 8, Norman Mackenzie to Sheldon-Williams, 12 August 1922; quoted in Hill, *The Group of Seven*, 120.
316. Andrew Carnegie, 'The Gospel of Wealth,' in Edward C. Kirkland, ed., *The Gospel of Wealth and Other Timely Essays* (Cambridge, MA: Belknap Press of Harvard University Press, 1962 [1900]), 23, 25, 28, 36.
317. Quoted in Margaret Beckman, Stephen Langmead, and John Black, *The Best Gift: A Record of the Carnegie Libraries in Ontario* (Toronto: Dundurn Press, 1984), 33.
318. Sir Henry A. Miers and S.F. Markham, *The Museums of Canada* (London: Museums Association, 1932), 18.
319. Quoted in Tippett, *Making Culture*, 151.
320. *The Voice* [Winnipeg], 13 October 1905; quoted in Beckman, Langmead, and Black, *The Best Gift*, 45.
321. Library and Archives Canada: Grand Trunk Railway Records, RG30, vol. 7055, Grand Trunk Pacific Development Corporation, pay ledgers for Fort Garry Hotel, December 1913.

322. Quoted in Reid, 'Our Own Country Canada', 183.
323. Quoted in E.J. Hart, *The Selling of Canada: The* CPR *and the Beginnings of Canadian Tourism* (Banff: Altitude Publishing, 1983), 36.
324. Quoted in Iain Stevenson, 'Books for Improvement: The Canadian Pacific Foundation Library,' *Papers of the Bibliographical Society of Canada* 43/1 (spring 2005), 37.
325. Quoted in Hart, *The Selling of Canada*, 109.
326. Quoted in ibid., 35.
327. Quoted in Hill, *The Group of Seven*, 188, 242.
328. University of Manitoba Archives: MSS 56 Ralph Connor Papers, box 33, f. 2, letter 28 February 1902.
329. Quoted in Tippett, *Making Culture*, 125.
330. Quoted in Hill, *The Group of Seven*, 38.
331. André Biéler and Elizabeth Harrison, eds., *Conference of Canadian Artists Held at Queen's University, Kingston, Ont., June 26–28, 1941* (1941), 21.
332. University of Calgary Library and Special Collections [UCLSC]: MsC 206 Agnes Aston Hill Papers, box 2, f. 7, editorial 'Alberta inspires poetic effort' [probably Calgary *Herald*], early 1930s.
333. Public Archives of Manitoba: P5389 Fort Garry Reading Club Papers.
334. UCLSC: MsC 253 Excelsior Glee Party Papers, box 1, f. 4, circular letter to local groups, 30 October 1930; box 1, f. 2, 'Excelsior Glee Party,' undated [1951].
335. Biéler and Harrison, eds., *Conference of Canadian Artists Held at Queen's University* (1941), 117.
336. Ibid., 7.
337. Quoted in Mollie Gillen, *The Wheel of Things: A Biography of L.M. Montgomery, Author of "Anne of Green Gables"* (Don Mills, ON: Fitzhenry and Whiteside, 1975), 184; quoted in John Coldwell Adams, *Sir Charles God Damn: The Life of Sir Charles G.D. Roberts* (Toronto: University of Toronto Press, 1986), 197.
338. Bertram Brooker, ed., *Yearbook of the Arts in Canada, 1936* (Toronto: Macmillan, 1936), xv, xvi, xxii, xxiii. Italics in original.
339. Quoted in L.B. Kuffert, *A Great Duty: Canadian Responses to Modern Life and Mass Culture, 1939–1967* (Montreal: McGill-Queen's University Press, 2003), 38.
340. Whyte Museum: M72 Helen Jo and Ernest Kennedy Papers, accession 361, f. 1, constitution, Banff Literary-Dramatic Club.
341. Biéler and Harrison, eds., *Conference of Canadian Artists Held at Queen's University*, 36.
342. Ibid., 44, 101–2; *Quill & Quire* 8/1 (February 1942), 9.
343. Quoted in Dean F. Oliver and Laura Brandon, *Canvas of War: Painting the Canadian Experience, 1914 to 1945* (Ottawa: Canadian War Museum, 2000), 167.
344. Biéler and Harrison, eds., *Conference of Canadian Artists Held at Queen's University*, 7; W.A. Bishop, foreword to G.L. Creed, *For Freedom* (Toronto: J.M. Dent & Sons, 1942), vii.
345. Amabel King, ed., *Voices of Victory: Representative Poetry of Canada in Wartime* (Toronto: Macmillan, 1942), v; Raymond Davies in *Saturday Night* 58/2 (19 September 1942), 19.
346. University of Regina Archives: 86-75 Dorothy Bee Papers, *Students' Bulletin* [Regina Conservatory of Music] 4/8 (30 November 1942).

347. Sheila MacDonald, 'Why Paint in Wartime?' in *The Empire Club of Canada: Addresses Delivered to the Members during the Year 1942–1943* (Toronto: Empire Club of Canada, 1943), 112.

348. City of Victoria Archives: PR182 29C8 Reginald Hincks Papers, concert program, 26–27 November 1943; Saskatoon Public Library: Doc 88 16A Saskatchewan Registered Music Teachers Association (Saskatoon Branch) Papers, newsletter to members, 27 June 1944.

349. Public Archives of Manitoba: MG10 G22 Edith Sinclair Papers, 'Consider the Play' notes.

350. Oliver H. Fletcher, *Songs of Our Empire's War and Praiseworthy Allies: Our Victory Book* (private, 1945); *Canadian Forum* 19/228 (January 1940), 324.

351. Quoted in Kuffert, *A Great Duty*, 62; Glenbow Museum: M2309 Alberta Theatres Association Papers, f. 1, letter to Premier Manning, 11 February 1948; f. 3, circular from Saskatchewan Motion Picture Exhibitors Association, 27 April 1948.

352. *Quill & Quire* 9/7 (August 1943), 20.

353. Biéler and Harrison, eds., *Conference of Canadian Artists Held at Queen's University* (1941), 9.

354. Arthur Lismer, 'New Type War Poster Artist Needed To Conceive New, Original Ideas' in *Marketing*, 19 June 1943, 2–3. Italics in original.

355. 'Strong Emotional Appeal Preferred By Most People for War Posters,' *Marketing*, 24 July 1943, 10.

356. John Grierson, 'A Film Policy for Canada,' *Canadian Affairs* 1/11 (15 June 1944), 4, 13.

357. Quoted in Jack C. Ellis, *John Grierson: Life, Contributions, Influence* (Carbondale: South Illinois University Press, 2000), 126.

358. Directorate of History and Heritage, Department of National Defence: Report No. 120, Historical Officer, Canadian Military Headquarters, 'The Canadian Women's Army Corps Overseas,' 31 July 1944, p. 29.

359. National Council of the YMCAs of Canada, War Services Committee, *C'mon and Sing!* (n.d.).

360. Quoted in Barry D. Rowland, *Herbie and Friends: Cartoons in Wartime* (Toronto: Natural Heritage/Natural History, 1990), 23; Bing Coughlin, *This Army*, vol. 2 (Rome: No. 2 Canadian Public Relations Group, 1945), 8.

361. Biéler and Harrison, eds., *Conference of Canadian Artists Held at Queen's University*, 21.

362. Ibid., x–xi.

363. Lawren Harris, 'Reconstruction through the Arts,' *Canadian Art* 1/5 (June–July 1944), 186.

364. Canada, House of Commons, Special Committee of Reconstruction and Re-establishment, Minutes of Proceedings and Evidence No. 10, 21 June 1944.

365. *Toronto Star*, 13 July 1944, 6.

366. Elizabeth Wyn Wood, 'A National Program for the Arts in Canada,' *Canadian Art* 1/3 (February–March 1944), 95; W.A. Deacon, 'The Arts in Canada Speak Out Before Parliamentary Committee,' *Globe*, 24 June 1944, 7.

367. Wyn Wood, 'A National Program for the Arts in Canada,' 93.

368. Quoted in Kalman, *A History of Canadian Architecture*, vol. 2, 565.

369. 'Art and Democracy,' *Maritime Art* 2/1 (October–November 1941), 8.

370. Bernard Ostry, *The Cultural Connection: An Essay on Culture and Government Policy in Canada* (Toronto: McClelland and Stewart, 1978), 41.

371. *Globe*, 25 August 1928, 15.

372. British Columbia Archives: MS 2834 Harold Lamb Papers, box 1, f. 3, Lamb to H.E. Young, Minister of Education, 30 September 1918.

373. Sir Henry A. Miers and S.F. Markham, *A Report on the Museums of Canada* (Edinburgh: T. and A. Constable, 1932), 3, 7.

374. Quoted in Phyllis Gale, 'The Development of the Public Library in Canada' (MA thesis, University of Chicago, 1965), 30.

375. Quoted in ibid., 99.

376. George Grant, *Lament for a Nation* (Toronto: Macmillan, 1965), 70.

377. Quoted in Marylin J. McKay, *A National Soul: Canadian Mural Painting, 1860s–1930s* (Montreal: McGill-Queen's University Press, 2002), 35.

378. Canada, *Proceedings and Report of the Special Committee on Radio Broadcasting* (1932), 565.

379. 'Community Art Centres: A Growing Movement,' *Canadian Art* (1944–45), 63, 77, 85

380. City of Victoria Archives: Audrey Johnson Papers, 'Art Centre Project,' undated.

381. Canada, Royal Commission in National Development in the Arts, Letters and Sciences, *Report* (Ottawa: King's Printer, 1951).

382. Quoted in Paul Litt, *The Muses, the Masses, and the Massey Commission* (Toronto: University of Toronto Press, 1992), 225.

383. Quoted in J.L. Granatstein, 'Culture and Scholarship: The First Ten Years of the Canada Council,' *Canadian Historical Review* 65/4 (December 1984), 460.

384. Library and Archives Canada [LAC]: RG69 vol. 423, f. 'Canadian Theatre Centre,' Dominion Consultants Associates Ltd, *A National Centre for the Performing Arts: A Study Prepared for the National Capital Arts Alliance*, October 1963, 9.

385. University of British Columbia Archives: June Binkert-Western Canada Art Circuit Papers, box 1, f. 6, "The Art Institute of Ontario: Objectives and History,' [1965].

386. Ibid., box 1, f. 6, 13–14 November 1964.

387. Ibid., box 1, f. 7, Mrs. ES Gregory, Powell River Fine Arts Club to WCAC, 8 March 1965; University of Regina Archives: 89–34 Norman Mackenzie Gallery Papers, brief to National Gallery of Canada by WCAC, 29 December 1965.

388. Thunder Bay Museum: Northwestern Ontario Art Association Papers, E22/1/1, constitution November 1960; E22/1/7, announcement to member clubs, 10 April 1966.

389. The correspondence between Hughes and Stern can be found in University of Victoria Archives: AR058 Galerie Dominion Papers.

390. Quoted in Betty Lee, *Love and Whisky: The Story of the Dominion Drama Festival* (Toronto: McClelland and Stewart, 1973), v.

391. Robertson Davies, 'Fifty Years of Theatre in Canada,' in Keith and Shek, eds., *The Arts in Canada*, 75, 77; letter of 29 April 1935 in Henry Borden, ed., *Letters to Limbo by the Right Honourable Sir Robert Laird Borden, PC, GCMC, KC, Prime Minister of Canada* (Toronto: University of Toronto Press, 1971).

392. *Royal Architectural Institute of Canada Journal* 37/4 (April 1960), 134; Banff Centre: 1990–58 Irene Prothroe Papers, box 3, Martin Lager and Charles Lawson, 'Prospectus for a Repertory Theatre in Calgary,' undated.

393. City of Vancouver Archives: AM1064 E.V. Young Papers, 606-A-1, f. 12, program for Theatre under the Stars, July 1947; f. 13, program for 1948 season.

394. Ibid., f. 17, program for 1952 season.

395. Arnold Edinborough, 'A New Stratford Festival,' in *Shakespeare Quarterly* 5/1 (January 1954), 50.

396. Thunder Bay Museum: Fort William Little Theatre Papers, E9/2/1, letter from Drama Advisor, Community Programs Branch, Department of Education, 18 July 1951.

397. British Columbia Archives: MS-0894 British Columbia Drama Association Papers, box 18, f. 2, constitution, January 1964; box 18, f. 7, unidentified farewell message.

398. University of Victoria Archives: AR001, accession 91-084 Elsie Allan Papers, f. 7, program for Bastion Theatre Studio 'Dark of the Moon', 4–8 May 1965.

399. Centennial Commission, *Architectural Requirements for the Performing Arts in Canada* (Ottawa, 1964), 3.

400. Ibid., 4; LAC: RG69 vol. 411, f. Status of Federal Programme, 'Historical Aspects of Canada's Centennial,' October 1961.

401. Canadian Centenary Council, *Making 1967 Work: Planning for the Centenary on the Community Level* (Ottawa: Canadian Centenary Council, n.d.), 8.

402. Ralph Hicklin, 'Cultural Workers in the Centennial Garden,' *Globe*, 15 October 1966, 13.

403. *Perspective '67: Art Gallery of Ontario, Toronto, Canada, July 8th to September 10th, 1967* (Ottawa: Centennial Commission, 1967), foreword.

404. Herbert Whittaker, 'Swinging Quebec Fares Best in Centennial Play,' *Globe*, 12 January 1967, 11; Herbert Whittaker, '1967: Year of the Canadian playwright—or is it?' *Globe*, 14 January 1967, 14.

405. Ron Evans, 'A Centennial Bomb,' Toronto *Telegram*, 12 January 1967, 68; Eric Nicol, *Anything for a Laugh: Memoirs* (Madeira Park, BC: Harbour Publishing, 1998), 228.

406. *Expovoyages*, 15 August 1966, 1.

407. Judith Shatnoff, 'Expo 67: A Multiple Vision,' in *Film Quarterly* 21/1 (autumn 1967), 3; Robert Fulford, *This Was Expo* (Toronto: McClelland and Stewart, 1968), 90.

408. Shatnoff, 'Expo 67,' 6, 11.

409. House of Commons, Debates, December 1963.

410. Dennis R. Reid, *A Concise History of Canadian Painting* (Toronto: Oxford University Press, 1973), 225.

411. Andrew Bell, 'Yes, Painting Might Be Better in Toronto,' in *Canadian Art* 8/1 (1950), 29.

412. Saskatoon Public Library: May Woodley Benson Papers, unidentified article, 20 April 1968.

413. *The Uncertain Mirror: Report of the Special Senate Committee on Mass Media*, 3 vols. (Ottawa: Information Canada, 1970), 11.

414. Canada, Revised Statutes, Telecommunications Act, 1993; University of Regina Archives: 87-16 Howard Leyton-Brown Papers, box 1 Canadian Music Council, The Development of a Music Policy for Canada, presented at annual conference, Banff, 5–7 May 1972.

415. Canada, Revised Statutes, Status of the Artist Act, 1992, c. 33, sec. 2(a) and (b).

416. Canadian Film and Television Production Association, Submission to the

House of Commons Standing Committee on Canadian Heritage, pursuant to its Study of the Canadian Feature Film Industry, 18 February 2005.

417. *Drawing Conclusions: The Report of the Provincial Arts Policy Committee* (St. John's: Department of Municipal and Provincial Affairs, 1990), 3.

418. *Change and Challenge: A Strategic Economic Plan for Newfoundland and Labrador* (St. John's: Government of Newfoundland and Labrador, 1992), 48; Ronald Rompkey, 'The Uncertain Past: Newfoundland Cultural Policy since Confederation,' presented to the Canadian Cultural Research Network Colloquium, June 1998.

419. *A Vision for Tourism in Newfoundland and Labrador in the 21st Century* (St. John's: Department of Tourism, Culture and Recreation, 1994), 11–12.

420. Quoted in Ted Magder, *Canada's Hollywood: The Canadian State and Feature Films* (Toronto: University of Toronto Press, 1993), 134.

421. *The Uncertain Mirror*, 194.

422. *Toronto Star*, 9 September 1952, 4.

423. *Toronto Star*, 8 September 1952, 10.

424. *Globe*, 9 September 1952, 1.

425. *Globe*, 22 July 1932, 18.

426. *Toronto Star*, 8 September 1952, 10.

427. House of Commons, Debates, 18 May 1932.

428. Royal Commission on Broadcasting, *Report* (Ottawa: Queen's Printer, 1957), 107.

429. Paul Gardner, 'Without Apology,' *New York Times*, 19 January 1964, p. X17

430. Canada, Secretary of State, *White Paper on Broadcasting* (Ottawa: Queen's Printer, 1966), 5.

431. *The Uncertain Mirror*, 206, 259.

432. Canada, Revised Statutes, Broadcasting Act, 1991.

433. *Mass Media: Report of the Senate Special Committee on Mass Media* (Ottawa: Queen's Printer, 1970).

434. *Report of the Royal Commission on Publications* (Ottawa: Queen's Printer, 1961), 4, 207.

435. *A Question of Balance: Report of the Task Force on the Canadian Magazine Industry*, co-chairs J. Patrick O'Callaghan and Roger Tassé (Ottawa: Minister of Supply and Services Canada, 1994), 77.

436. John Schofield, 'Subscribing to rules,' *Maclean's* 111/32 (10 August 1998), 38.

437. *A Question of Balance*, iii.

438. Department of Foreign Affairs and International Trade News Release #47, 14 March 1997, 'Canada to Appeal Ruling in Magazine Trade Dispute.'

439. Canada, Library of Parliament, Legislative Summary LS-323E *Bill C-55: An Act Respecting Advertising Services Supplied by Foreign Periodical Publishers.*

440. John DeMont, 'On guard for thee,' *Maclean's* 110/8 (24 February 1997), 25.

441. Cultural Industries Sectoral Advisory Group on International Trade, 'New Strategies for Culture and Trade in Canadian Culture in a Global World' (International Trade Canada, February 1999).

442. University of Victoria Archives: AR073 Audrey Johnson Papers, box 1, Janice Keys, 'Keith Turnbull on Canadian Content,' *Manitoba Theatre Centre Newsletter* 1/4 (February 1972).

443. Howard Leyton-Brown Papers, box 1 f. Canada Council Notes from Talks, André Fortier, 'Is There a Future for the Symphony Orchestra in Canada?,'

Joint Conference of the Association of Canadian Orchestras and the Ontario Federation of Symphony Orchestras, 28 April 1974; box 1 f. Memorandum to Chairman's Review Committee, 12 May 1971.

444. *RPM* 4/7 (11 October 1965).

445. *RPM* (fall 1969).

446. Canadian Music Publishers Association Position Paper, 'Canadian Content,' 5 March 2005.

447. William T. Stanbury, *Canadian Content Regulations: The Intrusive State at Work* (Vancouver: Fraser Institute, 1998).

448. Harold G. Fox, *A Synopsis of Canadian Laws of Copyright* (Toronto: Canadian Authors Association, 1949), 3.

449. Howard Leyton-Brown Papers, box 1, f. Canada Council, Canada Council News Release, 28 August 1972, speaking notes of director André Fortier for speech in Montreal to International Conference of Symphony and Opera Musicians.

450. Standing Committee on Canadian Heritage, *A Sense of Place—A Sense of Being: The Evolving Role of the Federal Government in Support of Culture in Canada* (June 1999), appendix 2.

451. *Copyright in Canada: Proposals for a Revision of the Law* (Ottawa: Consumer and Corporate Affairs Canada, 1977).

452. Joseph Jackson and René Lemieux, 'The Arts and Canada's Cultural Policy' (Ottawa: Library of Parliament/Parliamentary Research Branch Current Issue Review 93-3E, 15 October 1999), 9

453. Graham Henderson, 'Protect Artists: Reform Canada's copyright laws,' *National Post*, 11 May 2005; Steven Page, 'A Barenaked guide to music copyright reform,' *National Post*, 1 May 2006.

454. Jackson and Lemieux, 'The Arts and Canada's Cultural Policy,' 1.

455. Howard Leyton-Brown Papers, box 7, R. Murray Schafer, 'Planned Culture Seen,' uncited editorial.

456. Jackson and Lemieux, 'The Arts and Canada's Cultural Policy,' 2.

457. Canada, Library of Parliament, Parliamentary Information and Research Service PRB 99-25E, *Cultural Exemptions in Canada's Major International Trade Agreements and Investment Relationships*, 12 October 1999.

458. Cultural Industries Sectoral Advisory Group on International Trade, 'New Strategies for Culture and Trade in Canadian Culture in a Global World' (International Trade Canada, February 1999).

459. Donald W. Buchanan, 'The Changing Face of Canadian Art,' *Canadian Art* 15/1 (1958), 24; Gail Dexter, 'Jack Bush: A Sunday painter who made it at 58,' *Toronto Star*, 9 November 1968.

460. Robertson Davies, *The Diary of Samuel Marchbanks* (Toronto: Clarke, Irwin, 1947), 23–24.

461. Robertson Davies, 'A Canadian Author,' in *The Merry Heart: Selections, 1980–1995* (Toronto: McClelland and Stewart, 1996), 177–85.

462. Hill Strategies Research, *Government Spending on Culture in Canada, 1992–93 to 2002–03: Report Prepared for the Canadian Conference of the Arts* (July 2005).

463. Hill Strategies, 'Consumer Spending on Culture in Canada, the Provinces and 15 Metropolitan Areas in 2005,' *Strategical Insights on the Arts* (February 2007).

464. Silver Donald Cameron, *The Art of Development and the Development of Art: A Powerful Partnership—Business, Community and the Arts* (Ottawa: Canadian Conference of the Arts, 2004); letter of 6 April 1934, in Borden, ed., *Letters to Limbo by the Right Honourable Sir Robert Laird Borden*, 88–89.

465. Statistics Canada, Culture Goods Trade 2004, schedule 87-007-XIE (October 2005).

466. *From Script to Screen: New Policy Directions for Canadian Feature Film* (Ottawa: Canadian Heritage, 2000); Canadian Film and Television Production Association, Submission to the House of Commons Standing Committee on Canadian Heritage, pursuant to its Study of the Canadian Feature Film Industry, 18 February 2005.

467. Canda Council for the Arts, Funding to Artists and Arts Organizations, 2007–8: National Overview (Ottawa: CCA, 2008), 5. Hill Strategies Research, *Government Spending on Culture in Canada, 1992–93 to 2002–03.*

468. Quoted in Phillips, *Trading Identities*, 265.

469. Dorothy Eber, ed., *Cape Dorset Print Collection 1970* (Cape Dorset, NWT: West-Baffin Eskimo Co-operative, 1970), foreword.

470. Cameron, *The Art of Development and the Development of Art*, 9.

471. Hill Strategies Research, *Diversity in Canada's Arts Labour Force* (February 2005).

472. *The National Gallery of Canada Catalogue* (Ottawa: NGC, 1931), 195.

473. University of Calgary Library and Special Collections [UCLCS]: accession 362/85.8, Howard Cable Papers, box 5 file 2, '*Sing Sea to Sea.*'

474. Philip Marchand, 'What I Really Think,' *Saturday Night*, October 1997: 52–59.

475. Anne Kingston, *National Post*, 25 September 2005, WP2; quoted in Bentley, *The Confederation Group of Canadian Poets*, 242.

476. UCLSC: MsC Alan Brown Papers, box 1 file 14, Smith to Roy, 16 September 1976.

477. Kay Kritzwiser, 'Herman Geiger-Torel on Future of Opera,' *Globe*, 14 September 1963, 13.

478. Hill Strategies, 'Consumer Spending on Culture in Canada, the Provinces and 15 Metropolitan Areas in 2003,' *Strategical Insights on the Arts* 4/1 (May 2005).

479. Stephen Smith, 'Forty great works of Canadian fiction: A Q&Q panel selects the century's literary "best,"' *Quill & Quire* 65/7 (July 1999), 21.

480. Ditto.

481. Quoted in Tausky, *Sara Jeannette Duncan: Novelist of Empire*, 108.

482. Quoted in D.C. Harvey, 'The Intellectual Awakening of Nova Scotia'; *Christian Guardian*, 20 February 1839.

483. Quoted in Ann Davis, 'The Wembley Controversy in Canadian Art,' *Canadian Historical Review* 54 (1973), 63.

484. A.Y. Jackson, 'Two Views of Canadian Art,' address given 26 February 1925, in *The Empire Club of Canada Speeches 1925* (Toronto: The Empire Club of Canada, 1926), 113.

Picture Acknowledgements

The publisher is grateful to the following for their permission to reproduce the illustrations. Several illustrations are from the author's private collection; although every effort has been made to contact copyright holders, it has not been possible in every case and we apologize for any that have been omitted. Should the copyright holders wish to contact us after publication, we would be happy to include an acknowledgement in subsequent reprints.

6 Private collection
7 © Library and Archives Canada. Reproduced with the permission of Library and Archives Canada. Richard Harrington / Library and Archives Canada / PA-129586
9 Courtesy of the Royal Alberta Museum, Edmonton, Alberta
12 Dorset Mask Photo © Canadian Museum of Civilization, artifact QkHn-13:489, image S90-4013
16 Top: Private collection
16 Bottom: Library and Archives Canada, Acc. No. R9266-318 Peter Winkworth Collection of Canadiana
17 Library and Archives Canada, Acc. No. 1990-215-18
21 G.M. Dawson / Library and Archives Canada / PA-038148
22 Robert W. Reford / Library and Archives Canada / C-060823
25 © Library and Archives Canada. Reproduced with the permission of the Minister of Public Works and Government Services Canada (2008). Lawrence R. Batchelor / Library and Archives Canada / C-010522
26 Library and Archives Canada / C-013986
31 Library and Archives Canada, Acc. No. 1989-479-5
32 Image H-0453 courtesy of Royal BC Museum, BC Archives
33 Glenbow Archives NA-3421-9
34 City of Vancouver Archives, Photo No. LGN 583
38 City of Vancouver Archives, Photo No. In P8.3
42 Library and Archives Canada, Acc. No. 1989-472-1
44 Canadian Pacific Archives (A-31369)
45 Private collection
50 McCord Museum VIEW-14806
52 Centre for Newfoundland Studies, Memorial University Library
54 Library and Archives Canada, Acc. No. 1989-283-8
57 Library and Archives Canada, Acc. No. 1989-602-3
61 History Collection, Nova Scotia Museum
71 Private collection
72 McCord Museum M6109

75 Library and Archives Canada, Acc. No. 1943-121-22

79 Yukon Gold Co. / Library and Archives Canada / C-003069

80 Image B-07437 courtesy of Royal BC Museum, BC Archives

94 Private collection

95 McCord Museum M988.132

97 © W.R. Reid, courtesy of M.D. Vance

98 Library and Archives Canada, Record 4231

99 Glenbow Archives NA-1406-24

101 George E. Dragan / Library and Archives Canada / PA-088567

102 Ronny Jaques / National Film Board of Canada. Photothèque / Library and Archives Canada / PA-204120

109 Archives of Ontario, C 130-5-0-0-65

110 Private collection

112 Private collection

114 Hamel, Theophile, 622107, Government Art Collection, Archives of Ontario

119 McCord Museum M390.50.8.386

125 Courtesy of Lois Shewfelt

126 P37-257 Provincial Archives of New Brunswick

137 Library and Archives Canada / C-000057

138 Library and Archives Canada / C-000048

139 © Jonathan F. Vance

146 Canada. Dept. of Interior / Library and Archives Canada / PA-034427

151 Archives of Ontario, F 1140-7-0-3-3

154 Topley Studio / Library and Archives Canada / PA-028156

156 D.A. McLaughlin / Library and Archives Canada / C-003760

157 McCord Museum M930.50.8.269

167 McCord Museum MP-0000.871.4

172 Private collection

177 Public Archives and Records Office of Prince Edward Island, [Charlottetown Camera Club Collection, PARO Acc. 2320/53-10]

179 Archives of Ontario, C 6-2-0-0-25

181 Simpson Bros. / Library and Archives Canada / PA-164643

182 Private collection

184 William James Topley / Library and Archives Canada / PA-008927

189 Canada. Dept. of Mines and Resources / Library and Archives Canada / PA-021362

196 Archives of Ontario, C 3-1-0-0-311 (9508-10190)

198 William James Topley / Library and Archives Canada / PA-009273

200 Courtesy of Casavant-Frères Archives, Saint-Hyacinthe, Canada

204 University of Saskatchewan Archives, Gus Kenderdine fonds (MG 87), file 28, photo 1

207 Billy Rose Theatre Division, The New York Public Library for the Performing Arts, Astor, Lenox and Tildon Foundations

209 Library and Archives Canada, Le monde illustré, album universel Montréal: [Compagnie de Photogravure de Montréal, 1901?-1907]—10 janvier 1903—7 v. : ill.

211 Paul Peel, The Modest Model (1889), oil on canvas, 146.7 x 114.3 cm, Collection of Museum London, Gift of the estate of Allan J. Wells with the assistance of the Canadian Cultural Property Export Review Board, 1990

and conserved by the Canadian Conservation Institute of the Department of Canadian Heritage

221 Photograph LH-4064 courtesy of Saskatoon Public Library - Local History Room

222 Private collection

223 Canada. Dept. of National Defence / Library and Archives Canada / PA-023014

224 Canada. Dept. of National Defence / Library and Archives Canada / PA-000480

228 Archives of Ontario, F 1140-7-0-1

232 © J. Peter Vance

234 © J. Peter Vance

235 Top: © J. Peter Vance
Bottom: Private collection

239 Samuel J. Jarvis / Library and Archives Canada / PA-025077

240 CWM 19900076-410#1 George Metcalf Archival Collection © Canadian War Museum

251 Nova Scotia Archives and Records Management, Helen Creighton fonds, 1987-178, Album 12, no. 349

252 Archives of Ontario, F 1066

254 Archives of Ontario, F 1140-7-0-2.1

265 Whyte Museum of the Canadian Rockies (NA66-1691)

267 Photograph B-2552 courtesy of Saskatoon Public Library - Local History Room

268 William James Topley / Library and Archives Canada / PA-033973

271 Nova Scotia Archives and Records Management, Helen Creighton fonds, 1987-178, Album 14, no.2

272 C.N.R. / Library and Archives Canada / C-045102

274 Glenbow Archives NA-4210-2

283 City of Toronto Archives, Fonds 1244, Item 2150

285 Courtesy of the Provincial Archives of Alberta

287 Archives of Ontario, F 1125-1-0-0-108

292 © Toronto Public Library. Original: J.W. Bald, Carnegie Library, Penetan-guishene, Canada. 1910 c. Reproduced from the Toronto Public Library website http://www.tpl.toronto.on.ca.

295 Glenbow Archives ND-3-1504

299 William James Topley / Library and Archives Canada / PA-009563

300 Canadian Pacific Archives (A-31365)

311 Sgt. Karen M. Hermiston / Canada. Dept. of National Defence / Library and Archives Canada / PA-113772

313 University of Saskatchewan Archives, Mac and Beth Hone fonds (MG 183), series 8.2, file 4

317 Library and Archives Canada, Acc. No. 1983-30-245

319 National Film Board of Canada. Photothèque / Library and Archives Canada / PA-179892

321 Ronny Jaques / National Film Board of Canada. Photothèque / Library and Archives Canada / PA-179108

324 Canada. Dept. of National Defence / Library and Archives Canada / PA-152119

325 Private collection

327 Private collection
330 Private collection
331 Private collection
337 History Collection, Nova Scotia Museum
339 Archives of Ontario, RG 9-7-5-0-62
345 © MCpl Cindy Molyneaux, Courtesy of Rideau Hall, GG20040438-017
349 © Jonathan F. Vance
350 © Jonathan F. Vance
351 Image H-03098 courtesy of Royal BC Museum, BC Archives
353 Glenbow Archives NA-2771-14
356 Archives of Ontario, C 3-1-0-0-495
361 Glenbow Archives NA-3147-2
368 © Library and Archives Canada. Reproduced with the permission of
    Library and Archives Canada. Ken Bell / Library and Archives Canada /
    PA-153947
381 Photograph B-10295 courtesy of Saskatoon Public Library - Local History
    Room
383 Malak / Library and Archives of Canada / Acc. No. 1968-074
384 © Library and Archives Canada. Reproduced with the permission of the
    Minister of Public Works and Government Services Canada (2008). Frank
    Grant / Library and Archives Canada / e001098960
386 © Library and Archives Canada. Reproduced with the permission of the
    Minister of Public Works and Government Services Canada (2008). Library
    and Archives Canada / e001098962
388 © Library and Archives Canada. Reproduced with the permission of the
    Minister of Public Works and Government Services Canada (2008). Frank
    Grant / Library and Archives Canada / e001098960
389 Frank Grant / Library and Archives Canada / C-030085
392 Peter Croydon R.C.A., Courtesy of The Robert McLaughlin Gallery
394 Library and Archives Canada / e000001169
405 Glenbow Archives NA-5600-6090a
406 Gar Lunney / National Film Board of Canada. Photothèque / Library and
    Archives Canada / PA-169804
419 © Shawn Nagy / www.superoldies.com
420 Glenbow Archives M-8000-400
425 © Library and Archives Canada. Reproduced with the permission of
    Library and Archives Canada. Richard Harrington / Library and Archives
    Canada / PA-129944
433 Archives of Ontario, C 3-1-0-0-722
444 © Library and Archives Canada. Reproduced with the permission of the
    Minister of Public Works and Government Services Canada (2008). B.
    Korda / Library and Archives Canada / PA-145170
445 Isuma Distribution International
447 Private collection
448 © Great Big Sea 1995 Ltd.

Index